Praise for

DRESS CODES

"Essential reading whether you dress to the nines or prefer sweats . . . Ford's writing is steeped in extensive research and makes what could be a dull history lesson about fashion a deeply informative and entertaining study of why we dress the way we do, and what that tells us about class, sexuality, and power."

—*THE NEW YORK TIMES BOOK REVIEW*

"A sharp and entertaining history of the rules of fashion. Mr. Ford skillfully examines how fashion, far from being mere frivolity, has shaped people's lives from the fourteenth century to the present."

—*THE WALL STREET JOURNAL*

"An entertaining read, *Dress Codes* shows how fashion can both reflect and shape society."

—*THE ECONOMIST*

"Taking readers around the world from the 1200s to today, Ford embarks on an ambitious and comprehensive exploration of how fashion has been used by people both with and without money and power."

—*THE NEW YORK TIMES*

"*Dress Codes: How the Laws of Fashion Made History* is a new book by Richard Thompson Ford, a Stanford Law School professor who has terrific personal style. . . . The joy of Ford's book comes from learning about all the things people have historically been banned from doing to or with clothes."

—*New York* Magazine's *The Cut*

"In *Dress Codes*, Ford has created a thorough and well-thought-out history of fashion from a legal and societal perspective. . . . Readers will come away with a new understanding of—and critical eye for—what we wear and why."

—BOOKPAGE

"*Dress Codes* explores how for centuries fashion has marked a pathway for personal liberation and social critique even when it sought to reinforce class, race, and gender hierarchies. From nuns' habits to flappers' fringe to burkinis and hijabs, from Joan of Arc's armor to Martin Luther King Jr.'s Sunday best, Richard Thompson Ford reveals a history of individual imagination capable of outwitting and recasting even the strictest rules. Ford's writing is sharp, witty, and brilliant, with the elegance and craft of a bespoke suit."

—DANIEL SHARFSTEIN, professor at Vanderbilt University and author of *Thunder in the Mountains: Chief Joseph, Oliver Otis Howard, and the Nez Perce War*

"I think that *Dress Codes* is long overdue. Clothing is at the heart of culture, indeed it is almost a definition of what we mean by the term culture, a constructed but ever changing expression of social relationships, beliefs, and ideologies. We should all, as Richard Thompson Ford does so magnificently within this book, be taking fashion much more seriously."

—RUTH GOODMAN, author of *How to Be a Victorian* and *The Domestic Revolution*

DRESS CODES

*How the Laws
of Fashion
Made History*

Richard Thompson Ford

Simon & Schuster Paperbacks

NEW YORK · LONDON · TORONTO
SYDNEY · NEW DELHI

Simon & Schuster Paperbacks
An Imprint of Simon & Schuster, Inc.
1230 Avenue of the Americas
New York, NY 10020

Copyright © 2021 by Richard Thompson Ford

First Simon & Schuster trade paperback edition January 2022

SIMON & SCHUSTER PAPERBACKS and colophon are registered
trademarks of Simon & Schuster, Inc.

For information about special discounts for bulk purchases,
please contact Simon & Schuster Special Sales at 1-866-506-1949
or business@simonandschuster.com.

The Simon & Schuster Speakers Bureau can bring authors to your
live event. For more information or to book an event, contact the
Simon & Schuster Speakers Bureau at 1-866-248-3049
or visit our website at www.simonspeakers.com.

Interior design by Paul Dippolito

Manufactured in the United States of America

7   9   10   8   6

Library of Congress Cataloging-in-Publication Data has been applied for.

ISBN 978-1-5011-8006-4
ISBN 978-1-5011-8008-8 (pbk)
ISBN 978-1-5011-8009-5 (ebook)

For Richard Donald Ford

Fashion is instant language.

—MIUCCIA PRADA

Contents

Historical Milestones and Important Dress Codes   *xiv*

Introduction   *1*

PART ONE: STATUS SYMBOLS

Chapter One: Encoding Status   25

Concerning the Excessive Display of Trunk Hose,
Crowns, Ruffled Collars, Velvet, and Crimson Silk

Chapter Two: Self-Fashioning   38

Regarding Togas, Gowns, Robes, and Tailored Clothing

Chapter Three: Signs of Faith   46

On the Matter of Dresses with Indulgently Long Trains,
Earrings and Other Vanities, and on the Habits of Women
Religious—Inspired by Christian Dior

Chapter Four: Sex Symbols   67

On the Subject of Plate Armor and Associated
Undergarments, Masks, and Costumes

PART TWO: FROM OPULENCE TO ELEGANCE

Chapter Five: The Great Masculine Renunciation   79

On the Frock Coat, Tartan and Kilt, Civilian Uniforms,
and Powdered Wigs, Both Large and Modest

Chapter Six: Style and Status   100

The Importance of the Well-Dressed Man's Basic Black Suit
and the Elegant Woman's Eight Daily Toilettes; the Prevalence of
Silk and Velvet Waistcoats and the Art of the Perfectly Tied Cravat

Chapter Seven: Sex and Simplicity   109

*The Merits of Tailored Coats, Whaleboned Corsets, Full
Skirts and Petticoats, and Neoclassical Gowns*

Chapter Eight: The "Rational Dress" Movement   126

*The Inconveniences of Bloomers, Tight-laced Corsets,
Starched Collared Shirts, and Suits with Short Trousers*

Chapter Nine: Flapper Feminism   143

*The Scandal of Drop-waisted Shifts, Bobbed Hair,
Cupid's Bow Lips, Dancing Flats, Bakelite Earrings,
and the Symington Side Lacer*

PART THREE: POWER DRESSING

Chapter Ten: Slaves to Fashion?   157

*The Allure and Danger of Dressing Above One's Condition
in Pumps with Silver Buckles, a Hat Cocked in the Macaroni
Fashion, or a Jack Johnson Plaid Suit*

Chapter Eleven: From Rags to Resistance   168

*Seen on the Scene: Zoot Suits, Cotillion Gowns, Pressed Hair,
and Sunday Best; Afros and Overalls, Dashikis, Black
Turtlenecks, and Black Leather Coats*

Chapter Twelve: Sagging and Subordination   196

*Represent the Race! Don't Wear Sagging Pants, Gang Colors,
Hoodie Sweatshirts, or Decorative Orthodontic Devices (aka Grillz)*

PART FOUR: POLITICS AND PERSONALITY

Chapter Thirteen: How to Dress Like a Woman   221

*Your Personal Best: Teased, Curled, or Styled Hair, Lipstick,
Foundation, Eyeliner, Blush, Bunny Ears and Satin Maillot,
High Heels. Overdoing it: Bared Clavicles, Yoga Pants, Miniskirts,
"Smart" Jeans. In Re. Ladies in the Law: Skirts, Nylons, Makeup,
Nothing Low-Cut, a Feminized Morning Suit*

Chapter Fourteen: Recoding Gender 261

Clothing Not Belonging to Your Sex: Prom Night Tuxedoes, Blue (or Pink) for Boys, Pink (or Blue) for Girls, Miniskirts, Tutus, and Tailored Suits

Chapter Fifteen: Piercing the Veil 273

Outlawed as Indecent or Condemned as Sacrilegious: Headscarves, Burkas, Burkinis, Bikinis, Sexy Sheitels, Hip Hijabs, and Covergirl Makeup

PART FIVE: RETAILORED EXPECTATIONS

Chapter Sixteen: Merit Badges 295

Appropriate for the Workplace: Red-Soled Louboutins, a 21 Club Tie, a Blue Blazer, the Preppy Look, Red Sneakers, a Patagonia Vest, a Gray or Black T-shirt. Inappropriate: Designer Dresses, High Heels, Suits

Chapter Seventeen: Artifice and Appropriation 329

Outfits for Cultural Tourism: Bleached Blonde Hair, Dreadlocks, Hoop Earrings, a Cheongsam, a Pink Polo, an Abacost, European Luxury Tailoring

Conclusion: Decoding Dress Codes 355

Epilogue: Dress Codes Stripped Bare 373

Notes 375

Selected Bibliography 415

Acknowledgments 421

Index 425

Image Credits 441

Historical Milestones and Important Dress Codes

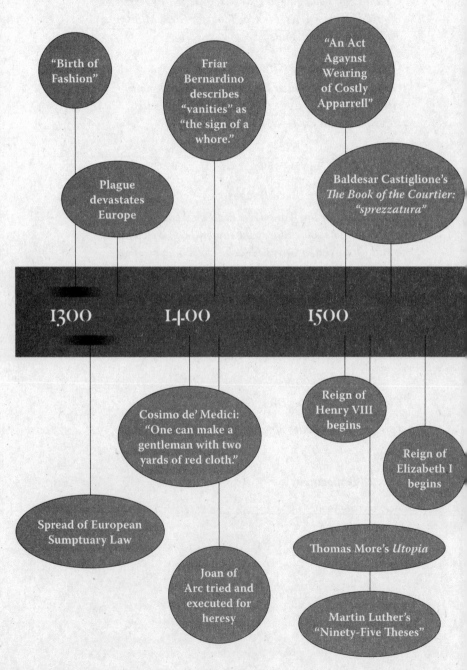

"Birth of Fashion"

Friar Bernardino describes "vanities" as "the sign of a whore."

"An Act Agaynst Wearing of Costly Apparrell"

Plague devastates Europe

Baldesar Castiglione's *The Book of the Courtier:* "*sprezzatura*"

1300

1400

1500

Cosimo de' Medici: "One can make a gentleman with two yards of red cloth."

Reign of Henry VIII begins

Reign of Elizabeth I begins

Spread of European Sumptuary Law

Thomas More's *Utopia*

Joan of Arc tried and executed for heresy

Martin Luther's "Ninety-Five Theses"

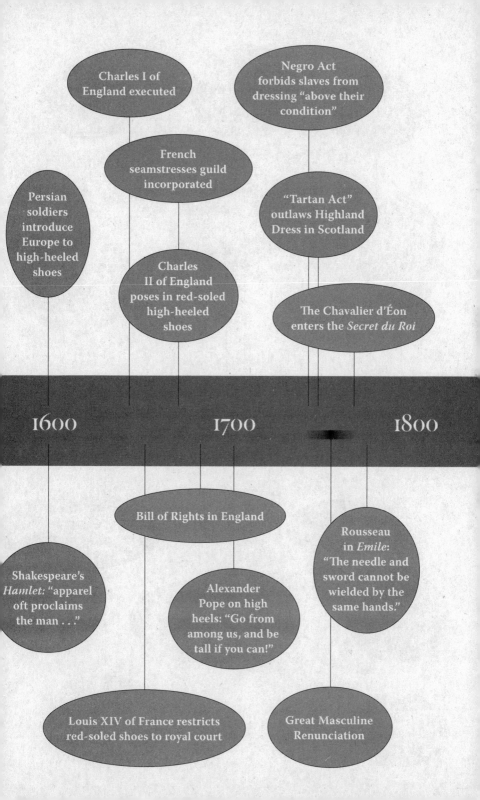

Charles I of England executed

Negro Act forbids slaves from dressing "above their condition"

French seamstresses guild incorporated

Persian soldiers introduce Europe to high-heeled shoes

"Tartan Act" outlaws Highland Dress in Scotland

Charles II of England poses in red-soled high-heeled shoes

The Chavalier d'Éon enters the *Secret du Roi*

1600   **1700**   **1800**

Bill of Rights in England

Rousseau in *Emile*: "The needle and sword cannot be wielded by the same hands."

Shakespeare's *Hamlet*: "apparel oft proclaims the man . . ."

Alexander Pope on high heels: "Go from among us, and be tall if you can!"

Louis XIV of France restricts red-soled shoes to royal court

Great Masculine Renunciation

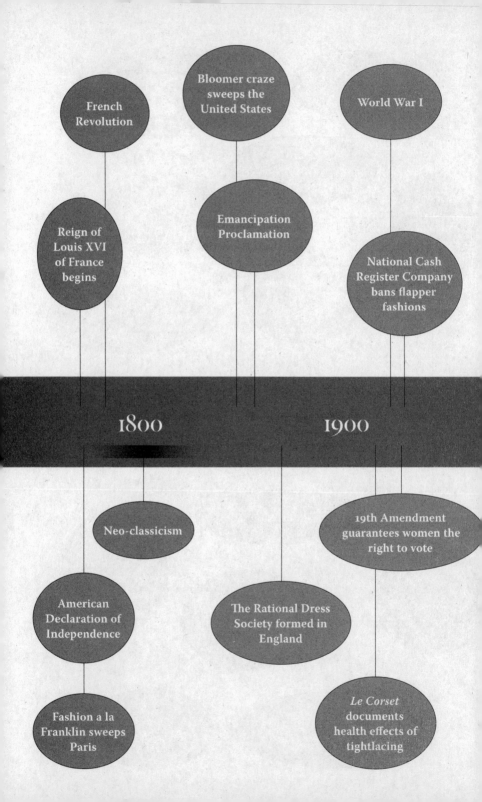

French Revolution

Bloomer craze sweeps the United States

World War I

Reign of Louis XVI of France begins

Emancipation Proclamation

National Cash Register Company bans flapper fashions

1800

1900

Neo-classicism

19th Amendment guarantees women the right to vote

American Declaration of Independence

The Rational Dress Society formed in England

Fashion a la Franklin sweeps Paris

Le Corset documents health effects of tightlacing

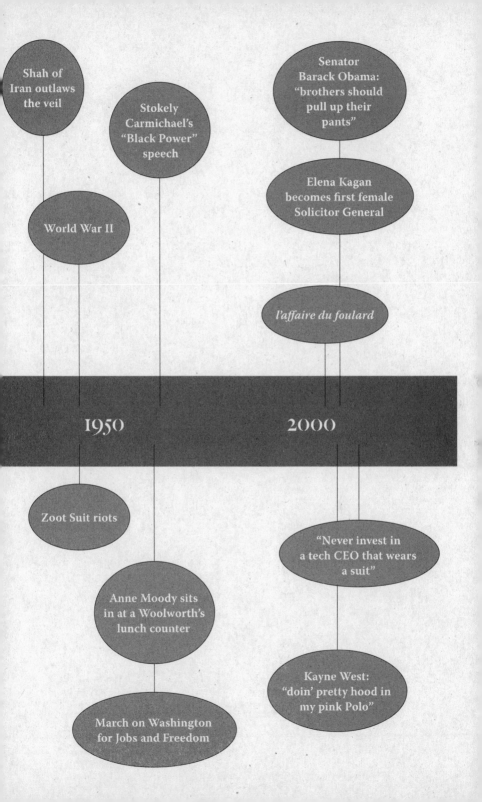

Shah of Iran outlaws the veil

Stokely Carmichael's "Black Power" speech

Senator Barack Obama: "brothers should pull up their pants"

World War II

Elena Kagan becomes first female Solicitor General

l'affaire du foulard

1950

2000

Zoot Suit riots

"Never invest in a tech CEO that wears a suit"

Anne Moody sits in at a Woolworth's lunch counter

Kayne West: "doin' pretty hood in my pink Polo"

March on Washington for Jobs and Freedom

Introduction

THE JANUARY 16, 1797 EDITION OF A LONDON GAZETTE RE-
ported that one John Hetherington, haberdasher of the Strand, was
arraigned on a charge of breach of the peace and inciting to riot and
required to post bond in the amount of 500 pounds for the following
offense:

> It was in evidence that Mr. Hetherington . . . appeared on the pub-
> lic highway wearing upon his head what he called a silk hat (which
> was offered into evidence), a tall structure having a shining lus-
> tre, and calculated to frighten timid people. As a matter of fact,
> the officers of the Crown stated that several women fainted at the
> unusual sight, while children screamed, dogs yelped and a [young
> man] was thrown down by the crowd which had collected, and
> had his right arm broken. For these reasons the defendant was
> seized by the guards and taken before the Lord Mayor.

What rule, written or implied but apparently known to all (even
dogs!), did Mr. Hetherington and his headwear violate? Tall, cylindrical hats were common well before the late eighteenth century: for
instance, the Puritans of the mid-seventeenth century wore a severe
black felt hat that is now familiar to every American schoolchild as
the headwear of the *Mayflower* pilgrims. And a scant thirty years after
Mr. Hetherington's arrest, the top hat had become an avatar of the
staid and self-satisfied plutocrat, marketed with names such as the
D'Orsay, the Wellington, and the Regent. What now-obscure code

allowed a top hat to be read as a provocation, "calculated to frighten" and deserving of legal sanction? Unfortunately, we can only speculate: the surviving record of the case begins and ends with this brief newspaper column.

It wasn't the first time a hat caused a riot and it wouldn't be the last. For instance, during the notorious Straw Hat Riot of 1922, marauding gangs in New York City violently enforced the rule that no man should wear a straw hat after September 15, knocking offending headwear off the heads of passersby, stomping on the hats and impaling them on pikes. The riots engulfed the city from the Bronx to the Battery: more than one thousand would-be fashion police gathered uptown on Amsterdam Avenue attacking straw-hatted bystanders, while downtown, fights between the vigilantes and citizens who attempted to defend their hats stopped traffic on the Manhattan Bridge.

One might think that such sartorial strictures and prescriptions are largely things of the past: the once-ubiquitous suit and tie, to say nothing of the dressy hat, are almost historical costume. But while dress codes may seem like a throwback, if anything they are growing more and more popular. For instance, in 1999 to 2000, 46.7 percent of U.S. public schools enforced a "strict dress code"—by 2013 to 2014, 58.5 percent did. Millions of people must conform to a dress code every day at work or school, and millions more confront dress codes after hours in restaurants, nightclubs, and theaters. Even the relaxed, bohemian domain of the American coffee shop is governed by dress codes: a 2014 dress code dictates that the Starbucks barista must eschew unnatural hair colors, nail polish, short skirts, and piercings other than earrings and subtle nose studs (no septum rings allowed). And dress codes aren't just for school-age kids and image-conscious private businesses: they are in force on the public streets, where clothing deemed provocative or threatening may be against the law. Those "sagging" pants favored by some rappers and their fans could be grounds for arrest in certain cities, and if police decide they mark you as a member of a gang, they could even turn a minor crime into a capital offense.

Some dress codes not only prescribe and prohibit specific garments but also obsessively dictate the minutia of attire. Consider the

2010 dress code of the Union Bank of Switzerland, a forty-four-page tome that directs employees to avoid chipped nail polish and scuffed shoes, make sure that jewelry matches the metallic color of eyeglasses, and that neckties just touch the tops of belt buckles. Exacting and detailed rules about what to wear are everywhere.

Consider one small but telling example: today's masculine formal and semiformal attire is almost a uniform, but it's a uniform one must assemble through the mastery and application of rules. The canons of menswear dictate that a black-tie ensemble consists of a black or midnight-blue jacket with a peak lapel or shawl collar faced in satin or grosgrain, and pants with the outside seam covered by a silk or grosgrain stripe. If the jacket is double breasted, it must have a peak lapel. If it is single breasted, it can have a peak lapel or shawl collar, but never a notched lapel, which is characteristic of a more quotidian business suit. A cummerbund, worn so that its pleats face up (a nod to the era when men tucked theater tickets into it), must cover the waist, unless the jacket is double breasted, in which case a cummerbund must not be worn. Trousers must be supported by suspenders or "braces"—never a belt—and indeed, the trousers of a semiformal suit must not have belt loops. In 2010, the *Wall Street Journal* offered many of these rules, as well as a few others, in response to a reader's inquiry:

> *Your shirt should be of white marcella . . . with a bib front. . . .*
> *French cuffs are a must. . . .*
> *[as is] The bowtie . . . and learn to tie it. . . .*
> *[P]ocket square, cuff links, watch (which should match your cuff links). . . .*

And even after following such detailed guidelines, you can still get it wrong: according to the men's style blog *The Art of Manliness,* when attending a black-tie affair, "the implication that you would check the time is considered rude to the hosts." In other words, when worn with a black-tie ensemble, a watch—even one that matches one's cuff links—is inappropriate.

And yet the typical black-tie soiree is a come-as-you-are shindig compared to a day at the races in the Royal Enclosure at Ascot, where:

Ladies are kindly reminded that . . .

Dresses and skirts should be of modest length defined as falling just above the knee or longer.

Dresses and tops should have straps of one inch or greater.

Trouser suits are welcome. They should be of full length and of matching material and colour.

Hats should be worn; however a headpiece which has a solid base of 4 inches (10cm) or more in diameter is acceptable as an alternative to a hat. . . .

Strapless, off the shoulder, halter neck and spaghetti straps are not permitted.

Midriffs must be covered.

Fascinators are not permitted; neither are headpieces which do not have a solid base covering a sufficient area of the head (4 inches/10cm).

As for men, even an immaculately correct dinner suit ensemble, watch left safely behind at home, would be out of place at Ascot, where:

[I]t is a requirement to wear either black or grey morning dress which must include:

A waistcoat and tie (no cravats)

A black or grey top hat

Black shoes

A gentleman may remove his top hat within a restaurant, a private box, a private club or that facility's terrace, balcony or garden. Hats may also be removed within any enclosed external seating area within the Royal Enclosure Garden.

The customisation of top hats (with, for example, coloured ribbons or bands) is not permitted in the Royal Enclosure.

Such nitpicking isn't limited to unusually fastidious businesses and old-fashioned festivities. In 2018, I asked Kate Lanphear, creative director of *Marie Claire* magazine and a self-described "punk-rock girl," about today's dress codes. She pointed out that even oppositional subcultures that pride themselves on breaking all of the rules still "follow a code. . . . The patches you put on a denim jacket or the pins, the band T-shirt you're wearing is still a code to other people to identify with . . . [they're saying] *I'm part of this tribe* . . . [they're] following the code of the rule breakers." In other words, those rule breakers replace the old rules with new rules—often as uncompromising as those they just broke. Here, I am reminded of the Pinnacle Peak Steakhouse in Southern California, known for its large portions and rustic atmosphere, where employees wielding scissors cut off the neckties of unsuspecting businessmen: the work-a-day rule requiring neckties is replaced by an after-hours rule forbidding them. Similarly, free-spirited college students who blanch at the idea of a dress code imposed by university administrators seem happy to conform to intricate unwritten rules about attire: campus social cliques are readily identified by their shared style of dress, and the fashions of just a few years ago are as completely absent as if they had been prohibited by law. Their professors, for their part, advertise their disdain for surface appearances with a *deshabillement* that has become a kind of academic credential: the naïve assistant professor who wears a Dolce & Gabbana dress to a faculty meeting may need years to recover an aura of scholarly gravitas. Even the Silicon Valley style of casual wear has become a kind of dress code: if a sweatshirt and flip-flops demonstrate a single-minded focus on innovation, a suit and tie betray an outmoded concern with appearances and status. Accordingly, one Northern California investor advised to "never invest in a tech CEO that wears a suit. . . ." These unwritten dress codes can be as powerful as rules inscribed in law and enforced by police.

A different kind of dress code gives our clothing social meaning. It is said that it takes about three seconds to make a first impression. What you wear is one of the most important parts of that introductory image. Clothing can magnify and embellish natural differences and can make the abstract statuses of social hierarchy tangible. The European aristocrat and blue-blooded New England preppy are defined by the subtleties of dress as much as by wealth and family lineage. Gender difference is marked by clothing, hairstyles, and cosmetics. Racial and ethnic groups maintain the bonds of kinship and solidarity through distinctive grooming and attire. Even religious faith—often thought of as a matter of private belief—is given public significance by prescribed and forbidden dress and grooming. And we don't just dress to impress others: our attire reflects our deepest commitments, aspirations, and sense of self. People often refer to a favorite item of clothing as a "signature": what we choose to wear can be as personal as our name. Yet we often take these most conspicuous elements of social standing and personal distinction for granted.

Why is attire so rule bound? Why and when is clothing important enough to become the subject of treatises, rules and regulations, legislative proclamations and judicial edicts? What happens—and what should happen—when those rules come into conflict with changing social norms about equality and personal freedom? When do dress codes serve useful purposes and when are they needlessly repressive or unjust? What does it mean to dress for success, or to flout the rules in the interest of self-expression? Is our choice of attire ever really personal, or do we always dress to impress—or provoke—other people? Are rules about clothing less important in the era of telecommuting and online dating or have our less frequent face-to-face interactions become all the more loaded with meaning? *Dress Codes* will answer these questions and many others, exploring the laws of fashion throughout history to uncover the personal, social, and political significance of clothing—our most intimate and most public medium of self-expression.

Decoding Dress: Communication and Self-Fashioning

Like a lot of men, I inherited whatever sense of style I have from my father. He was a man of rigorous and refined sensibilities—a trained tailor, a scholar, an activist, and an ordained minister. For years my dad endured my sartorial misadventures (asymmetrical "new-wave" haircuts, nylon parachute pants, the "punk" look, which consisted of deliberately torn garments held together with safety pins or duct tape) in quiet despair. It is said that the boy is father to the man, but, at least in this case, it turned out the father was the father: at long last I followed my dad's lead. I came to appreciate the virtues of well-cut tailored clothing, polished dress shoes, crisp shirts, even, on occasion, a necktie—though life in early twenty-first-century Northern California rarely calls for one. I learned how to tie a half and full Windsor and a four-in-hand knot and how to tie a bow tie—this last a skill needed only for rare black-tie events but, my dad insisted, worth mastering because "when the time comes, you won't be stuck wearing one of those ridiculous clip-ons." I learned how to tell the difference between a jacket properly constructed with a floating canvas and one that is fused ("glued together," Dad would grumble). Most of all, I learned that clothing could be both a form of self-constitution and a medium of communication, and how attire conveys respect or disdain, purpose or aimlessness, seriousness or frivolity. This combination of personal significance and social meaning explains why governments, businesses, and the institutions of civil society regulate attire and why individuals often consider such regulations oppressive and insulting.

My father had died twelve years before I decided to enter *Esquire* magazine's Best Dressed Real Man contest in 2009. My circumstances at the time will be familiar to any new parent: my second child was ten months old and my wife, Marlene, and I hadn't been out to dinner or a movie in as many months; our aspirations to a glamorous and urbane existence were a faded memory, our fashionable—or at least serviceable—festive attire pushed aside to make room for a slew of cotton onesies and bright plastic baby toys; our feeble attempts at grown-up merrymaking reduced to cocktails hastily mixed in the kitchen in between bottle feedings and diaper changes. One day after work I decided it would be a welcome change of pace to enter the *Esquire* contest and rally our friends to support my quixotic campaign: harried forty-three-year-old dad versus a bevy of lantern-jawed aspiring actors, sinewy fashion models, and athletic-looking frat boys: David against Adonis. The entry deadline was the next day. Marlene got out the camera and snapped a series of pictures. My five-year-

One of my wife's photos for my bid to be *Esquire*
magazine's Best Dressed Real Man. My son, Cole, is
stage right reading a magazine; daughter, Ella, is in
my lap, wriggling away to get to her mother.

old son Cole explored my stack of old magazines while ten-month-old Ella did everything she could to get her parents' attention. A few minutes later, with Ella screaming for a bottle or a diaper change, we called it quits. I uploaded the snapshots, filled out a short questionnaire, and hit "send."

Then I scoped out the competition. Other contestants had professional photos shot in exotic locations with exquisite backlighting. Some had already amassed tens of thousands of votes; I was hoping to break into triple digits. Several weeks later the website posted the top twenty-five semifinalists and, to my astonishment, there were the photos of me holding a squirming toddler while trying to show a favorite blue pinstripe suit to its best effect. It couldn't be right: I refreshed the browser and waited for the real list of semifinalists to appear. I was still there. A few days later my phone rang: *Esquire* had narrowed the field to ten, whom they were now interviewing in order to select five finalists who would fly to New York, receive fabulous prizes, and appear on the *Today* show. They wanted to talk to me about my personal style. *How did you choose what to wear? Can you be more specific? What tips do you offer others? "Be yourself" isn't very helpful, is it? Why is style important to you? Who are your style inspirations? C'mon, everyone says their father; who else? Everyone says Cary Grant. Everyone says Miles Davis too. David Bowie; that's better. Which era? Let's Dance? Really?* A few days later, the editor called again to break the bad news: I was number six, just short of the cutoff for finalists. It was all great fun, but also humbling. Talking about my personal style should have been easy: I'm a professor, someone who explains things to people for a living. But I blew the interview. I knew intuitively why I wore what I did, but I could not explain it to save my life—or my chances at a fabulous, all-expenses-paid weekend in New York City. My dad's guidance had—against all odds—helped me into the top ten, but he couldn't help me decrypt the inscrutable codes of dress.

In a sense this book is my response, in *l'esprit d'escalier.* In it, I will explore dress codes antique and contemporary: medieval sumptuary laws and modern indecency statutes, Renaissance vestimentary norms and Victorian-era sartorial etiquette, the sartorial rules of the road—and of the street, workplace, and school.

To understand why we care so much about what we—and other people—wear, I had to look at how clothing and fashion shape our behavior and perception of the world. That's not always easy to do because the way clothing affects our social interactions and worldview is a matter of habit, so reflexive and deeply engrained that we don't even notice it. Of course we *do* notice the multibillion-dollar fashion industry dedicated to offering us an array of clothes to choose from, the styles that change every few months, the clothes magazines and newspaper columns that report on the latest trends, the stores full of clothes, and all of those dress codes, rules, and expectations around clothing. But all this ever-changing detail, as overwhelming as it can seem, is just a small part of the world of fashion, like an eye-catching appliqué on top of a jacket.

We're immersed in these details, but we rarely question or analyze the larger patterns of dress. For instance, what makes some fashions masculine and others feminine? Why are some garments considered bold or edgy and others conservative or demure? What makes high heels frivolously sexy and flat shoes sensible but boring? We make small decisions about the fit, cut, and embellishments of our clothing, but almost no one questions its basic design. Two thousand years ago, a politician would have worn a draped garment—what we today might call a "toga"—when going to discuss affairs of state. The political leaders and elites of seven hundred years ago still wore draped robes not so different from the ancient toga. But most of today's politicians wear tailored trousers—the garb of the barbarian or the peasant to the ancients—and a matching longish jacket with lapels: the business suit. Why and when did this change take place? No one would dream of wearing a robe or a toga to an important meeting, but many women in more tradition-bound professions still eschew pants in favor of a dress or skirt, both essentially draped garments descended from the ancient toga. We take all of this, and much more, for granted. These larger and more long-lived trends in fashion organize society and shape how we think about ourselves. They are often the subject of explicit rules—dress codes—that determine both what clothing means and when and by whom it may be worn.

We need to look at changes in fashion over a long period of time—not seasons, years, or even decades but centuries—in order to see these larger trends. Looking at the rules that codified these changes alongside the historical events of the time helped me to understand what fashion meant then and what it means for us today. I learned that fashion is much more than just clothes.

Fashion is a way of communicating ideas, values, and aspirations through clothes. Through our attire, we announce who we are, what we care about, and where we belong—or aspire to belong—in society. Sometimes the message is obvious and direct, like the way an officer's uniform conveys authority; other times, more inchoate and figurative, like the way a punk-rock girl's denim jacket covered with patches and pins conveys rebellious swagger.

Less obviously, but perhaps more important, fashion is a means of transforming our sense of self and our sense of our place in society—what I will call, borrowing from the historian Stephen Greenblatt, self-fashioning. Attire can also change our self-perception and affect our learning, development, and sense of possibility. In a sense, we become what we dress for: our clothing trains us to occupy a social role—giving us confidence or sapping our courage, straightening our posture or forcing us to slouch, offering a sense of physical comfort and support or constraint and irritation. In this respect, in contradiction to the old saying, clothes actually do make the man (or woman, and they've long helped to establish the difference). Our clothing becomes a part of our bodies, both reflecting and shaping our personalities and helping us fit into various social roles—or making it hard for us to do so. An obvious example of this is women's clothing in the mid-1800s, which consisted of large full skirts, frills, and boned corsets. These outfits not only sent the message that women were decorative objects, valuable mainly for their beauty; they also made it impossible for women to move around easily or quickly and harder for them to perform many types of physical tasks, which in turn served as a visual "evidence" that women were less competent than men. Most women internalized the dress codes of the time and only felt comfortable in such clothing. This in turn led some to think of themselves as helpless and fundamentally decorative: their clothing determined their social roles and ultimately their sense of self. Here's another example of the self-fashioning power of clothing: psychological studies in 2012 and 2015 found that people who wore a white lab coat or dressed up for a job interview exhibited better abstract reasoning than people of comparable intelligence wearing jeans and T-shirts.

Dress codes are key pieces of evidence about both of these social functions of attire: communication and self-fashioning. "Dress code" has a double meaning: a code is a rule regulating action or behavior, such as a law, but a code is also a rule or a formula for interpreting or deciphering a text. So, a dress code is a rule or law regulating how we dress and also a rule controlling the meaning of our attire. In 1967 the semiologist Roland Barthes used the explicit discussions of clothing in high-fashion magazines as a guide to understand more mundane, day-to-day attire. He found that almost every detail of an ensemble— shirt collar, skirt length, color, pattern, fabric—could express passions, aspirations, fantasies, and convictions. The fashion magazine offered an incomplete lexicon of vestimentary meaning—it was at once a description of existing fashionable practices and a prescription for refining and improving them. I have a similar ambition for the study of dress codes. Dress codes simplify the often-overwhelming complexity of vestimentary custom because they take the form of *rules*. Because it must be specific in its prescriptions and prohibitions, a dress code—like fashion writing—makes the often implicit and unconscious meaning of attire explicit and deliberate. When a dress code requires or forbids an item of attire, it implies something of its social meaning. A dress code that excludes "unprofessional" attire simultaneously reinforces the perception that whatever attire it excludes is unprofessional. Ladies' "fascinators" are modish and informal in comparison to hats that cover the top of the head; septum rings are edgier than nose studs. A dress code can be the Rosetta stone to decode the meaning of attire.

We can get a hint about how people understood an article of clothing by looking at the rules that allowed and prohibited it. Sometimes dress codes are quite explicit about the meaning of the attire they regulate: for instance, some Renaissance-era dress codes said that red or purple symbolized noble birth, and others insisted that jewelry and sumptuous adornments were signs of sexual licentiousness. Moreover, these dress codes didn't just reflect preexisting associations between clothing and social status, sexual morality and political position—they also reinforced and at times even created those associations, changing the way people thought of those wearing a certain garment and how the people wearing it thought of themselves. Defining the social meaning of a garment can actually change the way it shapes individual self-image. For instance, remember that psychological experiment involving the white lab coat? It also found that people wearing an identical coat did not exhibit improved cognitive performance if they were told beforehand that it was a painter's coat instead of a lab coat.

The Law of Fashion

In 1974, one year before he would become an associate justice of the Supreme Court of the United States, John Paul Stevens wrote the following:

> From the earliest days of organized society . . . matters of appearance and dress have always been subjected to control and regulation, sometimes by custom and social pressure, sometimes by legal rules. . . . [J]ust as the individual has an interest in a choice among different styles of appearance . . . so also does society have a legitimate interest in placing limits on the exercise of that choice.

The case, *Miller v. School District No. 167*, involved a public school teacher who wore a "Vandyke" beard (a sort of abbreviated goatee shaped into a point at the chin, reminiscent of the Flemish painter Anthony van Dyck) in violation of his school's dress code. The court opined that "dress and hair styles [are] matters of relatively trivial importance" and rejected Mr. Miller's claim that the dress code violated his Constitutional rights.

I have no idea whether or not Miller deserved to keep his job as a math teacher. But I want to challenge the notion that dress and grooming are trivial—an idea all too common among lawyers, scholars, and other folks dedicated to weighty matters and serious causes. Most lawyers opt for safe and unremarkable professional attire, while the stereotypical intellectual exhibits a fashionable indifference to fashion: the best one can say of the attire of the typical professor is that it suggests a high-minded disdain toward clothes—a prejudice that has made any serious scholarly study of attire decidedly déclassé. Indeed, many years ago when I first wrote about disputes over dress codes, I too concluded that they were ultimately too trivial to merit the attention of lawyers or the courts. Today, I would insist clothing is as appropriate a subject for study, analysis, and even legal attention as any other art form or medium of expression. In this book I've tried to address these issues with more depth and nuance, stressing the importance of personal appearance in political struggles for equality and individual dignity and exploring the long history of efforts to shape and control it through dress codes.

For centuries, dress codes took the form of laws: medieval and Renaissance-era sumptuary laws assigned clothing according to social rank, the laws of American slave states prohibited Black people from dressing "above their condition," public decency laws required men and women to wear attire considered appropriate to their sex. These laws inspired and reinforced a host of rules surrounding attire: private business, enterprises, and clubs adopted explicit dress codes, etiquette guides promulgated rules of socially acceptable dress, and informal norms calcified into hard-and-fast unwritten rules—such as the rule against wearing a straw hat after September 15—enforced by social pressure and mob violence.

Today, the law, which for hundreds of years had underwritten dress codes, now often undercuts them. Legal rights to expressive liberty and laws against discrimination increasingly clash with many kinds of dress codes: for instance, in 2015 the New York City Commission on Human Rights informed business in the Big Apple that "dress codes . . . that impose different standards . . . based on sex or gender" are unlawful. The dress codes this edict legally proscribes include "requiring different uniforms for men and women . . . requiring employees of one gender to wear a uniform specific to that gender. . . ." and, in what seems to be a jab at the famous (but now suspended) policy of Midtown Manhattan's venerable 21 Club, "requiring all men to wear ties in order to dine at a restaurant."

But for the most part, the idea that dress and grooming are trivial has ensured that only a small fraction of disputes about dress get any attention at all, and those that do must be attached to some "more serious" claim, such as discrimination or expressive liberty. For instance, dress codes imposed by the government may violate the First Amendment guarantee of freedom of expression. But, for the most part, this is true only when the attire prohibited is "symbolic" in a fairly uninteresting sense of the term: a stand-in for a statement that could easily be translated into words. Accordingly, lawyers and judges look for an explicit, manifesto-like message in clothing or grooming. This ham-fisted literalism misses what is most profound about vestimentary self-expression: its unique ability to embellish, obscure, and reshape the human body. Fashion is a unique mode of expression that cannot be mirrored or conveyed through language or any other medium. Fashion sends messages, but the significance of attire isn't just a matter of literal meaning; it is more visceral and impressionistic than words on a page. A well-cut suit conveys wealth and sophistication by evoking other wealthy and sophisticated people—it is less an argument than a demonstration. An oversimplified idea of fashion-as-a-language leaves out everything distinctive about the expressive potential of clothing. It's like insisting that a Mark Rothko painting is *a statement about the loss of our authentic connection with nature in the condition of modernity*—overlooking the powerful aesthetic experience that is as obvious as it is inscrutable.

Some dress codes may violate laws prohibiting discrimination. But which do and why is obscure and confusing to anyone without legal training. For instance, an employer can have different dress codes for men and women without, legally speaking, "discriminating" as long as the dress codes don't impose "unequal burdens" on one sex or the other and are not "demeaning." In recent years some courts have concluded that a sex-specific workplace dress code may unlawfully discriminate against transgender employees, but oddly, it is not the obvious discrimination involved in a sex-specific workplace dress code that violates the law but only the decision to enforce it based on an employee's birth sex as opposed to the sex the employee identifies with. It's not clear where this leaves people who don't identify as either male or female. At the same time, in order to avoid "discrimination," employers must make special exceptions to dress codes that apply to all for religiously motivated attire—in effect creating different dress codes for employees of different religions. Workplace dress codes may ban hairstyles that result from artifice—such as teased hair or braids—but not those that are a consequence of the natural texture of hair. But, of course, a dress code can regulate the *length* of hair. Meanwhile, apart from this welter of conceptually inconsistent rules and surprising exceptions, a business can have pretty much any dress code it wants to, even when personal appearance has nothing whatsoever to do with the job.

Consider the plight of Chastity Jones, an African American woman who was denied a job as a call center operator because she wore her hair in dreadlocks in violation of a workplace dress code. She sued, claiming race discrimination, but the dress code, which applied to everyone regardless of race, wasn't obviously discriminatory and Jones couldn't prove it was applied inequitably. But step away from the legal complexities for a minute and it is obvious that Chastity Jones deserved to win as a matter of simple fairness. There's a powerful case to be made that hairstyles like locs are an important part of the struggle for equal respect and dignity. But we don't even have to make that case to see Ms. Jones's hair was important to her. What's more, it had nothing to do with the job she had applied for.

After all, the job in question was working at a *telephone call center*: no customer would ever see her hair! Because judges and lawyers—including no less a legal authority than John Paul Stevens—believe that dress and grooming are trivial, Ms. Jones couldn't make that straightforward case. She had to frame her objections in terms that law would recognize. Unfortunately, that frame didn't fit the picture well enough.

As a lawyer and scholar, I've spent much of my career studying, teaching, and advocating for reform in civil rights, a domain of the law where disputes involving attire and grooming are remarkably common. Because I also happen to be someone who is interested in fashion, I have always thought the legal arguments in many of these cases lost sight of some of the most obvious and important stakes of the disagreements. One reason I decided to explore the history of dress codes was to see more clearly what was at the center of these controversies. A look at earlier eras, before the idea that fashion is trivial and inconsequential had taken hold, revealed more candid discussions of dress—and the reasons for dress codes.

Status, Sex, Power, Personality

Our story begins in what many historians consider the end of antiquity and the beginning of a modern sensibility: the fourteenth century. The Middle Ages are coming to an end and the Renaissance is beginning to take shape. During this period, a new social sensibility emerges, one that places the individual at its center. This modern sensibility eventually inspired new forms of art, such as the novel, new conceptions of human consciousness in modern psychology, and the new political and ethical ideals of classical liberal thought, associated with theorists such as John Locke, Immanuel Kant, and Jean-Jacques Rousseau. New styles of attire accompanied and contributed to these developments: people sought out new ways of presenting the body as a reflection and extension of a unique individual personality. These new styles became the first "fashion" in the sense that I will use that term. While I would not go so far as to claim that fashion was an indispensable condition of modernity, the development of fashion played a role—and often a very important role—in contemporaneous social, intellectual, and political events. Throughout its long history, people thought fashion had political stakes; that's why some passed laws and developed rules regulating it and why others struggled to resist and overturn those laws and rules.

Trying to interpret the language of clothing is a daunting task. Attire can convey an almost infinite number of messages, drawing on centuries of garments, each of which may evoke a historical moment, a social institution, a political struggle, an erotic possibility. How can anyone hope to unweave the myriad threads of the long history of fashion? Thankfully, we don't have to. Using dress codes—rules, laws, and social strictures about clothing—as our Rosetta stone, we can identify four concerns underlying the major developments in fashion: *status, sex, power*, and *personality*.

Clothing is a status symbol, and history is replete with rules and laws designed to ensure that the social status of individuals is reflected in what they wear. Dress is also a sex symbol—social conventions and laws have ensured that clothing establishes whether one is male or female, sexually innocent or experienced, married or single, chaste or promiscuous. Attire is a uniform of power: it has helped define national belonging as much as any territorial border; it has differentiated ethnic groups and tribes as much as any language or cultural ritual; it has shaped religious sects as much as any scripture; and it has both established and challenged racial hierarchies. Finally, fashion is a medium for the expression of individual personality. We assemble our wardrobes and daily ensembles to reflect a distinctive point of view and confirm a distinctive sense of self. The history of fashion has run in parallel to the history of individualism: as individual freedom has grown, so has personal liberty in dress.

This book looks at how people tried to control fashion and why. Part One examines the use of dress codes to create *status symbols* in the late Middle Ages and Renaissance, just as fashion and the modern sensibility are born. The history of modern fashion and modern dress codes begins in the 1300s, when men stopped wearing draped garments and began wearing tailored clothing. With this technical innovation, clothing became a much more expressive medium than it had been before. For the next four centuries, fashion was the privilege of the elite and, accordingly, it often expressed royal power and aristocratic rank. In an era when most people were illiterate, social values were communicated through images: art, religious iconography, dazzling rituals, and, of course, sumptuous attire. But the emergence of modern fashion was a threat to an older social order. Fashion allowed individuals to assert distinctive personality, independent of—and even in opposition to—traditional social roles. Economic dynamism made a new class of people—merchants, bankers, and tradespeople—wealthy; they sought to show off their newfound success through fashion. Some upwardly mobile people copied aristocratic dress in order to pass themselves off as nobility, disrupting its exclusivity. Others used fashion to assert their own distinctive social status, challenging aristocratic preeminence. Many early modern dress codes were the efforts of elites to use fashion to reinforce familiar social roles and established prerogatives, and to outlaw, condemn, and ridicule the ambitions of social upstarts, religious minorities seeking social inclusion, and women asserting equality with men.

A profound change occurred in the late eighteenth century, when political revolutions and the influence of Enlightenment philosophy began to discredit aristocratic pretensions. Part Two explores the shift in fashion from *opulence to elegance*. The rise of Enlightenment ideals brought corresponding changes in dress codes. The display of opulence characteristic of elite attire in the Middle Ages and Renaissance gave way to a new ideal of understatement: the courtly display that advertised the divine right of kings and queens yielded to a new aristocratic wardrobe. In this new political context, high social status began to be associated with industriousness, competence, and enlightened reason as opposed to noble birth and honor, and it was marked by a new understated elite style. Men still distinguished themselves through their attire, but the mark of elite status was in subtle refinements rather than conspicuous adornment. In many respects, this shift was a way of *preserving* elitism under the guise of

attacking it: advances in manufacturing and trade along with a growing market in secondhand clothing had made many formerly rare
adornments and luxuries more widely available, diluting their value
as signs of exclusive privilege. The new status symbols of elegance,
by contrast, required education and acculturation, which were much
harder to fake. Meanwhile, the decline of dynastic power and the rise
of the nation-state as a political formation inspired new dress codes.
The eighteenth and nineteenth centuries witnessed proposals for national civilian uniforms in Western Europe and the United States, as
well as legislation outlawing the traditional dress of ethnic minorities
in Great Britain.

This shift from conspicuous opulence to understated elegance
was, for the most part, exclusive to men. Feminists and their allies
such as Amelia Bloomer resisted the restrictions of gendered roles
and gendered fashions, but their efforts to reform women's dress met
with ridicule and ended in failure. It would require a more fashionable form of resistance to begin to undo the gender norms that had
kept women in corsets and petticoats for over a century. As women
entered the workforce in large numbers during World War I, they finally achieved widespread acceptance of new, streamlined fashions
that began to adopt some of the sartorial innovations of menswear.
At first the "flapper" was ridiculed—as attempts to adopt practical,
unadorned women's wear had always been. But the clothing these
women pioneered formed the basis of a reformed feminine dress
code for the emancipated woman that is still with us today. Despite
these unquestionable advances, many feminists would rightly insist
that today's fashions still reflect ancient patriarchal ideals of feminine
decorativeness and compulsory modesty.

Part Three looks at *power dressing*. African Americans drew on
the evocative power of attire to reinforce their claims to equal dignity
and respect, first as slaves, runaways, and free Blacks struggling for
basic humanity in an unapologetically racist society; after Emancipation, under the vicious indignities of Jim Crow, and, of course, during
the civil rights struggle, when activists wore their "Sunday best" in
an effort to confound racial stereotypes. Later generations of activists

developed alternative sartorial vocabularies to the respectability politics of the early civil rights movement. These took the forms of a fashionable solidarity with agricultural laborers, the sleek, martial/beatnik garb of Black Power radicalism, and a romantic Afro-centrism. African Americans today still struggle over what some see as the elitism of respectability politics and what others condemn as the impracticality (and subtler elitism) of "radical chic."

Parts Four and Five examine the dress codes of the late twentieth and early twenty-first centuries. Our ideas about attire have become more relaxed, but we continue to control dress and to judge others by what they wear.

Part Four examines the changing dress codes regulating and defining gendered attire. As women demand equality and begin to enjoy prerogatives once reserved for men, the stakes of dress codes for women involve both *politics* and *personality*. Some women seek to escape the limitations of conventional femininity by rejecting compulsory feminine decorativeness in favor of a modest austerity while others reject compulsory feminine modesty in favor of a daring sexual assertiveness. Each of these new forms of power dressing comes with its own distinctive promise—and peril. Meanwhile, the next generation challenges the conventional association of sex and gendered attire, creating a new vocabulary of sex symbols that don't refer to biological reproductive roles.

Part Five explores today's remixing of sartorial symbols, made possible by the absence of consistent dress codes, and the *retailored expectations* this change has brought. We are much more accepting of individual choice in fashion than past generations were: indeed, we not only accept but *expect* that clothing will reflect personality. Today, we all have the centuries-long history of fashion at our disposal: everyone is free to adopt any of the status symbols of the past, whether or not one occupies the social roles that once defined them. But of course, dress codes persist: both the written rules that govern, for example, the attire of high school students and employees in the service sector and the unwritten expectations that ensure that Manhattan investment bankers all wear the same style of fleece sweater over identical light-blue oxford cloth dress shirts. Even if the formal authority of the government is no longer typically involved, social expectations and pressures constrain individual freedom. Most people still expect that clothing will reflect the social class, race, religion, and sex of the person wearing it, and some consider transgressions of older strictures disrespectful or even deceptive. Accordingly, many of today's dress codes are designed to make sure clothing continues to symbolize social position, both by censuring novel and unconventional uses of older sartorial symbols and by creating new status symbols that only a select few can decode. The triumph of individualism has created new opportunities for—and poses new challenges to—fashionable expression.

Dress Codes will look at what we wear and why to reveal how fashion made history.

Part One

Status Symbols

One can make a gentleman with two yards of red cloth.
—COSIMO DE' MEDICI

In difficult times, fashion is always outrageous.
—ELSA SCHIAPARELLI

Chapter One

Encoding Status

*Concerning the Excessive Display of Trunk Hose,
Crowns, Ruffled Collars, Velvet, and Crimson Silk*

IN 1565, THE HAPLESS RICHARD WALWEYN, SERVANT OF ROW-
land Bangham, Esq., was arrested for wearing "a very monsterous
and outraygeous greate payre of hose." For his crime of fashion, Walweyn was detained "untyll such a tyme as he had bought or otherwyse
provided himself of hoose of a decent & lawfull facyon [fashion] &
sorte . . . and also shewed himself in same new hose this afternoone"
to the Lord Mayor of London. The court ordered that the offending garment be confiscated and exhibited "in some open place in the
nether hall where they maye be aptly seen and consideryd of the people as an example of extreme folye."

Historian Victoria Buckley describes trunk hose as a "large pair
of inflated shorts . . . ballooning out from the waist and tapering in
around the upper thigh."

They "could often be . . . ludicrous, with enormous amounts of padding and stiffening and even . . . panels sewn into the hose, in gaudy
silks, which the wearer could pull through the outer fabric and puff up
before strutting off. . . ." If trunk hose were the parachute pants of their
day, Richard Walweyn was a Renaissance-era MC Hammer. And according to the authorities, trunk hose had become a public menace in
Elizabethan England. A royal proclamation in 1551 lamented "the use
of monstrous and outrageous greatness of hosen . . . crept a late into

Trunk hose were fashionable menswear during
the Elizabethan era.

the Realme, to the great slaunder thereof, & the undoyng of a number usyng the same, beyng dryven for maynetenaunce thereof, to seeke suche unlawful wayes . . . as . . . have brought them to destruction."

Accordingly, the law imposed severe penalties on those wearing such contraband clothing. Richard Walweyn's punishment was lenient in comparison to that suffered by Thomas Bradshaw, a merchant tailor, who, in the same year, was arrested for wearing overstuffed trunk hose "contrary to good order." The court that heard his case ordered "that all the stuffing & lyninges of his hose shalbe cut and pulled out . . . and he be put into his doublett [a fitted jacket] and hose, and so lead home through the streates into his . . . house, and there the lyninge and stuffing of th'other to be likewise cutt and pulled out." If crimes of fashion were thought to stem from the sin of vanity, perhaps it seemed fitting that the punishment should be public shaming.

But breaches of good taste were not typically punished with criminal sanctions, even under the reign of the fashion-conscious Queen Elizabeth I. However tacky or unsightly overstuffed trunk hose may have been, and however vain those who wore them had shown themselves to be, why did the government expend limited resources enforcing such a dress code? Richard Walweyn and Thomas Bradshaw did more than violate the canons of sartorial refinement—they disrupted the political order of a society that treated outward appearances a marker of rank and privilege. Their conspicuous dress was seen as a kind of counterfeit, which threatened to undermine an economy of aristocratic and noble prerogative by cheapening its sartorial currency. From the late Middle Ages until the Age of Enlightenment, both law and custom required that clothing announce the social class, caste, occupation, religion, and, of course, gender of the wearer. These dress codes made clothing into status symbols, establishing a sartorial language that remains with us to this day.

In one sense, the Tudor era laws banning outrageous trunk hose carried on an ancient tradition. The Spartans earned their reputation for austerity with one of the earliest known laws against opulent attire, and their erstwhile rivals, the Athenians, passed regulations limiting sumptuous clothing as early as the sixth century B.C. The Romans—who first used the term "sumptuary" to describe such legislation—passed numerous laws restricting luxurious clothing, as well as indulgent meals, opulent furniture, and the exchange of lavish gifts. The earliest medieval European law prohibiting excessive luxury was passed in Genoa in 1157 and by the late Middle Ages, sumptuary dress codes were widespread throughout Europe. These early dress codes served to promote the virtue of austerity and to prevent waste generally. They restricted not only sumptuous attire but also lavish expenditures on feasts and festivities such as weddings and funerals.

Beginning in the 1300s, sumptuary laws were increasingly concerned with clothing. Moralists condemned sumptuous clothing as, at best, a distraction from the more important matters of spiritual purity and religious piety; at worst, a corrupting pleasure of the flesh. For religious authorities, clothing itself was a consequence of the fall from grace, and bodily adornment was among the many lures wanton women used to tempt men into vice and profligacy. Queen Elizabeth herself cited more prosaic motivations in a proclamation of June 15, 1574, defending the regulation of attire as a matter of national security and insisting that expensive foreign imports of textiles, furs, and finished garments upset the balance of trade: "[T]he money and treasure of the realm is and must be yearly conveyed out of the same to answer the said excess." Sartorial competition also undermined law and order, as the cost of luxurious clothing threatened to bankrupt those of modest means, driving them to crime:

> [A] great number of young gentlemen, otherwise serviceable, and others seeking by show of apparel to be esteemed as gentlemen, who, allured by the vain show of those things, do not only consume themselves, their goods, and lands which their parents left unto them, but also run into such debts and shifts as they cannot live out of danger of laws without attempting unlawful acts.

These were the standard justifications for sumptuary legislation, but it's more likely that the main objective underlying the flurry of new dress codes was to reserve status symbols for the elite. The most urgent problem sumptuary laws addressed was not that "the meaner sort," as one Elizabethan proclamation put it, were tempted to buy clothing they could not afford; it was that a growing number of the meaner sort *could* afford to compete with the elite in their attire. Indeed, the preamble to a 1533 act restricting apparel declared:

> The sumptuous and costly array and apparel customarily worn in this realm, wherof hath ensued and daily do chance such sundry high and notable inconveniences as to be to the great, manifest and notorious detriment of the common weal, the subversion of good and politic order in knowledge and distinction of people according to their estates, pre-eminences, dignities and degrees.

Many sumptuary laws during the late Middle Ages and the Renaissance explicitly referred to social rank and status. For instance, in 1229 King Louis VIII of France imposed limits on the attire of the nobility in an effort to bring feudal lords under centralized control, and in 1279 King Philippe le Hardi III restricted the luxuriousness of attire on a sliding scale according to the amount of land owned. The English "Statute Concerning Diet and Apparel" of 1363 tied the luxuriousness of clothing directly to wealth: urban dwellers and landed gentry with comparable disposable incomes were subject to the same sumptuary restrictions. Milan's sumptuary law of 1396 exempted the wives of knights, lawyers, and judges from restrictions on clothing and jewelry, while the preamble to a subsequent Milanese law of 1498 frankly explained that it was a response to the complaints of nobles and elites about the erosion of their privileges and, accordingly, its proscriptions did not apply to senators, barons, counts, marquises, friars, nuns, physicians, and, in applicable cases, their wives.

As legislators struggled to keep up with social mobility and new fashion trends, the rules took on a frenzied character: almost every aspect of attire was a potential target for legal strictures. Genoa banned the use of sable trims in 1157. In 1249 Siena restricted the length of trains on women's dresses. In 1258 Alfonso X of Castile reserved scarlet cloaks for the king and silk for the nobility. The papal legate of the Romagna, in 1279, required all women in the region to wear veils; by contrast, Lucca in 1337 outlawed veils, hoods, and cloaks for all women other than nuns. A Florentine law of 1322 forbade women other than widows from wearing black. In 1375 in Aquila, only male relatives of the recently deceased were allowed to go unshaven and grow beards, and then only for a period of ten days.

Crowns were of particular concern. In late-thirteenth-century France, Philippe le Bel IV restricted the wearing of crowns to the upper echelons of society; his wife, Jeanne of Navarre, had, on at least one occasion, remarked caustically on the prevalence of opulent attire: "I believed myself to be the only queen and here I am seen with hundreds!" she complained. Outrage over the misuse of crowns was widespread: in 1439, an anonymous critic in Brescia complained that "builders, blacksmiths, pork-butchers, shoemakers and weavers dressed their wives in crimson velvet, in silk, in damask and finest scarlet; their sleeves, resembling widest banners, were lined with satin . . . fitting only for kings, on their heads pearls and the richest crowns glittered, crammed with gems. . . ."

"One can make a gentleman with two yards of red cloth," remarked Cosimo de' Medici, the powerful Florentine banker and effective ruler of Florence during the early fifteenth century, according to Niccolò Machiavelli. As the upper classes sought to maintain the status quo in the face of these disruptive innovations, the number of sumptuary laws increased dramatically, reaching a peak in the prosperous Renaissance era beginning in the fourteenth century. In cities up and down the Italian peninsula, republics and despots alike imposed new restrictions on the conspicuous display of luxury—especially clothing. European governments passed new dress codes in a desperate attempt to stay ahead of new fashions and new money. For example, according to historian Alan Hunt, the number of sumptuary laws in Florence increased from two in the thirteenth century to over twenty in the seventeenth, while Venice had one sumptuary law in the thirteenth century and twenty-eight by the seventeenth. England had no sumptuary laws in the thirteenth century but had put twenty in place by the sixteenth. Spain had only two sumptuary laws as late as the fifteenth century, but by the sixteenth century it had sixteen. France had one such law in the twelfth century and twenty in the seventeenth, by which time enforcement had been incorporated into both criminal law and the regulation of the economy: a 1656 law empowered the police to stop and search people on the streets of Paris for goods that violated the sumptuary codes, and merchants selling banned goods faced fines and could even lose the maitrise—the legal privilege to practice their trade—for repeated offenses.

The sumptuary laws of the late Middle Ages and Renaissance eras were attempts to define the social meaning of attire. These laws were a response to new social mobility and instability that came with economic prosperity. As Europe emerged from the Dark Ages, new technologies, new trade opportunities, increased migration, and population growth destabilized the older social order. The scope and magnitude of the changes in the late Middle Ages rivaled those of the

Industrial Revolution of the nineteenth century or of today's era of high technology and globalization. The twelfth century saw the development of manufactured paper, the invention of the magnetic compass, and the construction of the first known windmill. The Hanseatic League of cities, at its height in the thirteenth and fourteenth centuries, included outposts as far east as Russia and as far west as London and controlled trade in the Baltic and North Seas, bringing expanded trade, new wealth, and new ideas. The Silk Road trade route was dramatically expanded in the thirteenth century, bringing to Europe the technologies and goods of the East, most significantly China, then the greatest manufacturing power in human history. The first European universities were established in the twelfth and thirteenth centuries, and scholars in Italy, England, France, Spain, and Portugal began to translate Greek and Arabic texts, introducing both lost ancient and newly innovated mathematic, scientific, and philosophical ideas to Europe. This explosion of technology and trade allowed merchants, tradespeople, bankers, and other members of the petite bourgeoisie to indulge in conspicuous luxury previously exclusive to the landed aristocracy. Meanwhile, a thriving market in used—sometimes stolen—clothing threatened to further dilute the prestige, and confuse the social meaning, of attire.

Then, in the fourteenth century, the global pandemic of the plague devastated Europe, Asia, and the Middle East, killing hundreds of millions of people: historians estimate that 45 to 65 percent of the European population died between 1347 and 1351; tax records suggest that 80 percent of Florentines died in just four months in 1348. As the plague subsided, the resulting labor shortage allowed working people to demand higher compensation, better working conditions, and more respect, making social mobility more pronounced than ever.

Clothing was an indispensable status symbol of the established elite and the newly well-to-do alike. Clothing is an ideal means of displaying wealth and power: it is ubiquitous, personal, and portable. And any vestimentary embellishment that is not strictly functional demonstrates that the wearer can afford to squander resources;

hence, luxurious attire is a wearable advertisement of success. As the sociologist Thorstein Veblen puts it in his famous *Theory of the Leisure Class:*

> The basis on which good repute . . . rests is pecuniary strength . . . [demonstrated by] leisure and a conspicuous consumption of goods. . . . [E]xpenditure on dress has this advantage . . . our apparel is always in evidence and affords an indication of our pecuniary standing to all observers at the first glance. . . ."

If sumptuous attire was a way of asserting social dominance, sumptuary law was a way of keeping presumptuous upstarts in their place.

Fashion presented a distinctive opportunity because it alone could transform the body itself into a form of political persuasion. Most Europeans during the late Middle Ages were illiterate, and literacy spread only slowly during the Renaissance: for example, historians estimate that more than 90 percent of the English population was illiterate in 1500 and the majority remained so until the nineteenth century. As a consequence, these societies relied on verbal communication and images to convey messages that later societies conveyed through the written word. The church spread the Gospel through icons, paintings, ritual, and spectacle; the state addressed its citizens and the emissaries of foreign powers with magnificent celebrations, grand palaces, parades, and awe-inspiring monuments—visual arguments for deference and respect. Clothing was an integral part of these image-based polemics; a monarch could *show* other people she was extraordinary and destined to rule; a priest could suggest by his very physical presence the splendor of heaven and the glory of God. New developments in fashion amplified this type of visual persuasion: the tailor's art, which became widespread in the fourteenth century, allowed clothing to communicate not only through sumptuous fabrics, vibrant colors, and surface adornments but also through form and shape. Rather than simply draping a body in finery, tailored clothing could transform it into something otherworldly, superhuman. But because fashion offered almost infinite possibilities for sartorial expressiveness, it invited novel—and potentially unsettling—visual arguments. If the queen could suggest majesty in an elaborate gown, enhanced with padded shoulders and ending dramatically in large, structured skirts, then a lowly merchant tailor could make a bold play for his own importance in an especially imposing pair of trunk hose.

The Tudors were especially aware of the power of personal image, and jealously guarded their prerogatives with respect to sartorial spectacle. In 1510 the first Parliament of Henry VIII passed "An Act Agaynst Wearing of Costly Apparrell." It was misleadingly named as it did not actually outlaw expensive attire; instead it restricted clothing of prestigious colors, refined quality, and exotic place of manufacture to people of high status. For instance, the act forbade men under the degree of a lord to wear "any cloth of gold or silver, sables or woollen cloth made of out[side] of England, Wales, Ireland or Calais." Crimson or blue velvet was off-limits to anyone under the degree of Knight of the Garter. Similarly, velvet, silk, or damask was forbidden to anyone under the rank of knight, with the exception of "sons of lords, judges, those of the king's council and the mayor of London." Even the common people were sorted according to status; the act provided that "no serving man is to use above 2½ yeards [of cloth] in a short gown or 3 in a long one; servants of husbandry, shepherds, and labourers, not having goods above 10 pounds in value, are forbidden to wear clothing exceeding 2s [shillings] the yard or hose exceeding 10d [pennies] the yard, under pain of three days' confinement in the stocks." Subsequent Acts of Apparel were passed in 1515, 1533, and 1554.

Queen Elizabeth I used the spectacle of clothing more effectively than any monarch before her. She turned the disadvantages of her gender in the man's world of Renaissance England to her advantage, expressing through her attire an imposing otherworldliness that combined the sumptuous luxury of royalty and a severe, untouchable feminine virtue (Insert, Image #2). She understood the power of fashion and she was even more zealous than her infamous father, Henry VIII, in regulating the attire of others. Historian Wilfrid Hooper, writing in the early twentieth century, remarked that "the reign of Elizabeth marks an era of unprecedented activity in the history of restraints on apparel." Numerous new proclamations regulated the quantity and quality of fabric used in hose and stockings, always reserving more luxurious fabrics such as velvet and satin for the upper classes.

Such laws were hard to enforce and often flouted: after all, if a nobleman was to be distinguished from a commoner *by his attire,* how else could one tell whether a person dressed in red silk and ermine was entitled to wear it? But the laws were taken seriously. Elizabeth personally admonished the lord mayor of London to ensure the sumptuary laws were obeyed, and, to reinforce the point, the Privy Council summoned the lord mayor and the aldermen of the city to the Star Chamber to make the same demand. She enacted an elaborate scheme of surveillance, enlisting the nobility, local magistrates, and the common people to enforce these laws. Methods of enforcement included a kind of bounty hunting. Elizabethan sumptuary laws, for instance, in addition to imposing fines, authorized the private individual "to seize any apparel worn contrary to the statute . . . and keep it for his own use."

In November 1559, a letter sent from the Privy Council to the corporation of the city of London ordered two watchers appointed in each parish, armed with a list of everyone entitled to wear silk and the authority to detain anyone else caught wearing it. A proclamation of May 6, 1562, directed the mayor and Court of Aldermen of London to appoint in every ward four "substanciall & well meanying men" to apprehend sartorial scofflaws. In 1566, at the urging of the crown, the city appointed four "sadde and discrete personages" to stand watch at each of the entrance gates to the city beginning at seven in the morning:

> Ther conynually to remayn and watche until XI of the clock, and from I of the clock in the afternoone of the same daye until VI of the clock at night, havinge a diligent eye duringe all the said tyme to all and everye such personne & persons as they shall see there to enter into the Cytte of London . . . using or wearinge annye

greate and monstrous hosen, silk, velvet or weapons restreyned
and prohibited.

Subsequent royal proclamations against excessive apparel followed in 1574, 1577, 1580, 1588, and 1597, each an attempt to address
the powerful and varied seductions of fashion. For instance, a proclamation of 1580 added rules prohibiting "ruffes of excessive length and
depth"—a reaction to the development of starch and wire frames to
stiffen the folds of fabric and allow the fashioning of unusually large
ruffled collars.

Those who aided and abetted vestimentary villains faced legal
sanctions as well. According to the terms of a proclamation of 1561,
tailors and hosiers were forbidden to provide garments to those unau-
thorized to wear them and were required to post a bond of 40 pounds
to guarantee compliance; in addition, their premises were to be
searched once every eight days for contraband garments. Under the
provisions of the Act of Apparel of 1554, masters harboring servants
who had violated the act faced the astonishing fine of 100 pounds.

While the Tudors and their aristocratic contemporaries throughout Europe enacted sumptuary codes that reinforced traditional privilege, more radical thinkers imagined a world in which the symbolism
of attire would be turned upside down. Henry VIII's Lord Chancellor,
Thomas More, wrote of a fictional utopia in which all clothing would
be "of one and the same pattern . . . down the centuries. . . ." and "of
one color . . . the natural color. . . ." More's *Utopia* described an egalitarian society where the problem of promiscuous luxury was solved,
not by banning sumptuous attire or reserving it for the elite but
instead by deliberately degrading it. In *Utopia*, gold and silver were
used for chamber pots and to forge the chains of slaves, and criminals
were forced to wear gold medals around their necks and gold crowns
as punishment for their offenses, so that precious metals would become "a mark of ill fame." The Utopians gave gems to small children
as playthings, so that "when they have grown somewhat older and
perceived that only children use such toys, they lay them aside, not
by any order of their parents, but through their own feeling of shame,

just as our own children, when they grow up, throw away their marbles, rattles and dolls." In More's imagining, the change in symbolism was so effective that when foreign ambassadors visited, adorned in conspicuous finery, the Utopians mistook them for clowns or slaves.

More's utopian inversion of the social meaning of luxury was a sharp critique of the ethos of Tudor England, where dress codes made luxury the sign and privilege of high status. But *Utopia* also reflects an anxiety about the rapid pace of change in fashion, shared by the Tudor elite generally. In Utopia, clothing would be of one type *down the centuries*: for More, the good society was free not only of class distinctions but also of the vagaries of fashion. The elites of More's day attempted to confront changes in fashion with dress codes that defined clothing as a status symbol. Fashion was the enemy of both the spiritually inspired radical egalitarian and the aristocrat jealously guarding his privilege. The rapid increase in sumptuary dress codes between the fourteenth and sixteenth centuries reflects the speed with which new fashions—and new, disruptive ideas about social status—were being created. As new fashions proliferated, lawmakers responded with new dress codes to keep up with, control, and define the latest styles. A story written by the late-fourteenth-century Italian writer Franco Sacchetti dramatized this problem. In it, a group of women flouted the sumptuary law of their city through a devious sartorial innovation: when ordered to remove sumptuous buttons proscribed by local law, they replied that the articles in question were not, in fact, buttons at all because the garments to which they were attached had no corresponding buttonholes. Fashion was always one step ahead of the law, so each new fashion required a new dress code. In reaction to these contrast changes, the Venetian Senate, in 1551, bluntly proclaimed, "[A]ll new fashions are banned."

At the beginning of the Renaissance, in the era of trunk hose and fitted doublets, dress codes were, above all else, attempts to make sense of and control the meaning of attire. Upwardly mobile merchants, financiers, minor aristocrats, and successful tradespeople were transforming dress from a predictable and relatively stable marker of social position to a much more expressively rich and varied medium of self-expression. This happened because innovations in technique—especially the development of form-fitting tailored garments—coincided with changes in the economy that created new wealth and new mobility. As people flooded into cities in search of new opportunities, hierarchies based on established social relationships broke down. In a small village, everyone knew their place—and the place of their neighbors. In a big city full of strangers, the butcher's wife could pass as an aristocrat and one could make a gentleman with two yards of red cloth. Because the economy was also booming and creating new opportunities for wealth, that butcher might earn enough to buy a crown for his wife and two yards of expensive red silk for his own tailored doublet—or monstrously extravagant pair of trunk hose. For these social upstarts, fashion was a way of asserting status—not simply by passing as aristocrats, but, more dangerously, by insisting that *they* were a new kind of aristocracy: an aristocracy based not on inherited titles but on wealth, talent, and the force of individual personality. These changes threatened a social order based on status and on spectacle, where political authority was intertwined with the ability to look the part, and statecraft was an elaborate theater of rituals. Renaissance-era dress codes tried to control fashion and force it into the service of the older social hierarchies. Fashion, in turn, exploited such older associations between attire and status in the service of something new: the modern, expressive individual.

Chapter Two

Self-Fashioning

Regarding Togas, Gowns, Robes,
and Tailored Clothing

UNTIL THE LATE MIDDLE AGES, ANCIENT CUSTOMS AND HIER-
archical sumptuary laws defined the meaning of attire. But beginning
in the late Middle Ages and especially in the Renaissance—the era of
such outsize personalities as Shakespeare, Leonardo, and Michelan-
gelo as well as less illustrious figures such as Richard Walweyn of the
monstrous trunk hose—dress also became a mode of self-invention,
or self-fashioning.

In the ancient world and the early Middle Ages, significant clothing reflected lineage, tradition, and inherited status. Styles changed
slowly, and always in ways that were continuous with the familiar. Although attire was not unchanged and unchanging *down the centu-*
ries as Thomas More would have liked, it changed slowly enough so
that one could readily recognize new styles as slight variations on old
ones. But by the early years of the Renaissance, this traditional vestimentary symbolism was being displaced by fast-paced changes of
fashion. New technologies, new money, and new people contributed
to the emergence of fashion in the modern sense, with its relentless,
exhilarating, and exhausting pace. The new vestimentary imperative
was not to communicate continuity with the past but to express the
spirit of the present, the contemporary zeitgeist, the shock of the new.

Modern fashion emerged when economic mobility gave more

people the resources and ambition to express themselves through their attire and new technologies allowed for dramatic advances in the design of garments. The most important technological innovation was modern tailoring, developed in the fourteenth century. Before the introduction of tailoring, most elite European clothing was some form of a draped garment—for instance, the ancient Roman toga or the medieval gown or robe. In the ancient world, trousers were rare and either the lowly garb of laborers or the exotic attire of Eastern civilizations, such as the Persians. According to historians Glenys Davies and Lloyd Llewellyn-Jones, "leg-coverings, shaped to fit the waist and legs . . . were a distinctive hallmark of 'barbarians' according to Greek and Roman understanding." Historian Anne Hollander notes that tailoring was first used to make linen trousers and shirts designed to be worn under full-body plate armor, which was

Ancient clothing for both men and women
was typically a draped garment.

invented in the late Middle Ages. This new armor was a high-tech improvement over both chain mail and smaller plate armor that covered only discrete parts of the body such as the chest, forearms, or shins; it was expensive and cast for warriors and the elite, and so the tailored undergarments became a sign of high status as they evolved into outwear. Elite men adopted this, the first tailored clothing, and abandoned the draped robes previously common to both sexes.

Tailoring allowed for clothing that skimmed the body, emphasizing the individual morphology of the wearer—clothing that was more personal. While draped garments conveyed status through color, embellishment, and fabric, the innovation of tailoring allowed clothing to conform to the body, suggesting the form of the person underneath. Men's clothing adopted the new mode and the once-ubiquitous draped garments became the distinctive garb of tradition-bound occupations—the clergy, academia, and the law— and of women. Later, women's clothing began to borrow some—but never all—of the elements of tailored menswear: for instance, sleeves and bodices hugged the body but below the waist the old draped form remained. Both men's and women's clothing became more expressive as it became more form fitting. These developments allowed attire to express a much broader range of social meanings—even if these meanings were less familiar and less clear than those of older draped garments. As a consequence, meaningful attire was available for the first time to people from many different social ranks and vocations— the butcher and his wife in addition to members of the nobility and the clergy. Clothing could be a vehicle of personal expression. Some historians refer to this as the birth of fashion.

The historian Stephen Greenblatt notes that the term "fashion" was used in the sixteenth century "as a way of designating the forming of a self . . . [both] the imposition upon a person of physical form . . . [and] a distinctive personality." The emergence of sartorial meaning was part of this profound change in human consciousness: the rise of the modern individual.

This requires a bit of explanation. Of course, there have always been individuals, but the individual has not always been the focus of political and social ideals; indeed, people have not always thought of themselves, first and foremost, as individuals. Instead, they were members of groups, defined by collective enterprises and identities and by their role—or status—in such groups. The idea that we are, above all else, *individuals*, with personalities that transcend our social status, occupation, and family heritage, is relatively new. Individualism emerged in the late Middle Ages and the Renaissance—alongside fashion. Fashion, in the sense I will use the term, is an expression of individualism and could not exist without it. And it might not go too far to say that individualism also needed fashion to serve as its chief propagandist. According to philosopher Gilles Lipovetsky,

[a]t the end of the Middle Ages . . . we can observe an increase in awareness of subjective identity, a new desire to express individual uniqueness, a new exaltation of individuality. . . . [T]he passionate attachment to marks of personality, and the social celebration of individuality . . . facilitated the break with respect for tradition [and] . . . stimulated private imagination in a quest for novelty, difference, and originality. . . . By the end of the Middle Ages, the individualization of appearance had been legitimized: to be unlike others, to be unique, to attract attention by displaying signs of difference—these became legitimate aspirations. . . .

One can compare the birth of fashion with a contemporaneous turn in literature. Before the Middle Ages, Western literature typically took the form of the epic, which chronicled the important deeds of great men and women: kings and queens, warriors, knights, sages, and those who aided or hindered them in their weighty and momentous enterprises. The heroes and heroines of epics are defined by their status and by their place in history: the Father of the Nation; the Liberator of the People; the Seeker of Enlightenment. To the extent that the epic hero exhibits individual psychology, it is typically a relatively uncomplicated character trait that drives the epic narrative: the cunning of Odysseus, who outwitted the sirens; the vanity and pride of Achilles, who sulked in his tent while the Trojans routed

the Greeks; the torn loyalties of Orestes, driven to avenge his father
by killing his mother; the lust of Lancelot and Guinevere, who ruined
Camelot through their indiscretions. The character of epic heroes is,
by and large, not psychological: we care less about their motivations
than about their actions and less about their internal sensibilities than
about their status.

This pre-modern sensibility applied to politics and social life
more generally. The king was important because he was the divinely
ordained head of the state; the nobility were representatives of great
houses, administrators of the lands, and defenders of the realm in
times of war; the clergy were the representatives of God. These individuals were of interest because of what they represented. And so the
attire of such important people was significant because it symbolized
their status, not because it reflected their individuality. The clothing
of the common people was, for the most part, simply functional—
undistinguished and empty of symbolic meaning.

The emergence of the novel reflected—and perhaps helped to
create—a new emphasis on individual personality. In novels, the internal psychology of the *protagonist* (no longer a hero) and of those
he or she encounters drives the action, which need not involve great
deeds. Indeed, when historically significant events occur in modern
novels, they often serve as the context for individual psychological
drama. Many great novels contain nothing of broad political or historical interest; instead they are snapshots of everyday life, characterized by relatively mundane happenings and the subtleties of social
interactions and personal reflections. Contrast the exploits of Ho-
mer's Odysseus (already a figure of unusual psychological complexity
for an epic hero) and the ruminations of Proust's narrator in *À la re-
cherche du temps perdu (In Search of Lost Time)* or—more obviously—
James Joyce's *Ulysses*. This was a slow process, gathering steam over
the course of centuries. There are hints of this development in the
most sophisticated classical epics, and it was well underway as early
as the fourteenth century: for example, Boccaccio's *The Decameron*
added psychological depth to ancient allegories. But it culminated in
the seventeenth and eighteenth centuries in the liberal philosophy of

the Enlightenment and in what literary critic Ian Watt has called "the rise of the novel."

Of course, it's not that people did not express themselves through clothing, or that they lacked rich emotional lives before these developments. What they lacked was our modern sense of the centrality of psychological motivation. Today we are surrounded by psychological evaluations, examinations, and categorizations. "Personality type" is defined through rigorous psychological examinations and through the popular psychology of "personality tests" such as the Myers–Briggs evaluations. We decide guilt or innocence based as much on subjective motivation as on objective behavior: crime is defined by mens rea and violations of equal treatment by the concept of "discriminatory intent." Psychology defines the modern person—for us it is the very essence of what it is to be human. We have replaced the concept of sin with the idea of malice, the confessional booth with the therapist's couch, the immortal soul with the immutable psyche.

Because of its central focus on individual psychology rather than heroic deeds, the novel is a democratic medium—a chronicle of the common person. While only monarchs, warriors, and sages play a role in the epic theater of geopolitics, everyone has a rich psychological life entangled in the events of everyday life. The novel offers the wage laborer and middle manager the same attention and dignity it gives to the wealthy and powerful.

Fashion was (and is) democratic in the same way. By freeing vestimentary symbolism from tradition, it transformed the expressiveness of attire—once the exclusive platform of the powerful—into an inclusive showcase for individual personality. Fashion disrupted conventions. It allowed anyone who could afford it to use the sartorial symbolism of the elite, undermining its exclusivity and transforming its meaning.

To be sure, sometimes non-elites used fashion in an attempt to improve their reputation and esteem by passing themselves off as elites, or at least by demonstrating that they were as successful as elites. This is what Thorstein Veblen has referred to as "pecuniary emulation." But this idea, which the historian of sumptuary law Alan Hunt

calls a "rather simplistic model of envy [where] lower positions are pre-
sumed to aspire to . . . [emulate] their superiors," is not the whole story.
Today, empirical study has discredited the idea that fashions always
start at the top and trickle down as less privileged groups emulate the
elite. If anything, recent trends suggest the opposite: consider the development of expensive, high-fashion iterations of street culture such
as punk, grunge, and hip-hop. The use of status symbols by upwardly
mobile lower classes has never been *just* a matter of imitation; it also
involved using such symbols to reflect their own ambitions and sensibilities, born of their own new social positions. To be sure, the fawning
parvenu was ever-present, but the greater threat to the old social orders was a newly confident bourgeois class that insisted not on joining
or aping the nobility but on its own distinctive place in society. As historian Daniel Roche writes, the rise of fashion fostered "a new state of
mind, more individualistic, more hedonistic . . . more egalitarian and
more free." Fashion allowed for the assertion of individual personality,
independent of social class, ethnicity, occupation, or any other group
identity.

Clothing now involved showing off one's personal sensibility as
much as showing off one's wealth. Newly enriched and empowered
groups used old symbols of status in new ways: to insist on their own
place among the elite, to challenge and transform old hierarchies, and
to assert new social agency. The merchant's wife might wear a jeweled tiara not in order to imitate royalty but as a way of asserting a
new, higher status for, or among, merchants. Richard Walweyn might
have worn his puffy trunk hose not to copy the dress of a nobleman
but instead to insist on his own social significance. And perhaps, just
perhaps, the problem wasn't that he looked risible in his presumptuous attire but that he looked too good, and threatened to start a new
fashion trend, further complicating the association between social
status and apparel.

Dress codes have been a response to this profound change in
human sensibility. Sumptuary laws were not only a way to control social mobility, they were also—and increasingly, as time went
on—a way to decode the confusing new styles of clothing and the so-

cial roles and self-perceptions those new styles reflected. As a consequence, the dress codes that link clothing to ancient statuses are in constant tension with the modern desire for self-fashioning. For self-expression in attire is never as simple as bucking convention and wearing whatever one likes: it requires one to evoke dress codes and subvert them simultaneously.

Chapter Three

Signs of Faith

*On the Matter of Dresses with Indulgently Long
Trains, Earrings and Other Vanities, and on the
Habits of Women Religious—Inspired by
Christian Dior*

ALONG WITH THE NOBILITY, THE CHURCH WAS ONE OF THE
most important institutions of European society during the Middle
Ages and the Renaissance: one of the three estates of the realm in the
ancien régime of pre-Revolutionary France and one of the two lordly
estates in England. Like the nobility, the church marked its status with
distinctive attire, and it joined the aristocratic classes in condemning
the disruptive influence of fashion.

To the clergy, fashion encouraged sensuality, posed a challenge
to conventional gender roles, and blurred the symbolism that separated heathen from believer. Worst of all, it facilitated individual
self-assertion—an early form of the Enlightenment humanism that
eventually would displace God, the church, and theology from their
positions of cosmological centrality. Anticipating this threat—if not
the extent or exact form of these developments—the medieval and
Renaissance church waged holy war on fashion, using moral admonishment, the threat of divine retribution, and earthly political power
to enforce restrictive dress codes. Despite these efforts, fashion flour-
ished; indeed, it even influenced traditional religious dress, complicating and confusing its sectarian symbolism.

Wearable Ghettos

In 1427, Friar Bernardino of Siena authored a dress code—of sorts. Rather than legislative proclamations, he used rhetorical questions to assign meaning to fashionable attire and sanction the women who wore it:

> How do you know where to borrow money? By the sign on the awning. How do you know where wine is sold? By the sign. How do we find an inn? By its sign. You go to the taverner for wine because you see his sign. You say to him, "give me some wine. . . . [Now, what of] a woman who puts on clothes or decorates her head with vanities that are the sign of a whore? You'd ask for her . . . you know what I mean, as you demand a whore, or if you like as you demand wine from a taverner.

Such moral judgments about attire worked hand in glove with the sumptuary laws of the day. They made the confusing abundance of novel fashions understandable to a mass audience, and they created a justification for formal and informal sanctions of fashionable dress. The main object of secular sumptuary law was social status; by contrast, the primary concerns of such religious admonishments were to stabilize the relationship between attire, sex, and religious faith. Just as sumptuary laws made clothing signify social position, these religious and moral dress codes made clothing stand for sex, sin, and religious conviction. Attire would be a sign of gender, and it would also distinguish sinful from virtuous expressions of sexuality—especially for women.

Friar Bernardino's lecture was part of a long tradition of religious anti-fashion admonishment. The earliest Christians admonished the faithful to dress modestly, reserving special condemnation for women who used cosmetics or wore bright colors or jewelry. By the second century, Christian clergy began to formalize the customs of the church, some of the most important of which were detailed rules about clothing. Church Father Tertullian who, in the second century, authored the first Christian texts in Latin, advanced comprehensive strictures, based on principles of austerity and modesty. He inveighed against luxury of all kinds. Emphasizing the vanity of jewelry, he wrote, "Even though we call this thing a pearl, it certainly must be seen to be nothing else but a hard and round lump inside a shellfish." Against clothing dyed in rich colors, he cautioned, "We cannot suppose that God was unable to produce sheep with purple or sky blue fleeces . . . hence they must be understood to be from the Devil, who is the corrupter of nature." He advised Christian women to veil themselves, "so that they are content with one eye free, to enjoy rather half the light than to prostitute the entire face," and insisted that Christians should "hat[e] to be the object of desire of another." Against cosmetics, Tertullian wrote, "surely those women sin against God who anoint their faces with creams, stain their cheeks with rouge, or lengthen their eyebrows with antimony. Obviously, they are not satisfied with the creative skill of God." He railed against the use of hair dyes and elaborate hairstyles, wigs, and braids, pointing out that vain women would not be able to take their artifices with them when they met their final reward (or punishment): "[W]hy not let God see you today as He will on your day of judgment?"

Friar Bernardino followed in this tradition, traveling the Italian peninsula preaching against the excesses of luxury. He equated feminine adornment with the Tower of Babel: "[J]ust as Nimrod, building that great tower, tried to erect it against the will of God, so when the head fortifies itself . . . such erections are considered self-exultations and rebellion against God. You can certainly see the ramparts and arrow slits . . . above, the hair and precious stones; in front, the face and made up eyes and an infernal smile; on the cheeks, the glow of rouge." Medieval Christians saw Eve's transgression in the Garden as a prototypically feminine weakness: the inherent sinfulness of the female body became an article of faith. Women were thought to be preternaturally inclined to the sin of vanity—a predisposition they announced with their sumptuous attire. According to one medieval parable, a woman, appearing in church decked out like a peacock, did not notice that on the long hem of her luxuriant dress, a multitude of tiny demons was sitting. . . . [T]hey clapped for joy . . . for the woman's inappropriate attire was nothing other than the devil's snare.

Accordingly, many laws forbade prostitutes to enhance their attractiveness by wearing fur, silver, gemstones, and other finery considered to be an "expression of . . . feminine love of adornment." And all women who wore lavish, ostentatious, and fashionable clothing—even those entitled by their class position to do so—faced moral censure. But many medieval and early Renaissance-era dress codes did not seek to eliminate sumptuous attire; instead they made all clothing into a sex symbol—a sign both of biological sex and of virtue or sin. In fact, the laws of many cities *required* female prostitutes to wear bright colors and superfluous trimmings such as ribbons as a sign of their profession. In a sense, these laws sought to reinforce sumptuary regulations using the reverse psychology described in Thomas More's *Utopia*: by assigning showy finery to fallen women, the law would make it repellant to honorable women. For instance, fourteenth-century Siena assigned to prostitutes the silks and platform shoes its sumptuary laws otherwise banned. Similarly, in 1434 after a religious committee determined that dresses with trains were "indecent, immoral, and seriously excessive, the costume, in fact, of the prostitute," the Bishop of Ferrara decreed that only prostitutes could wear them. In the fourteenth and fifteenth centuries, the Italian cities of Pisa and Milan required prostitutes to wear bright yellow ribbons or distinctive mantles as symbols of their profession; in fifteenth-century Florence, prostitutes were forced to announce their approach with bells attached to their hoods.

In the summer of 1416, about a decade before Friar Bernardino gave his address condemning feminine vanities, a woman identified only as "Allegra, wife of Joseph" was arrested in the Italian city of Ferrara and fined ten ducats for appearing in public *without* her earrings. Her crime of fashion was in failing to exhibit a visible sign of her community. Allegra was a Jew and the law dictated that Jewish women wear "rings hanging from both ears . . . uncovered and visible to all." The symbolism could not have been clearer: in an era when superfluous adornment was condemned as a sign of sin, Jews were required by law to wear conspicuous jewelry. The dress codes that condemned jewelry as vanity also made it a mandatory sign of Judaism.

Until the fifteenth century, Jews in northern Italy had lived, for the most part, in harmony with Christians, sharing neighborhoods as well as many secular customs and fashions. According to historian Diane Owen Hughes:

> Jews often became full members of Italian cities, which not only recognized their rights to citizenship but also occasionally appointed them to public office. . . . [T]heir houses were scattered throughout the city, side by side with those of Christian(s) . . . [and] it had become extremely difficult to distinguish Jews from Christians. They spoke the same language, lived in similar houses, and dressed with an eye to the same fashions.

Not only had Jews become socially integrated into these cities, they were also vital to the local economies, supplying goods, skilled trades, and financial capital to the nobility and, ironically, often to the churches as well: "[W]hen the friars needed money, they pledged their bibles to Jewish money-lenders; when they needed a new roof, they went to Jewish iron-mongers . . . when the monastery's mattresses began to fall apart, they sought out a Jewish mattress maker. . . ."

In short, in their day-to-day casual interactions, the typical Northern Italian didn't—and often couldn't—distinguish between Christian and Jew. And that, for the authorities of the church, was the problem. Religious edicts had required that Jews wear distinguishing markings since the Fourth Lateran Council of 1215. For example, in 1221 Frederick II of Sicily demanded that the realm's Jews wear a distinctive mark, although according to Hughes, "no urban government seems to have made its Jews conform to the . . . legislation." In 1322, Pisa required "Jews . . . so that they might be recognized and distinguished from Christians . . . to have and wear on their clothes at the chest a clearly visible sign, that is an O of red cloth." In Rome, in 1360, Jewish men were required to wear a red tabard and Jewish women a red overskirt.

In the fifteenth century, the laws imposing a Jewish sign multiplied and enforcement intensified. In a 1423 speech in Padua, Friar Bernardino of Siena advocated an aversion to Jews that prefigured the atavistic racism of later eras: "[Y]ou commit a cardinal sin if you eat or drink with them. . . . [A] sick man seeking to regain his health must not repair to a Jew . . . [and] one must not bathe together with a Jew." According to historian Richard Sennett, an anti-Jewish canard condemned the Jewish banker who lent money at interest as a kind of sexual deviant who "puts his money to the unnatural act of generation"—combining the sins of avarice and lust. The clergy who insisted on sectarian segregation similarly tied the lust of the bejeweled temptress to the greed of the Jew. For example, Friar Giacoma della Marca insisted that feminine vanity was both a sign and an instrument of the avaricious Jew: the lust for luxury drove Christian families into debt and ultimately forced them "to pawn to the Jew for ten [soldi] a garment he will resell for thirty . . . Whence Jews become rich and Christians paupers." According to Hughes, "[T]he Jewish sign, which came to mark Jews throughout the Italian peninsula in the fifteenth century, can almost everywhere be traced" to such religious teachings that linked Jewish impurity to the corruption of cosmopolitan cities where Christian and Jew mingled promiscuously. The anti-Jewish campaign of segregation was also an anti-urban campaign. It claimed to defend supposedly pure and humble countryfolk against sinful and decadent city-dwellers: "[A] skillful association of the impurity of the Jew with the impurity of urban society. . . ."

Hence, new laws required Jews to wear distinctive attire so that they could be identified on sight. These dress codes made religious faith visible and so reinforced the idea that Jews were a physically distinct and deviant people.

Earrings became a symbol of Jewish vanity almost by accident, as Christian authorities capitalized on a chance association. According to Hughes, in northern Italy, as in other parts of Northern Europe, earrings were not widely worn: the sumptuary laws of northern Italian cities, like those of France, Germany, and England, do not mention earrings, and public records in those areas do not list them among the estates of the wealthy or property pledged to secure debts. But in southern Italy, earrings were fashionable among both Christian and Jewish women. When Jews first migrated north to escape the worst of the Inquisition, they brought their fashion sense with them and, for a time, the earrings of Jewish women made them stand out. But by the fifteenth century, when Allegra was arrested for her unadorned earlobes, most Jewish women in northern Italian cities had abandoned their earrings. As religious authorities condemned earrings as vanities, defining them as symbols of shame and of sin, new dress codes forced Jewish women to wear them again.

In many Italian cities—especially those in the south where earrings had never distinguished Jew from Gentile—Jews were required by law to wear distinctive clothing, such as red skirts, yellow veils, red or yellow circular badges, and red coats. New dress codes stigmatized Jews using the same colorful fabric or garments that marked prostitutes. For instance, in the fifteenth century, Roman Jewish women were required to wear a red overskirt that prostitutes also wore; Jewish women in other parts of Italy had to wear a yellow veil—a sign of the prostitute in Italian cities from the fourteenth through the sixteenth centuries. In 1397, Venetian law required Jews to wear a yellow badge, and a 1416 law required prostitutes and pimps to wear a yellow scarf. In Viterbo, any Jewish woman who dared appear on the streets without her yellow veil could be stripped naked by the first person to apprehend her—the same punishment prescribed in other cities for prostitutes who strayed from the districts where they were allowed to solicit customers.

Earrings became signs of exotic sexuality, shared by Jewish women and prostitutes as a matter of law. Religious art featuring anthropomorphic depictions of cardinal sins often dressed the sin of Vanity or "Vainglory" in sumptuous attire and jeweled earrings; respectable women, by contrast, were presented with unadorned earlobes. The sermons of Friar Bernardino inspired the faithful to burn luxuries such as jewelry, fine clothing, and cosmetics—rituals that prefigured the notorious Mardi Gras bonfire of the vanities in Florence in 1497, overseen by Friar Girolamo Savonarola. By then, the laws of many Italian cities forbade Christian women from wearing earrings. If, as Friar Bernardino insisted, vanities were the sign of the fallen woman, they would also become the sign of the Jew.

Italian Jews did their best to counteract these anti-Jewish stereotypes. In 1418 they devised their own dress codes, eschewing cloaks of sable, ermine, silk, and velvet unless the luxurious fabrics were completely concealed from public view, "In order that we may carry ourselves in modesty and humility before the Lord our God, *and to avoid arousing the envy of the Gentiles* [emphasis added]."

Propaganda that tied Jews to unhealthy and unnatural sexuality made it easier for Christians to blame them for the spread of disease. For instance, according to Sennett, when Venice suffered a syphilis epidemic, the city relied on its Jewish doctors to treat the disease, but at the same time blamed them for its spread: in 1520, the Venetian surgeon and scientist Paracelsus attacked the city's Jewish doctors who "purge [syphilitics], smear them, wash them, and perform all manner of impious deception." Jewish doctors who treated victims of disease—syphilis, leprosy, and especially plague—often wore distinctive clothing designed to protect the doctor from the vapors thought to spread the disease—a precursor of the iconic bird-beaked plague doctor's mask that developed in the seventeenth century. Because many doctors in Venice were Jewish—especially those called upon to treat the victims of communicable diseases—this strange costume and its associations with disease and death became associated with Jews. The resulting aversion culminated in 1516 in the physical segregation of Venetian Jews in the district after which isolated ethnic neighborhoods have been named ever since, the industrial ward named for the Italian verb "to pour," or *gettare*: the ghetto.

The mandatory distinctive clothing of Italy's Jews functioned as a movable ghetto, socially isolating them while still allowing them to bring their talents and resources to privileged members of society. But nothing as alluring as the earring could remain the exclusive property of the marginalized for long. Earrings soon became fashionable among the more powerful members of society. Whereas the sumptuary laws of many Italian cities in the fifteenth century forbade Christian women from wearing earrings, by the sixteenth century new dress codes made sumptuous attire and jewelry an exclusive sign of nobility, restricted to the social elite. For instance, in 1401 Bologna forbade all women, regardless of social status, to wear gold, jewels, silks, and velvets; by 1474 the daughters of prestigious guildsmen could wear gold and silver cloth; and in 1521 Bologna's Jewish women were limited by law to three finger rings and three gold pins— stripped, by law, of the earrings they had once been forced to wear as a badge of shame. Similarly, a Venetian decree of 1543 forbade prostitutes from wearing "gold, silver or silk . . . necklaces, pearls or jewelled or plain rings, either in their ears or on their hands."

Religiously inspired dress codes made earrings into signs of a stigmatized religion and a debased sexuality. But the unorthodox logic of fashion—perhaps drawing strength from the allure of the taboo— turned them into a coveted status symbol. So authorities changed tactics, legislating an association between luxury and privileged status and insisting that the Jew relinquish the adornment that had, despite the best efforts of church and state, become a status symbol.

Living Cloisters

The dress codes of fifteenth-century Italy forced Jews into wearable ghettos. Meanwhile, some of the most devout Christians willingly entered "living cloisters." The dress codes that established the religious costume of the Catholic woman religious, or "nun" in popular parlance, made clothing a symbol of religious devotion. Because each element in the distinctive ensemble has a specific symbolic meaning, the nun's habit may seem to be the purest of status symbols, elevating the iconography of faith over any idiosyncratic personal statement. But even here, self-fashioning was also at work—and at times at war with more conventional symbolism. The rules and customs surrounding the habit are both ancient and modern, and every attempt to establish a definitive meaning through dress codes was complicated by the mischievous dynamics of fashion.

Although the early Christian church had no authority to dictate the dress of its few and scattered members, many early Christians voluntarily adopted a distinctive dress code: a renunciation of worldly luxuries and an individual statement of religious devotion. According to historian Elizabeth Kuhns, "[T]he act of changing clothes *was* the action of religious profession by those who aspired to holiness." Indeed, in the early Christian church and throughout the Middle Ages, most monks and nuns did not take formal vows: distinctive attire was often the *only* explicit statement of religious devotion. By the sixth century, the habit was well recognized as a symbol of commitment to a life of religious service, as significant as formal vows. For example, a letter from the Archbishop of Canterbury to King Harorld's daughter, Gunnilda, written in the eleventh century reads, "[A]lthough you were not consecrated by a Bishop . . . the fact that you publicly and privately wore the habit of the holy way of life, by which you proclaimed to all who saw you that you were dedicated to God no less than by reading a profession, is in itself a manifest and undeniable profession."

In the Middle Ages, as clothing came to signify commitment, a dress code of Christian modesty was more forcefully encouraged for the most devout Christians. According to Kuhns, as some religious devotees began to succumb to earthly luxuries, "Bishops railed against nuns' finery, naming golden hairpins, silver belts, jeweled rings, laced shoes, brightly colored clothing, long trains and furs. . . ." Meanwhile, sumptuary laws and religious edicts alike sought to control the vestimentary lapses of religious men and women. For instance, King Alfonso X of Castile insisted in 1283 that "all of the clergy of his household be tonsured . . . and that they may not wear bright red, green or pink . . . they may not wear bright red or yellow tunics, shoes with strings, or closed detachable sleeves . . . they must wear conservative clothing. . . ." A fifteenth-century English mystic claimed to have had a vision of overdressed nuns suffering a poetic justice: "[I]n Purgatory wearing dresses made from painful hooks and headdresses from poisonous snakes." These admonishments against luxury helped to define the religious habit.

The habit, in whatever form it takes, is an austere and modest costume. The elements common to almost all its variations are a long tunic, a scapular—a long strip of cloth, fashioned with an opening for the head, which drapes over the front and back of the body, ending near the ankles—and a veil, which covers the hair and back of the neck (**Insert, Image #4**). Over time, various elements of the habit were formalized in dress codes and invested with spiritual significance: the "T" shape of the tunic echoes the cross of Calvary and the scapular came to symbolize the cross and the "yoke" of the religious calling. The cord or belt represents the bonds that immobilized Christ and held him to the cross. The color of the garments has significance as well: white for purity and innocence, brown for poverty and humility, black for mourning the death of Christ and for the renunciation of vanity. Although austerity is a common feature, the habit has taken many different forms throughout its history and among religious orders. According to Kuhns, some habits were "designed as monastic uniforms, specifically intended to distinguish women who had consecrated their lives to God. Other orders' habits . . . came about from a desire to blend into society and among those the sisters served."

Some aspects of the religious habit were originally common to men and women: the tunic was worn by both sexes and the nun's veiled hair was symbolically mirrored in the monk's tonsure—the distinctive haircut of shaven scalp and fringe of hair around the perimeter of the head. But for the most part, the nun's habit served as a symbolic assertion of a distinctive femininity—virtuous, chaste, and independent of the corrupting influence of men. The habit was also a response to the subordinate social status of women: by becoming brides of Christ, nuns could avoid becoming brides of fallen, earthly men and avoid the sexual advances endured by unattached women. Just as the convent provided a built environment free of the domination of men, the nun's habit offered the ability to move safely outside of that environment. Indeed, some nun's habits were originally a kind of disguise: for instance, in the seventeenth century, French nuns adopted the traditional costume of the widow—a modest black dress and veil—so that they could travel freely: while respectable single or married women required a male chaperone, law and custom allowed widows the liberty to travel alone. And in Catholic theology, nuns had the most unimpeachable chaperone: as brides of Christ, their husband accompanied them everywhere. As early as the tenth century and as late as the 1960s, many orders would consecrate a nun in a sort of marriage ceremony: she was given away by her father during a High Mass, she would change her name, she wore a white dress and veil, and in some sects received a silver wedding band. A reception following her induction might even include a wedding cake.

By the Middle Ages, the "life religious" served as an alternative to marriage for the nobility; the convent was, for women seeking independence, "the ideal setting to become great writers, thinkers and mystics." But the convent and the habit—the stone cloister and the cloth cloister—could also become traps. Historian Helen Hills describes the practice of veiling in a seventeenth-century Neapolitan convent as an act that drew attention to the sensuality it obscured: "[T]he nun's body—specifically her face—[was] the site of a potential contest between spiritual and mundane bridegrooms. The veil . . . signaled that Christ was the nun's bridegroom, but it also became a sign in itself, an acknowledgement of the beauty and temptation of the nun's face beneath it . . . the practice of veiling signified the sexual allure of the enclosed, veiled nun."

This more severe habit, with its full-face veil, coincided with an intensified enclosure of nuns within their convents, one of many reforms from the Council of Trent that established the Counter-Reformation: the Catholic Church's response to the threat of Protestantism. Nuns were forbidden to leave their convents except in cases of emergency—a rule that was to be enforced by the military if necessary, suggesting that the church anticipated resistance. Intriguingly, the closed convents featured ornate grilles, bars, screens, and curtains, which, like the veil, ensured that no one could see in or out, but which also drew attention to themselves: "paradoxically . . . wall apertures and points of potential access to nuns became the most conspicuous parts of the convent." According to Hills, the stone enclosure of the convent mirrored and supplemented the cloth enclosure of the habit—each creating an elaborate visual drama of concealment and revelation, modesty and seductiveness:

> [C]onvent architecture above all represented control over sexuality. . . . [T]he architecture of female monasteries responded with a rhetoric of fortification . . . focused on those areas of the convent where contact between inmates and outsiders was most possible, doors and windows—the symbolic orifices, which had to be shielded . . . [but] while bars and rustication may appear simply to fortify an opening, they also draw attention to [it] . . . and indeed, embellish it . . . fortification can also be a celebration of the temptation of symbolic orifices and their closure."

Here, under the influence of male authority, the symbolic significance of the habit was not to deny female sensuality but to advertise it while also obscuring it. The nun as bride of Christ was not asexual; instead, she directed her sexuality—all the more potent for its purity—toward God.

This mixed message was not merely a consequence of the paradoxes of Counter-Reformation dogma—it was tied to the broader social dynamics of sixteenth- and seventeenth-century Italy. The convents had a distinctive class structure in which the most isolated housed the daughters of the wealthiest families. To ensure that their unmarried daughters were chaste, wealthy families paid a sizable dowry to enroll them in a convent. These daughters arrived in their finest clothes, thereby emphasizing the wealth of their families. According to one commentator:

> As the day in which she must take the religious habit draws near, she dresses like a queen if she can . . . and so with all the great-

est imaginable luxury, she, magnificent, takes a turn around the city . . . [so that] there is no-one left who does not know the great sacrifice she is about to make.

Symbolically, the sumptuous attire of the novice was transferred from her body to the church, where lavish decoration graced the interiors of the convent. The dress codes of the convents forbade "precious clothes," jewelry—such as earrings—or "other secular profanities." But, according to Hills, "the richness of the decoration of aristocratic convent churches publicly demonstrated the familial, worldly and spiritual riches of the nuns." The symbolism of the nun's austere habit always suggested its opposite: the luxury she had relinquished in order to serve God. And so the seemingly self-effacing habit became not only a surrogate for the luxury of a family legacy but also an indication of a distinctive individual narrative: the woman who abandoned earthly privilege out of spiritual conviction. In this way, the nun's habit participated in the developing language of fashion, transforming ancient signs of asceticism and self-abnegation into more complex signifiers of social status and individual personality.

Bad Habits

The nun's habit was a complex and even contradictory vestimentary symbol, evoking forsaken sensuality through conspicuous modesty and suggesting forgone luxury through ostentatious austerity. As the Protestant Reformation swept through Northern Europe in the sixteenth century, the figure of the nun, with her distinctive attire, became an evocative symbol of Catholic corruption and hypocrisy. Many Protestant reformers, most notably Martin Luther himself, focused not only on what they considered to be the theological error but also the moral decay of the Catholic Church. In 1517 in his famous Ninety-five Theses, Luther attacked the sale of indulgences (through which the church claimed it would lessen the punishment for sins) as an example of the church's earthly corruption. Protestant critique also focused on the period of papal intrigue during the first

· half of the tenth century, later known as the "pornocracy" ("rule by prostitutes"), when many Popes behaved like the Roman aristocrats of the pre-Christian era, conspiring to control the succession of the papacy and, in some cases, keeping concubines. In these accounts, the Catholic Church was not only corrupt but also carnally deviant.

The religious schism split Europe into a Catholic south and increasingly Protestant north, where new theologies extended Luther's critique of Catholicism and both the state and private actors encouraged anti-Catholic sentiment. In the ensuring centuries, nuns, with their conspicuous clothing, became the targets of persecution—and the protagonists in salacious literature. The sexualized, sadistic, or victimized nun was a prevalent theme even in predominantly Catholic France. Denis Diderot's 1780 novel *La Religieuse* (*The Nun*) told of the gratuitous cruelty a young woman effectively imprisoned in a convent suffered at the hands of the Mother Superior, and Honoré de Balzac's 1837 collection, *Les cent contes drolatiques* (published in English as *Droll Stories: Collected from the Abbeys of Touraine*), included a ribald vignette titled "The Merry Tattle of the Nuns of Poissy."

In Victorian England, sordid accounts of debauchery, torture, and sacrilege in convents had become a minor literary genre. In these lurid tales, priests and monks, their sexuality twisted by the deprivations of celibacy, found an outlet for their repressed appetites in the women the church kept confined in cloisters; meanwhile, older nuns, withered, resentful, and armed with whips and other devices of torture, disciplined younger inmates with sadistic enthusiasm. Sensationalistic accounts of convent life depicted a dangerous cult that secretly rejected the Bible, tortured and prostituted nuns, and even immured rebellious novices inside the walls of convents, where they would die slow and painful deaths. One Reverend Coleridge authored a pamphlet titled *Awful Disclosures of Miss Julia Gordon, the White Nun or Female Spy!* that recounted the horrifying tale of a Protestant girl who ill-advisedly converted to Catholicism and entered a convent. She realized her mistake quickly, but still too late: the convent was in fact a prison, the priests, lecherous men who demanded sexual favors from the nuns. On a coerced trip to Rome, Julia saw the illegitimate offspring of priests and nuns thrown onto a lime pit in front of St. Peter's Basilica, along with the charred remains of Protestants who had refused to convert. After discovering that she had been impregnated by a priest, Julia fled and found refuge with a kindly Protestant family in Paris, but died in childbirth. Similar literature circulated in other countries: in the United States, an 1836 book, *The Awful Disclosures of Maria Monk,* offered the "firsthand" account of convents riddled with secret tunnels that allowed priests to creep into the bedchambers of nuns for illicit liaisons and of the infanticide of the resulting offspring.

Such stories inspired both mob violence and pornographic fantasy. In Victorian England crowds occasionally pelted nuns with

Nun's habits became a fetish object in the
Victorian era—a strange association that
continues to this day.

rocks in the streets. Meanwhile, the nun's habit became a fetish object: the whip-wielding nun was a popular titillating image and many Victorian-era brothels kept nuns' habits among their store of costumes. The habit, which began as an unassuming ensemble designed, in part, to protect single women from male harassment, had become eroticized—an association that continues to the present day.

In some cases, the elaborate designs developed in the Middle Ages and Renaissance survived long after the fashions that had inspired them had become museum pieces. Meanwhile, the pressure for distinctiveness among religious orders had led to a proliferation of new designs, some, according to Kuhns, with "bizarre characteristics, requiring excessive attention to minutiae." As a consequence, many orders retained habits that were first designed as stylized versions of conventional modest attire, even as secular fashions had moved in the opposite direction, becoming increasingly streamlined. For instance, the iconic habit of the Sisters of Charity was distinguished by a wimple or cornette—a large starched headdress, with upturned corners. The wimple was conventional headwear for aristocratic married women in the Middle Ages and into the seventeenth century, when the Sisters adopted it. But of course, women's fashions moved on while the habit remained anchored in the past: the Sisters abandoned the cornette only in 1964.

In 1917, the Code of Canon Law established a new dress code that required all "women religious" to wear the habit at all times and stipulated that new communities could not adopt the habits of established institutions—effectively codifying these anachronistic designs. By the mid-twentieth century, many nuns thought the habit symbolically alienated them from the people they endeavored to serve, hindering their missionary and charitable work. Echoing this concern, in 1950 Pope Pius XII advised: "[W]ith regard to the religious habit, choose one that expresses your interior lack of affectation, simplicity and religious modesty." After Pius XII's admonishment, Italian fashion designers presented new ideas for the habit, some practical prêt-à-porter; some elaborate haute couture. The trend gained new momentum in 1962 when Pope John XXIII announced the Second

Vatican Council, with the expressed intention to "shake off the dust that has collected on the throne of Saint Peter since the time of Constantine." In the same year Léon Joseph Cardinal Suenens, the Archbishop of Mechelen-Brussels, published a book titled *The Nun in the World*, which declared: "The world today has no patience with mere ornamentation, offerings or other oddities, whether starched or floating in the wind . . . anything contrived or lacking in simplicity is rejected . . . anything that gives the impression that the nun is not only apart from the world but also a complete stranger to its evolution." Religious orders looked to fashion for help finding a new look: the Sisters of Charity, for instance, turned to elite New York department store Bergdorf Goodman while the Daughters of Charity of St. Vincent de Paul adopted a new design with a chic box-pleated dress and kerchief-style veil inspired by the work of Christian Dior.

The Second Vatican Council reinforced this modern view: in 1965, the *Perfectæ caritatis*, subtitled Decree on the Adaptation and Renewal of Religious Life, insisted "the religious habit . . . must be simple and modest . . . suited to the times and place and to the needs of the apostolate. The habits, of both men and women, which are not in conformity with these norms ought to be changed."

During the 1960s, Catholic feminists trained a critical eye on the church's inequitable treatment of women, of which the habit was a striking symbol. In 1968, *The Church and the Second Sex* theologian Mary Daly complained of a Catholic Church that "pretends to put woman on a pedestal but which in reality prevents her from genuine self-fulfillment." According to Kuhns, "for some sisters the habit and veil represented the very ideal of male domination, and they compared the clothing to the burka of the Middle East." Even before the Second Vatican Council many newer orders had adopted simplified, modern habits: plain navy or black tailored dresses and plain veils or hats, only slightly different from contemporary secular clothing. In the wake of a growing feminist critique of the habit, in 1966 the Sisters of Loretto took the next logical step and abandoned it altogether in favor of modest suits.

Faced with these challenges to both tradition and traditional

The Daughters of Charity's updated habit,
inspired by Christian Dior, is on the left;
the traditional habit with dramatic cornette
appears on the right.

authority, the Vatican sought to establish the limits of modernizing reform, admonishing women religious to keep the faith, sartorially speaking: "[W]e cannot fail to mention how fitting it is for the
dress to be . . . a sign of their consecration and in some way different
from secular fashion," wrote Pope Paul VI in 1971. In 1972, the Sacred Congregation for Religious and Secular Institutes insisted that
"the basic criterion to be observed is that the habit prescribed by religious institutes, even as modified and simplified, should be such that
it distinguishes the religious person who wears it." By contrast, the
National Coalition of American Nuns echoed feminist critiques of
Catholic patriarchy, vowing to "protest any domination of our institutes by priests, no matter what their hierarchical status. We hold as
inviolable . . . rights of self-determination for religious women." By the

late 1970s, the habit had become a political symbol as well as a religious one: according to Kuhns, "Liberal and 'progressive' nuns wore secular clothing, and conservative nuns retained the habit. A nun's choice of clothing became a visual barometer of her politics, philosophy and loyalties."

In this sense, the habit became a kind of personal statement, invested not only with traditional spiritual significance but also with the social and political meaning characteristic of all modern clothing. This, of course, is precisely what Catholic traditionalists feared when they resisted the modernization of the habit. But these changes began long before Bergdorf Goodman started making designer habits and American nuns opted for pillbox hats over wimples; they started at least as early as the seventeenth century when Neapolitan novices conspicuously traded in their family jewels for a high-status enclosure in a living cloister. The dress codes governing the religious habit, like the sumptuary laws of Tudor England, were not simply a codification of ancient customs; they were a defensive reaction to the reuse of ancient vestimentary symbols in modern individual fashion statements.

Dress codes in the tumultuous years after the birth of fashion tried to ensure that clothing retained a specific and easily discernible meaning. For political authorities, the most pressing considerations were those of social class; for religious leaders, questions of faith and sexual morality were foremost. Dress codes—both those contained in law and those articulated in sermons and admonitory speeches—tied faith to sex and to sensuality by defining the attire appropriate to the virtuous woman in opposition to the clothing that would mark the fallen woman. But these dress codes were at war with the rising influence of a fashionable sensibility, which recycled, repurposed, and recoded older vestimentary symbols in the service of self-expression. The earrings assigned by law to Jews attracted the envy and attention of Gentiles. The attire of the sinful woman became fashionable among the respectable and God-fearing. The modest garb of the most devout inevitably suggested the status and sensuality it tried to obscure; fashion turned that unintentional play of conspicuous modesty into a form of self-assertion while masculine libidinal fantasy turned it into a sexual fetish. The transformation of traditional symbols—whether sacred or profane—into visual elements of personal stories inspired new dress codes in a desperate and often futile struggle to keep up with the accelerating pace of fashion.

Chapter Four

Sex Symbols

*On the Subject of Plate Armor and Associated
Undergarments, Masks, and Costumes*

GENDERED CLOTHING SEEMS A NATURAL CONSEQUENCE OF
human biology: just as a glove is designed to fit a hand, and a shoe, a
foot, so trousers were designed to fit male bodies and gowns suited to
the female form. This is a conventional understanding, not so much
articulated as implied in the rituals, customs, and moral strictures
surrounding our attire. But the sex of attire does not reflect human
biology—it is defined by habitual social roles and reflexive practices.
Gendered attire has always reflected our expectations, fears, and fantasies surrounding sexuality, reproduction, and family more than an-
atomical differences between men and women. Ancient dress marked
these cultural gender roles in the relatively simple ways draped clothing allowed for. Dress codes after the birth of fashion used a new,
more sophisticated and expressive vestimentary vocabulary that dramatically raised the stakes of gendered attire: tailored clothing could
more powerfully evoke traditional gender roles but it also created a
new sexual symbolism that challenged and subverted them.

How a Teenage Tomboy Became History's First Fashion Victim

In 1429, a seventeen-year-old girl who would soon come to be renowned as Jehanne la Pucelle ("Jeanne, the maiden") left a small town in northeast France to offer her services as a military strategist to Charles VII, the Dauphin—or heir to the throne—whose forces were losing a protracted war against English partisans threatening to displace him. At first, no one took her seriously, but Jehanne's determination overcame initial resistance: her skill and insight helped the French develop new battle plans and her courage inspired the demoralized troops. Under Jehanne's leadership, the French forces successfully thwarted a siege on the city of Orleans. Later she led a campaign to retake the city and cathedral of Reims, where the kings of France had been crowned ever since the Frankish tribes were united under one ruler, allowing the Dauphin to be crowned king in the ancient tradition. Jehanne's remarkable successes seemed divinely ordained, which necessarily implied Charles's divine right to rule France.

In 1430 Jehanne was captured in battle and imprisoned. An ecclesiastical tribunal stacked with English partisans tried her for heresy. But Jehanne's faith was beyond reproach. She showed an astonishing familiarity with the intricacies of scholastic theology, evading every effort to lure her into making a heretical statement. Unable to discredit her faith through her verbal testimony, the tribunal seized on the implicit statements made by Jehanne's attire. In battle, she wore armor, which required linen leggings and a form-fitting tunic fastened together with straps—both traditionally masculine attire—and, like the men she fought alongside, she adopted this martial attire when off the battlefield as well. Citing the biblical proscription in Deuteronomy 22:5 (KJV) which warns, "A woman shall not wear anything that pertains to a man, nor shall a man put on a women's garment, for all who do are an abomination to the Lord your God," the tribunal charged Jehanne with heresy. They burned her at the stake in 1431.

The church retried Jehanne posthumously and reversed her conviction in 1456, citing Saint Thomas Aquinas who allowed an exception to the biblical ban on cross-dressing: "Nevertheless, this [cross-dressing] may at times be done without sin due to some necessity, either for the purpose of concealing oneself from enemies, or due to a lack of other clothing. . . ." Similarly, Saint Hildegard von Bingen had written, "Men and women should not wear each other's clothing *except in necessity.* A man should never put on feminine dress or a woman use male attire . . . unless a man's life or a woman's chastity is in danger. . . ." The new tribunal concluded that Jehanne had worn male garb out of necessity.

Though she never used it in life, Jehanne became known in legend by her father's surname: D'Arc. Jeanne D'Arc—or Joan of Arc—was beatified in 1909 and canonized in 1920. As a consequence of her notoriety, her story has been told and retold, modified to serve numerous agendas. Her original trial concluded that she wore men's clothing for her own perverse gratification, in deliberate defiance of religious law, but the entire proceeding was a political vendetta based on trumped-up charges and falsified evidence. Her posthumous retrial found that a chaste and proper Joan wore men's clothing only out of necessity, but it was undoubtedly influenced by the desire to rehabilitate and embrace a woman who had, in the intervening years, become a religious and national icon. In recent years, some historians have suggested that Joan of Arc was transgender—a plausible hypothesis, but one that may be motivated by a desire to find historical inspirations for present-day social politics.

Did "Jehanne the Maid" wear male attire by choice, in belligerent defiance of religious law; or of necessity to protect her chastity; or as a transgender man? Or did she wear it simply because it looked good on her? Male clothing was certainly more practical under the circumstances; moreover, it was also more interesting and more symbolically potent than the women's wear of the time. Joan was coming of age just as fashionable clothing was beginning to supplement, if not displace, traditional clothing. And it was *men's* fashion, derived from tailored military garments, that was on the cutting edge—as it remained for the next three centuries. Using the sartorial techniques

first used to make undergarments for armor, men's styles in the fifteenth century featured form-fitting hose and trousers and short doublets. Menswear emphasized the body while women's attire obscured
it in fabric: although, in Joan's era, women's bodices revealed some of
the upper body, below the waist, women were draped—a convention
that endured until the twentieth century. Because men's form-fitting
attire revealed the shape of the body underneath, it was sexier than
the draped clothing prescribed for women, suggesting virility and
sexual assertiveness. According to historian Anne Hollander:

> Joan [of Arc] looked immodestly erotic in her men's gear. She
> wasn't disguised as a man, and she didn't just look soldierly and
> practical. . . . [Instead she was] abandoning the excessively roman-
> tic modesty of current women's dress without hiding the fact that
> she was a woman. . . .

The woman dressed in men's attire was already a familiar—and
popular—figure in medieval literature, which featured female knights
who competed in jousts and tournaments, girls who passed as boys
in order to inherit and protect family estates, and early Christian
saints who adopted male garb while on daring quests for spiritual
enlightenment. According to historian Valerie Hotchkiss, these stories demonstrated that medieval audiences were intrigued by the
blurring of gender categories and sympathetic to women who wore
men's clothing to facilitate virtuous endeavors. Joan of Arc's legend
fits squarely within this romantic tradition. A heroine in the chival-
ric tradition, Joan was not only a romantic figure but a sexy one as
well (Insert, Image #3). By adopting the masculine innovation of
form-fitting attire, Joan emphasized both her spiritual virtue and
feminine sexuality—a direct visual rebuttal to the religious morality
of her time, which tied a woman's virtue to unassuming modesty.

Cross-dressing was an established practice during Joan's era, but
also a controversial one that was tolerated only within well-defined
social boundaries. Cross-dressing of various kinds was a regular part
of medieval festivals, celebrations, carnivals, theater, and recreational

fantasy, always carrying with it a combination of the subversive and the erotic. Some was simply an instance of costume, which could involve crossing traditional boundaries of class and social role as well as sex. Balls and celebrations often featured costumes and masks, which allowed the wearer to escape the expectations of his or her social position and adopt the liberties of another. Some costumes truly concealed the wearer's identity, and many sumptuary laws forbade masks and disguises worn outside such festivities. But most costumes did not and were not intended to actually fool the observer; instead they were designed for lighthearted role-playing and a carefully limited and ritualized transgression of established social roles. For instance, the Renaissance-era Italian writer Baldassare Castiglione advises the aspiring courtier that "even though he be recognized by all . . . disguise carries with it a certain freedom and license." Skillful cross-dressing involved an instructive tension between outward appearance and inner truth; the costume became a commentary on the individual—an indirect form of self-expression.

Historians Judith Bennett and Shannon McSheffrey note that "cross-class dressing, both in brothels and on the stage, was highly charged in erotic terms. . . . [A] prostitute who dressed above her station" was a common fetish in Elizabethan England and had origins "as far back as the late thirteenth century, when London prohibited prostitutes wearing furred hoods 'after the manner of reputable ladies,'" in order to "mitigate the eroticism of over-dressed prostitutes." The attire of upper-class "matrons" or wives was an erotic fetish for working-class men "for whom such fantasies both spoke to anxieties about female domestic power and expressed social aspirations." Meanwhile, the upper classes dressed down and adopted the dress of exotic foreigners and outlaws in erotically charged masquerades. According to one account of such cross-class dressing, in 1509, shortly after his marriage to Catherine of Aragon, Henry VIII and several other noblemen burst into the "[q]uenes Chambre, all appareled in shorte cotes . . . with hodes on their heddes, and . . . bowe and arrows, and a sworde and a bucklar, like out laws, or Rokyn [Robin] Hodes [Hood's] men."

Despite—or perhaps because of—popular sympathy for some forms of cross-dressing, the sumptuary codes of the late Middle Ages and Renaissance prohibited a variety of practices of disguise to make sure clothing corresponded to status and to prevent the sexual titillation and illicit sex associated with cross-dressing of all kinds. For instance, a Florentine law of 1325 banned cross-gender dressing along with games in which young people dressed as old men or in which "anyone transformed himself." A 1481 Brescia law forbade the use of masks to disguise oneself. A 1476 Ferrara statute outlawed the covering of one's face for the express reason that masking made it easier for dishonest women and women dressed as men to misbehave. A 1507 law in the city of Gubbio made it a crime to wear a mask, to wear clothing of the opposite sex, or for laypersons to dress in religious garb.

Gender cross-dressing is probably as old as gendered clothing itself, but it became more conspicuous and more provocative in the 1300s, as fashions for men and women began to diverge. The sexier male attire of the late Middle Ages made female-to-male cross-dressing a provocative erotic costume. Cross-dressing—like sumptuous attire and other "vanities"—was associated with sexual transgression and often cited as evidence of adultery, "concubinage," or prostitution. For instance, in 1395 John Rykener, who dressed as a woman and used the name Eleanor, was arrested for having sex with another man; he testified before the mayor and aldermen of London that he learned from prostitutes how to dress and have sex as a woman and that he had had many sex partners, including "a fair number of priests and nuns." Katherina Hetzeldorfer was drowned in the German town of Speyer in 1477 after it was discovered that she had dressed as a man and had sexual relations with another woman. In the Flemish city of Bruges, Nase de Poorter was accused, in 1502, of cross-dressing in order to live in sin with a priest.

Most reported cases of unlawful cross-dressing involved women accused of prostitution or "ungoverned" sexual practice. In the Italian cities of the late Middle Ages, female prostitutes regularly dressed as men; indeed, according to Bennett and McSheffrey, cross-dressing

"so signaled a woman's sexual availability . . . that, when books depict-
ing fashions became common in the later sixteenth century, the typical Venetian courtesan was shown wearing men's breeches beneath
her womanly skirts." Similarly, in fourteenth- and fifteenth-century
London, "ecclesiastic and civic authorities . . . understood female
cross-dressing within the long-established category of women's sexual misrule. More than an offense in itself, cross-dressing was [treated
as] a signifier . . . of women's sexual disorder."

This historical record may leave one with the sense that
cross-dressing—especially of the female-to-male variety—was predominantly a fetish, used by prostitutes, "loose" women, and indulgent libertines to arouse and satisfy sexual appetites. But this is
undoubtedly a consequence of the available sources: other than in
fiction, most accounts of cross-dressing in this period appear in the
context of legal prosecutions. No doubt many cross-dressers who
were not accused of other unlawful activity did not appear in such
documents and their stories are lost to history. Moreover, even the
cross-dressers prosecuted for criminal offenses may not have committed them: the association of cross-dressing with sexual transgression was sufficiently powerful that cross-dressing itself could
have served as evidence—if not proof—of other offenses. To add to
the confusion, officials were not always careful to distinguish sexual offenses: homosexual sex, prostitution, and "ungoverned" sex by
women were sometimes lumped together. In all likelihood, the only
crime some people arrested for "whoring" actually committed was
fornication: sex outside of marriage. Finally, and especially in the
cases of women dressed as men, there were also practical, non-erotic
reasons for cross-dressing: women were excluded from many types
of employment, denied access to public entertainments, and always
at risk of predation. For independent women, cross-dressing offered
many advantages. Undoubtedly, some cross-dressers were "transgender" in today's sense of the term: people who deeply identified with
the gender in which they dressed and derived psychological comfort
and a sense of completeness from their attire. But it's not clear that we
can fully understand the cross-dressers of the past through the lens of

today's cultural politics. The meaning of gendered attire and the dress codes that enforced it has varied throughout the centuries and so has the significance of transgressing those strictures.

Ultimately, cross-dressing was one of the many ways of using the emerging vocabulary of fashion to create a distinctive individual visual persona. Clothing expresses personality only by taking the intelligible symbols of social status and combining them in distinctive ways to suggest something beyond status: a unique individual. As fashion became widespread, such playful and subversive use of clothing became more common—and more threatening. The medieval- and Renaissance-era prohibitions of cross-dressing—like the other dress codes of that time—were designed to reinforce traditional vestimentary meanings. These dress codes ensured that, for instance, a gown signified a female body while the pants worn beneath plate armor signified a male body.

Joan of Arc was among the individuals who violated the codes that made dress signify sex and disrupted the sartorial symbolism that distinguished virtuous and sinful bodies. She drew on conventional meanings of attire in an unconventional way, crafting a distinctive, modern persona that captivated her contemporaries and still fascinates us today. In doing so, she became one of history's first fashion victims.

In the late Middle Ages, the birth of fashion reflected and inspired dramatic changes in the nature of status, sex, power, and personality. Where ancient draped attire could express social status through adornment and luxurious fabric, the innovations of tailoring allowed clothing to have much more numerous and subtle effects. The evocative power of fashion was especially important in an era where literacy was uncommon and visual spectacle was the most important form of propaganda: both church and state communicated through images, icons, and grand displays of pageantry. Fashion made clothing one of the most important media of visual expression: because it transformed the body itself, clothing had a unique capacity to shape social relations. But unlike architecture, sculpture, music, and painting, fashion was immutably personal and unavoidably mobile—it made a statement about the individual who wore it and it moved with that individual. These qualities made fashion extremely seductive and especially difficult to control. The dress codes of the late Middle Ages sought to do just that, in order to create and safeguard *status symbols*, ensuring that clothing would symbolize social rank and position—class, religion, occupation, and, most of all, sex—to serve the interests of political power in both church and state. But fashion undermined these ancient social roles just as readily as it reinforced them because it secretly served a different master: individual personality. This would help to usher in a new era and new status symbols, formed from a new sartorial vocabulary—one that communicated in elegant whispers rather than in ostentatious shouts.

Part Two

From Opulence to Elegance

Costly thy habit as thy purse can buy, but not expressed in fancy; rich not gaudy; for the apparel oft proclaims the man.

—WILLIAM SHAKESPEARE

The boor covers himself, the rich man or the fool adorns himself, and the elegant man gets dressed.

—HONORÉ DE BALZAC

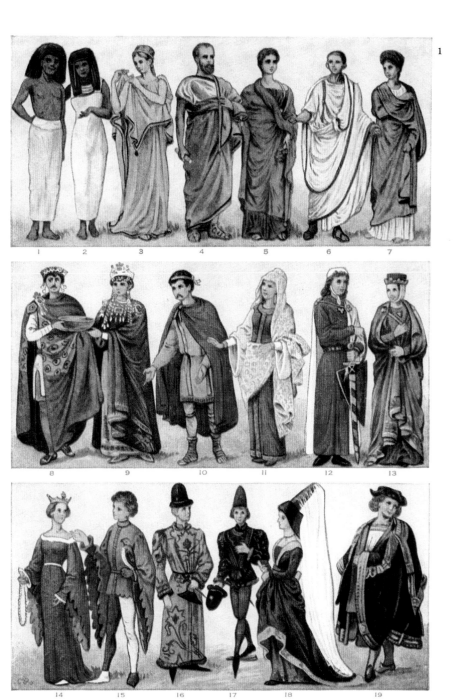

Until the late Middle Ages, most European clothing,
for both men and women, was draped.

2

Queen Elizabeth I used the evocative power of fashion to suggest an almost otherworldly magnificence.

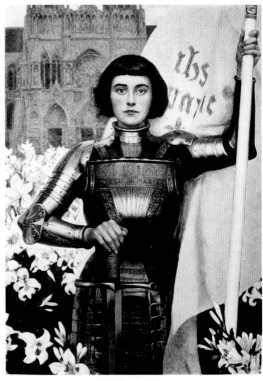

Joan of Arc seemed to assert masculine liberties and prerogatives by wearing men's clothing, which was more fashionable than the women's clothing of her era.

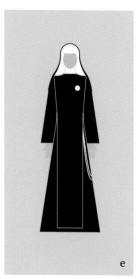

Some of the most common garments of the habits worn by women religious (colloquially referred to as *nuns*), each of which has a specific symbolic meaning: (a) Ring, indicating that the wearer is a bride of Christ, and sandals, symbolizing a disavowal of earthly wealth; (b) Tunic; (c) Cincture or cord, the knots of which may signify the virtues of the Virgin Mary; (d) Veil and/or wimple;
(e) Scapular, the shape of which evokes the Cross of Christ;
(f) Mantle, a cloak fastened at the neck

During the Seven Years' War, officers, such as Wenzel Anton
von Kaunitz, carried lip rouge, powder puffs, and eyelash
curlers into the field of battle.

The understated suit—a contrast to the sumptuousness of aristocratic courtly dress—became a symbol of political liberalism.

Beau Brummell, whose name is now synonymous with masculine flamboyance, was actually known for his understated attire.

Crinoline fires killed and injured
thousands during the style's heyday.

Camille Clifford's hourglass figure, draped in extravagantly decorative full skirts and crowned in a towering pile of upswept hair, reflected the turn-of-the-century feminine ideal.

10

Actress Louise Brooks epitomized the flapper of the 1920s: thin, athletic, and assertive in a streamlined knee-length skirt and bob hairstyle.

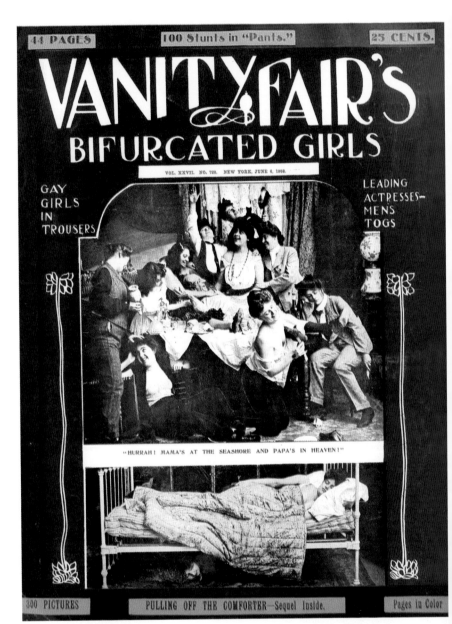

In the early twentieth century, the taboo against clothing that even suggested a woman's legs was so powerful that women dressed in trousers became a popular sexual fetish, known as *bifurcation*.

Chapter Five

The Great Masculine Renunciation

On the Frock Coat, Tartan and Kilt, Civilian Uniforms, and Powdered Wigs, Both Large and Modest

ACCORDING TO HISTORIAN FARID CHENOUNE, "[D]URING the Seven Years War [in the mid-eighteenth century] . . . officers carried campaign kits into battle that included perfume, rouge for lips and cheeks, powder puff and eyelash brush. . . . [T]he prince of Kaunitz . . . [Wenzel Anton von Kaunitz, a diplomat in the Habsburg monarchy and noble of the Holy Roman Empire] required four flunkys to dust him everyday with flour powder" (**Insert, Image #5**). Elaborate powdered wigs, brightly colored bonnets festooned with ostrich plumes, high-heeled shoes, and glittering jewelry were the height of masculine fashion throughout Europe well into the 1700s.

This changed beginning only in the late eighteenth century. In a span of about three decades—from 1760 to 1790—men throughout Europe abandoned the styles that had signified wealth and power for centuries. In their place, elite men adopted the sober, self-abnegating garb anticipated by Thomas More in *Utopia* and first favored by religious Puritans: simple wool and linen in sober hues of dark blue, brown, gray, and black. In 1930, the English psychologist and dress reformer John Carl Flügel described this as a "Great Masculine Renunciation . . . [of] sartorial decorativeness . . . at the end of the eighteenth century. . . . [M]en gave up their right to all of the brighter, gayer, more elaborate, and more varied forms of ornamentation, leaving these entirely to the use of women, and thereby making their own tailoring the most austere and ascetic of the arts."

The Great Masculine Renunciation was a political manifesto in cloth. It marked, in attire, the influence of religious severity in the seventeenth century and the triumph of Enlightenment idealism in the eighteenth century. The Great Renunciation had its antecedents in a simplification of courtly dress in both France and England that began in the seventeenth century. In England, after the execution of King Charles I in 1649, Oliver Cromwell established a Commonwealth. England was governed as a republic and the Church of England was stripped of some of its prerogatives, allowing other Protestants greater influence: Parliament passed laws closing theaters and banning many activities on Sundays. This combination of radical republicanism and religious severity inspired an austere wardrobe among elite men. Religious influence also inspired the renunciation of opulence in other places where Protestantism was influential, such as Germany, Switzerland, the Netherlands, and Scandinavia. Later, the Counter-Reformation ushered in a new austerity in Catholic-dominated societies, such as Spain and France.

The Protestant hostility to idolatry and religious vestments was part of a more general suspicion of sensuality. Max Weber's famous account of the Protestant work ethic explains the link between religion, capitalism, and this new austerity in dress:

[The religious denigration] of idle talk, of superfluities, and of vain ostentation . . . not serving the glory of God, but of man [led to] deciding in favour of sober utility as against any artistic tendencies. This was especially true in the case of decoration of the person, for instance, clothing. That powerful tendency toward uniformity of life, which to-day so immensely aids the capitalistic interest in the standardization of production, had its ideal foundation in the repudiation of all idolatry of the flesh.

Without their absolute monarch, Charles I, the English aristocracy had no need for the ritual that still animated political life and fashion at Versailles. In place of the ostentatious clothing of court, they adopted an eccentric style that would come to define modern menswear:

[A] sartorial blend of the chic plainness proposed by the Puritans of earlier days and by the country-dwelling yeomanry and gentry. . . . The startling modernizations in male dress that occurred in England at the very end of the eighteenth century were thus already well prepared for. . . . In England, a plain coat, useful boots, plain hat and plain linen were becoming signs of a gentleman possessed not only of many acres and full coffers, but of a sensible mind with an adult distain for primitive institutions and their personal fripperies.

Chenoune notes that, in eighteenth-century England, "ostentatiously expensive dress was associated with French fashion and Francophilia . . . particularly following the Puritan revolution and Cromwell's Commonwealth that had condemned the British royalty to a forced twenty-year sojourn at the court of France." Indeed, when the English monarchy was restored in 1660, Charles II—having learned from his father's tragic example—established a new, understated mode of court dress: a vest and frock coat ensemble that became the prototype for the three-piece suit. According to historian David Kuchta, "In introducing the three-piece suit, Charles II attempted to appropriate an iconoclastic, oppositional ideology [first developed as a critique of the monarchy] and use it to redefine court culture. . . . [C]ultural authority would be expressed by elite opposition to luxury, not by making conspicuous consumption the exclusive prerogative of the court." Subsequent events—most notably the Glorious Revolution of 1688 which established England's first Bill of Rights—reinforced the move away from aristocratic opulence and toward frugality: on the streets of London, highborn and commoner alike exhibited a new sobriety in dress. According to an early-eighteenth-century observer, Londoners were "rarely seen in gold braiding; they wear a small coat that they call a frock that is without pleat or adornment . . . they also have a little round wig, a plain hat and a stick in hand instead of a sword. . . . This attire can be seen on prosperous merchants, rich gentlemen and sometimes even lords of utmost distinction. . . ."

Enlightenment philosophy, with its emphasis on individual freedom, scientific rationality, and human flourishing reinforced this trend. The Enlightenment effectively codified the individualist mindset that coincided with the birth of fashion. René Descartes's famous dictum *Cogito, ergo sum* (I think, therefore I am) in 1637 neatly summarized a worldview that displaced the supernatural authorities of Church and Crown in favor of the centrality of individual human consciousness. The scientific method undermined religious cosmology in favor of a world that could be understood through human logic and human perception. With human beings at its moral center and human reason as its guide, the Enlightenment rejected ancient political arrangements based on tradition and dogma and began to develop the ideals that would mature into democracy and human rights.

Many of the English, who were among the first Europeans to renounce aristocratic decorativeness and display, began to associate their understated attire with these social and political ideals. For example, an English tourist who, on arriving in Paris in 1752, felt compelled to adopt the more ornate French costume complained that "I thought myself as much deprived of my Liberty, as if I had been in the Bastile [sic]; and I frequently sighed for my little loose Frock, which I look upon as an Emblem of our happy Constitution; for it lays a Man under no uneasy Restraint, but leaves it in his Power to do as he please." By the end of the eighteenth century, England had displaced France as the arbiter of masculine style (France would retain its primacy in women's fashion for at least the next three hundred years and arguably to this day). Some of the French nobility, who had lived under an absolute monarchy, saw the simpler English style of dress as an emblem of political freedom too. The frock coat and modest wig was the dress code of the partisan of individual rights and constitutionally limited government, and it became a fashion trend among free-thinking French nobles. When geopolitical conflict between France and England dampened French Anglophilia, French liberals looked to England's rebellious colonies: understated attire and a wigless head was dubbed *fashion à la Franklin*, after Benjamin Franklin.

Back in its country of origin, *fashion à la Franklin* was a patriotic imperative. An ethos of sartorial restraint began in the colonial period, in part as an attempt to improve relations with England, which controlled the colonial trade in luxurious textiles and garments. Sobriety and modesty in attire became a symbol of the American virtues of good sense and thrift and evidence of a healthy suspicion of the corruptions of European luxury and dishonest, excessively refined artifice. Franklin himself, writing in 1722 for the New-England *Courant* under the nom de plume Silence Dogood, inveighed against "the Pride in Apparel . . . growing upon us ever since we parted with our Homespun Cloaths. . . ." Echoing the rationale that Queen Elizabeth advanced in defense of sumptuary laws over a century and a half earlier, Franklin/Dogood remarked that:

> Persons of small Fortune under the Dominion of this Vice, seldom consider their Inability to maintain themselves in it, but strive to imitate their Superiors in Estate, or Equals in Folly. . . . By striving to appear rich they become really poor, and deprive themselves of that Pity and Charity which is due to the humble poor Man. . . . [T]hose airy Mortals, who have no other Way of making themselves considerable, but by gorgeous Apparel, draw after them Crowds of Imitators, who hate each other while they endeavor after a Similitude of Manners. They destroy by Example, and envy one another's Destruction.

As an alternative, Franklin advocated the "homespun Dress of Honesty," an ideal that swept the American colonies, inspired by both egalitarian idealism and Puritan fervor. American civic leaders advocated homespun clothing as a way to combine the virtues of personal industry and democratic equality: "Rich and Poor all turn the Spinning Wheel" became a patriotic slogan. As historian Michael Zakim notes, "[H]omespun erased the textured fineness of the cloth by which the 'respectable Ladies' of Narragansett and Newport had traditionally maintained their status." Religious zealotry also played a role, igniting in the New World, as it did in Renaissance Italy, bonfires of the vanities on which fancy clothing as well as books were burned. Nor was this the only echo of an older dress code: the homespun ideal inspired proposals for sartorial regulation reminiscent of the Elizabethan era as "[c]ollege orators debated 'whether Sumptuary Law ought to be established in the United States' and a[n] . . . attempt at legislative prescriptions on dress . . . was actually made at the Constitutional Convention."

The Great Renunciation took hold somewhat later in France than in England and the United States—the limited influence of *fashion à la Franklin* notwithstanding—but when French standards of dress did change, they did so with dramatic flair. The radicals of Revolutionary France were the sans-culottes, meaning without breeches and stockings—the characteristic aristocratic dress; the loose-fitting trousers of the working man became a symbol of solidarity, joining laboring classes and bourgeois radicals in protest against the inequality of the ancien régime. The reactionaries known as the *muscadin* dressed in skin-tight knee breeches, silk stockings, and fine buckled shoes or polished boots—the traditional attire of the eighteenth-century aristocrat. This refined costume was the extent of their gentility: their walking sticks—which they called their "Constitutions"—were in fact bludgeons used to subdue their political enemies.

The new French Republican government rejected the aristocratic dress codes of Versailles on October 29, 1793, declaring "everyone is free to wear the garment or garb suitable to his or her sex that he or she pleases." As John Carl Flügel noted, "One of the purposes of decorative dress was . . . to emphasize distinctions of rank and wealth. . . . It is not surprising . . . that the magnificence and elaboration of costume, which so well expressed the ideals of the *ancien regime,* should have been distasteful to . . . the Revolution." Political egalitarianism, combined with a new respect for work and working people, inspired new norms of attire:

> The new social order demanded something that expressed . . . the common humanity of all men. This could only be done by means of a greater uniformity of dress . . . the abolition of those distinctions which had formerly divided the wealthy from the poor, the exalted from the humble . . . a greater simplification of dress . . . to more plebian standards that were possible to all. . . .
>
> [T]he ideal of work had now become respectable. Formerly, all work or connection with economic activities of any kind . . . was considered degrading to the dignity of those classes who chiefly set the fashion. . . . The really significant moments of life were those that were passed on the field of battle or in the drawing-room, for both of which tradition had decreed a costly and elegant attire. With the new ideals of the Revolution . . . a man's most important activities were passed, not in the drawing-room but in the workshop, the counting-house, the office—places which had, by long tradition, been associated with a relatively simple costume.

The shift from aristocratic opulence to republican understatement reflected religious modesty, the humanism of the Enlightenment, and egalitarian political ideals in the New World and the Old. It began with the Protestant asceticism of Cromwell's Commonwealth, took hold as a secular fashion in the new understated wardrobe of a politically liberated English gentry, and became the new standard for male attire throughout the West after the French Revolution swept away the most influential remaining bastion of sartorial hierarchy and magnificence.

The Masculine Renunciation spread and intensified as sartorial refinements in each nation inspired further changes in others. For instance, just as the French had once been influenced by American *fashion à la Franklin*, Americans were influenced by the Revolutionary style of the French. According to Michael Zakim, Thomas

Jefferson adopted a sartorially refined version of the sans-culottes style during his time in France, abandoning knee breeches but swapping the loose pants of the laborer for closely fitted, highly tailored trousers. The new understated but elegant style became popular in the United States after he returned home. By the early nineteenth century, the term "silk stocking" had become an insult in America, denoting a hidebound older generation that clung to outdated aristocratic pretensions.

National Uniforms

The new ethos of sartorial understatement sweeping Europe symbolized distinctive political ideals: liberalism, egalitarianism, and, in some cases, national pride. Just as fashion could convey individual personality, it could also express ethnic and national identity: the liberated sensibility of the Englishman in his modest frock coat, the down-to-earth mentality of the American colonist in homespun, the radical politics of France's sans-culottes. It seemed natural that attire should reflect national identity during what some historians call the era of nationalism, beginning in the late eighteenth century. Western societies relied on common symbols such as flags, maps, national museums, an emergent national press—and common norms of dress—to define national identity. New dress codes also reflected and reinforced this emerging geopolitical ideal.

Although we take the nation-state for granted today, during the late eighteenth century, nationalism was only one of many forms of geopolitical organization; it was, in many places, novel and unfamiliar, and creating a sense of national identity was an urgent project. The political authority of the church and the rule of Europe's vast, interrelated imperial dynasties was in decline. Independent city-states, smaller regional principalities, and the sprawling political tributaries of the Holy Roman Empire were slowly but surely conquered in war or divvied up by treaty and consolidated into the contiguous, territorially, and ethnically defined sovereignties of European nation-states. As historian Benedict Anderson argues, this was a feat of imagination in which shared symbols were as important as shared experiences and traditions. Nationalism was an ongoing effort to convince people who thought of themselves as villagers, serfs, burghers of a free city, or the subjects of a prince or royal dynasty to identify, first and foremost, as citizens of a nation.

Dress codes became an important part of many struggles for national and ethnic identity. Distinctive ethnic dress could mark differences among ethnic groups within a nation. Some dress codes forbade ethnically distinctive attire that seemed to signal defiance but others redefined ethnic subgroups—and their characteristic garb—as integral parts of national culture. Meanwhile, proposals for official civilian uniforms, to be worn by all citizens of a nation, were surprisingly common in late-eighteenth-century Europe, reflecting a belief that divisions of status and ethnicity were threats to civic unity.

In 1746 the British Parliament enacted the Act of Proscription, which contained the following provision, subsequently referred to as the Dress Act of 1746, the Disclothing Act of 1746, the Act for Abolition and Proscription of the Highland Dress, or the Tartan Act. It held:

> That . . . no man or boy within that part of Great Briton called Scotland, other than such as shall be employed as Officers and Soldiers in His Majesty's Forces, who shall on any pretence whatsoever, wear or put on the clothes commonly called Highland Clothes (that is to say) The Plaid, Philabeg, or little Kilt, Trowse, Shoulder-belts or any part whatsoever of what peculiarly belongs to the Highland Garb; and that no tartan or partly-coloured plaid of stuff shall be used for the Great Coats or upper Coats, and if any such person shall presume . . . to wear or put on the aforesaid garments or any part of them . . . [he] shall suffer imprisonment without bail for the space of six months . . . and being convicted of a second offense . . . shall be liable to be transported to any of his Majesty's plantations beyond the seas, there to remain for the space of seven years.

The Tartan Act was a form of sartorial colonization. In the mid-eighteenth century, Great Britain—the union of England, Wales, Ireland, and, most tentatively, Scotland—was still fragile. England and Scotland had been united under one monarch since the death of Queen Elizabeth I and the ascension of James VI of Scotland, the only son of Mary, Queen of Scots, to both the English and Scottish thrones in 1603. James styled himself James I of Great Britain, but Scotland remained an independent state with its own laws and parliament until 1707, when, after years of tense negotiations, the English and Scottish Parliaments ratified the Acts of Union, which placed both nations under a single British Parliament.

The union was controversial in more heavily Catholic Scotland, where many resented rule by a Protestant-majority Parliament and Protestant monarchs. Scottish dissenters insisted that Scotland had retained its own independent line of succession, and some, the Jacobites (after Jacobus, Latin for James), sought the restoration of James I's line, the House of Stuart, as the rightful heirs to the throne. Many of the Scottish Highland clans were prominent among the Jacobite dissidents.

In 1746, Charles Edward Stuart, the descendant of James I, led an unsuccessful uprising against the British in Scotland, in which the Highland clans played a central role. Indeed, the Jacobite cause was so identified with the Highland clans that their traditional garb had become a sort of unofficial Jacobite uniform, worn by Highland and Lowland Jacobites alike. After quashing the rebellion, the British Parliament moved to subdue the Highland clans once and for all. New legislation disarmed the Highlanders, disbanded their armies, abolished the traditional authority of the Highland clan chiefs, and established British legal jurisdiction throughout Scotland. Imposing a final indignity, the Tartan Act banned the traditional Highland costume. The prohibition of the Highland garb was intended to destroy the last symbols of the Jacobite cause, break the spirit of the Highlanders, and speed their assimilation as British subjects.

But the Tartan Act backfired, instead encouraging widespread identification with the Highland costume. A mid-nineteenth-century commentary made these observations about the efforts to subdue the Highlanders:

> [F]orcing the discontinuance of the peculiar dress of the High-landers . . . instead of eradicating their national spirit and assimi-lating them in all respects with the Lowland population, it rather intensified that spirit, and their determination to preserve them-selves a separate and peculiar people. . . . The Act surrounded the Highland dress with a sort of sacred halo, raised it into a badge of nationality, and was probably the means of perpetuating and ren-dering popular the use of a habit, which, had it been left alone, might long ere now have died a natural death, and been found only in museums, side by side with the Lochaber axe, the two-handed sword, and the nail studded shield.

Moreover, by enumerating the precise elements of Highland dress, the Tartan Act may have helped to create a more easily identi-fied ethnic style than had existed before. According to historian Hugh Trevor-Roper, "[W]hen the great rebellion of 1745 broke out, the kilt, as we know it, was a recent *English* invention and 'clan' tartans did not exist." In 1715, many Highlanders fighting for the Jacobite army wore "neither plaid nor philbeg [kilt]," but instead the *leine*, a long, knee-length shirt or loose coat characteristic of both Scottish and Irish dress at the time. The Highlander elite wore trousers, either the same tight breeches worn by elites elsewhere in Britain, or, in the case of military officers, the "trews or truis"—a type of form-fitting hose, cut on the bias and made from tartan fabric. Indeed, Sir John Sin-clair of Ulster, who assembled the Scottish military regiments of the Rothesay and Caithness Fencibles in 1794 and 1795, was so convinced that the *trews* and not the kilt was the ancient garb of the Highlander that he not only designed the uniform of his regiment accordingly but also composed a marching song to advertise its greater antiquity:

> *Let others boast of philibeg*
> *Of kilt and belted plaid*

Whilst we the ancient trews will wear
In which our fathers bled.

In 1727 an English officer posted in Scotland described the "quelt" as a simple draped, un-tailored garment, "set in folds and girt round the waist to make a short pettitcoat that reaches half-way down the thigh, and the rest is brought over the shoulders and then fastened . . . " Perhaps this was an early distant ancestor of the kilt as we know it—again, suggesting that stereotypical Highland costume was a later invention. In fact, there is some evidence that the kilt that we now consider the ancient garb of the Scottish Highlander was the innovation of an *English* industrialist, Thomas Rawlinson, who, having established an iron-works in Glengarry and Lochaber, devised clothing more suitable to industrial labor for his Highlander workforce. A letter from one Ivan Baille of Aberiachan, Esq., published in *Edinburgh Magazine* in 1785 and titled "The Felie-beg, no part of the Ancient Highland Dress," stated that "Rawlinson, an Englishman . . . I can aver as I became personally acquainted with him . . . thought it no great stretch to abridge the dress [the "quelt"] and make it handy and convenient for his work-men. . . . [T]his piece of dress . . . was in the Gaelic termed *felie beg (beg* in that tongue signifies little) and in our Scots termed *little kilt.*"

As for tartan, the record is mixed. There is some evidence of regionally distinctive tartans in the early eighteenth century: for instance, in 1718, the Edinburgh poet Allan Ramsay wrote a poem titled *Tartana,* in which he arguably makes reference to distinctive clan tartans; the Scottish author Martin Martin writes in his *A Description of the Western Islands of Scotland,* published in the early eighteenth century, that "thru the mainland of the Highlands . . . at the first view of a man's plad [one can] guess the place of his residence." But the weight of opinion seems to be on the side of Trevor-Roper, who insists "contemporary evidence concerning the rebellion of 1745 . . . shows no differentiation of clans [by type of tartan], no continuity of setts [within clans]. The only way in which a Highlander's loyalty could be discerned was not by his tartan but by the cockade in his bonnet. Tartans were a matter of private taste."

The Tartan Act was repealed in 1782. A proclamation celebrated the sartorial liberation of the Highlanders:

[T]he King and Parliament of Britain have forever abolished the Act against the Highland Dress; which came down to the clans from the beginning of the world to the year 1746. This must bring great joy to every Highland heart. You are no longer bound down to the unmanly dress of the lowlander. This is declaring to every man, young and old, simple and gentle, that they may after this put on and wear the trews, the little kilt, . . . along with the belted plaid, without fear of the Law. . . .

But by then the Highland costume had fallen into disuse: "After a generation in trousers, the simple peasantry of the Highlands saw no reason to resume the belted plaid or the tartan. . . ."

It was the Scottish elite—who had never worn the kilt nor, in all likelihood, a family tartan before—who saw a reason to adopt them after the restrictive dress code was repealed. Scottish lawyers and noblemen formed the Highland Society of London in 1778. These elite Highlanders developed a modernized version of the traditional garb, and created an ancient pedigree for it. In this they were assisted, ironically, by the imperial ambitions of the British, who employed Highlanders to establish colonial rule in India and America. The overseas Highland regiments had been exempt from the Tartan Act and had begun to wear the kilt for reasons of expediency, just as Rawlinson's workers had done. The various Highland regiments also used distinctive styles of tartan to differentiate themselves from each other. Trevor-Roper argues that this military uniform was the origin of the distinctive tartan or "sett": the dress codes of the modern imperial military inspired the "revival" of ancient Highland garb.

According to Trevor-Roper, that ancient pedigree was established through unsubstantiated assertions, forged documents, and, of course, the collaboration of textile manufacturers, who knew an opportunity when they saw one and duly allied themselves with the Highland Society of London to certify that each pattern in their stock was in fact the tartan of a specific clan. Unbeknownst to the proud purchaser, the origins of many "clan" tartans were not to be found in the romantic and fog-shrouded Scottish Highlands but in the smoggy streets of England's industrial cities and the humid climate of the Caribbean colonies. For instance, Trevor-Roper reports that one "Cluny Macpherson . . . was given a tartan . . . now labeled 'MacPherson' . . . previously, having been sold in bulk to a Mr. Kidd to clothe his West Indian slaves, it had been labeled 'Kidd' and before that it had been simply 'No. 155.'"

But there is no doubt that the tartan became a powerful symbol of the Scottish people. The British, having first tried to ban it, next tried to incorporate it into a multiethnic national identity, an Anglo-Celtic *e pluribus unum*. Indeed, the history of the Jacobite uprising itself was braided into a unified British history, most famously in Sir Walter Scott's 1814 novel *Waverley*, in which a young English gentleman falls in love with a passionate Highlander woman and joins the Jacobite uprising. In the novel, young Waverley saves the life of a British officer in battle. When the uprising is put down, he is pardoned and marries the demure daughter of a Lowlander aristocrat. The two women seem to symbolize two Scotlands—the untamed Highlands of the Jacobite rebellion and the civilized Lowlands that favored British union. Such historical revisions, which romanticized the Jacobite uprisings and underplayed the fierce nationalism that inspired them, allowed the Highlander garb to be refashioned as a quaint regional custom. By 1822, King George IV was painted wearing Highland tartans and in 1853 Queen Victoria established a royal tartan, the Balmoral, which custom to this day reserves to the queen and the royal family.

The Tartan Act of 1746 addressed new concerns about the meaning of dress in the age of national consolidation. Distinctive garb could divide or unite a nation and dress codes could downplay or emphasize social divisions. Both national governments and ethnic groups used dress and dress codes to express collective ideals and ambitions.

•   •   •

According to historian Daniel Leonhard Purdy, "[T]he idea that all grown men should wear standardized dress was a recurrent minor debate of the eighteenth century." In Revolutionary France, freedom of choice in attire seemed to many a logical antidote to the hierarchical regulations of the old regime, but some wanted stronger guarantees of equality: a mandatory national uniform, to be worn by all citizens of the Republic. Similarly, Justus Möser, renowned jurist and advisor to the prince-bishop of Osnabrück (in what is now Germany), insisted in 1775 that a national uniform could bring together a fragmented people around common ideals of patriotic virtue:

> Nothing seems more fitting than that we request of our sovereign a uniform and make this the honorary dress for all those who make for the common good in equally praiseworthy manner and comport themselves as honorable men. To be sure, at first it will seem a new form of slavery to wear the prescribed color of a lord or to deny the noble freedom of being able to choose one's dress according to one's own preference. . . . However . . . a prince can now wear his fellow prince's colors without degrading his escutcheon, and the man who . . . risks his life for his country without pay, certainly has more than one right to respect and honor.

The national uniform would become a common symbol of patriotic virtue. But egalitarian promise did not completely overcome the ancient need for social distinction. Möser's national uniform—like the sumptuary laws of earlier times—would also make status visible, distinguishing noble from commoner, responsible citizen from derelict shirker, propertied taxpayer from indigent freeloader:

> Of course this will not come to pass without . . . determining the man . . . who should have a right to this uniform . . . that he possess either the requisite share of landed property or dependable capital . . . and thereby to exclude all worse persons. It is evident that there must be a reasonable number of gradations in this ar-

rangement and that the man of high rank must wear a uniform differently garnished than that of the common man.

Proposals for national citizen's uniforms were debated throughout Europe. For instance, in 1791, lawyer Samuel Simon Witte argued before the Danish Academy against a national uniform. He insisted that self-expression through clothing was one of the great accomplishments of Western civilization, which distinguished enlightened from repressive societies, advanced from primitive cultures. He observed that clothing was more than a sign of social status; it was a means of self-creation:

> [T]hrough which [a person] portrays, shows and announces himself and through which he is . . . presented . . . it can express, indicate and illustrate all type of moral and personal characteristics and feelings, such as grandeur, dignity, noble or humble origins, power, wealth, courage, pride, innocence, modesty, even the various gradations of virtue and age . . . .[T]he costume and its fashion have a greater power over the character and mores of a people than do all laws and police regulations; a power that is to be granted it all the more in that the costume exerts its effects silently, without force. . . .

A law mandating a civilian uniform, Witte insisted, would "suppress and stifle the taste of a people and reduce it to the barbarian's mere animal feeling. . . ."

Proposals for national civilian uniforms went nowhere. But ironically, in the subsequent decades an *international* civilian uniform slowly developed, not through legislation or decree but through custom and practice. As Möser would have hoped, it became a sartorial sign of civic virtue worn by heads of states and low-level bureaucrats, titans of industry and wage-earning clerks, the cultural elite and the petite bourgeoisie, and it allowed for infinite variations to signify social rank. Within the span of roughly half a century, men from Munich to Manhattan adopted, en masse, this modest, matching trouser-and-jacket ensemble. The business suit became the livery and regalia of Western society, and, as the influence of the West spread, it would become the global symbol of modernity, industry, and Enlightenment.

Wigged Out

The powdered wig was one of the last status symbols of the old regime and its norms of conspicuous display. But there were wigs and then there were *Wigs*. Look at a two-dollar bill and you will see Thomas Jefferson wearing a fashionable wig of his day (by contrast, George Washington, widely believed to have worn a similar wig, in fact did not; instead he powdered and styled his own hair to look like a wig). It's a modest wig befitting an elected representative of a democracy. Now find a painting of King Louis XIV, the Sun King, absolute monarch of ancien régime France. Now that's a *Wig*. The evolution of the masculine wig, from the outsize sign of royal privilege favored by Louis *Quartorze* to the small toupee sported by Jefferson, reflects the changing nature of status symbols in the years leading up to the Great Masculine Renunciation. Like clothing in general, the wig became less grand. Moreover, its social meaning was *transformed* and not simply muted as it shrank in size. The modest wig of Jefferson did not simply reflect the more modest political ambitions of the public servant of a republic as contrasted to those of an absolute monarch: it reflected a fundamentally different social status—one based on the modern human values of practicality and individuality as opposed to the ancient values of divine grandeur and magnificence. The Great Masculine Renunciation transformed the status symbols of the past, from markers of inherited privilege and formal rank into signs of individual merit and personality.

Louis XIV popularized the powdered wig—a status symbol first adopted by his father, Louis XIII (reportedly to disguise his baldness), but which reflected an ancient symbolism. Long hair had long been associated with royal blood; indeed, the great eighteenth-century authority on French culture Denis Diderot's *Encyclopédie* notes that, "long hair was a mark of honor and liberty among the ancient Gauls . . . a characteristic of princes of the blood . . . other subjects wore their hair cut short . . . [and] haircuts were more or less short, depending on the degree of inferiority in the ranks . . . the monarch's head of hair became . . . the yardstick of social rank."

In seventeenth-century France, the powdered wig became the height of fashion, and by the early eighteenth century, the wig trade was a vast industry employing thousands of skilled artisans. According to historian Michael Kwass, in 1771 there were almost one thousand master wigmakers in Paris alone, "[a]nd master wigmakers were merely the tip of the professional iceberg. Below the level of master, journeymen were . . . estimated in their ranks at nearly ten thousand. Such numbers do not include the countless . . . artisans who produced wigs without the guild's consent. . . ." The production of wigs in eighteenth-century France was controlled by an exclusive guild. While the official function of the guilds that controlled most skilled trades in France's old regime was to protect the livelihood of their members and the reputation of their trade, they also effectively guaranteed the exclusivity—and hence high price and high status—of their products. Even by the standards of the day, the production of wigs was extraordinarily controlled: master wigmakers acquired the right to practice their trade through the purchase of venal offices from the monarchy—an unusual and costly credential, the expense of which was, of course, passed onto the wig-buying customer. In addition, because the fashion was for wigs to be white, they had to be powdered with flour—an ongoing expense in maintenance. As a consequence, besides being impractical and cumbersome—indicating that the wearer lived a life of leisure—wigs were costly luxury goods—a perfect status symbol.

The popularity of wigs spread from the court of the Sun King across the channel to England and throughout the European continent to become an indispensable symbol of aristocratic status. They also trickled down the social register as courtiers, magistrates, clerics, lawyers, and wannabe nobles adopted the style in the classic pattern of Veblenian status emulation. Indeed, by the mid-eighteenth century, wigs were so widely worn that critics of luxury felt compelled to inveigh against them. According to historian Daniel Roche, Jean-Baptiste Thiers, curé of Champrond and Vibraque, decried the widespread wearing of wigs by the clergy, complaining that "[s]o many ecclesiastics today wear a wig that there is every reason to believe that they are persuaded . . . that this strange ornament is not wholly forbidden to them, and that it is not inherently unfitting to the seemliness of their profession." He went on to warn against the "seduction of appearances," insisting that wigs offended God by substituting human artifice for the blessing of nature; wasted time and resources in contradiction of the scriptural imperative for thrift; and betrayed the wearer's vanity. This left the bewigged cleric unable, without inviting the charge of hypocrisy, to chastise the faithful for their luxurious clothing and other indulgences. According to Kwass, the gentleman-economist Marquis de Mirabeau complained that wig-wearing members of the lower classes had put on airs: "Everyone . . . is a Monsieur. . . . [A] man . . . wearing black silk clothes and a well-powdered wig, and as I fell over myself offering him compliments, he introduced himself as the oldest son of my blacksmith. . . ." Another observer lamented the proliferation of wigs among the common people of Paris, including "[s]choolmasters . . . old choirmasters, public scribes, law court ushers, shop boys, legal and notarial clerks, domestic servants, cooks and kitchen boys."

In short, wigs were an exemplary status symbol. The longer story, however, is more tangled. According to Kwass, as the fashion for wigs spread among the merchant and laboring classes, the wig was described less and less often in terms of luxury or status and more frequently in terms of the modern, plebian value of convenience. Social critics, fashion experts, civility guides, and wigmakers themselves extolled the *convenience* of the wig: "[I]n an age when civility . . . prescribed the perpetual cleaning, combing, and styling of hair, it was easier to have your head shaved and don a wig than to groom your own hair. . . ." As wigs followed fashion, shorter and lighter styles were devised: the "full-bottom" or in-folio wig one associates with Louis

XIV was relegated to formal affairs of court while more practical styles served the day-to-day life of aristocrat, gentleman farmer, and blacksmith's son alike.

The wig became popular, not so much because commoners attempted to emulate aristocrats, but because wigmakers took an elite status symbol with a limited market and remade and remarketed it as a practical commodity for a mass market. The short, lightweight bobwig was not a poor man's imitation of the full-bottom wig but instead a modernized, streamlined, perfected version of it. As Kwass notes:

> Far from an object of Veblen-style conspicuous consumption . . . the post Louis Quatorze wig was . . . an accessory of convenience. . . . [T]aste leaders highlighted the physical ease and personal utility that . . . wigs provided. . . . [F]ashion critics argued that the convenience of wigs signaled the coming of a healthy, utilitarian aesthetic . . . [while] wigmakers exploited the concept of convenience to market wigs to what had become a relative broad customer base.

Instead, the mass appeal of the hairpiece was more like that of the timepiece: portable watches began life as an exotic contrivance to be shown off at high-society galas, but became popular as tools that could be strapped to the wrists of working people engaged in practical pursuits.

The wig also became a means of personal expression. The wigmakers' art was thought to lie in the ability to design a hairpiece that expressed individual character by accenting one's facial "air." Wigmakers touted their ability to tailor wigs and began to emphasize the personalized variety of their offerings—a wig to suit each individual face and sense of style. Wigs and hairstyles became expressions of individual sensibility and even philosophical conviction. For instance, Jean-Jacques Rousseau abandoned his long wig for a modest bobwig to signal his philosophical renunciation of social constraints, and Benjamin Franklin, when in France in 1776, abandoned his wig in favor of a plain cap that became an element of what the French dubbed *la mode à la Franklin*.

The powdered wig, of course, eventually fell out of fashion altogether. Today, it survives on the heads of English barristers who must wear the traditional "bench wig" when they argue in court. According to historian James G. McLaren, J.D., English judges and lawyers first wore wigs as a fashion accessory, in the aristocratic style of the early eighteenth century. Over time, as it became unfashionable everywhere else, the wig became a symbol of professional status, worn as a matter of custom and practice. No explicit dress code required the barrister's wig until the 1844 case of *Regina v. Whittaker*, in which a barrister who appeared without one was not "seen" by the judge (according to the librarian of Lincoln's Inn, one of the ancient English Inns of Court, "a judge indicates that counsel is improperly dressed by saying that he does not 'see' him.") Ever since, the wig has been mandatory attire for a barrister appearing before an English court.

Even as they were pared down for the common man, wigs were desirable in part because of their long association with aristocratic status. The modern, understated dress code that emerged in the late eighteenth century (and is with us to this day) didn't completely abandon status symbols. Instead, the Great Masculine Renunciation created a new kind of status symbol that was distinguished by its refinement, authenticity, and suitability. These became less an insignia of formal social position than a marker of individual virtue. This new kind of status symbol would retailor dress codes for the next two centuries.

Chapter Six

Style and Status

*The Importance of the Well-Dressed Man's Basic
Black Suit and the Elegant Woman's Eight Daily
Toilettes; the Prevalence of Silk and Velvet
Waistcoats and the Art of the Perfectly Tied Cravat*

BEFORE THE GREAT RENUNCIATION, SARTORIAL SPLENDOR
had been jealously guarded as a symbol of political power and economic status for centuries. Did men suddenly, in the late eighteenth century, lose interest in personal appearance as a marker of prestige? Did the English gentry, in their frock coats and stylized hunting garb, abandon the symbols of privilege? Did the pious Puritans and radical French followers of *fashion à la Franklin*, in their spare and modest costume, really give up on distinguished attire?

New social and political ideals of rationality, industriousness, and efficiency were displacing the older values of spectacle and display and, accordingly, new, subtle, and unwritten dress codes began to privilege understatement over the conspicuous luxury that had been encoded in the laws of the past. In the Age of Enlightenment, status became a matter of style.

In the early sixteenth century, Baldassare Castiglione, in *The Book of the Courtier*, advised the reader:

[I]n all human affairs, whether in word or in deed . . . to avoid affectation in every way possible . . . to practice in all things a certain *sprezzatura* [nonchalance] so as to conceal all art and make whatever is done or said appear to be without effort and almost without any thought about it. . . . [B]ecause everyone knows the difficulty of things that are rare and well done; wherefore facility in such things causes the greatest wonder; whereas . . . to labor . . . causes everything, no matter how great it may be, to be held in little account.

William Shakespeare expressed a similar theme several decades later, in *Hamlet*, where Polonius advises, "Costly thy habit as thy purse can buy, but not expressed in fancy; rich not gaudy; for the apparel oft proclaims the man." Similarly, the seventeenth-century English poet Robert Herrick advised the young woman seeking victory over her rivals in romance that "a sweet disorder in the dress / kindles in clothes a wantonness . . . / A winning wave, deserving note; / In the tempestuous petticoat; / A careless shoe-string, in whose tie, / I see a wild civility, do more bewitch me, than when Art, / is too precise in every part. . . ."

These exhortations to aristocratic understatement marked the beginning of the long trend toward sartorial refinement that would culminate in the Great Masculine Renunciation. Colonial expansion in the eighteenth century and the Industrial Revolution in the nineteenth century created new economic opportunities and new technologies, both of which undermined the exclusivity of opulence: a growing number of newly wealthy merchants, tradespeople, and financiers could afford even the most extravagant attire while new techniques of production brought well-made clothing to a mass market. As was true in the late Middle Ages, conspicuous luxury could no longer reliably distinguish the elite. But unlike their ancestors in the late Middle Ages and the Renaissance, elites in the eighteenth century could not enlist the state to shore up the exclusivity of sumptuous attire. European societies had or were in the process of overthrowing their old dynastic regimes, whether through the more gradual and episodic changes of England's transition to constitutional monarchy or through the more dramatic changes of the French Revolution. A splashy show of status privilege was not only out of step with the zeitgeist—it could be downright dangerous.

But, of course, status hierarchy survived in a new form and so did the dress codes that made it visible. Hence the eighteenth and nineteenth centuries saw the birth of a new sumptuary code that inverted the ancient values of the older ones: if the law could not deny luxury to upstarts and the nouveaux riches, then luxury alone would no longer be a sign of high status. From then on—and up to the present moment—a new reverse snobbery declared that too much opulence was a sign of poor taste and low breeding. Like Dr. Seuss's haughty star-bellied Sneetches, who had their stars removed when their social inferiors found a way to have stars applied to their abdomens, the elite renounced showy opulence when it became too widely available. Understatement, nonchalance, and relaxed elegance—once minor counterthemes in a social performance that emphasized showy opulence—became the featured status symbols of a new era. These had to be learned through constant and long-standing exposure to the elite. The etiquette manual superseded the statute and proclamation; the opinions of social peers, parents, and caregivers replaced the verdicts of constables and magistrates in establishing the dress codes of the post-Enlightenment era.

In the United States, homespun gave way to "ready-made"— epitomized by the democratic black suit of the Brooks Brothers catalog. Egalitarianism was expressed in a near-ubiquitous bourgeois standard of attire. The French intellectual and diplomat Michel Chevalier wrote, during a visit to the United States in 1834, "What a contrast between our Europe and America!. . . . Every man was warmly clad in an outer garment; every woman had her cloak and bonnet of the latest Paris fashion. . . ." In the mid-nineteenth century, the English poet Lady Emmeline Stuart-Wortley remarked "a mob in the United States is a mob in broad cloth. If we may talk of a rabble in a republic, it is a rabble in black silk waistcoats."

Many celebrated the democratization of fashionable attire and linked this refined dress with civic virtue; for example, Thomas Ford, who would later become the governor of Illinois, noted in 1823 that "with pride of dress came ambition, industry, the desire for knowledge, and a love of decency." Others longed for a return to an earlier era of simplicity—though not always for egalitarian reasons. For instance, one American critic complained that the prevalence of fine clothing undermines "every Distinction between the Poor and the Rich . . . people of the meanest parentages . . . vie to make themselves equal in apparel with the principle people of the place." By the mid-nineteenth century, elite New Yorkers openly worried that:

> The age is, perhaps, forever gone by, when a privileged class could monopolize finery of garb. . . . I have already seen a dozen at least cheap-booted apprentices wearing velvet waistcoats, which, a few years ago would have delighted [the famed French dandy] D'Orsay.

This comment reveals both the "problem" of widespread access to elegant clothing and its solution: the author is still able to spot the apprentices by their cheap boots. Quality footwear was both more difficult to imitate at low cost and more likely to be overlooked by the presumptuous social upstart—indeed, the opinion that one can most readily distinguish a well-dressed person by his or her footwear survives to this day. The democratization of fashion inspired new refinements and finer distinctions that could separate high-status fashions from superficially similar inexpensive garments.

The man whose name is synonymous with masculine fashion consciousness, Beau Brummell, was famous for his understatement (**Insert, Image #7**). His genius was to transform simplicity into an exacting perfection, requiring meticulous attention to costly details. George Bryan Brummell was a commoner who made friends with the Prince of Wales while at Eton in the late eighteenth century and thereafter became a figure in London high society. Much about Brummell is shrouded in mystery and distorted in legend. It is said that after the prince granted him a commission in the elite 10th Regiment of the Light Dragoons—or "Royal Hussars," as they were often called—Brummell insisted on altering the uniform to conform to his own standard of elegance. He was rumored to have hired two different glovers to produce a single pair of gloves: one to sew the fingers and another to construct the body. He was perhaps most well-known for the care with which he tied his cravat: he reportedly spent hours in front of a mirror, his floor littered with discarded scarves, which, having been creased in failed attempts at perfection, were unfit to be worn. Friends and admirers said that he took five hours to dress each day and he claimed to polish his boots with champagne. When asked the yearly cost to maintain the wardrobe of a well-dressed gentleman, Brummell answered that "with tolerable economy it might be done with 800 pounds"—the equivalent of 160,000 U.S. dollars today; at the time, the family of a skilled craftsman lived on about 60 pounds a year.

Despite his legendary extravagance, Brummell's great distinction was the simplicity of his attire. In the aristocratic salons he frequented, most men still favored brocade, jewels, and other opulent adornments. Brummell, by contrast, wore a simple frock coat during the day and a blue suit and white vest in the evening—an ensemble that "hardly varied, was not enhanced by jewelry or perfume, nor even discreetly highlighted by a special or distinctive detail." Brummell was, according to one of his contemporaries, "the most sober, most strict, and least extravagantly attired person of his acquaintance. Such unflagging moderation . . . made it impossible to imitate him, since there was nothing to copy."

Historian Philippe Perrot observes that in mid-nineteenth-century France, the elite were threatened from two sides: on the one, by "imitation . . . grocers in their Sunday best," and on the other, by "loud, vulgar parvenus who strive, clumsily and vehemently for the real thing . . . the cheap imitation of the poor, the overblown imitation of the rich." In reaction, a subtle and intricate, if largely unwritten, dress code ensured that class status was as visible as ever—to those who knew what to look for. There were correct outfits for early morning at home, mid-morning when seeing visitors, afternoon when strolling outside, late afternoon tea or relaxation, evening and dinner, fancy balls, entertaining at home, day services at church, evening services at church, weddings, funerals, baptisms, and shopping, all of which would change with the seasons and according to whether one was in the city or in the country and, needless to say, whether one was male or female.

Being well-dressed required both a lot of clothing and a lot of knowledge: one needed a different ensemble for each of a host of occasions and one needed to know which outfit went with a given event. Clothing was expensive and knowledge was closely guarded—usually conveyed by example or by word of mouth to those in the right social circles, or compiled into etiquette treatises, themselves exclusive in societies where bound books were luxury items and literacy still far from universal. The right clothing worn on the correct occasion was an unambiguous badge of high social position, while even small deviations from the rules signaled that either one's budget or one's savoir faire was inadequate. The greater the number and magnitude of the errors, the lower one's rank in society would appear to be. The showy, overcompensating parvenu revealed his ignorance, insecurity, and ineptness; by contrast, the elegant person demonstrated her knowledge by wearing the right thing at the right time, her self-confidence by choosing subtle signs of status that only her equals would recognize, and her skill by evincing a casual, devil-may-care attitude while still getting everything just right.

New subtleties of elegance were detailed in the etiquette manuals that flooded markets in both Europe and the United States. These texts, often written under an aristocratic-sounding nom de plume, offered detailed instruction on how the right sorts of people behaved, spoke, and—most important—dressed. According to one French guide on the *comme il faut* (or *as it should be*):

> Just as a single word is enough to betray someone's origins or reveal a dubious past or present, so to the eyes of a discerning man or woman a clumsy piece of lace, a flounce, a feather, a bracelet, and especially an earring or any pretentious ornament can reveal social status or assign a particular level in the social scale. Affectations in dress are breaches of elegance, just as certain expressions are incompatible with cultivated language.

Simplicity had a double, contradictory significance: it signaled a rejection of aristocratic privilege and—especially for men—an embrace of the bourgeois virtues of restraint. But at the same time, simplicity was a new way of asserting class status. The Great Masculine Renunciation did not mean that elite men had renounced luxury. Instead, they renounced a showy, obvious, and easily copied luxury and replaced it with the quiet, subtle, and elusive luxury we call "elegance." The luxury of costly adornment was replaced—or at least supplemented—by the much more precious luxury of time and knowledge necessary to be "cultivated." Sumptuary laws yielded to the often-unwritten rules of etiquette.

Especially for women—whose attire was still also governed by the older dress codes of vestimentary opulence and display—there was a gossamer-thin line between well-dressed and overdone. Too little adornment showed laziness and a lack of propriety; too much showed a vulgar sensibility or insecurity. An etiquette treatise from nineteenth-century France, for example, advises that,

> [a] woman who wants to be well dressed . . . needs at least seven or eight toilettes per day: a morning dressing gown, a riding outfit, an elegant simple gown for lunch, a day dress if walking, an afternoon dress for visiting by carriage, a smart outfit to drive through the Bois de Boulogne, a gown for dinner, and a gala dress for evening or the theater. . . . [I]t could be more complicated . . . in summer with bathing costumes, and in the autumn and winter, with hunting and skating costumes. . . .

Of course, these requirements alone put the status of *well-dressed* beyond the reach of anyone of modest means. But the most rigorous test was not whether one could afford the required wardrobe but whether one knew when and how to wear it. For instance, while precious gems remained de rigueur for certain society occasions, the "Comtesse de Bassanville" warned that "those who know how to dress well will never wear diamonds . . . during the summer, even at a ball; they will substitute flowers [or] ribbons. . . ." Meanwhile, when at worship, the chic set practiced what Perrot has called "conspicuous under-consumption," which added the moral legitimacy of Christian humility to elegant understatement. "Comtesse Drohojowska" admonished her readers with the following cautionary tale:

> I was seated along one of the principle aisles; but as wide as it was, the belles dames found a way to brush against my chair with their vast skirts, causing their silken dresses and starched bouffante underskirts to cry out . . . a deafening froufrou made louder by the incredible movements of their shoulders, their rapid hurried gait . . . I asked myself: "Are there the manners of a woman who is *comme il faut* and should she appear to be so preoccupied with herself in the house of the Lord?

According to Perrot, the aristocratic families of France's Second Empire practiced a type of reverse snobbery "by relinquishing obvious display":

> [T]he eloquence of aristocratic simplicity lay in its distance from acquisition, its casual attitude toward possessions—itself the supreme possession—[which] separated them from the parvenus for whom triumphant ownership compensated previous deprivation. . . .

Of course there was in fact nothing casual about this elitist simplicity in dress, which wielded exacting attention to detail as a weapon in a ruthless fight for status. The seemingly ascetic sensibility of the elite was carefully calculated to send a message of effortless elegance. As "Comtesse Dash" advised her readers: "[I]f you want to compete with someone in elegance, the only way to win is with exquisite simplicity. . . . The great merit of an outfit is to seem natural and improvised when it has cost hours of study and preparation for those who wear and those who made it."

In the nineteenth century this became a widespread ethos. The legal regulation of status through sumptuary rules was replaced by the informal regulation of status through the rules of elegance, the rigors of the *comme il faut*, the subtleties of sprezzatura. The potentially democratic renunciation of luxury was turned into a new and more insidious form of status consciousness, disguised as the promotion of virtue. Simplicity of dress was a sign of a sensible, businesslike mind and an admirable lack of pretense. The move from conspicuous opulence to subtle elegance is doubled-edged: it symbolizes the rejection of overt status hierarchy—in line with Enlightenment ideals— but it also enforces a new class stratification that is marked by the less obvious but more demanding display of "correctness." This can take the form of rules—new dress codes—knowledge of which separates the highborn from the commoner. They can also take the more elusive form of taste, which, it is often said, can be neither taught nor learned.

Ostentatious simplicity, conspicuous understatement—these transformed the renunciation of sumptuousness from a puritanical and ascetic phenomenon into a new form of indulgence; from an egalitarian gesture to a power play. For the elite, renunciation was an adaptation to a world where the old symbols of privilege were readily copied.

Chapter Seven

Sex and Simplicity

*The Merits of Tailored Coats, Whaleboned
Corsets, Full Skirts and Petticoats, and
Neoclassical Gowns*

WHY WAS THE GREAT RENUNCIATION MASCULINE? WHY DID
men and only men give up luxurious and glamorous attire, leaving
the field of fashion to the fairer sex?

In an important sense, they didn't. Instead, men only abandoned
the cumbersome and increasingly obsolete symbolism of conspicuous ornamentation to women, who would embody this as surrogates
for men. Men would still enjoy much of the ancient privilege of opulent display through their wives, mistresses, and daughters, while
maintaining enough distance from it to avoid any impression of vanity. At the same time, in place of the older, degraded symbolism of
opulence, men adopted new, modern sartorial signs, which they reserved for themselves.

As historian Anne Hollander points out, until recently it has been
men, not women, who have driven and followed fashion most assiduously: "[L]ooking just at clothing since 1200, you can see that spurts
of cultural advances . . . [and] sharp new visualizations of human
looks . . . were initially masculine. . . . It's clear that the fastest and sex-
iest advances in Western costume . . . were made in male fashion. . . ."
From the birth of fashion in the thirteenth century up until the Masculine Renunciation of the eighteenth century, those advances in

fashion were *sartorial* advances: improvements in the technique of tailoring. Tailoring allowed garments with articulated limbs to displace simple draped garments, and it allowed a single ensemble to include both form-fitting shapes (tights, pants, bodices, sleeves) as well as sculpted elements (the ballooning pants of trunk hose, similarly ballooning sleeves, skirts that were increasingly constructed rather than simply draped). It created a visual drama that seemed to alter the body itself. New innovations were usually made in menswear and then adopted by daring and fashionable women and finally incorporated into more conventional women's dress: for example, the fitted bodice of the Renaissance-era gown borrowed from the form-fitting doublets first developed for men to be worn under plate armor.

Because tailors created feminine versions of clothing first designed for men, men's and women's fashions were complementary variations on a theme, expressing the same social values, overlaid, in a sense, with distinctive gendered symbolism. But that changed after the Great Masculine Renunciation, when fit and basic form became paramount and surface ornamentation anathema. In a sense, the Masculine Renunciation made the most advanced and dynamic aspects of fashion—those of sartorial technique—into a new kind of masculine status symbol. At the same time, it transformed the more decorative surface embellishments that had been the markers of elite privilege into signs of anachronistic values and social backwardness— or of the female sex.

The Needle and the Sword

The idealism and vanity of men may have inspired the Masculine Renunciation, but a group of working women trying to get ahead in a man's world helped to make fashion into a woman's prerogative. A league of French dressmakers changed the way clothes were made and sped up the divergence of masculine and feminine attire.

To explain how, I must make a slight digression into the unfashionable subject of political economy. In much of seventeenth-century Europe, many businesses and most skilled trades operated with the permission of the government. A corporate charter or the privileges of a legally recognized guild provided both a license to do business and an oligopoly guaranteed by the power of the state. The economic theory of the time—mercantilism—held that commerce should be planned and controlled by the government in order to benefit the nation and avoid unfavorable balances of international trade. In theory, the entire mercantile economy was organized according to specific legal privileges, granted at the discretion of the crown, legislature, or parliament. Moreover, the legal theories of the era made no clear distinction between governmental agencies and private enterprise: all organizations operated under some grant of legal authority from the government, many of which combined economic rights and regulatory powers. For instance, many charters granted a corporation both a commercial monopoly and the authority to enforce the law in a particular domain. Commercial and artisans' guilds both participated in commerce and regulated it, making and selling their products and also ensuring fair terms of trade, honest weights and measures, and standards of quality.

Such broad powers came with social responsibilities and limitations. The corporations and guilds of the mercantile era could do only what their charters specifically authorized. A corporation chartered to make and sell wigs in Paris could not start making perfume or expand its operations to the city of Reims without unlawfully usurping the prerogatives of another corporation. Similarly, tailors in seventeenth- and early-eighteenth-century France could make and sell completed garments but could not sell raw cloth, which had to be purchased from a licensed mercer; "drapers" could make dresses and robes but not tailored clothing. Any corporate act not authorized by the charter was ultra vires—beyond their powers—and hence illegitimate and invalid. Agreements made beyond the scope of a charter were unenforceable; goods produced outside the jurisdiction of the guild were subject to seizure by the officers of the offended entities.

Until the late seventeenth century in France, male tailors made clothing for both sexes. Women were excluded from the guilds, with a few exceptions: for instance, the wife of a tailor could work alongside her husband and the widow of a master tailor was permitted to carry on the family business as long as she did not remarry outside the guild. Consequently, male tailors controlled the design of clothing for both men and women and, as historian Anne Hollander maintains, "for four centuries [from the fourteenth until the eighteenth] a certain harmony was maintained between the separate kinds of sexual symbolism in dress. . . . [T]hey were . . . conceived and made on the same principles of craftsmanship, out of the same materials; and for centuries neither sex was more ornate than the other."

In the mid-seventeenth century, a group of Parisian seamstresses challenged the monopoly of the tailors. According to historian Jennifer Jones, French seamstresses were not organized into a guild, but some were quite successful and had powerful noblewomen as clients. Tailors seized and destroyed the goods of those seamstresses whom they deemed to have usurped their exclusive legal prerogatives, often violently. In order to protect their livelihoods, the seamstresses had to assert their own right to make clothing. But the seamstresses didn't push for equal access to the masculine domain of tailoring. Instead, they argued for their own, feminine sphere of influence, using the gendered norms of their day. They insisted that respect for feminine modesty required that women have the option of being fitted by a female dressmaker. Therefore, they argued, seamstresses needed the legal authority to manufacture all forms of women's clothing (and that of young boys, reflecting the convention that children belong to the feminine sphere). In 1675, a royal edict incorporated the female seamstresses as an artisan's guild. Tailors retained their exclusive jurisdiction over clothing for men and boys over eight years of age and *all* tailored clothing, whether for men or women. Seamstresses could make draped garments for women and young boys but tailors retained a monopoly on women's formal dress, bodices, skirts with trains, and sewn ornamentation such as ribbons, lace, and braid.

This tense and unstable compromise invited new conflicts. For instance, seamstresses were entitled to use whalebone and other stiff materials to construct an otherwise draped gown, but tailors insisted that they alone had the legal authority to make clothing that required that whalebone be *sewn* into the cloth, such as corsets and hoop skirts. According to Jones, in one especially dramatic conflict in 1725, tailors and officials of the tailors' guild "noisily demonstrated outside of [seamstress] Marie Therese's house, hurling . . . insults. Then they stormed into her workroom, tossed several boned bodices . . . onto the floor, and denounced her for having no right to make them. . . . Without regard to her advanced state of pregnancy, the men violently seized the garments . . . Marie Therese . . . began to vomit and bleed profusely. . . . Her distress ultimately resulted in . . . the stillbirth of her child. . . ."

Several similar disputes found their way to court. The tailors emphasized their superior skills and the importance of their work: because whalebone corsets were used not only for fashionable attire but also to correct serious medical conditions, such as malformed spines and misaligned organs, the public interest required that the construction of such garments remain under the exclusive control of skilled artisans. Tellingly, the seamstresses countered, not by insisting that their skills were equal to those of the tailors or that their work was equally important, but instead reiterating the claim that "propriety, decency and modesty" demanded that women be allowed to choose members of their own sex for the intimate task of fitting and dressing. They added, for good measure, that their work was one of the few honest means of sustenance for a community of "girls and women"— implying that if deprived of their livelihood as seamstresses, many would be forced into disreputable work in a much older profession.

These arguments for a distinctively feminine role in the creation of attire still inform our thinking about fashion today. In arguing that fashion provided women with one of the few honorable livelihoods appropriate for them, the seamstresses tacitly accepted the subordinate place of women in society and helped to develop the now-common view that fashion is distinctively feminine and less serious than typically masculine endeavors. As Hollander explains:

The new craft of dressmaking, now carried on by women, actually consisted of simply applying the fabric, often in folds and with

very little cutting, to fit onto an already shaped torso. . . . [I]mag-
inative cutting and construction were not required. . . . [because]
the cut and fit that made the essential shape of the torso were devised by the male corset maker. . . .

[E]legance for women was . . . created by the enormously expensive . . . *marchandes de modes [fashion merchants],* women
who specialized in making and arranging the ephemeral trim and
small accessories that gave feminine fashion its increasingly bad
reputation for frivolity and extravagant costliness. . . . "Fashion"
was gradually perceived anew, and soon appeared to be largely the
unserious province of the women who created and consumed it.

As fashion became associated with women and women with fashion, an interest in beautiful and luxurious clothing began to acquire
the stigma of effeminacy. By the late eighteenth century, many believed that women should have the exclusive right to make women's
clothing; some went further and insisted that even the tailor's art
was beneath male dignity and that women should make all clothing.
For instance, in his influential treatise *Emile*, Jean-Jacques Rousseau
insisted,

[n]ever did a young boy by himself aspire to be a tailor. Art is required to bring to this woman's trade the sex for which it is not
made. (There were no tailors among the ancients. Men's costumes
were made at home by women.) The needle and the sword cannot
be wielded by the same hands. If I were sovereign, I would permit
sewing and the needle trades only to women and to cripples reduced to occupations like theirs.

Sewing of any kind was increasingly apprehended as emascu-
lating, and men working in fashion became objects of ridicule and
scorn. One author mockingly suggested that men making and selling
female fashions "should wear women's clothing, so that the metamor-
phosis can be complete, and the feathers of this bird will respond to
his pretty song." Another insisted that,

men who hold the needle . . . who are merchants of linen and fashion . . . usurp the quiet life of women while women are dispossessed of the arts they should exercise to sustain their lives and are instead obliged to . . . abandon themselves to prostitution. . . . I blush for humanity when everywhere I see, to the shame of the name of man, strong and robust men cowardly invading a state which nature has particularly destined for women. . . . One should condemn all men who forget their estate . . . the male fashion merchants, the tailors who make women's clothes . . . to wear women's clothing.

Tailors fought this characterization by emphasizing the technical skill required to make form-fitting clothing. They emphasized the distinction between the sartorial technique underlying fitted garments such as coats, shirts, and trousers—primarily men's clothing—and the "mere" draping and decoration that produced a skirt. Tailors were artisans, they insisted. The construction of a garment demanded the rigorous application of technical knowledge; building a jacket was like building a bridge. By contrast, dressmaking—apart from the few elements that included tailoring—was a mere decorative art, in which superfluous surface adornments mattered more than structure. Women may have been naturally well-suited to selecting eye-catching fabrics and gussying them up with spangles, frills, and ribbons, but the precise work of building a form-fitting tailored suit was man's work.

The argument succeeded: as Anne Hollander observes, "Male clothing, and by extension male regard for personal appearance altogether, continued to receive . . . the respect given to all serious male enterprise. . . ." The terms of a new détente were established. Fashion was given over to the aesthetically intuitive but stylistically uninventive women who made and decorated sumptuous gowns and to the graceful but ornamental women who wore them. Tailoring was to remain the domain of the skillful male artisans who made functional and streamlined clothing for the serious men of the world. From then on, masculine and feminine fashions began to diverge, not only in their details, but in their fundamental symbolic vocabulary. The first, indispensable step in this divergence was to insist that masculine fashions were not fashions at all.

Neoclassical Renunciation

Fashion in the late eighteenth and early nineteenth centuries was not only a sartorial response to changing political ideals and to economic mobility, it also reflected a new aesthetic sensibility that extended beyond attire, inspired by the art and architecture of ancient Greece and Rome. The excavation of Pompeii and Herculaneum in the mid-eighteenth century and the arrival of the Parthenon Marbles in England in the first decade of the nineteenth century encouraged a neoclassical turn in fashion, architecture, and design.

Both men's and women's fashions in the early nineteenth century exhibited the neoclassical influence, but in very different—indeed opposed—ways. Feminine fashions essentially copied classical attire and updated it to reflect contemporary standards of female modesty. As always, women's clothing retained the basic form of the draped garment that was once common to both sexes. Because dressmakers, following the mode of the French seamstress, were practiced in draping and surface adornment but not in tailored construction, it was natural for them to invoke classicism by creating stylized versions of classical draped dress itself. Accordingly, women's neoclassical clothing mimicked the robes of Greek and Roman statuary: it was light, diaphanous, and ultimately fanciful, as any literal revival of an anachronistic style is. This aligned with and magnified an age-old association of women with both tradition and with whimsy.

Menswear also reflected the influence of classical antiquity. But neoclassical men's fashion did not copy classical attire: instead it evoked the ideal male nude *underneath* a streamlined, modern costume—an effect achieved through the tailor's art of careful construction and subtle padding. The neoclassical influence of the eighteenth and nineteenth centuries appeared as a highly stylized suggestion of an ideal male nude and not as a reinterpretation of ancient-draped garments, as it did in early nineteenth-century women's fashions. Neoclassicism pared down the bulky, almost pear-shaped silhouette of the seventeenth- and eighteenth-century masculine ideal: coats shed their long heavy tails, padding moved up from the hips and waist to the shoulders, waists were nipped. Tailors sculpted a heroic masculine silhouette using the same methods they had always used, innovating to create new forms from a solid base of well-established techniques. As a consequence, the modern suit evoked the classical ideal through the reshaping of discrete body parts: arms, legs, torso. The attire was dark, spare, and functional—woolen armor. This streamlining continued, following the aesthetic developments of modernity generally: form followed function and the male wardrobe gradually lost almost all of its embellishments; its references became less and less literal and more abstract. The end result was the modern business suit: a distinctively modern design that evokes a sleek functionalism and has scarcely changed to this day.

The Great Masculine Renunciation was less an abandonment of luxury than it was an application of technological and aesthetic refinements that were transforming all of the visual arts. The simplification of the male wardrobe was part of a much broader shift away from ornamentation and formal literalism and toward a streamlined aesthetic that would mature into high modernism at the beginning of the twentieth century. Indeed, masculine attire after the Great Renunciation has not always been more practical than contemporaneous women's apparel of the same era, or even than the more sumptuous menswear that it superseded. Instead it has been designed to *look* practical. By way of comparison, consider that the famous designs of modern architecture were often more impractical (and more costly) than the baroque and neoclassical structures they superseded: flat roofs *looked* streamlined but were prone to leaks as a result of ponding water; the absence of ornate molding looked economical but actually required much more precise construction to eliminate gaps and unevenness that molding simply covered; the seemingly unadorned structural columns of Mies van der Rohe's iconic Seagram Building are in fact needlessly clad in expensive and structurally superfluous bronze. Similarly, men's tailoring can be as elaborate as many formal gowns—the difference is that while a gown exhibits its adornment on the outside of a draped garment, most of the intricate work in a suit is hidden in the seamwork, canvassing, and padding that give the ensemble its seemingly natural shape. As historian Anne Hollander puts it, "the male body received a complete new envelope that formed a flattering modern commentary upon its fundamental shape, a simple and articulate new version that replaced the naked frame, but this time without encasing it, upholstering it, stiffening it, or overdecorating it. . . ."

Because men's fashions took a modern form and expressed their anachronistic influences abstractly rather than exhibiting them literally, men could follow fashion assiduously while appearing to be concerned only with practical matters of function. Just as tailors were concerned with "serious work" of fit and construction, rather than fashionable decoration, respectable men were not "fashion conscious" but "well-dressed"—a description that suggested not vanity but civility. A sober but flattering wardrobe was considered an indispensable emblem of virtuous citizenship in both the Old World and the New. This new ideal was expressed as the Great Masculine Renunciation began: "The difference between a man of sense and a fop is that the fop values himself upon his dress; and the man of sense laughs at it, at the same time he knows he must not neglect it," insisted Lord Philip Dormer Stanhope, the fourth Earl of Chesterfield, in the mid-eighteenth century in a letter to his son. Echoing this sentiment almost a century later, the *American Gentleman's Guide to Politeness and Fashion* opined that "while care is taken to avoid the display of undue attention to the adornment of the outer man, everything approaching to indifference or neglect, in that regard, should be considered equally reprehensible." As men's attire simplified under the neoclassical influence, it became common wisdom that men who appeared to care too much about their appearance were effeminate fops or superficial dandies; the well-dressed gentleman left his appearance to trained professionals: "While a fop is the slave of fashion, a philosopher surrenders himself to his tailor, whose duty lies in dressing him becomingly," opined the American tailor George P. Fox.

Although both masculine and feminine styles were simplified, the neoclassical influence did not inspire a feminine equivalent of the Great Masculine Renunciation. The meaning of simplicity itself was gendered. The simplicity of men's neoclassical clothing suggested the rigors of virtuous labor. The unadorned styles of fashionable neoclassical women's clothing were rooted in fantasy and whimsy and hence suitable only for those who could afford to eschew productive work in favor of leisure. Although the gendered division of attire was centuries old, this particular symbolism was new, prefiguring the ideal of feminine domesticity most completely expressed in the Victorian-era cult of pure womanhood.

As the men's suit has become ever more streamlined and functional, women's fashions have careened between countless fanciful, dramatic, and beautiful but often impractical styles: layers of petticoats, elaborate bustles, tight-laced corsets, and the drama of ever-changing necklines and hemlines. Of course, this division in the symbolism of attire corresponded to and furthered male chauvinism in politics and the economy: men and only men could present themselves as serious and stalwart, while women were required by law and custom to dress in essentially anachronistic ornate costume, reminiscent of a discredited social order.

How Fashion Made a Bad Boy Into a Good Feminist

According to the prejudices of the time, the impediments of women's clothing matched the limited capacities of the "weaker sex." Thankfully, history has provided some instructive natural experiments that undercut this chauvinistic claim. Many involve women who rivaled the most accomplished men in feats of prowess and daring when freed from their skirts and corsets; a few feature men who chafed under the physical and socially imposed constraints of feminine attire. Clothing may not make the man, but it can unmake and remake him—as is shown in the unlikely story of how a woman's wardrobe converted a shameless rake into a committed feminist.

Charles-Geneviève-Louis-Auguste-Andrée-Timothée d'Éon de Beaumont was a French diplomat, a decorated soldier, and a spy in the *Secret du Roi*, King Louis XV's secret service. According to his memoirs, in 1756 the king sent d'Éon on a secret mission to Russia to gain the trust of Empress Elizabeth and conspire against the enemies of one of France's greatest geopolitical rivals, the Habsburg Monarchy. According to some accounts of his exploits, d'Éon adopted the persona of the *Lady* Lea de Beaumont in order to evade a blockade imposed by the English (another rival of France) and, still disguised, served as a maid of honor to Empress Elizabeth. So disguised, he completed his mission and avoided capture. This ruse would later have profound consequences for his career and social status.

Less than a year after returning to France, d'Éon became a captain of dragoons in the Seven Years' War. He received the Order of Saint Louis for his military service, an honor which came with the title Chevalier. He later traveled to London as a diplomat while secretly continuing to spy for the *Secret*. But after running up large debts and clashing with his superiors in both the foreign ministry and the *Secret*, he was demoted and ordered to return to France to face accusations of embezzlement and disloyalty. Having fallen out of royal favor and fearing imprisonment in the Bastille, d'Éon defied the order and remained in London, where he published the first volume in what he threatened would be a series of pamphlets that would contain all of his secret diplomatic correspondence. As a result, d'Éon became a minor celebrity in England and enjoyed the protection of the British government. The French quietly abandoned the effort to arrest him and eventually secretly recruited him back into the *Secret* at substantially increased pay: having established his bona fides as a traitor to and enemy of France, he was all the more valuable as a spy.

But d'Éon had what would turn out to be an even bigger problem than the threat of extradition. Sparked, perhaps, by his earlier mission

The Chevalier d'Éon, depicted in a
contemporaneous caricature.

in the Russian court, rumors had begun to spread that the Chevalier
was a woman. French society was atwitter about what one aristocrat
claimed was "final incontestable proof" that d'Éon was female; meanwhile, in London, bookmakers gave 3:2 odds that d'Éon was a woman.
Instead of denying the claims, d'Éon refused to dignify the rumors
with a response, fueling speculation. In May 1772, an agent of the *Secret* came to London to investigate the claims and reported that d'Éon
had indeed been born female.

King Louis XV died in 1774 and the *Secret du Roi*—along with d'Éon's royal protection—died along with him. In 1775, a representative of the French government approached d'Éon seeking a return of all documents related to his tenure as a spy. In return, d'Éon demanded to return to France as a hero—or heroine. Here accounts differ: one account of d'Éon's story holds that French authorities capitalized on the rumors about d'Éon's sex and demanded that he accept life as a woman—and consequently, exclusion from political life—in return for immunity from prosecution. An alternative account from historian Gary Kates suggests that d'Éon cleverly engineered his gender transition by planting rumors that he was a woman and deliberately fueling speculation in order to support a more flattering narrative about his activities in England. That narrative—which was widely accepted at the time—was that d'Éon was in fact "born female . . . [and] raised male by a father who wanted a son; he excelled as a diplomat and a soldier; and was now coerced by the new king and propriety to adopt the appearance of his birth gender." This story would allow d'Éon to return to France as a "heroine who had dressed . . . as a man in order to perform patriotic acts for Louis XV" in the style of Joan of Arc instead of as an effeminate "trickster" who had betrayed his country.

While historians differ as to the reason for his transition, by all accounts d'Éon did not settle easily into the life expected of a woman in the waning days of France's old regime. In 1777, when ordered to appear in women's clothing, d'Éon reportedly complained, "I do not yet know what I need . . . I only know it is more difficult to equip a lady than a company of Dragoons from head to foot." When d'Éon lobbied for permission to again wear a dragoons uniform and fight with the French in the American Revolutionary War, she was imprisoned until she agreed to accept the conventional limitations—and attire—of her sex.

The French Revolution swept aside the dress codes of the old regime, but this didn't help d'Éon. Although the new government decreed on October 29, 1793, that "No person of either sex can force any citizen *male or female* to dress in a particular way," the decree added a qualification: "[E]veryone is free to wear the garment or garb *suitable to his or her sex* that he or she pleases." French dress codes would continue to require d'Éon to dress and act as society demanded a woman should. After the Revolution, d'Éon's pension was discontinued and she was soon destitute. She returned to England where she eked out a modest living as a curiosity, putting on fencing exhibitions as an Amazon swordswoman, dressed in petticoats and full skirts. d'Éon died an impoverished shut-in.

When d'Éon's body was prepared for burial, the question that had vexed French diplomats, Russian aristocrats, and London bookies alike was finally settled: d'Éon had "male organs in every respect perfectly formed."

Was d'Éon, as National Portrait Gallery curator Lucy Peltz put it in 2013, "Britain's first openly transvestite male who was able to live out the life that his gender orientations demanded of him"? Was he a dissolute rake, who passed as a woman in order to more easily seduce married women, as a nineteenth-century biographer claimed? Or did he identify as female only under duress? According to historian Simon Burrows, d'Éon had racked up significant debts in England; when offered the chance to escape his creditors and return to France, "d'Eon really has little option but to agree. . . . He needs money. . . . And in Britain there's risk he'll be locked up as a debtor." Accepting a female identity allowed him to escape debtor's prison, but it also ensured that d'Éon was unable to reenter political life when back in France, satisfying his enemies. According to Burrows, d'Éon was "to some extent tricked into [identifying as a woman] . . . it wouldn't have been his first choice."

There may be some truth in all of these accounts. Perhaps d'Éon's transition was incremental, driven by a combination of convenience, necessity, desire, and moral conviction. According to historian Gary Kates, d'Éon became a feminist before living as female. He amassed "one of the largest collections of feminist writing in Europe" and came to believe that women were naturally more virtuous than men: "[L]iving as a woman comes to him as a way to transform himself morally and a way to escape this hyper-masculine" ideal of his era. Indeed, d'Éon referred to his gender transition as a "conversion from

bad boy to good girl." Whether by choice, chance, or coercion, the attire of a woman gave d'Éon a woman's perspective on a man's world.

Since the late Middle Ages, the rise of fashion transformed clothing from a sign of social status and traditional allegiance into a statement of individual identity. As people asserted their own distinctive
personality through attire, recycling and reusing ancient dress codes
to create new, modern meanings, it was inevitable that they would
eventually find new uses for the most powerful vestimentary symbolism of all: that of gender. Unconventional uses of gendered attire allowed women to create new and distinctive individual narratives: the
pious woman who seeks spiritual enlightenment or holy war in the
garb of the knight or pilgrim; the irreverent woman who expresses
her defiance of social strictures by adopting the sexually expressive
attire of men.

But d'Éon's gender transition was more dramatic—and more vex-
ing for his contemporaries—not only because it involved the rarer
case of a man dressing as a woman, but also because it occurred just
as the Great Masculine Renunciation was transforming male fashions
from sumptuous and ornate to austere and spare, increasing the symbolic distance between masculine and feminine attire. The Chevalier
d'Éon was a dashing figure of the honor-based value system of the old
regime. He was a man who lived large and had extravagant tastes: he
was chastised for his general profligacy while in the Foreign Ministry, and he ran up such large debts while in London that many believe
he had to flee to avoid debtor's prison. His life of derring-do, military
honor, and conspicuous excess was esteemed in the courtly world of
the ancien regime, but less so in the world at the end of the eighteenth
century—a world that d'Éon would have seen all the more clearly in
London, where the Great Renunciation was born and already well advanced. Perhaps d'Éon came to see himself as a bad boy because what
it meant to be a good man had changed.

Those same changes made it more improbable than ever that a
woman could live the life of influence that d'Éon craved. Although

French society hailed d'Éon as a heroine, her attempts to reenter political life in France were rebuffed at every turn: she was pressured
to join a convent and told that her only hope of influence lay—as it
did with almost all women of her era—in marriage. It's telling that
even after she accepted the life of a woman, it required a royal decree to separate d'Éon from her cherished dragoon's uniform, and
she repeatedly and unsuccessfully petitioned for the legal right to
wear it again. Jean-Jacques Rousseau had insisted that the needle and
the sword could not be wielded by the same hands—an assertion of
strictly delimited gender roles. Fifteen years later d'Éon wielded a
sword while wearing a dress. Unfortunately, d'Éon's feminine attire
conspired against her—just as it was designed to do.

Chapter Eight

The "Rational Dress" Movement

*The Inconveniences of Bloomers, Tight-laced
Corsets, Starched Collared Shirts, and Suits with
Short Trousers*

THE *CHEVALIER* D'ÉON BECAME A FEMINIST WHILE TRYING to overcome the cumbersome, anachronistic dress that burdened women of her era. Nineteenth-century feminists fought a similar battle, applying the principles of the Enlightenment to the customs of clothing to reform feminine attire.

One of the earliest protests against conventional gendered clothing was that of Amelia Bloomer, whose name became synonymous with a new garment: a pair of women's trousers designed to be worn under what was for the time a relatively short skirt. "Bloomers" reflected the same stylistic changes that had transformed menswear over the previous several decades. By 1850 the democratic and utilitarian ethos of the suit had taken firm hold. Quality was a matter of construction, refined fabrics, and proper fit—never of surface decoration. Echoing the ethos of England's Beau Brummel, American and European pundits admonished men to "Dress so that it may never be said of you, 'What a well-dressed man!'"

For men, freedom of movement was of paramount importance: "Every garment should leave the wearer perfectly free and uncontrolled in every motion" declared an American tailoring periodical in 1850. But women's attire seemed purposely designed to impede

The bloomer fashion, as depicted by
Currier & Ives.

movement. Long skirts dragged in the dirt that covered the street of
every nineteenth-century city, requiring "respectable" women to travel
by carriage and lift their skirts—but not too much!—when climbing in and out of their coaches and condemning those who could
not afford private conveyances to wear soiled garments. Numerous bulky underskirts made navigating narrow passages challenging:
nineteenth-century feminist Elizabeth Cady Stanton contrasted her
own encumbered movement with that of her bloomer-clad cousin
Elizabeth Smith Miller, who, "with a lamp in one hand, a baby in the
other, walk[ed] upstairs, with ease and grace, while, with flowing robes,
I pulled myself up with difficulty, lamp and baby out of the question."

For American feminists, gendered dress was as serious an imped-
iment to equal opportunity as it was to physical mobility. Susan B.
Anthony insisted, "I can see no business avocation, in which woman

with her present dress *can possibly* earn equal wages with man." Apparently some employers agreed that reformed attire would be a boon to women's success at work: according to *The Lily*, a women's newspaper edited by Amelia Bloomer, in 1851 the managers of textile mills in Lowell, Massachusetts, hosted a banquet in honor of their female workers who adopted the more practical bloomer style. During what became known as the bloomer craze of 1851, a pamphlet titled *Declaration of Independence from the Despotism of Parisian Fashion* circulated at lectures advocating dress reform and among the members of new dress reform societies. The same year, bloomer advocates hosted a festival in New York City. In February 1856, participants in a dress reform convention held in Glen Haven, New York, formed the National Dress Reform Association. Its constitution declared that "[t]he objects of this Association are to induce a reform in Woman's Dress, especially in regard to long skirts, tight waists, and all styles and modes which are incompatible with good health, refined tastes, simplicity, economy and beauty." *The Lily* reported that the association would "assist in the translation of woman from slavery to freedom . . . from the kingdom of fancy, fashion and foolery, to the kingdom of reason and righteousness."

Across the Atlantic, English women formed the Rational Dress Society, which ran a clothing store stocked with "underclothing, rational corsets and divided skirts," and published a quarterly newsletter in 1888 and 1889. The January 1889 issue of the *Rational Dress Society's Gazette* began with this statement of purpose:

The Rational Dress Society protests against the introduction of any fashion in dress that either deforms the figure, impedes the movements of the body, or in any way tends to injure the health.

It protests against the wearing of tightly-fitting corsets, of high heeled or narrow toed boots and shoes; of heavily–weighted skirts, as rendering healthy exercise impossible; and of all tie-down cloaks or other garments impeding the movement of the arms.

It protests against crinolines and crinolettes of any kind as ugly and deforming. . . .

The *Gazette* demanded comprehensive reform of women's dress, advocating a new distinctively feminine costume based on the principles of comfort, fit, and ease that had remade menswear a century earlier. The idea that women would enjoy the kind of practical clothing worn by men alarmed many. For instance, a critic of Rational Dress reform sought to preempt the more startling implications of the movement, insisting that even the most extreme reformers would not "go so far as to recommend" that women "make such a revolution in their attire as would enable then to dispense with the assistance of [corset] stays" or "venture to suggest that women should wear outer garments adapted to the natural form of the body." Rational Dress Society founder Lady Harberton retorted: "On the contrary, the recommendation of a complete alteration is . . . what almost everyone who has lectured or written on the subject of late years has most strongly insisted on."

Rational dress reform got a boost from a growing sense of alarm over a novel fashion trend: the tight lacing of corsets. Corsets had been around for centuries and had changed along with notions of the ideal body. For instance, Renaissance-era corsets had been almost cylindrical, elongating the torso and compressing the chest. Until the early nineteenth century, both men and women had worn corsets, which not only ensured a trim figure but also were thought to be medically beneficial, correcting defective posture and keeping internal organs in place. But by the 1800s corsets were a strictly feminine affair. They had morphed to create an hourglass shape, pushing breasts upwards and out, tapering in to define a narrow waist, and flaring outward at the base of the hips. Some women took the style to extremes, using the corset not only to define the natural waist but also to severely constrict it, at the expense of comfort, good digestion, and easy breathing.

Popular opinion of the corset was mixed. Most people in nineteenth-century Europe thought that corsets were a necessary element of feminine attire. Corset advocates believed its structure provided necessary support for what they considered to be weak feminine bodies and deficient feminine morality alike. "The corset is the framework of a woman's body. It is the foundation and the edifice," opined Dr. Casmir Delmas in *Hygiene and Medicine.* Similarly, the 1870 treatise *Hygiene for Fashionable People* insisted that corsets "are beneficial because they brace and support the body and internal organs that tend to be dragged down by their weight or are badly contained in their cavities."

But other physicians denounced corsets—especially tight-lacing— as injurious to good health, blaming them for fainting spells, infertility, and damage to the internal organs. For instance, in 1857 Dr. Auguste Debay published statistics demonstrating the perils of the corset:

> May the following . . . open the eyes of those blind mothers who, in the hope of giving their daughters an elegant waist, imprison them from an early age in an inflexible corset. . . .
>
> Of 100 young girls wearing a corset:
>
> 15 succumbed to diseases of the chest;
>
> 15 died after their first delivery;
>
> 15 remained infirm after delivery;
>
> 15 became deformed;
>
> 30 alone resisted, but sooner or later were afflicted with serious indispositions.

In 1892 Benjamin Orange Flower published a pamphlet titled *Fashion's Slaves,* which described the "evil effects of tight-lacing, or of any lacing at all" and promised that if the "needed reform in fashionable dress" was achieved, "the resulting health and happiness of the human race would be incalculable." Dr. Flower insisted that "every vital organ is either functionally obstructed or mechanically disordered" by the corset and as a consequence, the corseted woman suffered a "constant liability to headache, vertigo, or worse affections . . . length of life is shortened . . . [and] life is rendered correspondingly useless and miserable while it does exist." According to Flower, the corset not only threatened the health of those who wore it but also the future of all humanity: "[I]f women will continue this destructive habit, the race must inevitably deteriorate. . . . [T]he salvation of the race depends on the correction of this evil habit." The invention of the x-ray offered dramatic new evidence of the deleterious effects of the corset. In 1908, Dr. Ludovic O'Followell published *Le Corset*, which included images of women's rib cages distorted by compression from tight lacing.

Opposition to corsets was not limited to the medical profession. Etiquette maven Countess Drohojowska also warned her readers away from the tight-laced corset, asking, "How many cases of gastritis, liver complaints, migraines and anxious depressed moods would have been easy to cure at the onset by loosening a corset? But, having reached a certain stage, they become incurable and dig a premature grave before the eyes of a weeping family, who often, by admiring

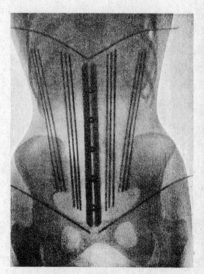 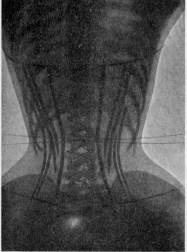

X-ray photographs showed the deleterious effects of the corset.

bodies deformed by deliberate distortions, have encouraged this ab-erration." Moralists had their opinions too. Many insisted that the corset provided a necessary physical constraint on loose sexual appe-tites, but they nevertheless condemned tight lacing as evidence of fe-male vanity. Some believed the exaggerated hourglass figure created by the tight-laced corset inspired male lasciviousness, even as they also insisted that the corset itself was indispensable to feminine mod-esty and propriety. For instance, one guide to "good form" advised women to wear a corset "early, accustom yourself to not being able to do without it" but also warned that "if decent women knew that a slim waist and crinoline please men only because they arouse secret im-ages of shameful debauchery, they would give them up."

Such contradictory attitudes left women dammed if they wore a corset and dammed if they didn't. Indeed, what seemed like enlight-ened opposition to the corset often made matters worse for women who were still expected to maintain a wardrobe made possible by the rigid bracing of the midsection. An article in the *Rational Dress So-ciety's Gazette* lamented that half-reforms could be worse than none at all:

[A] country doctor made the lives of his wife and daughters a bur-den to them by insisting on their leaving off stays [a stiff corset or undergarment, often supported by boning or metal strips] while still wearing the fashionable heavy skirt and tight bodice. Everyone who has worn them knows that bands of skirts pulling in different directions, and the bones of bodices pricking and chafing here and there, cause an amount of comfort not to be endured without the pressure of stays to deaden the sense of feeling. [But] their lord and master [was] . . . only exercised with regard to the one gar-ment he knew to be injurious. . . . He was obeyed with fear and trembling while he was at home, but the moment he took himself off . . . [his] wife and daughters laced themselves up again. . . .

Although women clearly had the greatest cause to complain, men advanced their own movement for dress reform. The poet and playwright Oscar Wilde was a pioneer in this movement. He wrote a series on women's dress reform for the *Pall Mall Gazette* and an essay for the *New York Tribune*, in which he advocated clothing based on sound design principles, made to complement, rather than obscure, the human figure. The psychologist John Carl Flügel, who first described the Great Masculine Renunciation, helped to establish the Men's Dress Reform Party in England in 1929. Like the Rational Dress Society, it advanced dress reform as a way to improve health and hygiene. The reformers insisted that men's clothing was physically and psychologically damaging, contributing to the degeneration of the "British race." Starched collars were uncomfortable, suit coats were hot, trousers impeded free movement, underwear cut off circulation, and the drab colors of masculine apparel had a "depressing effect." As a consequence, men were "hot, uncomfortable, tired and bad-tempered." In place of these oppressive garments, the reformers advocated blouses with soft collars, worn with loosely knotted scarves, and—instead of long trousers—skirts, kilts, or short pants. They advised that coats and hats were to be worn only as needed to protect against cold or rain.

Unlike the women's rational dress movement from which it took its inspiration, men's dress reform was not always motivated by egalitarian sentiment. Indeed, it was, at times, frankly misogynistic. One detects a hint of this resentment in Flügel's own description of the Great Masculine Renunciation as the beginning of the era when "woman was to enjoy the privilege of being the only possessor of beauty and magnificence." According to historian Joanna Bourke, "[Dress reform] required men actively to protest against their clothing *and* stand defiantly against the horror and anger of women. All symbols of men's inferiority to women were to be tackled." A satirical cartoon in a 1924 edition of the periodical *Punch* showed a man conservatively dressed in bowler hat, jacket, tie, and carrying a walking stick but wearing short pants, glaring defiantly at a nonplussed woman wearing a knee-length skirt. The implicit message, Bourke writes, was that "both sexes should be entitled to expose their legs."

The stakes of dress reform were high because cross-dressing brought not only social ostracism but legal penalties as well. For example, Section 2343.04 of the Columbus, Ohio, Municipal Code, passed in 1848, read:

> No person shall appear upon any public street or other public place in a state of nudity or in a dress not belonging to his or her sex. . . .

A similar local ordinance passed in San Francisco in 1863 decreed that,

> if any person shall appear in a public place in a state of nudity, or in a dress not belonging to his or her sex, he should be guilty of a misdemeanor, and on conviction, shall . . . pay a fine not exceeding five hundred dollars.

By the early twentieth century more than forty-five American cities expressly enforced gendered attire and prohibited cross-dressing. Laws against disguise were also used to punish cross-dressing: for instance, police enforced an 1845 New York state law that made it a crime to appear "disguised" in public to prohibit cross-dressing, and cross-dressers were detained under an 1874 California law making it illegal to "masquerade" in another's clothing for unlawful purposes. Many of these laws seemed designed to target deception, just as some Renaissance-era laws had; indeed, many required an intent to deceive or an unlawful purpose as an element of the offense. In at least one case a cross-dresser arrested for wearing women's clothing avoided legal sanction by agreeing to wear a sign declaring "I am a man." But police often saw deceit in any attempt of a woman to assert male prerogatives by adopting male attire. According to historian Clare Sears, cross-dressing bans were enforced against "feminist dress reformers, female impersonators, and 'fast' young women who dressed as men for a night on the town."

Despite the support of physicians, philosophers, playwrights, moralists, and feminists, rational dress reform was a failure. "Bloomers" initially enjoyed some positive mainstream press: *The Ladies'*

Wreath, for instance, described the garment as "a dress altogether American and unique in its character, distinguished from any of those imported from abroad by its surpassing neatness and simplicity." But despite this praise, *The Ladies' Wreath* ultimately declined to endorse bloomers. Other periodicals were scathing in their assessments. Cartoons in an 1852 edition of *Harper's New Monthly Magazine* depicted a dystopian future in which women wore the pants: bloomer-clad wives bullied their cowering husbands or proposed marriage to blushing men. Critics of bloomers "warned that Wellingtons [tall men's riding boots], canes and even cigars couldn't be far behind."

Faced with such fierce and unrelenting opposition, the vogue for

This cartoon depicts a "bloomer" admonishing her emasculated husband. The caption reads, "Now, do, Alfred, put down that foolish Novel, and do something rational. Go and play something. You never practice, now you're married."

This cartoon depicts a bloomer-clad woman proposing marriage—the accompanying caption reads, "Say! oh, say, Dearest, will you be mine?"

bloomers was short-lived. Amelia Bloomer herself abandoned them in favor of the soon-to-be-despised cage crinoline, which, she said, because of its lighter weight, was an improvement over layers of heavy, full skirts.

It may look comically impractical today—and indeed it was the subject of numerous jokes at the time—but crinoline was lightweight and cheap: two profound improvements that changed the nature of women's attire. Although the United States had led the way in inexpensive ready-made men's suits with companies such as Brooks Brothers in the early nineteenth century, according to historian Michael Zakim there was no mass production of women's clothing in America until after the Civil War. But by the late nineteenth century, the crinoline was being made by the thousands in both Old World and New. Because it replaced layers of underskirts with a steel frame, it was comparatively light and allowed for greater circulation of air and freedom of movement. Because it was also relatively in-expensive, women of varying social statuses could afford it, and so it helped introduce to women's clothing some of the social equality that the ready-made suit had offered men. The predictable dynamic of status emulation and jealousy followed: according to design his-torian Malcolm Barnard, many nineteenth-century publications fea-tured the comic figure of "the indignant and crinoline-clad lady of the house [who] orders her identically dressed maid to go and change." An essay in the *Dundee Courier* in 1862 called for legal regulation, complaining,

> [w]e should not care so much if a sumptuary law could be passed, prohibiting any but ladies, who are ladies enough not to have any-thing to do, from wearing crinolines; but everybody takes to the nuisance. . . . [F]rom the highest to the lowest grade of society. . . . [A] servant maid . . . drags the chairs, and jostles the table, and puts the dishes in danger, and flounces papers away, as though she was a whirlwind; and when she puts coals on the fire, occa-sionally carries away the tongs as an appendage to her skirt. . . . It says a great deal for the cautiousness of servant girls, that more of them have not fallen victims to crinoline fires. . . . In factories, the factory lasses, though barefooted, are becrinolined, better fenced than the machinery they work among. . . . But putting aside ugli-ness and danger . . . many crinolines are simply depots for stolen goods.

The relatively light weight of the crinoline allowed skirts to ex-pand to theretofore unknown dimensions, ushering in dramatic new fashions—and dramatic new hazards: the large skirts inevitably brushed up against bystanders, doorways, furniture, and active fire-places, with calamitous results: some estimate that crinoline fires killed thousands of women on both sides of the Atlantic during the decade or so when the garment was fashionable (**Insert, Image #8**). The crinoline quickly inspired the potent mixture of social anxiety and ridicule that so often accompanies women's clothing. Some cartoons depicted women crushing hapless men or keeping unwanted suitors at a safe distance with crinolines of excessive size. Others showed women trapping love interests or hiding adulterous lovers beneath their voluminous skirts.

The crinoline was three steps forward and two steps back in terms of practicality, but even Amelia Bloomer eventually concluded that a steel cage was as much liberation as nineteenth-century women could hope for. Dress reform produced an impressive number of newsletters, pamphlets, and manifestos but few lasting changes in dress codes. Feminine attire continued to feature full skirts, sup-

The crinoline became a new source of old
fears about feminine artifice and deceitfulness:
here, a faithless wife hides her lover under her
voluminous skirts.

ported by bustles, underskirts, and crinoline until the early twentieth century. Corsets remained popular in Europe and the United States until women entered the work force during World War 1. Men's dress reform fared no better. The professional journal *Tailor & Cutter* expressed the dominant sentiment in a 1931 article that insisted on the importance of "restraint, [and] on such articles of discipline and control as buttons, studs, and braces.... [A] loosening of bonds will gradually impel mankind to sag and droop bodily and spiritually. If laces are unfastened, ties loosened, and buttons banished, the whole structure of modern dress will come undone ... society will fall to pieces." Another commentator warned that conventional menswear, uncomfortable as it may have been, was essential to "keeping the social fabric together." In 1932, in a debate titled "Shall Man be Redressed?" one D. Anthony Bradley defended the traditional strictures of men's apparel in terms that reflected the consensus of the day: "The man who, alone in the jungle, changes into his dinner jacket does so to convince himself that he is not a savage—soft floppy clothes are symbolic of a soft, floppy race ... [the] sturdy and virile man [is] capable of withstanding the rigors of a stiff shirt."

Dress reform movements for both men and women were based on the false premise that the primary purpose of clothing is to be comfortable; in fact, its primary function is to be expressive and transformative. Cumbersome, uncomfortable, dramatically gendered clothing persists despite its impractical and objectively useless features because both men and women have consistently preferred the symbolic power of fashionable gendered clothing to any comforts promised by reform. Pointing out that a garment is "impractical" in the narrow sense of physical comfort and ease of movement is not a convincing indictment. Our choices of attire are never based solely on practicality—whether one opts for refined business suits or whimsically elaborate gowns, chunky brogues (the now purely decorative perforations of which were originally meant to allow water to escape from a shoe that was designed to be worn tromping through marshes and bogs) or sexy stilettos (derived from the shoes of Persian military equestrians). This is why, as Anne Hollander pithily notes, "[dress] [r]eform on the basis of good sense was, of course, an ill-conceived and losing battle."

No doubt, women often wore corsets, hoop skirts, bustles, and crinolines at the behest of men. At the same time, it would oversimplify matters to say that women's clothing was nothing more than a symptom of masculine domination. For much of the period in question, women's attire was designed and produced primarily by female seamstresses or commissioned and custom made according to the instructions of wealthy women. The stereotypical Pygmalion-like dictatorial fashion designer, remaking Woman according to male fantasy, was not a significant phenomenon until 1858, when the English tailor Charles Frederick Worth set up shop in Paris and transformed women's fashions by introducing elements and techniques of male tailoring. Ever since, to be sure, male designers have done a great deal to make women "look like detailed concrete visions, in one style or another, of men's abstract and well-categorized fears and dreams about the female sex," as Anne Hollander puts it. The resulting sexualized apparel and the attitudes it reflects and fosters have contributed to women's subordination. But fantasy in and of itself is not oppressive; indeed, it had long been a powerful element in all fashionable clothing—masculine as well as feminine. Menswear, for its part, has its own distinctive sexual appeal, not because it is sober and practical, but because it is formally sophisticated and evocative of woodland, maritime, and military adventures.

For better and for worse, the gendered division in clothing has also offered a sense of identity, satisfying eroticism, and comfort in one's own skin for generations of men and women. Fashion often sacrifices physical comfort to style and symbolic impact because there is a lot more to comfort than how something feels as a tactile matter. As Hollander insists:

It should not be assumed that all the women in the past were angry victims in their long skirts and tight stays. . . . [Female] heads of state . . . steered their nations through difficult times with great political talent, energy and application . . . dressed in garments of great weight and stiffness . . . skirts and sleeves of immense size. . . . [T]heir own sense of their authority . . . was enhanced and supported by those clothes. . . . Generations of laced-up, long-skirted women went up and down stairs all day doing household tasks, bending over washtubs, beating carpets, reaching up to clotheslines and running after children. . . . [T]his normal female gear provided deep general satisfaction for centuries. It gave women the sense of completeness that acceptable clothing always gives, which is its true comfort.

Rational dress reform was ill conceived for both women and men—but for very different reasons. Men's dress reform was simply redundant: the Great Masculine Renunciation had *already* reformed menswear over a century before the men's dress reform movement started. To be sure, men's clothing was still more uncomfortable than necessary, but comfort was never the point. Women's dress reform, on the other hand, was necessary but misdirected: it focused on the physical discomfort and impracticality of feminine attire, which, while real, were only symptoms of the gendered segregation of *symbolic meaning* in dress. The Great Masculine Renunciation did not reform men's dress simply by making it more comfortable; it made menswear into a new, subtler status symbol—a symbol of a new kind of political and civic virtue. Even the most refined feminine clothing could not compete with masculine attire in this respect. This was not the case before the Masculine Renunciation, when men's and women's clothing was designed and produced by the same artisans using similar styles, materials, and techniques, each, in many ways, a variation on a single theme. Even in an unapologetically patriarchal society, Queen Elizabeth I could assert her status through her sumptuous attire, deploying essentially the same sartorial language used by powerful men of her era. The Great Renunciation created a new exclusively masculine symbolic language, which became a sartorial lingua franca. This gendered symbolic division, more than any objective hindrances of feminine attire, was and remains the most appropriate target of dress reform.

The nineteenth century brought greater sartorial equality to men but not to women, and as a consequence, the gap between the sexes grew larger. The nineteenth century, despite the flourishing of egalitarian idealism, was also, in at least some respects, an era of regression in gender equality marked by an increasing obsession with an idealized feminine virtue epitomized by what feminist historians of the Victorian era call the Cult of Pure Womanhood. It would take a new generation to revive the work of Amelia Bloomer, Lady Harberton, and Elizabeth Cady Stanton, but this time the most persuasive arguments for reform appeared not in political pamphlets but in fashion magazines.

Chapter Nine

Flapper Feminism

*The Scandal of Drop-waisted Shifts, Bobbed
Hair, Cupid's Bow Lips, Dancing Flats, Bakelite
Earrings, and the Symington Side Lacer*

IN 1920, THE *SATURDAY EVENING POST* PUBLISHED A SHORT
story by F. Scott Fitzgerald titled "Bernice Bobs Her Hair." The title
character is a young woman who is goaded into cutting her lovely long
hair into a short bob by a social rival. The ill-advised decision ruins her
social life and brings scandal on her family. The cautionary tale ends
with Bernice exacting poetic revenge by shearing her rival's hair off in
her sleep, and, after "swinging the braids like pieces of rope," flinging
them onto the porch of her rival's soon-to-be-astonished—and, if Bernice's experience is any guide, soon-to-be-ex—boyfriend. The lesson:
humiliation and social ostracism awaited any young woman foolish
enough to flirt with the radical fashions of the day.

The dress reform movement of the nineteenth century ended in
failure. But women's dress was eventually reformed nevertheless—
albeit according to the logic of fashion rather than the logic of feminist theory. Roughly fifty years after Amelia Bloomer abandoned her
pantaloons for the crinoline, a new generation of fashion-conscious
feminists changed women's wear forever. The women of the early
twentieth century donned lightweight, form-fitting clothing: snug

one-piece bathing suits; short, easy-wearing sportswear; and slinky fringed minidresses. This *feminine* renunciation came 150 years after men cast off conspicuous and cumbersome adornment in favor of form-fitting, lightly constructed, functional clothing. As men had in the late eighteenth century, women in the early twentieth century adopted a youthful, athletic silhouette. The feminine ideal in the Victorian and Edwardian eras was full figured and mature—the décolletage was the focus of erotic interest, legs were shrouded in fabric, and an hourglass shape was defined by the rigid whalebone of the ever-present corset. In the twentieth century, the ideal became young and lithe; women finally rid themselves of the constraint of the corset; legs, freed from their cocoons of tulle and taffeta, replaced breasts as the erotic focal point; the heavy, cumbersome upswept hair of the Gilded Age matron was sheared off into a sleek bob haircut; and ladylike high heels ditched for flat dancing pumps. The woman who succeeded, where the serious and earnest Rational Dress Reformer failed, in reforming gendered dress codes was the sexy, jazz-age flapper.

Picture a flapper and you probably see a carefree young woman in thrall to the latest trends in music, sports, art, and fashion, speeding around unchaperoned in an open-topped car, dancing to hot jazz in the wee hours fueled by speakeasy cocktails and illicit tobacco. Fitzgerald's spoiled, callous Daisy Buchanan is the literary archetype. But the real flappers were a lot more interesting and more thoughtful than the object of Jay Gatsby's tragic obsession. First of all, the flapper look was an overt challenge to conventional gender ideals. Sheath dresses were form-fitting in the way the men's suit was form-fitting: for the first time, women's clothing skimmed the body. The flapper look was angular, athletic, and boyish; it borrowed from the aesthetics of high modernism in rejecting ornamentation in favor of purity of form, an innovation menswear had made over a century earlier with the Great Masculine Renunciation. In this sense, the flapper—like androgynous dressers since Joan of Arc—claimed masculine prerogative by adopting masculine sartorial symbolism. This suggested sexual liberation, which made it titillating, just as any adoption of menswear by women had been since the late Middle Ages. Flappers increased the dissonance in gendered symbolism by shearing their hair into boyish bob cuts. And they emphasized the sexual provocation by exposing their arms and, more scandalously, their legs, which had been obscured in draped fabric since ancient times.

Indeed, the taboo against clothing that revealed or even suggested a woman's legs was so complete that women wearing loose-fitting trousers became a popular sexual fetish, known in the trade as "bifurcation." In 1903, the men's magazine *Vanity Fair* (unrelated to the current magazine of the same name) ran a special issue titled "Bifurcated Girls" that featured photos of provocatively posed young women dressed in trousers **(Insert, Image #11)**. According to Dian

Flappers abandoned full skirts and upswept coifs for form-fitting clothing and short, practical "bobbed" hair.

Hanson, magazine editor and author of *History of Men's Magazines,*
"[T]he biggest thrill of all was . . . [b]ifurcation, meaning 'split in two,'
[a term that] referred to the contours of a woman's legs revealed by
her donning men's trousers."

Many flappers also wore heavy makeup—previously the adornment of the prostitute, the dance-hall entertainer, and the disreputable thespian. This signaled a rejection of the guileless maidenly
virtue of the Edwardian era. It also turned the face into a canvas for
modern art. Technological advances had only recently revolution-
ized the cosmetics business, facilitating the new fashion for makeup.
Blush or rouge in portable compact cases and lipstick, in small re-
tractable tubes, replaced brushes and jars of pigment. New face pow-
ders also came in portable compacts. In 1926, with the flapper look
a full-blown trend, cosmetics mogul Helena Rubinstein introduced
"Cupid's Bow," a "self-shaping lipstick that forms a perfect cupid's bow
as you apply it." Eyeliner, mascara, and nail varnish all went mainstream in the era of the flapper.

This transformation in women's fashion was almost as dramatic as
the Great Masculine Renunciation was for men's, and, to some extent,
it was motivated by the same aspirations and ideals: to create a costume for an emancipated and enlightened citizen. The growing popularity of sports—especially cycling—played a role in encouraging
less cumbersome women's attire, although these considerations also
weighed in favor of dress reform in the mid-nineteenth century and
did not save the bloomers from an ignominious end. Weightier needs
may have made the difference: in 1917, as men left their jobs to fight
in World War I, women joined the workforce in large numbers. The
Nineteenth Amendment extended the franchise to women in 1920,
removing the last legal barrier to full citizenship. Women gravitated
toward simple, modern styles, which symbolically reflected their
newly won roles as publicly engaged citizens. Flapper style was not
just an indulgent fashion trend for the leisure class. Personal liberation, sexual freedom, and play were certainly a part of flapper ethos,
but so were industriousness and competence.

Flapper styles weakened older gender and class boundaries. A

Presenting

Cupidsbow

THE SELF-SHAPING LIPSTICK CREATED BY HELENA RUBINSTEIN

*An entirely new kind of lipstick—forms a perfect cupid's-
bow as you apply it—ends fussing, shaping and smudging.
In the new shades that are now taking Paris by storm!*

"FEMININE lips should resemble as closely as possible a cupid's-bow." To this, painters, poets and authorities on beauty the world over, agree.

The new CUPIDSBOW lipstick created by Helena Rubinstein gives you this greatly desired and much admired effect instantly. *The veriest amateur at make-up gets the professional touch at once!*

Cupidsbow stays on . . . scientifically safeguards even the most delicate skin . . . is simple to use and molds itself to the individuality of the lips in exquisite curves.

Made in two typically Parisian tones—Red Raspberry (medium) rich and becoming to every type, Red Geranium (light) vivacious, flattering to blondes and an evening shade for all.

This intriguing lipstick can be had in containers of stunning Chinese Red with a band of gun-metal black—or in handsome silvered and golden casings, both also banded with black. Each $1.50

Other Beauty Essentials made by Helena Rubinstein

The basis of beauty

VALAZE PASTEURIZED FACE CREAM—a marvelous cleanser—keeps complexion smooth, protected. Excellent for all normal skins, also the only cream that positively benefits an oily, pimpled or acne blemished skin. 4 oz. 1.00, ½ lb. 2.00, lb. 3.50.

To clear and whiten, follow with

VALAZE BEAUTIFYING SKINFOOD—the skin-clearing masterpiece—lightens, and refines skin. Bleaches tan, freckles and sallowness. The ideal beauty cream for daily use, the year round—1.00, 2.50.

For very obstinate freckles or a heavy coat of tan, use VALAZE FRECKLE CREAM. Bleaches, freshens and tones up the skin. 1.50.

Tone and Brace

VALAZE SKIN-TONING LOTION. Closes pores, keeps tissues firm, erases and prevents fine lines, a cooling, soothing, liquid day cleanser to which skin responds rapidly. 1.25, 2.50.

Oily skin, Blackheads

VALAZE BEAUTY GRAINS—a wonderful lather-forming wash—unsurpassed for correcting oiliness—clears away blackheads, whiteheads, greasiness, refines enlarged pores, and leaves the complexion smooth and velvety. 1.00, 2.00.

VALAZE LIQUIDINE—a beauty lotion that instantly absorbs oiliness and shine—use always before going out, especially on nose and chin. Leaves a mat-like smoothness. Excellent, also, for removing travel stains from face and neck. 1.50, 2.75.

Complimentary Beauty Service

You are invited to visit the trained counsellors at Helena Rubinstein Salons for individual diagnosis and expert advice on all beauty problems.

Cupidsbow and all Valaze Beauty Preparations dispensed by trained and competent advisers at the better stores—or order direct from Dept. N-10.

Helena Rubinstein

46 West 57th Street, New York

PARIS
52 & 126 Rue du Fg. St Honoré

LONDON
24 Grafton St. W 1

Flapper fashion included dramatic use of makeup,
such as the "Cupid's bow" lip.

new cadre of financially independent and liberated young women delayed marriage and indulged in leisure time activities once reserved for men: sports, gambling, drinking, and nightclub dancing. Flapper styles blurred class distinctions too. The flapper look first appeared in "working class neighborhoods and radical circles in the early 1900s before it spread to middle-class youth and college campuses," and the flapper's bob haircut and dropped-waist sheath skirt "united blacks and whites under a common hip-culture." Indeed, critics lamented that flapper fashions eliminated "all difference among people. You can no longer tell who is the daughter of the common laborer and who belongs to the better circles." The new functional styles cut against the traditional role of women as ornamental trophies that had been theirs since men renounced adornment in the late eighteenth and early nineteenth centuries. More threatening still, flapper styles "seemed to call attention to the body beneath the clothing. . . . [T]he amount of fashionable female underwear was reduced to brassieres, underpants, and light corsets . . . merely a few layers of delicate fabric shrouded the female body. . . ."

These challenges to the older norms of virtuous femininity fueled the negative stereotype of the irresponsible flapper. The flapper look was condemned as unfeminine, or alternatively, as scandalously seductive. Some detractors insisted that short-haired flappers were unattractive—like Fitzgerald's "Bernice" after her haircut—and had condemned themselves to live out their lives as spinsters. Others warned that short, form-skimming flapper dresses would arouse uncontrollable sexual desire in men. For instance, a Danish journalist worried that "[w]omen are becoming more and more beautiful, and still more seductive under the devilish rule of his majesty King Fashion, and the rest of us are undeniably—only men. . . ." Another commentator made the implication explicit, arguing that "all sections of criminal law pertaining to rape ought to be abolished" if women insisted on wearing the new fashions in public. Newspapers and magazines blamed the unfeminine—or too seductive—flapper look for inspiring divorces, domestic abuse, and even murder. A characteristic opinion came from an unlikely source, the film actress Betty Blythe, known for her provocative attire, who wrote in 1926:

> Most of the frocks worn by girls and women today are a terrible temptation, not only to men but to themselves. . . . [T]hey inflame the senses, rouse the passions, and the rest follows as the night the day! We see the consequences . . . broken lives, deluded women, a nameless child . . . and perhaps the river out of sheer desperation . . . who can estimate accurately the full toll of that urgent lure that a display of long silken legs, the glitter of bare white shoulders, the gentle curves of a close fitting dress . . . who can tell what toll this takes on the morality of men and women?

Even the practical advantages of the new fashions were seen in a negative light. Simpler, less cumbersome clothing allowed women to dress quickly and without assistance. But critics insisted that these fashions invited sexual promiscuity: it was as easy, they worried, to *undress* as it was to dress.

Unsurprisingly, given this moral panic, new dress codes restricted flapper styles. Many hairdressers initially refused to cut women's hair into the short bob. Employers banned bobbed hair and fired women who adopted the new styles. For instance, according to a 1922 article in the *Morning Tulsa Daily World*, a New Jersey bank adopted a new dress code in response to an "illegally attractive" female teller:

> Her hair was bobbed, her hidden ears were hung with jade earrings, her low-cut waist allowed certain exciting revelations, and suggested even more. And as she walked toward the back of her cage, a pair of low-cut, flat heeled sport shoes with champagne colored legs springing out of them came into view. . . .

The bank manager responded with an edict requiring all female employees to wear a prescribed dress "in either blue, black or brown and sleeves must not be shortened above the elbow. The dress must not be worn higher than twelve inches from the ground." The article also listed several other businesses and employers who had implemented dress codes targeting flapper fashions:

> [E]mployees of the Federal Reserve Bank in New York were told emphatically that they could take no time off during the day for beautifying. She could have bobbed hair, but she could not fluff it on the bank's time. . . . [A] committee of employees was delegated to prevent any ultra-flapper from wearing anything extreme. . . . [O]ne of the oldest department stores in New York found it necessary to . . . prescribe blue and black dresses for winter to be varied by a white waist in summer. The stockings and shoes must be black at all times and the dress must not be too high at the bottom and not too low at the top. In Detroit, telephone girls have been given a uniform and in Dayton the National Cash Register Company has placed bobbed hair, short skirts and silk hose under the ban. . . . Big Business has apparently decided that the Flapper must go.

Despite these efforts, flapper fashions only grew in popularity. By the mid-1920s, the once-remarkable "flapper look" was simply the fashion for women of all ages. In 1925, the *Washington Post* in an article titled "Economic Effects of Bobbing" reported that bobbed hair was so popular that it had been a boon to the economy. Hairdressers multiplied from five thousand in 1920 to twenty-one thousand in 1924, buoyed by demand for the new hairstyle. Barbershops also did "a rushing business with bobbing." Flapper dresses and bob haircuts were featured in the Sears, Roebuck and Co. catalog in 1926. A 1925 article in the *New Republic* titled "Flapper Jane" insisted that the once-extreme fashions of the flapper had become "The Style, Summer of 1925 Eastern Seaboard. These things and none others are being worn by all of Jane's sisters and her cousins and her aunts. They are being worn by ladies who are three times Jane's age, and look ten years older; by those twice her age who look a hundred years older."

The triumph of flapper fashions was a Great Feminine Renunciation. Inspired by political emancipation and new roles in the workplace, women renounced ornamentation, heavy draped garments, and cumbersome padding in favor of lightweight, body-skimming, practical attire that allowed for ease of movement and communicated a rational sensibility and a readiness for action. Women's clothing suggested the classical ideal of the athletic nude—as menswear had for over a century—instead of an hourglass. This shift, from clothing that symbolized femininity while obscuring most of the actual female body to clothing that expressed the feminine form by suggesting its actual contours, was a visual manifesto for gender equality, an implicit statement that women's bodies were fit for public view and physically capable too. The *New Republic* saw flapper fashion as the uniform of an almost militant women's liberation: "[W]omen to-day are shaking off the shreds and patches of their age-old servitude. . . . 'Feminism' has won a victory so nearly complete that we have forgotten the fierce challenge which once inhered in the very word. Women have highly resolved that they are just as good as men, and intend to be treated so."

And yet . . . this Great Feminine Renunciation was neither as complete nor as definitive as its masculine counterpart. Instead, the new liberated feminine ideal became, in many ways, as compulsory as the old Victorian one. The trim, athletic flapper look was almost boyish—it downplayed womanly curves to such an extent that many women, having finally cast off their corsets, resorted to binding their breasts. The Symington Side Lacer, for instance, was a flapper-era brassiere with corset-like laces on both sides designed to compress the chest to allow fuller-figured women to slip into fashionable drop-waisted sheath dresses: the athletic ideal could be as punishing as any whaleboned, laced corset. Moreover, the renunciation of feminine adornment was far from complete: the flapper styles included a profusion of heavy and elaborate jewelry and a new emphasis on makeup, as if the loss of feminine curves and adornment in clothing required an exaggeration of femininity elsewhere as compensation. Consequently, from the 1920s to the present day, the bare female face has been seen as a naked face, inappropriate and unfinished.

What's more, many of the older aesthetic ideals of femininity did not die but lurked in remission, to reappear in time. As a consequence, women's wear since the flapper era has veered back and forth between opposed aesthetic extremes, using disparate elements in arresting combinations. The flapper combined an angular, almost androgynous silhouette with dramatic, hyper-feminine makeup; Christian Dior's "New Look" in the 1940s and poodle skirts in the 1950s revived the impractical full skirts of the Victorian and Edwardian maiden in an abbreviated, leg-baring form; the feminine ideal of the 1950s, personified in Marilyn Monroe or Jayne Mansfield, combined the exaggerated hourglass silhouette of the nineteenth century with the form-fitting fashions of the flapper; the "Twiggy look" of the 1960s was a throwback to the flapper's trim, boyish athleticism and heavy eye makeup; the sex symbols of the 1970s and 1980s mixed the flapper's boyish athleticism below the belt with the Edwardian maiden's full-figured bustiness above—the archetype for Charlie's Angels, Daisy Duke, the Victoria's Secret supermodel, and the *Baywatch* babe; the fashions of the Reagan era mixed boxy suit jackets with skintight miniskirts and dramatic, flowing, teased hair.

Men's fashion since the Great Masculine Renunciation has progressed in a straight and unbroken line toward ever more streamlined, formally refined, and unadorned styles—a modernizing coherence, punctuated by a few anachronistic details, such as vestigial lapels and pockets. By contrast, even after the Feminine Renunciation of the 1920s, women's fashion has been marked by ambivalence: liberation in the shadow of the lofty pedestal of pure womanhood; refinement offset by superfluous opulent display; austere practicality embellished with dramatic flourishes. This tension is often productive—every drama requires conflict, after all. It—along with the mere fact that women's fashion retains the added flourishes of conspicuous ornamentation— is why women's fashion today is usually more interesting than men's. But the clash of opposed aesthetics also ensures that women's fashion sends mixed messages, open to misinterpretation—hence the familiar misogynistic slurs that modern women are coquettish teases or conniving minxes. Even today, the ambitious woman often finds that her clothing conspires against her. The tug-of-war between a modern, liberated practicality and an ancient, conspicuous ornamentality has defined the gendered dress codes of the twentieth century.

The Great Masculine Renunciation overturned the symbols of status, sex, and political power established in the late Middle Ages and created a new sartorial vocabulary for the expression of individual personality. It made understatement into a new kind of status symbol, which required savoir faire as well as ready cash to exhibit. In turn, elegance and style became new modes of self-fashioning. But the Great Renunciation contained the contradictions of the Enlightenment ideals from which it emerged: its understatement reflected the ideal of social equality but it also magnified status-based divisions by making status symbols harder to copy. And, because it was a *masculine* phenomenon, it excluded women who sought power and status. Their struggle, and the struggles of other groups left out of the egalitarian promise of the Enlightenment, would define the dress codes of the next two centuries.

Part Three

Power Dressing

Fashion is part of the daily air and it changes all the time,
with all the events. You can even see the approaching
of a revolution in clothes.

—DIANA VREELAND

The Great Masculine Renunciation made understatement into a new, exclusive status symbol, disguised as a sign of civic virtue. But it was reserved for a privileged few. Just as women sought to break free of gendered limitations of their clothing, members of stigmatized ethnic and racial groups who adopted refined attire implicitly challenged a well-established hierarchy. New dress codes responded to this challenge in a way that echoed the sumptuary laws of the past—in this case, by requiring each race to wear attire appropriate to its social position. Hostility toward members of stigmatized racial groups who "put on airs" and "dressed above their condition" was a constant feature of social life in eighteenth- and nineteenth-century America, and an insistence on dignified dress was an important part of the struggle for social justice and equality in the nineteenth and twentieth centuries.

Chapter Ten

Slaves to Fashion?

*The Allure and Danger of Dressing Above One's
Condition in Pumps with Silver Buckles, a Hat
Cocked in the Macaroni Fashion, or a Jack
Johnson Plaid Suit*

SOUTH CAROLINA'S NEGRO ACT OF 1740 PROVIDED THAT

whereas, many of the slaves in this Province wear clothes much above the condition of slaves . . . no owner or proprietor . . . shall permit or suffer [any] Negro slave, or other slave . . . to have or wear any sort of garment or apparel whatsoever, finer, other or of greater value than Negro cloth, duffels, coarse kerseys, osnabrigs, blue linen, check linen, or coarse garlix, or calicoes, checked cottons or Scottish plaids. . . . [A]nd all and every constable and other persons are hereby authorized, empowered, and required . . . to seize and take away the same, to his or their own use, benefit and behoof; any law, usage or custom to the contrary nowithstanding.

Echoing earlier sumptuary laws, the Negro Acts justified their proscriptions in practical terms, lamenting the large number of Negroes wearing "clothes much above the condition of slaves, for the procuring of which they use sinister and evil methods." But the true purpose of the laws was clear enough: the Negro Acts were comprehensive regulations designed to ensure that the subordinate status of

Black slaves was always visible. The Negro Acts effectively created a *racial* dress code under the guise of regulating the attire of slaves, often using the terms "Negro" and "slave" interchangeably: for instance, one clause forbids any *"Negro or slave"* from carrying a gun without a "ticket or license, in writing from his master. . . ." The provisions authorizing the seizure of fine clothing effectively gave white people license to take the clothing off the backs of Black people.

Such sumptuary legislation was thought necessary because refined clothing was a potent sign of status, suggesting both social position and social virtue. American elites studied English etiquette guides or "courtesy books" and followed their instructions on elegance in comportment and dress. According to historians Shane and Graham White:

> [T]he clothing of the genteel had to be close- rather than ill-fitting, clean and brushed rather than soiled, and above all, smooth in texture rather than coarse . . . made from silk, chintz and super-fine wools rather than plain cottons or poorer quality wools . . . from which the clothing of those lower down the social scale was cut. . . . [T]he tailored shirts, stylish coats and velvet breeches of the gentry contrasting with the loose shirts . . . short jackets, and trousers or leather or osnaburg breeches worn by the lower orders. . . . [T]he silk gowns and lace accessories of the elite women were easily distinguishable from the coarse dresses and aprons of their social inferiors.

In a similar vein, historian Jonathan Prude notes that eighteenth-century America was "a culture . . . of sumptuary regulations . . . sensitive to plebian overdressing. . . . [S]laves who dressed in 'excessive and costly' apparel . . . struck many whites as arrogant."

Blacks who dressed "above their condition" seemed, to status-conscious whites, to threaten or even mock the sartorial social order. The Negro Acts punished Blacks for their perceived challenge. Black women in particular inspired calls for vigorous enforcement of the Negro Act's dress codes: "[I]t is apparent," complained a Charleston grand jury in 1744, "that Negro women in particular do not restrain themselves in their Cloathing as the Law requires, but dress in Apparel quite gay and beyond their Condition." A 1772 letter to the editor of the *South Carolina Gazette* worried that "many of the Female Slaves [are] by far more elegantly dressed, than the Generality of White Women below Affluence." In a society stratified by class as well as by race, well-dressed Black women provoked resentment and envy. Well-dressed slaves—especially female slaves—suggested forbidden intimacies and the illicit blurring of racial divisions, as implied in another letter that lamented that "there is scarce a new mode [of fashion] . . . which *favourite* black and mulatto women slaves are not immediately *enabled* to adopt." Hinting at the open secret of interracial sexual relations, the *Gazette* railed against the "scandalous *Intimacy* . . . [between] *Sexes of different Colours.*"

Some slaves dressed in luxurious clothing at the behest and for the gratification of their masters, but many valued fashionable attire for their own reasons. Indeed, according to Shane and Graham White, the slaves who were allowed the greatest autonomy by their masters and "allowed to . . . [hire] out their own time" in the city were primarily responsible for "the often-commented-on [ostentatious] dress of Charleston blacks." A letter to the *South Carolina Gazette* commented on "[a] great Difference in Appearance as well as Behavior, between the Negroes of the Country, and those in Charles-Town. . . . [Those from the country were] generally clad suitable to their Condition [but those from town were] the very reverse . . . insolent and shameless."

Even runaway slaves were often surprisingly well-dressed. For instance, "Bacchus," the personal servant of a Virginia plantation owner, escaped in June 1774, taking with him:

Two white Russia Drill Coats, one turned up with blue, the other quite plain and new, with white figure Metal Buttons, blue Plush Breeches, a fine Cloth Pompadour Waistcoat, two or three thin or Summer Jackets, sundry Pairs of white Thread Stockings five or six white Shirts, two of them pretty fine, neat Shoes, Silver Buckles, a

fine Hat cut and cocked in the Macaroni Figure, a double-milled
drab Great Coat, and sundry other Wearing Apparel.

With respect to Bacchus's "Macaroni" hat, today most of us know
the term only from the children's song "Yankee Doodle Dandy," in
which the risible American "stuck a feather in his cap and called it
'Macaroni.'" In eighteenth-century English slang, a "Macaroni" was
an especially—to many, scandalously—fashionable man who wore
costly imported clothing, often acquired while on a grand tour of
Italy. A hat "cocked in the 'Macaroni' figure" suggests a sophisticated
fashion sense.

Despite his trendy hat, Bacchus was no superficial fop. His disgruntled former master described him as "cunning, artful, sensible"
and "very capable for forging a Tale to impose on the Unwary." He
feared that Bacchus planned to use his refined wardrobe to pass as a
free man and travel to England, where he could follow the example set
by escaped slave James Somerset and demand his freedom. Somerset
had traveled to England with his master Charles Stewart in 1769 and
escaped in 1771. When Somerset was found, his master arranged to
transport him to Jamaica and sell him for plantation labor. An English
abolitionist, Granville Sharp, hired five lawyers to argue on Somerset's behalf that the laws of England did not permit chattel slavery.
If Somerset's legal arguments prevailed, the roughly fifteen thousand
slaves in England at the time would be free. The presiding judge, Lord
Mansfield, having heard the legal arguments and, aware that the law
favored Somerset's claim, urged an out-of-court settlement:

> In five or six cases of this nature, I have known it to be accom-
> modated by agreement between the parties: on its first coming
> before me, I recommended it strongly here. . . . If the parties will
> have judgment, *fiat justitia ruat caelum* let justice be done, what-
> ever be the consequences. . . . [The consequence may be the ab-
> olition of slavery in all of England. To avoid this upheaval,] Mr.
> Stewart may end the question, by discharging or giving freedom
> to the Negro.

Coincidentally, Lord Mansfield, also known as William Murray, the Earl of Mansfield, and Lord Chief Justice of England and Wales, had an unusual insight into the questions of race and slavery. His nephew, John Lindsay, had fathered a daughter with Maria Belle, an African slave from the British West Indies and, after Maria died, brought his daughter to live with the Murrays in London. The girl, Dido Elizabeth Belle, was brought up as a gentlewoman and became a close companion of another of Lord Mansfield's nieces, Elizabeth Murray. A contemporaneous portrait of Dido and Elizabeth suggests an affectionate relationship. Elizabeth is seated and dressed in the most sumptuous formal attire of the era, her hand extended to touch Dido's arm; Dido stands next to Elizabeth dressed in very luxurious and fashionable clothing, albeit less traditional and arguably more exotic: she wears a kind of turban, a garment worn by some of the more fashion-forward women of the time (**Insert, Image #12**). A visiting American remarked unapprovingly of Dido's social integration into the household and Lord Mansfield's affection for her:

> A Black came in after dinner and sat with the ladies and after coffee, walked with the company in the gardens, one of the young ladies having her arm within the other. . . . This girl . . . was taken care of by Lord M., and has been educated by his family. He calls her Dido, which I suppose is all the name she has. He knows he has been reproached for showing fondness for her—I dare say not criminal.

In his will, Lord Mansfield confirmed Dido's status as a free woman and bequeathed to her a sizable inheritance.

Some speculated that Lord Mansfield's affection for Dido would influence the judge's opinion in Somerset's case. The same American visitor recounted that:

> A Jamaica planter being asked what judgement his L'dship would give? "No doubt" he answered "he will be set free, for Lord Mansfield keeps a Black in his house which governs him and the whole family."

The slave owner, Stewart, ignored Lord Mansfield's suggestion that he free Somerset voluntarily, and one month later, Lord Mansfield delivered the opinion of the court:

> The state of slavery is . . . so odious, that nothing can be suffered to support it. . . . Whatever inconveniences, therefore, may be . . . the black must be discharged.

Somerset v. Stewart repudiated the notion that slaves were property, to be bought and sold "like stock on a farm" and was the beginning of the end of slavery in England. The case was well known in the American colonies: in Massachusetts, several slaves sued for their freedom citing *Somerset* and, after American independence, the reasoning in the case inspired courts to find slavery inconsistent with new state constitutions in Vermont, Pennsylvania, Massachusetts, and Connecticut. As the report of Bacchus's master suggests, *Somerset* made slave owners anxious even in states that did not accept its reasoning. That probably gave hope to potential runaways.

Like Bacchus, many runaways carefully selected the clothing they would take with them. In 1775, a North Carolina master described an escaped slave's "[a]ffected gaiety in dress" and reported that she had taken with her "a homespun striped jacket, a red quilted petticoat, a black silk hat, a pair of leather shoes, with wooden heals, a chintz gown and a black coat." A Maryland man sought the return of two runaway slaves who had taken a large quantity of clothing with them, including "a crimson velvet cape . . . a deep blue camblet jacket, with gold lace at the sleeves, down the breast and round the collar . . . a pair of pumps and buckles. . . . [T]wo calico gowns, one purple and white, the other red and white . . . a black silk bonnet, a variety of handkerchiefs and ruffles . . . [and] several white linen shirts. . . ."

Historian Jonathan Prude, in a study of late eighteenth-century advertisements seeking the capture and return of runaway slaves, indentured servants, convicts, and AWOL soldiers, found that "[m]ore than three-quarters . . . made some mention of garments: the clothing runaways 'had on' when they left as well as the apparel [they] . . . 'took with' them. . . . When clothing was noted, moreover, it was often in extraordinary detail." Many runaways had expensive tastes: according to Prude, "11.4 percent of all runaways taking . . . buckles took buckles of silver, and at least 10 percent of individuals taking . . . garments took items made of expensive materials . . . nearly a quarter of fugitive males taking hats covered their heads fashionably. . . ."

Shane and Graham White note that "[i]t was not uncommon for slave-owners to remark on their slaves' great love of fine clothing." Fine clothing was often a reward for good service and accordingly, a status symbol: in the 1780s, one master, the Reverend Henry Laurens, told his overseers that "any . . . Negro who has behaved remarkably well" should be rewarded and "distinguish[ed] in their clothing by something better than white plains." But well-dressed Black slaves were not just fawning "house Negroes" desperate for the approval of whites. Fashionable attire brought tangible advantages. Some masters allowed their slaves to earn money by doing extra work in town or on neighboring plantations, or by selling the produce grown or raised on small plots of land set aside for their personal use and likewise, some allowed slaves to sell clothing. Shane and Graham White write of a "quasi-licit trade in apparel. . . . Not only was clothing valued by slaves for its own sake but, since it was so readily disposable, it could function as a form of currency." Fashionable clothing could easily be sold or traded while on the run, offering ready income as well as the possibility of disguise. One "Wanted" poster noted that a slave who escaped bondage with a large quantity of fine clothing "probably will exchange for others if in her power." According to Prude, some "Wanted" advertisements warned that runaways might "pose as Methodist preachers . . . shave [their] head[s] . . . adopt different names, and . . . use fake documents to facilitate their escapes . . . [and many] would change costumes. Indeed, it was . . . to transform their 'looks' (so the ads speculated) that some fugitives took or stole extra apparel."

Of course, slaves also cared about fashion for the same reasons people always have: they took pride in their appearance and expressed themselves through their apparel. According to Prude, "Unfree laborers . . . used fine clothing to punctuate personal advancements or special occasions . . . [and] dressing up could express a quiet bid for equality and autonomy. . . ." Even during desperate attempts to escape slavery, "the tendency to seek out alternative outfits never undercut the runaways' evident attachment to the garments they already held . . . [indeed] the limited size of plebian wardrobes may actually have tightened personal connections with specific garments. . . . [B]reeches and petticoats could well have been more fully invested with personal significance among the poor than among the more amply costumed genteel."

Slaves, runways, and free Blacks alike used fashion as a political statement. While some Black slaves dressed with scrupulous fidelity to European standards of elegance, others adopted a more personal approach, combining elements of African and European dress or blending elements of disparate styles. Jonathan Prude notes that "chattel laborers actively preserved strands of African-West Indian heritage through clothing . . . [and] fashions . . . that were neither wholly African nor wholly Anglo-Saxon but Afro-American 'creolizations.'" Shane and Graham White describe slaves using eclectic dress as a means of "subverting white authority. . . . [T]here was a light mocking touch to the activities of slaves, an elusive characteristic that is . . . difficult to discern two hundred years later." Descriptions of runaway slaves detailed the "odd blendings . . . so different from the coordinated apparel of gentility that fugitives must often have seemed to be . . . mocking proper attire." And Prude suggests that an "expression of anti-elite sensibilities . . . may have been a way for laboring folk to lay their own claim to stylish 'looks' . . . . [T]he many laboring men . . . with hats 'cocked in the fashion' [may] have been making their own comment about the legitimacy of prevailing rankings. . . ."

In short, African Americans defied racist dress codes and expectations, using attire to express identity, affinity, and self-respect. Free Blacks as well as many slaves avoided the rough, plain garments assigned to slaves by the Negro Acts: Prude notes that "blacks who were not slaves seemingly sought to underscore their nonchattel status by insistently avoiding the color (white) that was most intensively used in slave work garments." Many slaves valued refined clothing and often defied the efforts of whites—including their masters—to limit their choices. They used clothing to oppose the laws and social mores of white supremacy and insist on their dignity by appropriating the status symbols of whites, by subverting and mocking elite sartorial etiquette or by combining European and African styles to create distinctively African American fashions.

As a consequence, well-dressed African Americans were a conspicuous symbolic challenge to white supremacy. After Emancipation—which occurred at different times in different American states north of the Mason–Dixon Line—racist whites resorted to verbal and written abuse and, that failing, physical violence to do so. In 1845 the prominent Philadelphian John Fanning Watson complained about the attitudes of recently emancipated Blacks (Pennsylvania provided for the gradual abolition of slavery in 1780):

> In the olden time dressy blacks and dandy coloured beaux and belles, as we now see them issuing from their proper churches were quite unknown. Their aspirings and little vanities have been rapidly growing. . . . [Now they have] an overweening fondness for display and vainglory. . . . [J]udicious men wish them wiser conduct, and a better use of the benevolent feelings which induced their emancipation among us.

Watson's complaint was not that "dressy blacks" were forced to resort to crime to fund their wardrobes, nor did he find them guilty of any antisocial behavior—indeed, his ire is directed toward people leaving their "proper churches." Instead, their only social transgression was their "display and vainglory," which, one must presume, was unwise because it would provoke the envy and resentment of status-conscious whites. Satirists mocked Blacks for emulating their "betters" in their dress and cartoons included grotesque caricatures of Blacks in exaggerated finery. As was true of the descriptions of social climbers in earlier eras, both mistakes and "overly" correct practices were ridiculed. Unconventional sartorial combinations or overly flamboyant adornment were taken as proof of an inherent lack of refinement and stereotypically Black speech patterns were the butt of jokes in newspapers, pamphlets, and popular entertainments. At the same time, popular depictions compared Black people in refined clothing to apes in fancy dress and their etiquette-book-perfect diction and attire were considered a risible parroting of the superior race. White schoolchildren taunted well-dressed Blacks, pelted them with snowballs in the winter and with rocks in warmer seasons. As often as not, adults joined in.

As bad as race relations were in the North, they were worse in the South. The defeated Confederacy was forced to accept Emancipation in 1863, but by the turn of the century, the Jim Crow system was firmly in place, replicating most of the conditions of slavery in a new form. Black slaves became sharecroppers, no less tied to the land and its owners than their ancestors had been. Idle Black people were arrested under anti-vagrancy laws and forced to work in prison chain gangs. The definition of vagrancy was, by design, imprecise, inviting overzealous enforcement: as waves of African Americans sought to leave the South for better opportunities in the North, authorities used these laws to prevent their exit, continuing the practices used to detain and return fugitive slaves.

As was true before Emancipation, whites demanded deferential treatment and subservient demeanor from Blacks. According to Shane and Graham White, "Blacks understood . . . that it could be dangerous to wear expensive clothes or . . . to don Sunday attire during the week." When Taylor Gordon, a Black train porter working for John Ringling's circus, came to Houston, Texas, for the first time, he set out to see the sights wearing his "new Jack Johnson plaid suit, patent leather shoes, [and] hotcap." Before he had left the train station, Gordon was stopped by a police officer armed with a billy club. "You're a Yankee Nigger, ain't cha?" the policeman challenged. Gordon thought fast and replied, "No, I'm a Ringling's Niggah." "Well, by God! that saves yah . . . You sure *look* like a Yankee Nigger. They're too damn smart." The police officer then warned Gordon against venturing into town "in them clothes" and suggested he change into his porter's uniform.

Even those who had served their country in war were not exempt from the expectation that African Americans appear in humble attire. When Black soldiers returned home from World War I to Vicksburg, Mississippi, in 1917, white mobs threatened to strip their uniforms off their backs. "What did they do to the niggers after this first world war?" Alabama tenant farmer Ned Cobb, aka Nate Shaw, asked, rhetorically. "Meet em at these stations where they was getting off, comin' back into the United States, and cut the buttons and armaments off their clothes, make em get out of them clothes and if they didn't have another suit of clothes . . . make em walk in their underwear." In the same year in Jackson, Mississippi, an officer walking down a public street dressed in his uniform had to run from an angry white mob in fear for his life. In Blakely, Georgia, in April 1919, a former soldier was fatally beaten by a mob for wearing his uniform for what they thought was too long after the end of the war. White resentment of well-dressed, "uppity" Blacks persisted throughout the Jim Crow era, and beyond. One Black man living in South Carolina during the 1940s remarked that whites "don't like nobody who don't wear overalls and don't work like digging ditches. If a man dress decent, he's a smart nigger."

For both the African Americans who wore refined clothing and those who resented them, dress had important social and political stakes. An elegantly dressed Black person was a direct challenge to a racist society because race itself was a social status determined largely by outward appearance. Just as women wore masculine clothing as a way of claiming the social privileges of men, elegantly dressed African Americans made a sartorial statement that they deserved and would insist on the esteem and respect that their attire symbolized. At the same time, personal investment in refined attire went beyond a social protest: being well-dressed brought a sense of personal satisfaction and psychological comfort: the political was also personal. This combination of political statement and self-assertion became a potent and enduring, if often overlooked, part of the history of social transformation in the twentieth century.

Chapter Eleven

From Rags to Resistance

Seen on the Scene: Zoot Suits, Cotillion Gowns,
Pressed Hair, and Sunday Best; Afros and
Overalls, Dashikis, Black Turtlenecks, and
Black Leather Coats

"THE ZOOT SUIT HAS BECOME A BADGE OF HOODLUMISM,"
exclaimed Los Angeles Councilman Norris Nelson. "We prohibit
nudism . . . [and] if we can arrest people for being under-dressed, we
can do so for being over-dressed." A few days earlier, on June 4, 1943,
a group of about two hundred sailors stationed in Los Angeles had
roamed the streets of East Los Angeles looking for young Mexican
American men wearing zoot suits. The sailors attacked the young
Mexican American men and often stripped them of their distinctive
clothing: wide-brimmed hats, broad-shouldered, long, drape-cut suits
with high-waisted trousers cut voluminously in the thigh and tapering
dramatically at the ankle. The zoot suit was a mid-twentieth-century
echo of the Renaissance-era's overstuffed trunk hose. It had become
the de facto uniform of the young Latinos in Southern California who
called themselves *pachucos*. What would become known as the "Zoot
Suit Riots" raged for weeks as other servicemen and some white civilians joined the sailors. One observer witnessed a "mob of several
thousand soldiers, sailors and civilians proceed to beat up every zoot
suiter they could find. . . . Streetcars were halted while Mexicans, and
some Filipinos and Negroes, were jerked from their seats, pushed

into the streets and beaten with a sadistic frenzy." The mobs hunted zoot suiters throughout Latino neighborhoods, in theaters, clubs, and bars. One account of the riots described a mob that stormed a theater, dragged the *pachucos* they found onto the stage, stripped them of their clothing, and urinated on the offending suits.

Popular sympathy was with the vigilantes enforcing an ad hoc anti–zoot suit dress code. When the *pachucos* fought back—and sometimes even when they didn't—the police arrested them; by contrast the rioting servicemen were quietly remanded to military authorities or simply released without charge. The press depicted the riots as a long-overdue "cleansing" of the city streets, as if the riots were a disciplined military campaign rather than a drunken melee. A typical article reported favorably that:

> Zoot-suits smouldered in the ashes of street bonfires. . . . Searching parties of soldiers, sailors and Marines hunted them out and

Zoot suiters detained by police during the 1943 "Zoot Suit Riots" in Los Angeles.

drove them into the open like bird dogs flushing quail. Procedure was standard: grab a zooter. Take off his pants and frock coat and tear them up or burn them. Trim the 'Argentine Ducktail' haircut that goes with the screwy costume.

What was so objectionable about the zoot suit? Some contemporaneous accounts suggested that the extravagant ensemble, with its almost knee-length coat and voluminous trouser, was unpatriotic—a conspicuous waste of fabric during wartime rationing. Others speculated that the pricey, often custom-tailored suits were purchased with the ill-gotten gains of crime. But these explanations were oversimplified at best and post-hoc rationalizations at worst. The real offense of the zoot suit was symbolic: it was an assertion of self-determination and personal pride at a time when America's racial hierarchy was experiencing its first signs of vulnerability.

According to a *New York Times* story of June 11, 1943, the first bespoke zoot suit was bespoken by one Clyde Duncan, a young African American from Gainesville, Georgia, in 1940. He astounded his tailor by requesting a suit with a thirty-seven-inch-long coat, and trousers twenty-six inches at the knees and fourteen inches at the ankles. The tailor sent a photograph of the suit to a trade publication, the *Men's Apparel Reporter*, which published an article about the curiosity in 1941. From there, the suit went viral, catching on in Mississippi, New Orleans, Alabama, and Harlem. The *Times* speculated that the zoot suit was inspired by Rhett Butler's clothing in *Gone with the Wind*, which had opened in theaters in 1939—a somewhat improbable account given the racial politics of that film. The African American press had a more plausible theory: the zoot suit's inspiration was that paragon of sartorial daring, the Duke of Windsor. Prince Edward VIII was notorious for his sartorial innovations and transgressions, which included drape-cut suits with folds of fabric in the chest and shoulder blades, and "Oxford Bags"—a voluminous cut of trousers popular with college students in the 1930s. The *Amsterdam News* quipped that "what the reporters [of the *Times*] seem to have forgotten . . . and what the Duke of Windsor would like to forget, is that he, as Prince of Wales, wore the first, and is truly the father of the present-day Zoot Suit. . . . [H]e was young and fly, too, in those days."

Whatever its origins, the zoot suit became associated with jazz, flamboyance, and a carefree lifestyle. In his autobiography, Malcolm X recalls that before his conversion to Islam, when he was known as "Detroit Red," he often wore a sky-blue zoot suit, broad-brimmed hat, and gold watch chain. Perhaps the most famous of zoot suiters (other than perhaps the Duke of Windsor) was the magnificent big band leader and singer Cab Calloway, who often wore a zoot suit on-stage and, famously, in the classic African American musical *Stormy Weather*. Ralph Ellison's protagonist in *Invisible Man* begins his journey away from ideological dogma and toward self-knowledge after observing and pondering a group of seemingly apolitical zoot suiters; he later dons a zoot suit himself and finds that: "by dressing and walking in a certain way I had enlisted in a fraternity in which I was recognized at a glance—not by features, but by clothes. . . ."

That sartorial fraternity was not racially exclusive: one observer noted that "youths of Scotch-Irish Protestant, Jewish or Italian, Russian or Negro backgrounds" wore zoot suits. It was a brotherhood of common alienation from the American mainstream, a defiant new mode of self-assertion and a countercultural sensibility that would come to define subsequent generations of beatniks, hipsters, and hippies. It was also a sisterhood: young women who wore a feminine zoot suit ensemble were labeled *pachucas*, "Zoot suit gangsterettes," and "zooterinas." The zoot suit was unconventional, demonstrating an indifference—if not a disdain—for American standards of good taste. It was attention grabbing, a bold provocation from people who American society expected to be meek and unobtrusive. It was ostentatiously expensive, its voluminous draping requiring skilled custom tailoring and yards of fabric. The zoot suit was an almost belligerent repudiation of the American sartorial ethos set by the understated, modest, black and gray ready-made suits of Brooks Brothers in the nineteenth century. It was made all the more threatening because the black- and brown-skinned people who made it popular had every reason to question the bourgeois ethos of sober, restrained masculine virtue and the false promise of equality that the standard suit symbolized. As the poet Octavio Paz wrote of the *pachuco*, "They are instinctive rebels. . . . [T]he pachucos do not attempt to vindicate their race or the nationality of their forebears. Their attitude reveals an obstinate, almost fanatical will-to-be, but this will affirms nothing specific except their determination . . . not to be like those around them."

In that way, the *pachucos* were the spiritual descendants of the nineteenth-century dandies celebrated and castigated in the writing of Charles Baudelaire, Jules-Amédée Barbey d'Aurevilly, and Thomas Carlyle. Baudelaire described dandies as "beings [who] have no other calling but to cultivate the idea of beauty in their persons, to satisfy their passions, to feel and to think." Barbey d'Aurevilly wrote that dandyism's "most general characteristic—is its ability always to produce the unexpected . . . the revolt of the individual against the established Order . . . Dandyism . . . plays with the regulations, but at the same time pays them due respect. . . ." The very existence of the dandy was a rebuke to the bourgeois moral order, which, consistent with the Protestant work ethic, defined virtuous citizenship in terms of the productive vocation. Carlyle, in his idiosyncratic work *Sartor Resartus* (*The Tailor Retailored*), suggests that the dandy's obsessions rushed in to fill the void left by the decline of religious conviction:

In these distracted times when the Religious Principle, driven out of most Churches either lies unseen in the hearts of good men . . . or else wanders homeless over the world, like a disembodied soul—into how many strange shapes of Superstition and Fanaticism, does it not tentatively and errantly cast itself. . . . [T]hese people, animated with the zeal of a new Sect, display courage and perseverance. . . . They affect great purity and separatism; distinguish themselves by a particular costume . . . strive to keep themselves unspotted from the world.

The nineteenth-century dandy was typically an aristocrat, by predisposition an enemy of democracy and its leveling influences. Dandies were, of necessity, rich, "with fortunes ample enough to pay without thinking of all of their extravagances." But the twentieth century created a new dandyism of the dispossessed: poor, unemployed, and underemployed people who, though they lacked money, had free time with which to pursue their passions. Like the dandies of the nineteenth century, the zoot suiters were alienated from the mainstream of their society: they were the children and grandchildren of immigrants, stripped of the language and culture of their ancestors and held in wary contempt by their adopted homeland or African American migrants fleeing the unapologetic racism of the rural South for the disdainful racism of the Northern cities. Excluded from the American cult of democratic virtue and profitable industriousness, the zoot suiter expressed a studied and flamboyant indifference to the mainstream.

This defiant stance, combined with the ubiquitous racism of 1940s America, was enough to provoke both the sporadic and undisciplined violence of mobs and the sustained antagonism of politicians. California state senator Jack B. Tenney presided over an un-American activities investigation "to determine whether the present zoot-suit riots were sponsored by Nazi agencies attempting to spread disunity between the United States and Latin-American countries." A witness testifying in the investigation insisted that the zoot suiters were instigated by "fifth columnists" and domestic Nazi sympathizers: "[W]hen boys start attacking servicemen it means the enemy is right at home."

The zoot suit riots did not stay contained to the Golden State; Detroit and Harlem experienced their own riots later in the same year. While the mainstream press consistently denied that that the riots were a form of "racial persecution," the Black press begged to differ. In an opinion piece in *The Crisis*, Chester Himes succinctly insisted "Zoot riots are race riots," while another editorial in *The Crisis* opined: "These riots would not occur . . . if the vast majority of the population, including more often than not the law enforcement officers and machinery, did not share in varying degrees the belief that Negroes are and must be kept second-class citizens."

The novelist Ralph Ellison offered perhaps the most insightful comment on the zoot suit—an admonishment to civic leaders of all races:

> A . . . major problem . . . is that of learning the meaning of myths and symbols which abound among the Negro masses. For without this knowledge, leadership, no matter how correct its program, will fail . . . perhaps the zoot suit conceals profound political meaning . . . if only leaders could solve this riddle.

A similar riddle still perplexes many leaders today who confront the obscure symbolism of sagging pants, body piercing, tattoos, and many other fashion statements of alienated youth. The mid-twentieth century witnessed the birth of a new type of collective dandyism: that of a youth group defined by an obsessive attention to a specific mode of attire and type of popular music. The *pachuco* was the prototype for the beatnik and hippie movements of the 1950s and 1960s, and of the mod, punk, New Wave, New Romantic, and goth subcultures of more recent decades.

The zoot suit was as enigmatic as the politics of the *pachuco*, but as the struggle for racial justice developed its own dress codes, the political meaning of attire came to be a subject of explicit ideological debate. Was the desire to be well-dressed a dignified challenge to the status quo, or a pathetic capitulation to bourgeois norms of respectability?

The Black Bourgeoisie

The eminent Morehouse College sociologist E. Franklin Frazier wrote in 1955 that the "black bourgeoisie" had created a "world of make-believe" centered around "the activities of those persons who constitute its 'society.'" Black "society" was defined by exclusive social clubs, dinner and cocktail parties, debutante balls, awards ceremonies, and the Black fraternity and sorority system of Black colleges and universities. Frazier, writing in the spirit and tradition of Thorstein

Veblen's *Theory of the Leisure Class,* first published *Bourgeoisie Noire* for a French-speaking audience, but it was the 1957 English-language translation, *Black Bourgeoisie,* that found a large audience among the community that was subject of the book. Like Veblen was for the elite of the Gilded Age, Frazier was unsparing in his assessment of the Black bourgeoisie. For Frazier, the social rituals of the Black elite were a pathetic imitation of the grander rituals of white society—rituals from which Blacks were, of course, excluded. Indeed, for Frazier, almost every aspect of the culture of the Black bourgeoisie was motivated by their deep feelings of inferiority to whites and their desperate, unrealized desires to separate themselves from poor Black people:

> Since the black bourgeoisie live largely in a world of make-believe, the masks which they wear to play their sorry roles conceal the feelings of inferiority and of insecurity and the frustrations that haunt their inner lives. Despite their attempt to escape from the real identification with the masses of Negroes, they cannot escape the mark of oppression any more than their less favored kinsmen. . . . [T]hey have developed a self-hatred . . . revealed in their pathological struggle for status . . . and craving for recognition in the white world. Their . . . sham "society" leaves them with a feeling of emptiness and futility which causes them to constantly seek an escape in new delusions.

Clothing played a central role in the make-believe world of Black "society." Indeed, clothing was literally the costume that accompanied the "masks" worn by the Black bourgeoisie to play their "sorry roles." The Black bourgeoisie "are constantly buying things—houses, automobiles, furniture . . . not to mention clothes. . . . Negro school teachers who devote their lives to 'society' like to display twenty pairs of shoes, the majority of which they never wear." Consumerism fed a "delusion of wealth" whereby the Black bourgeoisie pretended to greater social status and importance than they in fact had—or ever could have in a racist society.

Frazier reserved special scorn for the tradition of the debutante ball or "cotillion," which he insisted the Black bourgeoisie had borrowed from the wealthy white households in which their ancestors had served. The cotillion "provides an opportunity . . . for the so-called rich Negroes to indulge in lavish expenditures and create a world of fantasy to satisfy their longing for recognition." Frazier lamented that these debutante balls were breathlessly reported on in the Black press, which "noted . . . the money spent on decorations and the expensive gowns and jewels worn by the women. . . .[The] weekly accounts in the Negro press . . . include a catalogue of the jewelry, the gowns, and the mink coats worn by the women, often accompanied by an estimate of the value of the clothes and jewelry. . . ." For Frazier, the Black debutante ball was the apotheosis of Veblen's conspicuous consumption: frenzied acquisition and anxious status-seeking driven by an insatiable thirst for affirmation. Worst of all, the whole gaudy circus was underwritten by a noxious mix of snobbery and self-hatred: Frazier's Black bourgeoisie used conspicuous consumption to separate themselves from the unrefined, uncouth, struggling masses of Black people because, ultimately, they yearned to separate themselves from their own blackness.

When Frazier's book appeared in the 1950s, it was a sensation, and it remains a classic study by one of the most celebrated Black sociologists of the twentieth century. Anyone familiar with the social life of middle- and upper-class African Americans will find something familiar in Frazier's account. Even today, status consciousness and a preoccupation with luxury, while widespread among Americans of all races, are especially pronounced among Black professionals and businesspeople. As I write, I have my father's well-worn copy of *Black Bourgeoisie* in front of me. My dad took Frazier's concerns seriously. That, combined with an asceticism inspired by Calvinist theology and a dash of mainline Protestant reverse snobbery, made him disdainful of luxury and showiness, even as he insisted on quality and style. My dad shared Frazier's contempt for "high-society" events and exclusive clubs. He would not hear of having me or my sister join "Jack and Jill"—an elite social club for Black young people—and when the notion of a "coming-out" party for my sister was broached by a visiting relative, he responded with a lengthy critique that came straight from Frazier.

The influence of *Black Bourgeoisie* has been long-lived. Just as Marx transformed the term "bourgeoisie"—originally the title of propertied urbanites in pre-Revolutionary France—into the title of an economic class responsible for capitalist exploitation, Frazier turned the term "bourgeoisie" (which in recent decades has morphed into the slang epithet "bougie") into a sociological caste defined by its political apathy, social ambition, and bland consumerism. Ever since, the term has become something of a free-floating insult and, as a consequence, politically aware Black people have sought to avoid exhibiting any sign of it. One might say that the affectations of the bourgeoisie are now decidedly déclassé. But the history of Black elegance is long and much more varied than Frazier's attack on bourgeois pretensions suggests. Indeed, the commonplace observation that all revolutions begin with the bourgeoisie could not be more apt as a description of the revolutionary struggle for racial justice in the United States.

Sunday-Best Activism

On a hot May afternoon in 1963 five people sat down at a Woolworth's lunch counter in Jackson, Mississippi. They were well mannered and well-dressed. One of the women, Anne Moody, recalls that she wore a dress, stockings, and closed-toe pumps and the pressed and curled hair popular at the time among middle-class women. Two of the group of five were white, the other three were Black. Anyone fleetingly familiar with the history of the American South can guess what happened next. A group of high school boys pummeled the group with "ketchup, mustard, sugar . . . pies." Eventually Moody was dragged across the floor by her pressed and curled hair. Officials from a nearby college rescued the group from a large and growing mob. "Before we were taken back to campus," Moody recalled, "I wanted to get my hair washed. . . . I stopped in at a beauty shop across the street from the NAACP office."

My first reaction when hearing this account was admiration and

Anne Moody and companions after a mob pelted them with
food during a lunch counter sit-in.

awe: Moody was fierce! Like James Bond straightening his tie after
a near miss from an assassin, Moody had such style and sangfroid
that even after narrowly escaping a racist mob, she was determined
to make sure she still looked good. I was half-right: Moody *was* fierce.
But her concern with her appearance had very different roots than
007's vanity.

Respectable appearance was a mandatory part of the civil rights
struggle. Professor Anthony Pinn, an expert on the history of the
Black church and the struggle for racial justice in the United States,
describes the importance of attire in the civil rights movement: "Although there was no formal dress code, [civil rights activists] wore
their best as a way of indicating their seriousness and importance.
It forced people to move beyond the stereotypes of blacks and black
bodies. . . . [W]hat they wore . . . [had] deep meaning in the politi-

cal realm. . . ." Racist whites threw food at Moody and her friends in order to deprive them of the psychological and symbolic power of a respectable appearance. Moody needed to scrub that violation clean and restore her dignity.

To be sure, "well-dressed" was, in important respects, defined by and for privileged white people. As the racial justice struggle evolved, an activism premised on such "respectability" became both practically and ideologically untenable. The contradictions between the demand for racial justice and white-centered standards of respectability were most conspicuous in the case of Black women. Consider Anne Moody, who lost one of her dressy pumps and had her carefully set hairdo ruined by a racist mob. Wouldn't lace-up flats have been more sensible? And what about her pressed, curled, shoulder-length hair, an easy target for an assailant to grab? Tying it up or cutting it short would have been more practical.

Some would insist that a different hairstyle might have been more psychologically empowering as well. When Moody sought solace

Civil rights activists wore suits and ties during the famous
March on Washington in 1963.

in a local beauty salon, she also sought to restore her hair to a fashionable style made popular by white women. Conventional women's hairstyles in the early 1960s were demanding enough for those born with the long, straight hair the styles were designed for—straight hair had to be set in curlers to achieve the upturned curl that signified the well-coiffed bourgeois woman of the 1960s. Most Black women first had to straighten their hair *and then* reset in curlers. Straightening hair is notoriously difficult: a hot comb is typically insufficient, yielding unsatisfactory and fleeting results, and chemical straighteners are time consuming, and potentially dangerous: in the 1960s the main ingredient in hair "relaxers" was lye, which straightens the hair shaft but also burns any unprotected skin.

"Respectable" hair was time consuming and expensive for Black women. Worse yet, the conventions of this grooming implied that Black people's hair required extensive transformation to be presentable. This standard of respectability was—and is—tied up with gender politics: although some Black men straightened or "conked" their hair, by the 1960s most did not. Short cropped hair was the norm among well-dressed Black and white men—no processing required. Longer hair was the exclusive prerogative and obligation of women—a sign of femininity. This was not only especially burdensome for Black women; in addition, the norms of femininity that required such hairstyles were insulting, implying that Black women were naturally less feminine than white women.

The attire and grooming of civil rights activists became less "respectable" as they pressed into rural areas to organize poor sharecroppers and laborers. In the early 1960s—around the same time many younger racial justice activists began to describe themselves as "revolutionaries"—the activists of the Student Nonviolent Coordinating Committee, or SNCC, abandoned suits and dresses for denim skirts, jeans, and overalls—the clothing of the farm and factory workers they hoped to organize. SNCC's new, more radical image included "abandoning processed hairstyles and opting to wear . . . natural hair." According to Tanisha Ford, a historian of the civil rights movement, this clothing was practical as well as symbolically appropriate: "The

A younger generation of civil rights activists wore overalls and
workwear in solidarity with the poor people they hoped to
organize in a 1965 march.

various pockets [of overalls] served as storage space for flyers, pens
and leaflets. . . . Like sharecroppers, SNCC activists labored long
hours in their 'field' canvasing rural communities for African Americans who were bold enough to attempt to register to vote. . . . SNCC
activists also used [attire] to present their political alliance with sharecroppers and to critique the . . . politics of the black middle class."

Class divisions among African Americans were a problem for civil
rights activists. Many civil rights organizers were relatively urban and
privileged—college students and professionals such as lawyers. They
had the sensibilities and mannerisms of middle- and upper-middle-
class urbanities—quite literally, the bourgeoisie. For them, the politics
of respectability wasn't *just* a strategy; it also reflected their sincerely
held values. Civil rights activists who had engaged in "respectability
politics" weren't simply catering to the sensibilities of a white majority;
to a large extent, they shared those sensibilities. As with other members of the bourgeoisie, they saw unrefined mannerisms, unkempt

grooming, and disheveled clothing as evidence of poor character. But a new generation of civil rights activists needed to organize rural laborers who lacked the signs of bourgeois respectability. Moreover, the moral principle underlying the civil rights movement—equal dignity and respect for all—was at odds with such denigrating assessments of the poor. And worst of all, as Black women's experiences with their hair so dramatically demonstrated, conventional respectability wasn't really available to Black people on equal terms. It was easier for a white woman to have a proper coif because the hairstyles that counted as proper were designed for white women. Maybe it was also easier for a white person to come across as respectable because the ideal of respectability itself was designed for white people. SNCC's new proletarian style reflected that growing suspicion.

Radical Chic

"We Want Black Power!" In 1966, SNCC activist Stokely Carmichael rallied a crowd in Greenwood, Mississippi, with a phrase that would define a new social movement. Black Power was the mainstream civil rights movement's wilder, younger sibling, combining radical ideology, confrontational tactics, strident rhetoric, and a new style that was simultaneously flamboyant and down-to-earth. When asked to define Black Power, Carmichael replied that it meant "bringing this country to its knees any time it messes with the black man . . . any white man in this country knows about power. He knows what white power is and he ought to know what black power is."

After the Greenwood rally, both SNCC and the Congress of Racial Equality repudiated the nonviolent ethos of Martin Luther King's Southern Christian Leadership Conference and embraced militant separatism and Black Power. The Black Power movement insisted that meaningful equality and liberation for African Americans could come only through fundamental changes in American culture, economy, and politics. The right to enter white-dominated schools, businesses, and workplaces on formally equal terms was not enough: Black Power challenged the unstated norms and practices that benefited whites at the expense of Blacks. Black Power sought self-sufficient Black-controlled institutions organized around ideals and values developed by, and suitable for, Black people.

Fashion and aesthetics were an important part of the Black Power agenda, a priority reflected in the slogan "Black is Beautiful." In 1962, Eldridge Cleaver, who later became a leader of the Black Panther Party, wrote that the "Caucasian standard of beauty has been—and is now—one of the corner-stones of the doctrine of 'White Supremacy.'" He argued that conventional depictions and standards of beauty, which featured "creamy white skin, sparkling blue eyes, and long flowing blonde tresses," demoralized Black people and encouraged them to waste time and money on "hair-straighteners, wigs, and skin bleaches." Black women who could not coax their "crinkly" hair into fashionable styles were "looked upon as an especial abomination." For Cleaver, a reexamination of such cultural standards was as important as any change in public policy. "It would be facetious of us to campaign for a law to ban the Caucasian standard of beauty," Cleaver quipped. Instead, Black liberation required a change in cultural consciousness. "We must see ourselves as beautiful people," Stokely Carmichael insisted in a 1967 interview. "We keep thinking the only thing that is beautiful is white, a chick with long blonde hair. We've got to understand that we have thick lips and flat noses and curly hair and we're black and beautiful. And we're not going to imitate the white man anymore."

The charismatic Black nationalist leader Malcolm X of the Nation of Islam also saw personal aesthetics as an integral part of Black liberation. He ruefully recalled his youthful attempts to meet white standards of beauty by chemically straightening his hair:

[T]his was my first really big step towards self-degradation, when I endured all of that pain, literally burning my flesh with lye, in order to conk my natural hair until it was limp, to have it look like a white man's hair. I had joined that multitude of Negro men and women in America who are brainwashed into believing that the black people are inferior . . . they will even violate and mutilate their God-created bodies to try to look "pretty" by white standards.

For this younger generation of activists, pride—or lack thereof—in one's appearance was far from trivial; it was among the most profound political issues facing the Black community. As one contemporaneous article put it, natural hairstyles "are part of the de-brainwashing of . . . our people." In a 1965 speech, Malcolm X said, "When you teach a man to hate the lips that God gave him, the shape of the nose that God gave him, the texture of the hair that God gave him, the color of the skin that God gave him, you've committed the worst crime that a race of people can commit." Given the magnitude of the injuries African Americans had suffered—injuries Malcolm X had been extraordinarily forceful in recounting—this is a dramatic claim, attesting to the importance Malcolm X and the Black Power movement attributed to grooming and pride in personal appearance.

The Black Panthers combined countercultural and quasi-military styles.
UC Santa Cruz, Ruth-Marion Baruch and Prickle Jones Collection.
Photograph. © UC Board of Regents.

In the 1960s, a younger generation of Black women rejected artificially straightened hair in favor of natural hairstyles that reflected racial pride.

UC Santa Cruz, Ruth-Marion Baruch and Prickle Jones Collection.

Photograph. © UC Board of Regents.

The Black-is-beautiful ideal inspired radical changes in style, fashion, and grooming for millions of people. Black men and women rejected the "respectable" fashions of the white mainstream—and the mainstream civil rights movement. While SNCC activists adopted the tough, practical garb of tenant farmers or factory workers, the Black Panther Party devised a novel, quasi-military style that combined berets, aviator sunglasses, bohemian turtleneck sweaters, and long, sleek leather jackets. Meanwhile, Afrocentrists wore dramatic robes or "dashikis" in brightly colored African kente cloth and African-inspired jewelry, an aesthetic turn to Africa that echoed the nineteenth- and early-twentieth-century movements that sought a literal return to Africa, inspired by a belief that integration with whites on equal terms was impossible and that liberation required a dramatic separation from a society and culture premised on white supremacy and Black inferiority. By reclaiming the African names, language, and cultural styles that slavery had wrested from them, African Americans could begin to build a society suited to their distinctive, African-derived virtues.

The SNCC activists who abandoned respectable Sunday-best activism for grassroots organizing in proletarian garb and natural hairstyles were, for the most part, middle-class urbanities. They had dressed accordingly for much of their lives before joining SNCC. Blue jeans, overalls, and denim skirts were part of a contrived style, calculated to make a political point—not an authentic expression of their inherited culture. That style may have helped the activists relate to some of the poor farmers and factory workers they hoped to organize, but to others it was off-putting. Many rural and small-town residents of every race felt that "anybody wearing old work clothes all the time couldn't be about very much." For some, the objections to such affectations were more profound. Stokely Carmichael's then girlfriend and later wife, the South African singer Miriam Makeba, felt the SNCC activists romanticized a poverty they were safely insulated from:

> When I was growing up we were poor. But we were clean, and we took great pride in the way we dressed and looked. Stokely and his American friends, who are not poor, dress like vagabonds. . . . He and his friends say that being dirty and wearing tattered clothes means that a person identifies with the masses. This makes me mad . . . it sounds patronizing. . . . We were not proud of our poverty.

Ironically, because the new radical and Afrocentric styles were self-conscious stylistic affectations, they were open to the critique of inauthenticity. In 1969, the Black radical sociologist Robert Allen complained,

> [B]lack culture has become a badge to be worn rather than an experience to be shared. African robes, dashikis, dresses and sandals

have become standard equipment, not only for the well-dressed Black militant, but even for middle class hipsters who have gone Afro. Business firms advertise hair sprays especially suited for natural styles, and some of the shrewder cultural nationalists have turned a profit peddling African trinkets and clothes to naïve young Blacks.

The journalist Tom Wolfe coined the term "radical chic" to describe the politics of the late 1960s and early 1970s—with the implication that many political commitments were as shallowly rooted as the latest fashion trends:

> *Christ, if the Panthers don't know how to get it all together, as they say, the tight pants, the tight black turtlenecks, the leather coats, Cuban shades, Afros. But real Afros, not the ones that have been shaped and trimmed like a topiary hedge and sprayed until they have a sheen like acrylic . . . but like funky, natural scraggly . . . wild. . . . These are no civil-rights Negroes wearing gray suits three sizes too big. . . . The Panther women . . . are so lean, so* lithe, *as they say, with tight pants and Yoruba-style headdresses . . . as if they stepped out of* Vogue, *although no doubt* Vogue *got it from them.*

Wolfe mocked the rich white liberals who fawned over the Panthers, not the Panthers themselves, but his observations raised some uncomfortable questions for the movement. Did the new styles overcome racially denigrating standards of beauty or just rework them? Would Black radical chic inspire equal respect for African Americans, or did even sympathetic whites see the Panthers and other chic Black radicals as late-twentieth-century Noble Savages, dressed up for the post–civil rights era?

The rejection of bourgeois respectability walked a thin line between an urgent critique of soulless materialism and a patronizing *nostalgie de la boue.* The philosopher Roland Barthes described this tightrope of countercultural symbolism in a pointed commentary on the contemporaneous "hippy" aesthetic:

Clothing . . . is . . . the main choice made by the hippy; in relation to the norms of the West. . . . Cleanliness . . . the most important of American values . . . is counteracted in spectacular fashion: dirt on the body, in the hair, on the clothes; clothes dragging along the street . . . but somehow it is still different from real dirtiness, different from a long-engrained poverty, from a dirtiness that deforms the body . . . hippy dirty is different, it has been borrowed for the holidays, sprinkled over like dust. . . .

Despite this superficiality, Barthes thought that the hippy aesthetic was a valid symbolic reaction to American bourgeois moralism because "it strikes exactly . . . at the good consciences of the well off, the guardians of social morals and of cleanliness. . . ." By contrast, hippies slumming in a "fairly poor country," conveyed a "fragmented" and "contradictory" meaning:

[O]nce out of its original context, hippy protest comes up against an enemy far more significant than American conformism . . . poverty. This poverty turns the hippy's choice into [an irresponsible] . . . copy of poverty. . . . For most traits invented by the hippy in opposition to his home civilization (a civilization of the rich) are the very ones which distinguish poverty . . . [in poor countries,] bare feet, dirtiness, ragged clothing . . . are not used in the symbolic fight against the world of riches but are the very forces against which we should be fighting. . . .

In this sense, the SNCC organizers and Black Panthers were African American hippies, reacting to the respectability of the older generation of civil rights activists with the same sartorial symbolism white hippies used to attack the moralistic prosperity of the white mainstream. But unlike hippies in wealthy America, Black activists worked with genuinely poor people—inner-city low-wage laborers and rural farmers stuck in a sharecropping economy. Here, as Barthes would have predicted, their rejection of respectability risked looking like a patronizing copy of real poverty or a reckless provocation. Unsurprisingly, many Black people decided that radical chic was a luxury they could not afford.

The Return of Respectability

In 1969, arguably the height of the Black is Beautiful movement, fewer than half of African Americans approved of the natural Afro hairstyle. Prominent African Americans attacked the new styles as counterproductive posturing. For instance, Joe Black, one of the first African American Major League Baseball players and later an executive at Greyhound Bus Lines, asked rhetorically, "Do you know . . . an employer who will offer you a job with a future because you're wearing an Afro?" Black questioned radical politics generally, emphasizing the importance of respectable dress and demeanor for success: "Chanting slogans, spewing hate and changing your physical appearance won't stop hunger pains, or get you a solid job. . . . Remember it for yourself, for your future and self-respect, and for the dignity of black people everywhere." Even the hated practice of hair straightening had its defenders. For instance, in 1969, one letter to *Ebony* magazine read, "I think it's time that the black woman started pressing her hair again and even buying an assortment of wigs to keep her looking sweet, delicious and desirable and feminine. . . . The men look great and masculine in their Afro styles—our women look great and masculine too."

By the late 1970s, much of the menace and the glamour had gone out of Afrocentric styles. They had become another fashion trend, backed by a large industry selling clothing and jewelry with an African influence and grooming products and services designed to maintain "natural" hair. The beauty parlor that civil rights activist Anne Moody visited after her ordeal in the Mississippi Woolworth's lunch counter would, fifteen years later, most likely have offered, as an alternative to straightening her hair, to condition and shape it into an Afro or style it into long, tight braids. All of these hairstyles had their fans and their detractors: straightened hair was respectable to some, a sign of self-hatred to others; a natural hairstyle was either proud and practical or needlessly provocative; an all-braided style might be apprehended as daring and chic or an affectation suitable only for the beach.

Renee Rogers had worked for American Airlines for eleven years when, on September 25, 1980, she arrived for work wearing cornrows—so named because the braiding exposes some of the scalp in parallel lines, like the furrows between crops in a field. American Airlines prohibited employees from wearing all-braided hairstyles and insisted that Rogers change her hairstyle or cover it with a hairpiece that satisfied their dress code. Rogers refused and eventually sued American Airlines for race and sex discrimination. Rogers argued that the cornrow hairstyle

> has been historically, a fashion and style adopted by Black American women, reflective of cultural, historical essence of the Black women in American society. . . . It was analogous to the public statement by the late Malcolm X regarding the Afro hair style. . . . There can be little doubt that, if American [Airlines] adopted a policy which foreclosed Black women/all women from wearing hair styles as an 'Afro/bush', that policy would have very pointedly racial dynamics and consequences reflecting a vestige of slavery . . . a master mandate that one wear hair . . . consistent with the 'white master' dominated society. . . .

American Airlines had made respectability a job requirement. But was this race discrimination under the law? Not according to the federal court that heard Rogers's case. Judge Abraham Sofaer pointed out that the dress code applied to all employees, regardless of race or sex. Moreover, he noted, the cornrow hairstyle was not a natural or exclusive characteristic of the Black race: it was a product of artifice, potentially available to anyone. The judge noted that Rogers had first started wearing cornrows shortly after the Caucasian blonde actress Bo Derek popularized the style in the film *10*. In addition, American

Airlines didn't demand that Rogers cut her hair or remove her corn-rows; instead it "permitted her to pull her hair into a bun and wrap a hairpiece around the bun during work hours"—thus allowing her to "wear her hair as she liked while off duty."

The no-braids rule that Rogers challenged as discriminatory was just a small part of the detailed and exacting dress and grooming regulations every major airline imposed during the 1960s, 1970s, and well into the 1980s. Airlines were heavily regulated until the 1980s with fares, routes, and the configuration of the aircraft largely set by law. Because they couldn't distinguish themselves based on price or basic service, they competed fiercely with respect to image. Uniforms were designed by high-fashion houses such as Emilio Pucci and Christian Dior, and every element of the appearance of staff, from ticketing agents to flight attendants, was controlled. The dress codes included exacting regulations with respect to height, weight, makeup, jewelry, fingernails—and, of course, hair. In the 1972 book *Flying High: What It's Like to Be An Airline Stewardess*, the author advises:

> Don't let your hopes soar about keeping your waist length hair. Count on its being cut to perhaps an inch or two below your collar, and then later, if you are lucky enough to conceal longer hair in a chignon or knot, you can be happy. Many training schools offer hairpieces at a discount price, and the instructors will show you how to manage them.

Arguably, American Airlines wasn't singling Rogers out for special scrutiny because of her race. The company forced almost everyone to conform to a rigid dress code.

Even today, such exacting dress codes are commonplace in the hospitality industry, where image is as much a part of the product as food, lodging, or service. For instance, Disney's amusement parks are renowned for the precision with which they are operated and maintained. This is the "magic" that transforms an amusement park into "The Happiest Place on Earth." Similarly, Disney's employees conform to a strict code—the "Disney Look"—in which "every detail counts." The Disney Look is "clean, natural, polished and professional, and avoids 'cutting edge' trends or extreme styles." Hair dyed unnatural colors is prohibited. Men's hair must not cover the ears or extend below the collar. "Bi-level" hairstyles are not allowed. Too much hair gel is a problem because the Disney Look requires "a soft, natural hairstyle." Men's fingernails must not extend beyond the fingertip while women are allowed nails 6 millimeter beyond the fingertip, provided that any polish is of a natural color and not "black, gold, silver, multicolored or neon." Women may not have any part of their head shaved. The Disney Look flatly prohibits "visible tattoos, brands, body piercing (other than traditional ear piercing for women), tongue piercing or splitting, tooth filing, earlobe expansion and disfiguring skin implants."

Similarly, the Ritz-Carlton Hotel enforces a strict dress code. Its "Service Values," to which every employee must commit, states, "I am proud of my professional appearance, language and behavior," and according to the Ritz-Carlton leadership center, "the dress code at The Ritz-Carlton ensure that . . . the Ladies and Gentlemen of the Ritz-Carlton . . . maintain a professionalism and dignity in their appearance . . . [and] you never want to be a distraction to your customer." Although the hotel does not circulate its dress code to non-employees, the *Los Angeles Times* reported in 1996 that the Ritz-Carlton in Dana Point, Orange County, required "that hair be a 'natural color,'" forbade "beards and goatees, 'mutton chop' sideburns, dreadlocks, big hair (buns, twists or bangs higher than 3 inches from the top of the head), earrings larger than the size of a quarter, more than two rings on each hand, skirt lengths higher than 2 inches above the top of the knee and long fingernails." According to a manager at the Ritz-Carlton, the dress code is simply part of the luxury experience, like the furnishings: "Guests staying at the property are paying for a nice ambience. They're also paying for well-groomed people." Employees who don't make the grade are sent home—or out for a manicure and hair styling: "[W]e've made appointments for them in our beauty salon . . . if they refuse, they can be terminated. We're so strict, we have employees rat on other employees."

In the decades since the *Rogers* case, many employees have complained about workplace dress codes that forbid cornrows and other hairstyles. In 1986, Cheryl Tatum lost her job at a Hyatt hotel in Washington, D.C., because she refused to change an all-braided hairstyle that management deemed to violate a rule prohibiting "extreme and unusual hairstyles." In response, almost fifty women picketed the hotel and Black community leaders threatened a boycott. Hyatt and American Airlines were far from alone in banning such styles: the Washington, D.C., Metropolitan Police Department, the Atlanta Urban League, and Howard University Hospital all prohibited all-braided styles at the time.

Today, the all-braided hairstyle is commonplace and uncontroversial. But as fashions change, new hairstyles pose similar challenges and inspire new dress codes. Dreadlocks may be the early twenty-first century's version of cornrows: a style favored by a growing number of African Americans but seen as unconventional and even subversive by many people of other races. In 2013 Chastity Jones lost out on a job at an insurance claims company when she refused to change her dreadlock hairstyle to comply with a dress code requiring a "professional and businesslike image." She convinced the U.S. Equal Employment Opportunity Commission that the employer's rule was discriminatory, using an argument much like the one Renee Rogers had made: "dreadlocks," the EEOC insisted on Jones's behalf, "are a manner of wearing the hair that is physiologically and culturally associated with people of African descent . . . hairstyle can be a determinant of racial identity." But despite the EEOC's support, Jones lost: the Eleventh Circuit Court of Appeals held that although "we respect that intensely personal decision [to wear dreadlocks] and all it entails . . . [the EEOC] did not state a plausible claim that [the employer] intentionally discriminated against Ms. Jones because of her race."

It's not only employers that prohibit braids, dreadlocks, and other styles associated with racial identity: many schools do so as well. For instance, in 2013, seven-year-old Tiana Parker was sent home from the Deborah Brown Community School in Tulsa, Oklahoma, for wearing dreadlocks, in violation of a dress code that states, "hairstyles such as dreadlocks, afros, mohawks, and other faddish styles are unacceptable." The 2016 dress code for Butler Traditional High School in Kentucky banned "hair styles that are extreme, distracting or attention-getting" and specifically listed "dreadlocks, cornrolls (sic), twists," and "afros . . . more than 2 inches in length." In 2016 at Durham, North Carolina's School for Creative Studies, Black students were told to remove their African-inspired head wraps. And the Mystic Valley Regional Charter School near Boston insisted in 2017 that African American students Mya and Deanna Cook "fix" their long, braided hair to comply with a dress code that banned hair extensions.

In most circumstances, civil rights laws allow schools and employers to require "respectable" dress and grooming, as long as the rules are applied equally to everyone. In fact, the stricter the dress code, the more likely it is to be seen as evenhanded: an employer, like the Ritz-Carlton that makes almost everyone change their hair, is an equal opportunity stickler for style. But that may be changing: in 2019 the New York City Commission on Human Rights announced that it would protect "the rights of New Yorkers to maintain natural hair or hairstyles that are closely associated with their racial, ethnic or cultural identities," including a "natural hair, treated or untreated hairstyles such as locs, cornrows, twists, braids, Bantu knots, fades, Afros, and/or the right to keep hair in an uncut or untrimmed state." Later that same year, California passed the CROWN Act, which amends state civil rights laws to prohibit discrimination based on "traits historically associated with race, including . . . hair texture and protective hairstyles." If New York and California can start new trends in the law, as they do in fashion, a legal right to racially expressive coiffure may be coming soon to a town near you.

In the mid- and late twentieth century, the movement for racial justice was split between those who adopted a strategy of respectability and those who favored the tactics of rebelliousness. The use of respectable attire could be a challenge to racial stereotypes and a bold assertion of dignity. But it also could be seen as a sycophantic form

of status emulation in the classic Veblenian mode. By contrast, ethnically distinctive garb and grooming was a rejection of mainstream
norms, expressing racial activists' demand for equality and respect
on their own terms. But "radical chic" could also be self-indulgent
and naïve, romanticizing poverty and marginalization in the name of
combatting them. In this turbulent era, dress codes always had double meanings. As social justice struggles divided the nation, what
would become known as the politics of respectability would divide
advocates for racial justice.

Chapter Twelve

Sagging and Subordination

*Represent the Race! Don't Wear Sagging Pants,
Gang Colors, Hoodie Sweatshirts, or Decorative
Orthodontic Devices (aka Grillz)*

COMEDIAN BILL COSBY'S REMARKS AT THE 2004 NAACP'S 50TH Anniversary Commemoration of *Brown v. Board of Education* became infamous as an example of what has come to be known as the "politics of respectability." Cosby harangued the crowd with a "get-off-my-lawn"-style rant, attacking the attitudes, mannerisms, activities, names, and clothing of poor African Americans:

> People marched and were hit in the face with rocks to get an education and now . . . the lower economic . . . people are not holding their end in this deal. . . . [P]eople with their hat on backwards, pants down around the crack . . . she's got her dress all the way up to the crack . . . and got all kinds of needles and things going through her body. . . .With names like Shaniqua, Shaligua, Mohammed and all that crap and all them are in jail. . . .

To his many critics, Cosby came across as an uptight curmudgeon or worse—a calculating sell-out. Cosby's remarks came to symbolize everything that was wrong with the Black bourgeoisie: snobbish, judgmental, obsessed with the approval of whites, and eager to distance themselves from the less fortunate.

But Cosby's speech was only one of many similar exhortations. For instance, on August 7, 2011, Philadelphia mayor Michael Nutter addressed a predominantly Black audience at the Mount Carmel Baptist Church in the aftermath of a riot. He lamented that the rioters had "made shame on our race" and insisted:

> If you want . . . us to respect you . . . if you want folk to stop following you around in stores . . . if you want somebody to offer you a job . . . then stop acting like idiots and fools . . . take those doggone hoodies down . . . pull your pants up . . . and buy a belt because no one wants to see your underwear or the crack of your butt.

Members of the congregation joined in with a chant: "Buy a belt! Buy a belt!" Similarly, during a 2013 celebration of the 50th anniversary of the 1963 March on Washington, Black filmmaker Tyler Perry remarked, "I would be a fool to walk around with my pants around my ankles"—behavior that, he opined, would squander the sacrifices previous generations of Black people had made in the struggle for equality. In 2008, then-senator-and-presidential-hopeful Barack Obama told an audience of MTV viewers that "brothers should pull up their pants. You are walking by your mother, grandmother, your underwear is showing. . . . Come on. Some people might not want to see your underwear. I'm one of them."

Obama qualified his remarks by insisting that *outlawing* sagging pants would be a "waste of time." Some did not agree. In that same year, the police chief of Flint, Michigan, announced that "sagging" pants violated the city's disorderly conduct and indecent exposure ordinances—each offense punishable by up to a year in jail and up to $500 in fines. Flint was far from alone in criminalizing the scourge of sagging. In 2007, Delcambre, Louisiana, prohibited intentionally wearing trousers to show underwear. In 2008, Hahira, Georgia, banned wearing pants with the top below the waist so as to show skin or undergarments. In 2010, the city attorney of Albany, Georgia, reported that police had issued 187 citations and the city had collected $3,916 in fines in less than a year under a law that banned wearing pants or skirts more than three inches below the top of the hips. Opa-locka, Florida, banned sagging in 2010, and in 2011 the public transportation authority of Fort Worth, Texas, prohibited passengers from wearing pants that exposed their underwear or buttocks: "Pull-Em Up or Find Another Ride" read signs announcing the new policy. Also in 2011, the state of Florida banned sagging pants in public schools. The town of Wildwood, New Jersey, banned sagging pants from its boardwalk in 2013. And, in 2016, Timmonsville, South Carolina, threatened sagging pants scofflaws with up to a $600 fine.

Anti-sagging sentiment affected the administration of justice as well as the content of the law. In 2012 Alabama judge John Bush sentenced defendant LaMarcus Ramsey to three days in jail for wearing sagging pants during a judicial proceeding: "[Y]ou are in contempt of court because you showed your butt in court," admonished the judge, "when you get out [of jail] you can buy pants that fit, or at least get a belt to hold up your pants so your underwear doesn't show."

The American Civil Liberties Union has consistently opposed these dress codes. In reaction to an East Baton Rouge proposal to "end public exposure to baggy pants," the ACLU of Louisiana's executive director Marjorie Esman remarked that "instead of . . . fashion commentary . . . the Council should protect the rights of all people to . . . be judged by the 'content of their character' and not by their choice of clothing." She noted that the ban "targets young African-American men" and worried that "if the government can affect the height of someone's waistband, it can control other aspects of dress and personal appearance. Choice of clothing is a personal one . . . in which the government has no place." In reaction to a Terrebonne Parish, Louisiana, sagging pants ban, the ACLU insisted "to ban a particular clothing style would violate a liberty interest guaranteed under the 14th Amendment. The government does not . . . have the right to use clothing as a pretext to engage in otherwise unlawful stops of innocent people."

The use of the term "pretext" had important legal implications. The "pretext stop" is a notorious policing tactic, used to detain, interrogate, and search people based on vague suspicions—and too often these suspicions can be linked to race. Lacking a good reason to interfere, the unscrupulous officer will look for an excuse—a pretext—to justify the stop. To civil liberties advocates, sagging pants laws turned the wrong clothing into an excuse to harass otherwise innocent people and fish for evidence of a crime.

Sometimes, the wrong clothing can be that evidence itself; a sign of gang membership, which in turn can connect otherwise innocent actions or minor infractions to much more serious crimes. For instance, under California law, if members of rival gangs begin a "rumble" that ends in death, all of the members of both gangs may be prosecuted for murder under the theory that the death was a "natural and probable consequence" of the rumble they participated in. Gang membership is the link that ties a minor infraction—like a brawl—to a serious felony: a punch in the nose becomes a deadly provocation when the fist and the face belong to members of rival gangs. But gang members don't carry membership cards or keep membership rosters. Sometimes, clothing serves as proof of membership.

Take the case of rival California gangs the *Sureños* and the *Norteños*. Both are loose confederations of smaller local groups from, as their names suggest, southern and northern California respectively. Police and prosecutors have argued that gang members signal their affiliation by displaying various gang signs: distinctive tattoos and graffiti tags often incorporate regional references such as telephone area codes. Colors can have gang affiliations too: blue for the Crips and *Sureños,* and red for the Bloods and *Norteños.*

Prosecutors have also argued that sports jerseys and hats can be a sign of regional and gang affiliation: Oakland Raiders and San Francisco 49ers gear identified a *Norteño* while an L.A. Clippers jersey or a Dodgers cap might mark one as a *Sureño.* In my hometown of Fresno, the Fresno State Bulldogs football and basketball games have long been the hottest tickets in town and the Bulldog is a symbol of local pride. More recently, the Bulldog also became the symbol of one of the largest gangs in California: in 2013, the Fresno County district attorney estimated that the gang had as many as thirty thousand members. The Bulldog gang has adopted the team's jerseys, hats, and mascot insignia as their own. Like most gangs, the Bulldogs will pun-

ish anyone outside the gang who dares to wear "their" gear. Moreover, other gangs, such as the *Norteños* and *Sureños*, consider anyone
in Bulldogs regalia a potential enemy. As a consequence, wearing the
wrong team shirt in the wrong neighborhood can be dangerous. In
2003 Fresno State sophomore Lyndsay Hawthorne went for a run
in Atwater—seventy miles north of Fresno—when a car of *Sureños*
yelled at her about her Bulldogs shirt and shot at her feet, sending
sparks flying off the pavement. Stephen Maciel—a father of four with
no gang ties—was shot and killed by a Bulldogs gang member in 2011
for wearing a red Fresno State Bulldogs shirt. Local high schools
banned Fresno State clothing and soon had to extend the ban to include Georgetown Hoyas gear, which also features a bulldog. Some
schools have banned all clothing featuring a sports logo.

Prosecutors point to such clothing to show that a seemingly isolated criminal act was in fact part of much more serious gang activities. In 2015 *New York Times Magazine* reporter Daniel Alarcón
covered a gang conflict that ended in the death of a young man, Erick
Gomez, in Modesto, California, a small town about an hour north of
Fresno. The actual shooter had escaped capture and was believed to
have fled the country. Prosecutors put another man, Jesse Sebourn,
on trial for the murder. They argued that Sebourn set off a deadly
chain of events that led to the murder when he "tagged" or defaced a
mural that honored dead members of the *Norteño* gang. The prosecution claimed that a group of *Norteños* attacked Sebourn in retaliation
for tagging the mural; Sebourn then went out with a gang of *Sureños*
looking for revenge and one of them killed Gomez. But the prosecution couldn't prove that Sebourn was even present at the scene of
the crime: they needed to link Sebourn's defacing of the mural to a
murder that happened several hours later, perhaps without his direct
involvement. The theory of the case was that Sebourn, as a *Sureño*,
knew that tagging the mural was a declaration of war, "the equivalent
of firing a shot:" the death of one or more gang members was a natural and probable consequence of his defacing the mural. It followed,
by this logic, that Sebourn was as guilty of murder as if he had pulled
the trigger himself, prosecutors alleged.

At trial, prosecutors showed the jury numerous photos of Sebourn and his friends scowling at the camera, drinking malt liquor from the bottle and dressed in blue jerseys. They *looked* like gang members—a fact that was not legally relevant but would certainly influence a jury. Moreover, by wearing blue jerseys, they had marked themselves as *Sureños*—the gang responsible for the murder of Erick Gomez. The wrong clothes could send Jesse Sebourn to prison for murder.

Seabourn's defense attorney also used gang dress codes to show that his client was innocent. He showed the jury a photo of Seabourn and his six-year-old son, who was dressed in a *red* shirt and shorts. "Would someone who was a *Sureno* criminal street gang member . . . be taking photographs of his son wearing all red . . . ?" he asked the expert witness for the defense, former gang member and criminal defense consultant Dr. Jesse De La Cruz. "Of course not," De La Cruz replied. De La Cruz thought Sebourn and his friends were "pretenders. Poseurs." After the trial, one juror, who worked at a local Head Start program, told reporters that children as young as three years old refused to "sit on a blue square or use a red crayon" because of a parent's gang loyalties. She remembered when the young son of a *Sureño* "told her in tears that he wanted to give his mom a Valentine's Day card but was afraid if he made it red, he would get a spanking." A real *Sureño*, she concluded, would never even let his son wear red, much less take pictures of him like a proud father. Sebourn's trial had ended in a hung jury. Dress codes could make clothing evidence of guilt or proof of innocence.

"I am urging parents of black and Latino youngsters particularly not to let their children go out wearing hoodies." Television pundit Geraldo Rivera offered this helpful parenting advice on *Fox & Friends*—an unlikely medium through which to reach Black and Latino parents perhaps, but a good one through which to find a sympathetic audience for such remarks. "I think the hoodie is as much responsible for Trayvon Martin's death as George Zimmerman was." Trayvon Martin was a young African American who, in 2012, was shot and killed by a vigilante in Sanford, Florida. A neighborhood resident, George Zimmerman, thought Martin looked "suspicious" walking on a rainy night. Zimmerman followed Martin in his truck and called police, who advised him not to continue his pursuit, but Zimmerman, concerned that Martin would get away, got out of his truck to confront Martin and, shortly thereafter, shot and killed him. Zimmerman claimed he shot Martin in self-defense after Martin attacked him. But Martin had been unarmed and police investigating his death found no evidence that he had been involved in any crime. Martin's death caused a national outcry and renewed debates about gun violence, race, and vigilantism.

Trayvon Martin was wearing a hoodie when he died. And according to Rivera, that sweatshirt was a symbol of criminality:

> Every time you see someone sticking up a 7-Eleven, the kid's wearing a hoodie. Every time you see a mugging on a surveillance camera or they get the old lady in the alcove, it's a kid wearing a hoodie. You have to recognize that this whole stylizing yourself as a gangsta—people are going to perceive you as a menace. . . . [Martin was] an innocent kid. . . . But I bet you money, if he didn't have that hoodie on, that nutty neighborhood watch guy wouldn't have responded in that violent and aggressive way.

Rivera echoed the "respectability politics" of Bill Cosby but with much higher stakes: *a Black kid in a hoodie looks like a thug—no surprise he was treated like one.* But he also spoke as a concerned parent of a "dark skinned kid;" he had "yelled" at his own son because he believed hoodies and sagging jeans would make him a target for harassment. Perhaps this was simply posturing, but many Black and Latino parents had drawn similar conclusions. For instance, when young people in San Francisco's Mission District told *New York Times* reporter Daniel Alarcón that they would not wear red, the reporter first assumed that these kids belonged to a *Sureño* gang whose rivals wore red. But one of boys added, ruefully, "*my* Mom doesn't let me wear red, either." These boys weren't gang members engaged in symbolic warfare—they were kids with worried parents who were trying to keep them out of harm's way. And their parents certainly weren't bourgeois snobs trying to distance themselves from the lower classes—they were realists who understood that wearing the wrong clothes can be a matter of guilt or innocence and even of life or death.

Race and Respect

It is our expectation that students who select Morehouse do so because of the College's outstanding legacy of producing leaders. On the campus and at College-sponsored events and activities, students at Morehouse College will be expected to dress neatly and appropriately at all times.

Students who choose not to abide by this policy will be denied admission into class and various functions and services of the College if their manner of attire is inappropriate. Examples of inappropriate attire and/or appearance include but are not limited to:

1. No caps, do-rags and/or hoods in classrooms, the cafeteria, or other indoor venues. This policy item does not apply to headgear considered as a part of religious or cultural dress.

2. Sunglasses or "shades" are not to be worn in class or at formal programs, unless medical documentation is provided to support use.

3. Decorative orthodontic appliances (e.g. "grillz") be they permanent or removable, shall not be worn on the campus or at College-sponsored events.

4. Jeans at major programs such as, Opening Convocation, Commencement, Founder's Day or other programs dictating professional, business casual attire, semi-formal or formal attire.

5. Clothing with derogatory, offensive and/or lewd messages either in words or pictures.

6. Top and bottom coverings should be worn at all times. No bare feet in public venues.

7. No sagging—the wearing of one's pants or shorts low enough to reveal undergarments or secondary layers of clothing.

8. Pajamas shall not be worn while in public or in common areas of the College.

9. No wearing of clothing associated with women's garb (dresses, tops, tunics, purses, pumps, etc.) on the Morehouse campus or at College-sponsored events. . . .

Morehouse College boasts an illustrious group of alumni: activist and politician Julian Bond, Surgeon General David Satcher, filmmaker Spike Lee, actor Samuel L. Jackson, and, of course, the icon of the civil rights movement, Reverend Martin Luther King Jr. We can be certain that no one in MLK's graduating class of 1948 wore pajamas, high-heel pumps, or decorative orthodontic devices to lectures or campus events. But in 2009, the Morehouse dress code was a declaration of war. To its critics it was snobbish: "Morehouse is no longer a safe place for all black male intellectuals, but rather only open to those who can tie a Windsor knot and clasp cufflinks to suit jackets. . . . *[Author's note: cufflinks attach to shirt cuffs, not jackets.]* To promote the idea that to dress the part is as important as the standard of education is to mock the legacy of empowerment Morehouse has held fast to for so many decades." It was discriminatory: "Morehouse is instituting a de facto uniform that normalizes and privileges the upper-class, gender conforming, cissexual, heterosexual, black male who has an array of suits, neckties, slacks and other fixtures of that life . . . the administrators at Morehouse should be ashamed of themselves." It was repressive: "[O]nce you try to stop people's expression, everything that is unique about people is going to start to crumble, and you will produce robots. . . ." It was nothing less than a betrayal of the civil rights movement: "[T]he new dress-code policy . . . is a stunning retrenchment of the prophetic vision once made famous by Morehouse's most celebrated alumnus, Dr. Martin Luther King, Jr. . . . who prophesied the dawn of a political landscape where men would be judged . . . by the 'content of their character' rather than by the superficial trappings of color (or by extension, clothing.)"

Are dress codes the twenty-first-century's Jim Crow laws? To be sure, a strict dress code is an anachronism in a college or university setting. While many K–12 schools and many employers enforce dress codes, higher education is, for many, a privileged interlude between childhood and the working world when young people can experiment, free of parental constraint and professional responsibilities. After the countercultural upheavals of the 1960s, college students complained that the traditions and mores of the past were restrictive and chauvinistic. Most colleges and universities responded by abandoning many traditional rules: just as curfews and chaperoned dances gave way to coed dorms on campus and keggers on the fraternity house lawn, dress codes yielded to a new informality in attire.

Morehouse was an exception: one of a handful of colleges and universities that retained the discipline of conventional sartorial norms. Indeed, Morehouse was a holdout in a more important way: it was one of only four remaining all-men's colleges in the nation. One of the others, Hampden-Sydney, located near Richmond, Virginia, shares with Morehouse a focus on self-presentation: each student receives a copy of "To Manner Born to Manners Bred—A Hip-Pocket Guide to Etiquette for the Hampden-Sydney Man," which includes several pages of advice on attire, from blue blazers and seersucker suits to the more rarified domain of formal wear: *Dress trousers made of a family tartan can be very striking.* Not so long ago, many colleges and universities aspired to provide a holistic education, in which academic mastery was part of a larger process of acculturation. Not coincidentally, most of these colleges were all male: hence the hoary notion of the "Harvard Man" or "Princeton Man." Hampden-Sydney and Morehouse have retained this holism: they work to create a distinctive culture while most other schools have drifted toward a cosmopolitan careerism. These schools are defined by an ethos of bourgeois masculine virtue: Hampden-Sydney's code of conduct demands that every student "behave as a gentleman at all times," while Morehouse admonishes its students to live up to its "outstanding legacy of producing leaders" by behaving and dressing respectably.

In a sense, critics complaining that the Morehouse dress code was "exclusionary" were merely stating the obvious. As an all-men's college, Morehouse unapologetically excludes one half of the human race. As a historically Black college, it expressly tailors its offerings to a small minority of the remaining half. Its historical mission has been to further narrow that field to those men willing and able to become leaders of the Black community.

Of course, there was a more pointed objection to the Morehouse dress code: it was not just exclusive, but bigoted. Parts of the dress code seemed to be a response to the appearance on the Morehouse campus of a small but very visible group of cross-dressers (it's not clear if they were transgender or identified as women) who called themselves "the Plastics"—a reference to a clique of fashionable young women featured in the 2004 film *Mean Girls*. *Vibe* magazine picked up the allusion in an article titled "The Mean Girls of Morehouse," which describes "a subgroup of gender benders who rock make-up, Marc Jacobs tote bags, sky-high heels and Beyonce-style hair weaves." The article went viral and, to the chagrin of the administration, for fifteen or so minutes the "Mean Girls" became famous as the public face of Morehouse College. Morehouse's vice president for student services, William Bynum, fueled suspicions of bias when he remarked: "[W]e are talking about five students who are living a gay lifestyle that is leading them to dress in a way we do not expect in Morehouse men."

Bynum insisted that the dress code didn't target gay men: "Morehouse is completely supportive of our gay students. This [the dress code] isn't about them, but about all students." Morehouse had consulted the campus LGBTQ organization, "Safe Space @ Morehouse," before adopting the dress code. The co-president of Safe Space at the time said that, dress code aside, overall Morehouse was "more committed to equality for gay students than ever before; as an openly gay student, I feel privileged to have matriculated now." And even some of the more vocal opponents of the dress code conceded that it wasn't motivated by anti-gay prejudice: for instance, a Morehouse graduate who attacked the dress code as "a stunning retrenchment" and a "lazy attempt to shift the focus away from a failing administration," also said that "it is unfair to assume that the policy is directed toward gay men at large." Instead, he argued, it targeted "the subset of gay men who choose to express themselves in women's clothing."

Still, for those who saw transgender rights as the social justice struggle of the twenty-first century, the dress code was a betrayal of Morehouse's legacy of civil rights activism, and the dress code's prohibition of do-rags, caps, shades, and "grillz" seemed to many to reflect the mores of an out-of-touch bourgeoisie. Moreover, there was a philosophical conviction behind the opposition: that individual opportunity should depend on intrinsic virtue—not on surface appearance: a Morehouse student should be judged by the content of his character, not by the content of his closet.

The dress code did have its supporters. A columnist for the news website *The Root* argued that it was part of Morehouse's institutional mission: "[I]f saying 'anything goes' is a sign of progress, count me out. For the record, I'm a big fan of dress codes. . . . Yes the . . . [Mean Girls] of our community need places where they're free to be themselves, in all their glory. But Morehouse isn't obligated to be one of those places. . . ." For its defenders, the Morehouse dress code reflected the civil rights tradition of Sunday-best activism, exemplified by the elegant, Harvard-educated W. E. B. Du Bois and, of course, Martin Luther King Jr. Civil rights protestors sat in at lunch counters and marched in demonstrations dressed in their Sunday best. Their attire was a visual repudiation of racist stereotypes. By dressing to confound racist images of Black ignorance, sloth, and slovenliness, the well-dressed Black person used clothing to repudiate racism on the visual and visceral levels on which it operated.

My father wasn't a Morehouse graduate, but he might have sympathized with some parts of the school's dress code. An educator and social worker, he dedicated his life to reversing injustices and improving the lot of the unfortunate; an ordained minister of the Presbyterian church, he held himself (and, to my occasional chagrin, his children!) to the highest ethical and moral standards; a cosmopolitan university professor, he was open-minded and appreciative of many different ways of life. He trained as a tailor at a time when aspiring Black professionals typically learned a skilled trade, both as a mental discipline and as a fallback in the event racism denied them access to their chosen profession. He knew quality rags and was a natty dresser, and while he did not believe that clothes make the man, he did recognize that they reflect on him, for good or for ill. That— along with the fun of it and perhaps a little vanity (a trait I'm afraid I have inherited)—is why he wore a dress shirt, tie, and jacket to work every day, even in the often-withering heat of Fresno, California, and despite the decidedly more casual attire of all of his colleagues.

"It's 100 degrees out there—why are you wearing a jacket?" I would often ask.

His inevitable answer: "Because this is how a professional dresses for work."

"But none of the other professors wear a jacket. None of the other *deans* wear one either. I bet even the president of the university isn't wearing a jacket *today*," my mother might have added.

"That's their business. You can't let yourself be defined by what other people do," Dad would reply, his shift to the second person sig- naling that the statement was also an admonishment to his offspring within earshot.

The issue of race was not far beneath the surface of this conversa- tion. The 1970s was not an especially enlightened time when it came to race relations, and while Fresno was a long way from Birmingham, Alabama—where my father was born—some of the attitudes he en- countered at work were all too familiar. My father was the first Black dean at California State University, Fresno, and I am certain that— at least at first—many faculty and students did not let him forget it. He never complained, but it had to have been rough going for some while. That jacket and tie were armor—both protection and an as- sertion of status. Though he was on friendly terms with every jani- tor in the building, he could not afford to be mistaken for one. This was not something his white colleagues needed to worry about, and it may have played some role in his careful approach to his attire. Dad knew that clothing sends a message and he wasn't going to let the hot weather speak for him. But I think the most important motivation was more personal: he felt *himself* in a jacket and tie—the polished ensemble offered a comfort that outweighed the bodily inconveniences of intemperate climate (and it didn't hurt that the garment in question was a half-lined silk-and-linen sport jacket—more breathable and perhaps even cooler than the permanent-press, short-sleeved dress shirts that would reveal the damp underarms of many of his colleagues on a hot day).

My father was also a former community organizer, compatriot of *Rules for Radicals* author Saul Alinsky and intellectual disciple of E. Franklin Frazier. He would have hated Cosby's "Pound Cake speech." He had nothing but contempt for those who blamed the poor for their misfortunes: "We were poised to take advantage of the opportunities civil rights opened up. Many weren't so lucky," he often insisted. But, although he didn't think people should have to pull themselves up by their own bootstraps, he might have agreed that they should pull up their pants and put their best foot forward.

Morehouse continues in an older tradition, characteristic of Black colleges, in which colleges and universities aspired to provide a holistic education, including lessons in comportment, etiquette, and attire. Not so long ago, many colleges and universities aspired to provide a holistic education, in which academic mastery was part of a larger process of acculturation to refined norms of civility. Such training is necessarily controversial (although so is contemporary training in any area of humanistic study: literature, history, philosophy, or legal ethics), but it serves a purpose, *especially* for those students who have not been exposed to it before college. Critics of the Morehouse dress code understandably worried that it was elitist: it promoted a bourgeois ethos, that of *the Black male who has an array of suits, neckties, slacks, and other fixtures of that life.* But maybe that's the point: Morehouse required attire that some of its *students* were unfamiliar and uncomfortable with to make sure that all of its *graduates* would be familiar and comfortable with the written and unwritten dress codes of the professional world most of them aspired to enter.

In a sense, Morehouse has simply retained a type of cultural education that was once commonplace in higher education. For instance, in 1965, Yale University had a twenty-point dress code, recommending cotton trousers in white, cream, and solid blue, striped button-down shirts, and penny loafers, plus a dark-colored suit for formal occasions and a sport jacket and tie "when going on a date in a restaurant." It warned against "jackets with excessively elaborate designs or . . . that include flashy patterns" and advised students to choose sweaters with "a mixed yarn of charcoal, grey or olive" in an "orthodox style." It insisted that "a black . . . knit tie is essential."

Today, the most elite and exclusive institutions of higher learning in the nation—the Ivy League schools of New England and their few rivals in prestige, such as my own alma mater and employer, Stanford University—do not have such dress codes. They don't need them: the majority of their students come from privilege and understand its symbolism almost instinctively; they are, as Shakespeare put it centuries before Hampden-Sydney adopted the phrase, *to the manner born.* The few who are not can suffer when it's time to look for that first job. Every fall, during recruitment season, our students anxiously pace the halls outside conference rooms where elite law firms conduct interviews for coveted summer internships. Most look predictably sober and boring: precisely what is required. A few take small chances with personal flair, but well within the bounds of conservative good taste. But every year there are some who haven't quite refined their professional look to conform to the norms of the notoriously hidebound legal profession: they wear sideburns too long, a skirt that's too tight, a suit that's too shiny, a tie that's too loud. Having worked in Big Law, I know that these details can detract from an otherwise solid résumé. I made the mistake of wearing a double-breasted suit to work a few times as a first-year associate in a prominent San Francisco law firm. It was a nice, conservative suit, but still. . . . The partner in charge of my practice group commented a couple times that I was wearing "quite a suit, there." I got the hint and decided to save that suit for nights out on the town—or when *I* made partner. Even when an interviewer has the best of inclusive and egalitarian motivations, small transgressions of style can affect an all-important impression.

What are my obligations as an educator and mentor to these students? The reactions to the Morehouse dress code tell me all I need to know about how any advice, however well intentioned, would be received. I keep my mouth shut. But I worry that such reticence reflects its own elitism, smugger and more insidious than any restrictive dress code. Most of our students at Stanford grew up surrounded by professionals—they don't need instruction on professional norms. But we leave the few who might need it—those from "underprivileged backgrounds" and "underrepresented groups" who we congratulate ourselves for recruiting and admitting—to work out a lifetime's worth of knowledge on their own. By contrast, Morehouse, like most historically Black colleges, has made upward social mobility a central part of its institutional mission; it deliberately focuses on cultivation and socialization—things that many other schools take for granted. I have misgivings about some of the proscriptions contained in the Morehouse dress code—particularly those that concern gender identity—but I'm convinced that it is not simply bigoted and elitist. It seems an honest, if imperfect, effort to spare its students, who will suffer the unavoidable disadvantages of racism, the avoidable disadvantages that come with inappropriate attire and grooming.

A defining ideal of the civil rights movement is that we should be judged based on the content of our character instead of the color of our skin. Unfortunately, many judgments are based on fleeting first impressions and character is not as immediately apparent as skin color. People of color often never get the chance to demonstrate their fine manners, eloquent speech, upstanding morals, or encyclopedic knowledge. But we can all demonstrate a grasp of sartorial norms and a willingness to adhere to them. As any dress-for-success treatise will attest, this can make a big difference, even for people whose race gives them the benefit of the doubt. And for those laboring under racist contempt, it can turn a hopeless cause into a fighting chance. This is why dress and dress codes have been a surprisingly important part of the struggle for racial justice.

Today, many activists use "the politics of respectability" as a term of derision, synonymous with snobbery and contempt for the less

fortunate—the twenty-first-century's version of what Frazier criticized in the Black bourgeoisie of the mid-twentieth century. But that
is not how the author who coined the phrase understands it. Harvard
historian Evelyn Brooks Higginbotham first used the idea of respectability politics in her 1994 book, *Righteous Discontent: The Wom-
en's Movement in the Black Baptist Church, 1880–1920,* to describe
a fierce, uncompromising, and dignified political activism that compelled the respect of those who witnessed it. Higginbotham wrote
of civil rights activists who commanded respect by behaving—and
dressing—respectably. In an interview, she corrected widespread
misinterpretations of the politics of respectability:

> Imagine yourself back in the 1950s . . . you have to go through the
> back door. There's lynching. There's everything from the outside
> society that's telling you you are inferior and you are not worthy of
> respect. . . . Think of the Civil Rights marchers . . . .when they are
> walking in there you see them in their Sunday clothes but they're
> defying the laws aren't they? . . . When you see all these white thugs
> are coming and they're throwing coffee on them and cursing at
> them, the world looks at that and sees who is respectable. . . . They
> wanted to look clean cut because they wanted people to see them
> and say, "These are the respectable people. . . . Their cause is some-
> thing that we can identify with." . . . . [This was not about snobbery
> or a bid to be part of high society.] Do you think Fannie Lou Hamer
> had fancy clothes? They believed in the respectability of their lives.

The activist and philosopher Cornel West, who, unlike most of his
peers in activist circles and academia, typically wears a three-piece
suit and tie, made a similar point about the connection between attire
and self-respect:

> The Victorian three-piece suit—with a clock and chain at the
> vest—worn by W. E. B. Du Bois . . . dignified his sense of intellec-
> tual vocation. . . . [By contrast] the shabby clothing worn by most
> black intellectuals these days may be seen as symbolizing their

utter marginality behind the walls of academe and their sense of impotence in the wider world of American culture and politics.

In the spring of 2020, marches and protests for racial justice erupted nationwide in reaction to several horrific deaths suffered by African Americans at the hands of police that year. Most of the protests were organized over social media. Many had the character of almost spontaneous outpourings of rage and grief. Protesters from all walks of life and, notably, of all races, poured into the streets, both in the United States and worldwide, to demand racial equality, justice for the victims of police violence, and systemic change in policing. There was no dress code: people came as they were and the diversity of attire reflected the diversity of a rapidly growing movement; as the *Washington Post*'s style critic Robin Givhan put it, "[T]here is no cohesion in the look of the marching multitudes, which is part of the deep resonance of these images. Humanity is arrayed in its countless forms. No one is costumed to play the game of respectability politics."

But within a few weeks, that started to change. On June 4, 2020, many of those attending a demonstration in New York City in honor of George Floyd, who was killed by police earlier that year in Minneapolis, wore tailored suits and ties as a sign of respect. On June 14, a crowd supporting transgender African Americans—a group routinely mistreated by police—wore all white when they gathered in Brooklyn. And in Columbia, South Carolina, a group organized a June 14 march for racial justice in which protesters arrived "fully adorned in their Sunday Best" (**Insert, Image #13**). Perhaps one reason for these new dress codes was that activists wanted to demonstrate not only conviction but also the discipline required to coordinate a common mode of dress. While a lack of sartorial cohesion was a symbol of the breadth of the movement, it also suggested a lack of centralized organizing, which could undercut its long-term influence. Sociologist Zeynep Tufekci—who participated in and studied protest movements in Turkey—noted that decentralized protests organized quickly through social media haven't had the same impact as similar protests had had in the past, when organization was a more time-consuming and arduous task:

[T]he 1963 March on Washington . . . took 10 years of sustained movement-building to get to the point where you could even think about it and then it took six months of organizing. . . . [I]f you're a person in power, you look at that, and you're thinking, "If they can pull this off, they have logistics, they have organizational capacity, they have collective decision-making ability. . . ."

[By contrast, in the case of more recent protests organized on social media] it came together very quickly. You know it came from a Facebook post. . . . [I]t's not the same length of time and the same building of capacities as the 1963 march. While it looks the same, it's not signaling to the powerful the same thing because digital technologies . . . give us springs on our feet. . . . [But] that means when you need to do the next thing, you don't necessarily have the muscle.

There's no going back to an era before Facebook and Twitter, but perhaps the symbolism of a dress code could suggest the discipline and organization of the momentous social movements of the past.

The Sunday-best attire of the South Carolina march was hardly the sober bourgeois attire that characterized the activism of the 1960s: electric-blue, cherry-red, and dusty-rose suits replaced blue and gray; one young woman sported a hot-pink chiffon minidress and lime-green close-cropped hair instead of the prim skirt, pressed hair, and pearls worn by earlier activists, such as Anne Moody. The South Carolina march paid homage to the civil rights leaders of the past, but it was an expression of the present moment. As Eddie Eades, one of the organizers of the march, explained, "As a young African-American man, it was powerful to me to see a well-adorned person who had my skin color. To see how he carried himself, how he moved. . . . [I]n the history books one day . . . a young person may see it, as I once saw images from the civil rights movements, and say: 'This is who we are, and who we were.'" A new generation of African American activists used fashion to repudiate derogatory stereotypes and also to challenge the status of the "respectable" bourgeois by appropriating their status symbols: the transgression of vestimentary stereotypes signaled a refusal of social and political limitations.

Struggles for racial justice animated some of the most profound and influential political movements of the nineteenth and twentieth centuries. The inventive uses of dress and dress codes in those movements remade older status symbols, transformed the sartorial signs of power, and created new modes of shaping and expressing personality. Disfavored groups have used the evocative power of fashion to challenge social hierarchies and advance bold new visions of equality and justice. The dignified African American in Sunday best, the defiant *pachuco* in a flamboyant zoot suit, or the chic Black radical in a turtleneck sweater and leather coat all asserted themselves as representatives of communities demanding respect and fairness and as unique individuals. Self-fashioning was inseparable from the social and political function of attire: the personal was political. As the civil rights movement of the mid-twentieth century inspired new struggles for dignity, equality, and self-respect in the following decades, new dress codes revitalized cherished traditions and challenged older customs as never before.

Fashioning Personality: 1960–Present

The cultural upheavals of the 1960s radically changed the expectations, customs, and laws surrounding dress throughout the Western world. The counterculture of the 1960s introduced a host of new garments to day-to-day wardrobes: workwear in the form of denim and boots and vaguely exotic clothing derived from the real or imagined traditions of Asia, Africa, and the indigenous people of North America. In the last decades of the twentieth century, these styles moved from the fringe of the counterculture to the mainstream and, as a consequence, individual idiosyncrasy in attire was not only more acceptable than in the past, it was an expected demonstration of authenticity and sincerity.

Yet dress codes have persisted. They regulate the attire of millions of employees in restaurants, hotels, coffee shops, retail stores, investment banks, and law offices as well as that of high school students, airline passengers, and restaurant patrons. Moreover, unwritten dress codes are as prevalent and insidious as ever, from the blunt expectation that women "dress like women" as they are imagined in chauvinistic fantasy to the subtle strictures of Silicon Valley's reverse snobbery. Indeed, the absence of dress codes provides a greater justification for judgment based on attire: unconstrained clothing choices would seem to reflect only individual taste, judgment, and character. The dress codes of the late twentieth and early twenty-first centuries, whether written or unwritten, represent a clash between the familiar effort to use attire to mark status, sex, and power and the increasingly widespread and jealously guarded prerogative to express individual personality.

Part Four

Politics and Personality

Fashion is the armor to survive the reality of everyday life.

—BILL CUNNINGHAM

In order to be irreplaceable one must always be different.

—COCO CHANEL

Chapter Thirteen

How to Dress Like a Woman

*Your Personal Best: Teased, Curled, or Styled Hair,
Lipstick, Foundation, Eyeliner, Blush, Bunny Ears
and Satin Maillot, High Heels. Overdoing It: Bared
Clavicles, Yoga Pants, Miniskirts, "Smart" Jeans. In Re.
Ladies in the Law: Skirts, Nylons, Makeup, Nothing
Low-Cut, a Feminized Morning Suit*

CHANGING GENDER NORMS HAVE INSPIRED SOME OF THE most important developments in fashion—and some of the most aggressive uses of dress codes—throughout the twentieth century. Inspired by the feminist movement, women in the late twentieth century insisted on social, economic, and political prerogatives that had previously been reserved for men. Their attire reflected their newly earned freedoms: new styles reused and recombined older sartorial symbols with unprecedented creative license. The Western woman of the late twentieth century—be she wealthy socialite, up-and-coming young professional, or low-wage laborer—combined conventionally feminine and traditionally masculine garments, contemporary Western dress with items from Eastern cultures, the garb of ancient societies, and the imagined fashions of a fantasized future. Political liberation and self-assertion were inseparable: here too the personal was political, as the old feminist slogan asserts.

The sartorial liberation of women started with the form-fitting attire of the flapper and continued, in fits and starts, through the twentieth century, finding new momentum in the counterculture of the 1960s. The second wave of feminism that followed the pioneering efforts of women such as Amelia Bloomer and Elizabeth Cady Stanton extended the progressive-era themes of equality in employment, politics, and social life. At the same time, the sexual revolution carried on the Jazz Age emphasis on personal fulfillment and women's assertion of traditionally masculine social prerogatives. But the dress codes that these two aspects of the flapper ethos suggested were increasingly hard to reconcile: equality in work and politics seemed to require women to exhibit the understatement characteristic of men since the Great Masculine Renunciation, while sexual liberation suggested an assertive sensuality. As a consequence, with large numbers of women entering the workforce and demanding social and political equality, many faced contradictory demands and desires: social pressure to exhibit feminine vulnerability and sex appeal along with a professional imperative to demonstrate masculine assertiveness. For gender equality, this was three steps forward and two steps backward, in high heels. Women, at long last, had adopted some of the privileged sartorial vocabulary that had been reserved for men since the Great Masculine Renunciation, but they needed to emphasize whatever womanly characteristics remained in order to still convey a socially acceptable degree of femininity, much as flappers counterbalanced their short hair and tailored clothing with dramatic eye makeup and cupid's bow lipstick. In some ways, the demands of conspicuous decorative femininity, while less precise, were as pronounced as ever. And because the remaining feminine affectations were often exaggerated as compared to those of past generations, they also invited ancient criticisms of seductive feminine artifice.

Laws, workplace rules, and social customs codified these contradictions. Meanwhile, the restless creative energy of fashion—whether on the streets, in the shopping mall, or in the rarified salons of haute couture—made the gendered meaning of attire a moving target. Men and women alike resisted older strictures on both political and personal grounds: fashion had become a matter of both social justice and self-actualization. The resulting new dress codes established new styles and redefined older fashions, creating an ever-changing and often bewildering catalog of sartorial meaning. Women accepted, resisted, and negotiated these new dress codes in a wide variety of ways. But these new styles could never please everyone. The new feminine ideal—like the older one—was less a settled expectation than an excuse for continual and relentless regulation: women's wear, like women's work, was never done.

Dressing for Success

In the 1967 book *How to Dress for Success*, Hollywood columnist Joe Hyams and legendary film costume designer Edith Head—the creative mind behind the style of women such as Audrey Hepburn, Grace Kelly, Ginger Rogers, and Elizabeth Taylor—described both the employment market and the marriage market as fields of battle in a war between the sexes, where the right clothing was a woman's armor and secret weapon:

> No matter in which direction your strivings for success are pointed, what you wear and how you look can make the difference. . . . Your basic virtues, assets, attractions, talents and loving heart may be far and away superior. . . . Your family and friends may think you're the greatest thing since Eve—but Eve, remember, had an edge. She was one of kind, with no competition.

How to Dress for Success advised women on how to select clothing that flattered their figures, harmonized with the tastes of their mates or potential mates, exuded confidence while not upstaging their superiors, and matched their complexion and hair color. It warned against fads and flamboyance, whether at work or in social life:

> Extremism in make-up, hairdos, length of skirts or brilliance of color are likely to be frowned upon. The interviewer will think 'This one has just cooked too long—she's overdone in every way.' . . .

[W]hile the boys ogle the charms of Venus Unadorned in art galleries, night clubs and between the covers of some magazines, it's the covered girls rather than the Cover Girls they invariably marry.

The book counseled care and constant vigilance with respect to personal appearance. A subchapter titled "How to Hold on to that Husband" disapprovingly describes the scene at a resort hotel popular with honeymooning couples: "[A]ll the brides made their daytime appearance with their hair up in rollers . . . [giving] . . . the impression we'd just been invaded by Mars. An assortment of weird, unattractive, bubble-headed, ugly creatures was all over the place—and their poor, too-soon suffering spouses looked as frightened as the conquered males they were. . . .We wondered . . . whether [this phenomenon] has anything to do with the current divorce rate of three out of five marriages. . . ."

The overarching lesson of *How to Dress For Success* echoed the sentiment of cosmetics magnate Helena Rubinstein who once said, "There are no ugly women, only lazy ones"—a convenient motto for someone who made a fortune on women who worked diligently on their looks. According to *How to Dress For Success*, there were also no ugly men—only lazy wives. The chapter "How to Dress Your Family for Success" tells the reader that she must "take the responsibility for his [her husband's] wardrobe in your own hands. . . . Keep a constant check on the condition of his clothes as he drops them with abandon around the house. . . . If necessary, lay his clothes out each morning so you're sure things go together." Nor should this responsibility be cause for resentment; instead, wives should welcome the sloth and indifference of their husbands. "[H]is apathy about his clothes will stand you in good stead" the authors insist; while by contrast, the unfortunate woman who marries a rare "Dapper Dan" would have to worry about "how you can keep up with him and stop him from spending the entire family clothing budget on himself."

How to Dress for Success reflected the gendered expectations of the late twentieth century. Women must take scrupulous care to present themselves in just the right way: attractive but not too sexy; professional but not too stuffy; stylish but not overdone—always bearing in mind that each new circumstance requires a reassessment and recalibration of clothing choices. All of this must look effortless (find a way to style your hair without eating breakfast in rollers). Now rinse and repeat for the men in your life.

The dress codes of the working world changed dramatically in the decades following the publication of *How to Dress for Success,* but the challenges associated with clothing choices did not.

In February 2000, Harrah's Operating Co. adopted the "Beverage Department Image Transformation" program. The program included a new dress code, part of what the company called the "Personal Best" program. It required all bartenders to wear a uniform of black pants, vest, bow tie, and white shirt and to be "well groomed, appealing to the eye, be firm and body toned, and be comfortable with maintaining this look while wearing the specified uniform."

The dress code also contained a few other general guidelines:

Overall Guidelines (applied equally to male/female):

Appearance: Must maintain Personal Best image portrayed at time of hire.

Jewelry, if issued, must be worn. Otherwise, tasteful and simple jewelry is permitted; no large chokers, chains or bracelets.

No faddish hairstyles or unnatural colors are permitted.

And many gender-specific provisions:

Males:

Hair must not extend below top of shirt collar. Ponytails are prohibited.

Hands and fingernails must be clean and nails neatly trimmed at all times. No colored polish is permitted.

Eye and facial makeup is not permitted.

Shoes will be solid black leather or leather type with rubber (non-skid) soles.

Females:

Hair must be teased, curled, or styled every day you work. Hair must be worn down at all times. No exceptions.

Stockings are to be of nude or natural color consistent with employee's skin tone. No runs.

Nail polish can be clear, white, pink or red color only. No exotic nail art or length.

Shoes will be solid black leather or leather type with rubber (non-skid) soles.

Make up (face powder, blush and mascara) must be worn and applied neatly in complimentary colors. Lip color must be worn at all times.

Darlene Jespersen tended bar at Harrah's in Reno, Nevada. She had never worn makeup, either at work or in her free time. She felt makeup made her look like a "sex object" and a "clown," and she wasn't about to start wearing it after twenty exemplary, lipstick-free years on the job. Instead, she sued Harrah's, claiming that because only women were required to wear makeup, the dress code was a form of sex discrimination.

Title VII of the Civil Rights Act of 1964 prohibits sex discrimination in employment. In a strict sense of the term "discrimination," Harrah's dress code obviously qualifies: it required women and only women to wear makeup. But the Ninth Circuit Court of Appeals rejected Darlene Jespersen's claim—a decision that surprised many people, although few civil rights lawyers. The court was following legal precedent set decades earlier that makes an exception to employment discrimination laws for gendered dress codes. Jespersen was not the first woman to complain about sex-specific dress codes, nor was she the last—and it wasn't only women who complained about them. For instance, after complaints from customers about the "careless grooming of some company representatives," the National Cash Register Company—which, you may remember, banned flapper fashions back in the 1920s—issued the following dictum to its male employees: "Hair will be neatly trimmed and combed. The length of hair will taper down the back of the head and terminate above the collar. This eliminates the appearance of long hair." Unfortunately, the "appearance of long hair" was what employee Gerald Fagan wanted. "I wear my hair long . . . it is below the ears and below the collar in the back and styled in the vogue and fashion of the times in projection of my image of self and consistent with the consciousness of my peer group," he wrote in 1973 in connection with his sex-discrimination claim.

In the early years of Title VII litigation, courts had come to inconsistent conclusions about such dress codes. Some held that sex-specific dress codes were discriminatory. For instance, in 1971 an Ohio court held that the General Mills Company unlawfully discriminated by requiring men in a food processing plant to cut their hair short while it allowed women to wear hairnets to contain their long hair. In 1972 a California court held that although an employer was entitled to have different dress codes for different *jobs*, any dress code had to apply to everyone in a given job category, regardless of sex. But other courts thought it was just common sense to have different rules for different sexes and held that such dress codes are lawful as long as they didn't undermine equal employment opportunity. For instance, in 1972, a California court held that the employment discrimination law would not prohibit "general rules of employment . . . where the . . . economic effect upon the employee was nominal . . . merely because [a male employee] wishes to wear his hair longer than the company rules prescribe." Similarly, a court in Washington, D.C., opined in 1972 that the law prohibited only "outmoded and unjustifiable sex stereotypes . . . [which] had distinct employment opportunity disadvantages for one sex. . . . Congress by this Act did not give the federal court the task of deciding whether hair at the collar level or one-half inch below is [acceptable.]" Likewise, in 1972 a federal court in Georgia insisted:

> It is not unreasonable for an employer to expect differences in grooming between men and women—and such expectations are not indicative of [discriminatory] sexual treatment. . . . [If we were to hold otherwise] it must logically follow that men, if they choose, could not be prevented by the employer from wearing dresses to work if the employer permitted women to wear dresses. . . . This court . . . will not be party to . . . a ridiculous, unwarranted encroachment on . . . the right to prescribe reasonable grooming standards which take cognizance of societal mores.

The court in Gerald Fagan's dispute, like most federal courts from then on, shared this assessment—it rejected Fagan's claim. Ever since, it has been settled law that employers can impose sex-specific dress codes, provided they are not "demeaning" or "unequally burdensome" to one sex.

For instance, when San Francisco reporter Christine Craft was hired to host the nationally televised *CBS Sports Spectacular* "Women in Sports" segment in the late 1970s, management made her dye her hair blonde and wear heavy makeup; the new look was awkward and the segment was ultimately discontinued. And when in 1981 a St. Louis television station, KMBC, hired Craft to co-anchor the evening news, she told management upfront that she didn't want to go through another makeover. Nevertheless, KMBC hired image consultants to rework Craft's wardrobe and makeup. And when focus groups suggested that makeover was unsatisfactory, the station demoted her. Craft sued for sex discrimination, pointing out that none of her male counterparts were put through comparable makeovers or held to similar standards of physical appearance. Although the station had ordered men to lose weight, change hairstyles, switch eyeglasses for contact lenses, and wear better-fitting clothing, Craft was held to much tougher standards. For instance, an image consultant told Craft not to wear the same outfit more than once every three or four weeks; by contrast, men could wear the same suit twice in the same week with a different tie. According to the station, Craft was held to a higher standard because of the demands of audiences: "[V]iewers . . . criticize women more severely than men for their appearance on camera and . . . women's dress is more complex and demanding." According to KMBC this wasn't *their* fault: "[S]ociety has made it that way."

The federal court rejected Craft's claim, holding that "appearance regulations making distinctions on the basis of sex" are lawful, provided "the standards are reasonable and are enforced as to both sexes in an evenhanded manner. While we believe the record shows an overemphasis by KMBC on appearance, we are not the proper forum in which to debate . . . questions of substance versus image—in television journalism. . . . KMBC's appearance standards were shaped only by neutral professional and technical considerations and not by any stereotypical notions of female roles and images."

It's hard to escape the conclusion that such "neutral professional considerations" based on the gendered expectations of the general public often lead employers to embrace and enforce "stereotypical notions of female roles and images." In practice, if not in principle, the law often allows this, as it did in the case of Christine Craft. But there are limits. For instance, when the accounting firm of Price Waterhouse refused to promote Ann Hopkins, a promising and highly qualified candidate for partner, among the reasons the firm cited was her wardrobe. The partnership advised her to try again the next year and, in the meantime, to "walk more femininely, talk more femininely, dress more femininely, wear make-up, have her hair styled, and wear jewelry." Hopkins didn't think this de facto dress code was fair—in fact, she thought it would undermine her authority and make it harder for her to do her job. So she sued for sex discrimination and took her case all the way to the Supreme Court of the United States in 1989, inspiring a change in the law in the process. Justice Sandra

Day O'Connor—then the only woman on the court—pointed out that Price Waterhouse had demanded that Hopkins act out a gender stereotype in order to move up in her career. Worse yet, that gender stereotype was inconsistent with the prevailing norms of professionalism, authority, and competence. Hopkins was in a "Catch-22 bind": she had to confirm gender stereotypes to get the promotion but those same stereotypes would undermine her professional credibility with the coworkers and clients whom she needed to impress to succeed. Hopkins won her lawsuit in the Supreme Court. Her case prompted Congress to amend the Civil Rights Act in 1990 to strengthen civil rights protections. Justice O'Connor's opinion remains highly influential, both as an interpretation of the law and as a statement of the challenges faced by professional women.

Despite *Price Waterhouse v. Hopkins*, when a business deliberately sells sex appeal, employers can insist that employees look and dress the part. For instance, Hooters restaurant hires only female waitstaff, who have to dress in orange hot pants and skintight, low-cut tops. According to the company, "[T]he essence of our business is the Hooters Girl. . . . They audition for their roles and, once hired, they must maintain a glamourous appearance . . . to provide a unique Hooters experience." This is legally questionable. But the eroticized "Hooters Girl" has survived multiple complaints and an investigation by the federal Equal Employment Opportunity Commission.

Before Hooters, there were the Playboy clubs in the 1960s and 1970s. In 1963, a young Gloria Steinem wrote a damming exposé about her short stint as a Playboy Bunny, titled "A Bunny's Tale," describing her bunny uniform:

> She gave me a bright blue satin. It was so tight that the zipper caught my skin as she fastened the back. . . . The bottom was cut up so high that it left my hip bones exposed as well as a good five inches of untanned derriere. The boning on the waist would have made Scarlet O'Hara blanch, and the entire construction tended to push all available flesh up to the bosom. I was sure it would be perilous to bend over. . . . A blue satin band with matching Bunny

ears attached was fitted around my head like an enlarged bicycle clip, and a grapefruit-sized hemisphere of white fluff was attached to hooks at the costume's rear-most point. 'Okay baby . . . put on your high heels and go. . . .'

The Playboy clubs, needless to say, required women and only women to wear this uniform because it employed only women as "bunnies." The Playboy clubs established the following guidelines for ranking its female employees based on their appearance:

1. <u>A flawless</u> beauty (face, figure <u>and</u> grooming).
2. An exceptionally beautiful girl.
3. Marginal (is aging or has developed a <u>correctable</u> appearance problem).
4. Has lost Bunny Image (either through aging or an <u>uncorrectable</u> appearance problem).

These criteria became the subject of a civil rights lawsuit. In 1971, the New York State Division of Human Rights board noted that,

Playboy Bunnies picket to protest restrictive workplace rules.

because the Playboy Club basically sold sex appeal, "the restriction to females only of the eligibility for employment as a Bunny constitutes a bona fide occupational qualification and as such is exempt from [laws prohibiting sex discrimination in employment]." The board summarized the dispute and rendered its judgment as follows:

> The members of [the Playboy clubs] are attracted thereto, in large measure, by the allure of young and beautiful female employees who serve the patrons and who are called 'Bunnies.' By this exploitation of female youth and pulchritude respondents have made the employment of 'Bunnies' the cornerstone of its business. . . . Complainant's services were terminated . . . because . . . she did not meet acceptable standards in reference to physical proportions. . . . [I]n this respect she is being measured against standards of near perfection within her own sex. . . . Although it is this writer's opinion that a business . . . which is based upon the commercial exploitation of sex appeal and deliberately seeks so to titillate and entice has little to recommend its establishment or perpetuation, its existence is not in violation of the Human Rights Law.

The last of the original Playboy clubs closed its doors for good in 1988, but there have been several reboots: one in Las Vegas in 2006, which lasted for six years, and another in Manhattan in 2018. When Ms. Steinem was asked what she thought of these, she was characteristically resolute: "Playboy clubs were a parody of patriarchy." The Bunnies, she insisted, are "the gendered version of a minstrel show." Another famous former Playboy Bunny, Mary Laurence Hutton, adopted a shortened version of her middle name when she started work at the Playboy Club and went on to become one of fashion's first supermodels: Lauren Hutton. She had a comparatively blithe take on the return of the Playboy Club: "I'd like to point out it's a one-piece bathing suit," she said of the Bunny costume. "Nowadays in fact it's probably a pretty sober one-piece I guess for what's out there. And you're wearing ears, which is pretty funny."

The bunny's bathing suit, rabbit ears, shirt collar, and bow tie are an extreme, stylized example of gendered symbolism—eroticized femininity combined with decontextualized elements of traditional male attire that both call attention to its wearer's femininity and also titillatingly suggest the masculine prerogative of sexual license, in the classic mode of the female-to-male cross-dresser. It's an outfit shaped by very familiar, stereotypical notions of the female role and images, an outfit that "makes sense"—by which I mean one that is titillating rather than just bizarre—only because of the rich, complex symbolism that the fashion system has generated over the centuries. The Playboy Bunny reflected, in exaggerated form, the demands and constraints of the late-twentieth-century feminine ideal.

Well Heeled

The cover of my colleague Deborah Rhode's powerful polemic against the injustices of gendered standards of beauty, *The Beauty Bias*, consists of a black background, white text, and a silhouette of a single high-heeled shoe. High heels are so strongly associated with feminine artifice, sexual allure, erotic power, and patriarchal domination that they are as much an abstract icon as an article of clothing. They are text message emojis, indicators of female sex on public restrooms, and symbols of sexualized entertainment used on signs and in advertisements. As clothing, high heels are symbols of conventional femininity, required in many contexts by custom and express prescription. If any single item of clothing can contain the controversies, contradictions, pleasures, pain, and prejudice of gendered clothing, it is the high-heeled shoe.

In 2000, cocktail waitresses in Reno and Las Vegas carried signs that read "Hey Boss, Kiss My Foot" in protest against dress codes that required high-heeled shoes. "Why do women have to suffer physical pain for the visual pleasure of men?" demanded one cocktail waitress. Cocktail servers made similar protests in 2013 against the Mashantucket Pequot Tribe, owners of the Foxwoods casino in Connecticut, which required its cocktail waitresses to wear heels. The cocktail servers considered high heels a health hazard and some saw dress codes requiring them as a way to force out older employees, who were less able to endure the physical stress caused by those shoes: "Most of us girls have been here for 20 years, 15 years. This job has really done a number on our feet and they know it," complained one Fox-woods server. In defense against such protests and against litigation challenging high-heel dress codes as sex discrimination, some casinos have redefined the job itself to make sexy outfits an indispensable part of it. On the Vegas Strip, young women are now hired as *bevertainers*, echoing the rhetoric of the Playboy clubs of the 1970s: according to an exposé in *Slate*, "besides serving drinks, bevertainers . . . entertain by dancing and parading through the casino. Casinos believe that the new job descriptions will help them evade sex and age discrimination lawsuits because looking young and sexy is a legitimate job qualification. . . ."

Dress codes that require high heels apply to the rich and famous as well as to the working women of the hospitality industry. For instance, in 2015, several women were turned away from the Cannes Film Festival for wearing flat shoes in violation of the event's formal dress code. Many women were outraged, citing both the medical hazards of high-heeled shoes (one attendee complained that "even . . . older women who can't wear heels for medical reasons" were turned away) and the inequitable gender norms underlying the dress code. The following year at Cannes, several A-list actresses made a point of wearing flat shoes or even going barefoot. Actress Kristen Stewart captured the mood of protest, asking rhetorically, "[D]oes [a man] have to wear heels? . . . I get the black-tie thing but you should be able to do either version—flats or heels."

Outright defiance can work for Hollywood celebrities—after all, bare feet and evening wear are a cinematic combination as old as Anita Ekberg's fountain scene in *La Dolce Vita*—but for women living paycheck to paycheck, flouting the dress code is risky. Still, some run the risk and, occasionally, reap the rewards of their defiance. For instance, in 2016, British receptionist Nicola Thorp was sent home from work for wearing flat shoes. Her sensible footwear served her well as she walked the halls circulating a petition to prohibit dress codes that require high heels. More than 150,000 people signed the petition, which prompted a parliamentary committee to call for more "reasonable" workplace dress codes. The struggle against the hegemony of high heels has reached Tokyo, where women have rallied behind #KuToo—"a pun on the Japanese words for shoe (kutsu) and pain (kutsuu)." Like Nicola Thorp, Japanese actress Yumi Ishikawa submitted a petition calling for a law banning employer dress codes that require high heels.

How did high-heeled shoes become an established part of conventional feminine attire? Women's feet have, of course, been an object of aesthetic and erotic fascination in many eras and many cultures. The infamous practice of footbinding in Imperial China is an obligatory citation here, although it may have less in common with Western footwear fashions than some suggest. The origins of this ancient practice are uncertain: many historians speculate that it began as a way of guaranteeing the sexual fidelity of the emperor's thousands of wives and concubines by literally hobbling them; subsequently the practice became a status symbol and spread through the familiar process of status emulation. In any event, once it became established as a status symbol, it was remarkably persistent: when the Manchus overthrew the Ming dynasty in 1644 they tried to eradicate footbinding, issuing numerous decrees forbidding it, but the practice endured and was still common in the nineteenth century.

Another possible high-heel antecedent is the chopine—a vertiginous platform shoe first worn by Venetian courtesans and aristocratic women in the fifteenth century (**Insert, Image #14**). Some *chopines* were more than twenty inches high and required the wearer to be flanked with servants to help her walk, although contemporaneous etiquette treatises claimed that, with practice, a woman could learn to move gracefully and even dance while wearing them. In 1430, Venice limited the height of *chopines* to three inches by law, a dress code that was apparently widely ignored: *chopines* remained in fashion in Venice and in Spain until the seventeenth century.

While both footbinding and the *chopine* bear a superficial similarity to the high-heeled shoe, today's high heels are probably neither a variant of Chinese footbinding nor a descendant of the *chopine*. Instead they are an artifact of female-to-male cross-dressing that became a convention. High heels were a *masculine* fashion for centuries. The story of the high-heeled shoe involves the transformation of a practical shoe into, by turns, a status symbol, an icon of femininity, a fetish object, and, of course, a personal fashion statement.

According to Elizabeth Semmelhack, curator of the Bata Shoe Museum in Toronto, the original high-heeled shoe was a Persian riding shoe, meant to keep soldiers secure in their stirrups as they fought on horseback (**Insert, Image #15**). High-heeled Persians soldiers first visited Europe in 1599; their heeled shoes fascinated the European aristocracy and became a fashion craze.

Heeled shoes became a sign of both status and virility, so naturally they were emphasized and exaggerated: the aristocracy adopted higher and higher heels to outpace members of the lower classes. Moreover, the very impracticality of high heels made them a status symbol: cumbersome garments are a form of what Thorstein Veblen called conspicuous waste, a clear indication that one does not need to work—or, in extreme cases, even walk. King Louis XIV of France, only 5 feet, 4 inches tall, wore shoes with four-inch high heels. He emphasized his shoes by having their soles and heels tinted with red dye, which at the time was expensive and thus itself a sign of wealth (**Insert, Image #17**). A status symbol was born. Imitators soon followed: England's Charles II is pictured in conspicuous red heels in his 1661 coronation portrait, and by the 1670s the shoes were so popular that their high status was at risk: the Sun King declared that only members of his royal court would be allowed to wear shoes with red heels.

Daring women first adopted the masculine style as a provocation: high heels, like menswear generally, suggested a liberated woman who claimed masculine license for herself. The feminization of high heels began as women turned this masculine status symbol into an element in a feminine ensemble. The feminine high heel might have remained an aberration but for another, larger change in the cultural codes of dress: the Great Masculine Renunciation. With aristocracy under attack and new ideals of equality and industriousness in ascendancy, the symbols of the ancien régimes, such as showy, impractical fashions, became anachronistic. By the early eighteenth century, men in heels were considered risible. For instance, the English satirist and poet Alexander Pope threatened to expel from his gentlemen's club anyone who "shall wear the Heels of his shoes exceeding one inch and a half. . . . Go from among us, and be tall if you can!"

High heels became an exclusively and stereotypically feminine adornment. For moralists, they soon also became yet another example of feminine vanity, but in fact, the women who wore high heels often wore them for men—and in more than one sense. Women in fashionable high heels could show off wealth and privilege in a way that the sober, practical man of the Enlightenment no longer could do himself. The "trophy wife," then as now, was evidence of her husband's wealth. High heels became a status symbol through which a man showed off his wealth through a woman he supported. Also, high heels were sexy: they flattered by lengthening the visual line of the leg—as they had always done for men and women alike—and, because they required small careful steps and impeded forceful movements, they also suggested vulnerability, adding an erotic charge.

High-heeled shoes evolved into symbols of a rarified femininity that could look either virtuous and dutiful—like a Counter-Reformation-era nun's habit—or exotic and transgressive—like the jewelry that Friar Bernardino condemned as the sign of a prostitute. High heels belong exclusively to the female sex and so demonstrate adherence to gendered conventions of female propriety. But they are also fundamentally impractical and decorative, inviting the age-old condemnation of feminine vanity. Consequently, for every dress code that requires high heels, there is at least one that condemns them as frivolous and even perverse. Like the earrings of the fifteenth-century Italian Jew or the "vanities" of the early Renaissance woman, high heels have been both status symbols and signs of a debased, corrupt femininity. For instance, a *New York Times* opinion piece from 1871 complained,

the shoe worn by the young woman of the period is surely
one of the most abominable contrivances ever brought into
vogue. . . . [W]ith a toe like a bird's bill, and a heel three inches
high . . . there is hardly a young woman now who regards herself as
at all fashionable who has not bunions, callosities, corns and enlarged joints. . . . No degree of sense or independence, or stability
of character seems to absolve any woman . . . from slavery to fashion. Suffrage! Right to hold office! Show us first the woman who
has independence and sense and taste enough to . . . walk down
Fifth Avenue wearing . . . a shoe which does not destroy both her
comfort and her gait.

In the early twentieth century, dress codes proposed in Massachusetts and Utah would have banned shoes with heels higher than an
inch and a half. Utah, in 1921, considered a bill that provided for fines
of up to $1000 and up to one year in prison for anyone with high heels
in her possession. When shoemakers appeared before a Massachusetts legislative in 1921 to complain that the proposed Massachusetts
law would outlaw 60 percent of all women's shoes, representatives of
the Massachusetts Osteopathic Society responded that "the high heel
[is] the worst epidemic any country has ever known" and insisted that
"87 per cent of women's ills come from wearing high heels," echoing
earlier critiques of the corset. Worst of all, the president of the society insisted, "maternity is . . . affected." High-heeled shoes, it seemed,
threatened to destroy the very essence of virtuous femininity.

Even today, high heels still suggest feminine vanity, leading many
to condemn both the shoes and the women who wear them, just as
the moralists of the nineteenth century and Prohibition era did. For
instance, in 2013, Jorge Cortell, CEO of high-tech start-up Kanteron
Systems, surreptitiously photographed a woman wearing high-heeled
pumps at a conference and tweeted the photo along with the caption,
"These heels . . . WTF?" and "#brainsnotrequired." Cortell elaborated
in later missives, insisting that high-heeled shoes are "STUPID, bad
for your health," a symptom of the "superficiality of putting image
ahead of health" and anathema to "a culture that appreciates data, sci-

This portrait depicts Elizabeth Murray and Dido Elizabeth Belle. Dido, holding a basket of fruit, was the daughter of a British naval officer and a West Indian slave. Both women were the grandnieces of Lord Mansfield, Chief Justice of England and Wales and lived with him as young girls. Both wear sumptuous and fashionable gowns; Dido's is decidedly more exotic than Elizabeth's.

In 2020, racial justice activists in South Carolina demonstrated
against police violence "fully adorned in their Sunday Best,"
in homage to the civil rights leaders of the past.

The chopine, popular in Venice and on the Iberian Peninsula in the fifteenth century, was distinguished by a platform that could be as tall as twenty inches in height.

Today's high heels evolved from the heeled shoe worn by Persian mounted soldiers and introduced to Europe in the late fifteenth century.

High heels are now distinctively feminine and can also be an exclusive status symbol—Christian Louboutin is the only designer with the legal right to make such shoes with contrasting red soles.

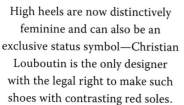

Louis XIV made the high-heeled shoe an elite status
symbol; he eventually decreed that only members
of his court could wear shoes with red heels.

Arizona senator Kyrsten Sinema stands out in her
unapologetically feminine styles, a stark contrast to an
older generation of professional women who needed
to wear more sober styles to be taken seriously.

President Mobutu of Zaire banned European fashions in favor of the *abacost*—short for *a bas le costume*, or "down with the suit."

After the end of the Mobutu regime, the *Sapeurs* of the
Congo revived Western fashions in dramatic style and are
now an indispensible presence at celebratory events.

Donald Trump flouts the norms of good taste with a poorly tied necktie, kept in place with Scotch tape.

ence, health, choices, improvement . . . not . . . superficiality." Many
women bristled at Cortell's remarks: "[S]o you see nothing wrong
with calling women stupid?" one demanded. Cortell's comments implied that women who wear high heels are either brainless, or at best
do not need a brain because they can exploit sex appeal to get ahead;
their stiletto heels were a weapon in the battle for career advantage, a
way to, as *The Atlantic* writer Megan Garber put it when interpreting
Cortell's tweet, "game a system based on meritocracy using . . .femi-
ninity." Coming from a man in a male-dominated industry, Cortell's
attack on high heels smacked of chauvinism. But much of it echoed
many feminists, who saw high heels as symptom and cause of wom-
en's subordination—an impractical encumbrance that undermined
women's autonomy and reinforced the perception of women as primarily decorative. For instance, in 2000 my colleague Deborah Rhode
wrote in the *New York Times* that the "women's shoe industry is the
last acceptable haven for misogynists," and described high heels as
"footwear that maims" and the "functional equivalent of footbinding," concluding that although "no one is forcing women to wear
[them] . . . such small indignities . . . get in the way of women's lives."
An understandable reaction from someone who has suffered the tyranny of the high heel for much of her professional life. But as Cortell's comments demonstrate, it's a fine line that separates a critique of
women's fashions from a critique of the women who wear them, and
few things make that line harder to walk than a pair of high heels.

The dress codes for high heels are still complicated. For every
woman who attacks high-heeled shoes as impractical, sexually provocative, or patriarchy on stilts, another sees them as chic, flattering, and
even empowering. For instance, in 2013, style consultant Chassie Post
replied to high-heel detractors: "I embrace the high heel in every form.
I would jog in them if I could. . . . I love the way they look, as well as the
way they make me feel: taller, sleeker and more powerful. . . . Heels not
only say 'chic,' but they provide polish and elevate the workplace wardrobe. . . . Footwear can be a powerful statement. . . ."

In any event, high heels seem as popular as ever, even among
women who can ignore just about any dress code. In 1992, the shoe

designer Christian Louboutin began using red soles on all of his wom-
en's shoes **(Insert, Image #16)**. It would be an understatement to say
that the shoes are popular: Louboutin was declared the most prestigious maker of women's shoes in the world by the Luxury Institute's
Luxury Brand Status Index in 2007, 2008, and 2009; today, his shoes sell
for over $600 a pair and the priciest can cost over $6,000. Fashionable
women rush to retail stores to buy his latest creations—sometimes in
multiple styles and colors. "These is red bottoms, these is blood shoes.
Hit the store, I can get 'em both, I don't wanna choose," intones Cardi B
about her spike-heeled Louboutins. The novelist Danielle Steel reportedly owns more than six thousand pairs of Louboutins, buying as many
as eighty at a time. Over the years, Louboutin has sued several rival
shoemakers who have produced shoes with red soles, arguing that red
shoe soles were its exclusive trademark, and in 2011 the U.S. Court of
Appeals for the Second Circuit held that Louboutin had an exclusive
right to produce women's shoes with contrasting red soles. More than
230 years after the sumptuary codes of Louis XIV and ancien régime
were repealed, the law still restricts who may buy and sell high-heeled
shoes with coveted red soles, ensuring their exclusivity and high status.

Fashion Victims

The ancient imperative to separate virtuous from fallen women still
defines today's dress codes, and many use it to justify obsessive control over women's bodies. While some dress codes punish women like
Darlene Jespersen and those who reject high heels for refusing sexual
objectification and decorativeness, equally potent rules and expectations demand feminine modesty. Modesty may seem the opposite of,
or even an antidote to, sexual objectification and decorativeness, but
in fact *both* dress codes require women to cater to the desires of men:
while the sexualized, decorative woman must make herself pleasing to
the eye, the modest woman is obliged to avoid drawing attention to herself. The demands of decorativeness and modesty are opposites sides of
a single patriarchal coin, which the modern woman must balance on its
edge.

•   •   •

In the nineteenth century, feet were erotic objects whose power to titillate surpassed the décolletage. According to historian Philippe Perrot, the foot was "at the heart of all male fixations, the spark that informed their desires, the anchor of all their fantasies." Hidden from view by dresses that skimmed the floor, women's shoes and feet became "the object of a universal, ardent and fanatical cult." The clever coquette danced along the boundary of propriety, lifting her skirts when sitting or dismounting from a carriage just enough to reveal "the tip of a dainty foot that attracts you . . . to the point of giving you an immoderate desire to see what is concealed . . . [and] very little need to be shown in order to suggest even more." By contrast, when too much was revealed, erotic tension was diminished and off-putting flaws became all too apparent: "[A] damsel . . . innocent and naïve, will . . . reveal her foot all the way to the ankle, without suspecting that the top of her boot may gape, that her stocking is creased. . . ." Ironically, dress codes that require modesty can eroticize the boundary between permissible and illicit, encouraging lust rather than preventing it. Concealment contains the timeless allure of forbidden fruit.

In the twenty-first century, the clavicle may have displaced the foot as the unlikely object of erotic interest and social taboo: in 2015, Stephanie Dunn was sent to the principal's office from Woodford County High School in Kentucky for wearing a shirt that exposed her collarbones. Earlier that year, Gabi Finlayson was stopped at the door of a dance at Lone Peak High School in Highland, Utah, because her calf-length, high-necked sleeveless dress—something Doris Day might have worn in a 1950s Hollywood comedy—did not have the regulation two-inch shoulder straps. When sixteen-year-old Florida student Miranda Larkin wore a skirt that administrators deemed too short for school, she was forced to don an oversized Day-Glo-yellow T-shirt emblazoned with the words "Dress Code Violator." In 2013, a Petaluma, California, junior high school held a special assembly for girls to announce a ban on yoga pants, leggings, and tight jeans.

Such rigid dress codes may seem like a throwback, but in fact they are more and more popular: in 2000, 46.7 percent of U.S. public schools enforced a "strict dress code"—by 2014, 58.5 percent did. And a growing number of schools take "strict" to a new level. For instance, in 2014, Tottenville High School in Staten Island implemented a new dress-for-success policy that prohibits hats, headbands, hoodies, sunglasses, tank tops, low-cut blouses, halter tops, and bare midriffs. On September 5, 2014, one hundred students were sent to the Dean's Office for dress code violations and then corralled in the school auditorium until their parents arrived with new clothing that satisfied the dress code. In the first two weeks, two hundred students were sent to detention for dress code violations.

Defenders of these strict dress codes insist that many adolescents test the boundaries of propriety by wearing what they know is inappropriate clothing. Some studies have suggested that dress codes can promote learning by prohibiting unnecessary distractions, and, like school uniforms, dress codes can help school administrators undermine gangs and cliques and reduce the social shaming that can surround status and body image. Even what seem to be unreasonably strict restrictions are often really attempts at clarity. Rules of thumb govern the length of skirts and shorts: for instance, the well-known "fingertip rule" dictates that such garments must extend to the fingertip when the student's arm is hanging at her side, fully outstretched, while the equally widely used "credit card rule" holds that shirts cannot be cut lower than the length of a credit card from the throat. Dress codes that require shirts to cover the collarbone may have a similar justification as a rule of thumb. Few have been aroused by the sight of a woman's collarbone, but perhaps that's not the point: as Scott Hawkins of Woodford County High School put it, "There's nothing magical about the collarbone itself . . . that's just a point of reference."

According to their defenders, even when strict school dress codes go beyond prohibiting the most scandalous attire, they teach students about the importance of presentable appearance and prepare them for an unforgiving work world. One of the most controversial of recent school dress codes may be understood in this light. Carlotta Outley Brown, principal of James Madison High School in Houston,

Texas, made headlines when she imposed a dress code on the *parents* of her students, banning hair rollers, leggings, pajamas, undershirts, and shower caps. Brown observed that adults who arrived on campus inappropriately dressed set a bad example for the children: "[Y]ou are your child's first teacher" she admonished in a letter to parents explaining the dress code, and "we want them to know what is appropriate and what is not appropriate. . . ." Outraged parents and bystanding commentators alike accused Brown of snobbery, insensitivity, "respectability politics," and even racism (many of the students at James Madison High School are Latino and Black—Brown herself is Black). A candidate for Houston City Councilor insisted that Brown should be fired, complaining, "Most of the parents likely cannot afford to comply with this dress code." The president of the Houston Federation of Teachers said the dress code was "classist," adding, "[T]his principal may have plenty of money and time to go to the hairdresser weekly and have her stuff done. Who are you to judge others who may not have the same opportunities. . . ." Brown stood firm, insisting that the dress code required effort—not ample finances. She pointed out that many of the parents would not wear the offending clothing "to church. If I could be very frank, [they would not wear such clothing] if they were going out on the town at night. . . . This is a professional place. . . . [Some attire that] is permissible in the home, with your family . . . [is] not permissible in the school setting." And the idea of a dress code for parents of school-age kids may be catching on: Tennessee state representative Antonio Parkinson sponsored legislation that would create a statewide dress code for parents of children in public schools: "There are parents who are showing up at schools with lingerie on . . . Imagine the teasing and bullying that comes with that," he said.

Of course, most schools limit their dress codes to the kids. Unfortunately, kids are especially vulnerable to anxiety about their bodies, which insensitively enforced dress codes can trigger and magnify. In the fall of 2018 while researching for this book, I spoke on a panel involving school dress codes in Washington, D.C. The panelists included a bright and engaging high school student who had been sent home several times for dress code violations, a school administrator for the Washington, D.C., public schools, an attorney from the National Women's Law Center, and an educator from a nonprofit organization dedicated to helping at-risk young women. The panel discussion centered on the publication of a report titled *Dress Coded*, which discussed the inequities in dress code enforcement: for instance, schools with a large percentage of Black students typically had the strictest dress codes and both the text of rules and the patterns of enforcement disproportionately targeted girls. Black girls fared worst of all, often facing racially discriminatory enforcement of already sex-specific rules regulating skirt length, cleavage, and yoga pants as well as blanket prohibitions of hairstyles and head coverings typically worn by Black women. The student panelist movingly described her experience as she entered puberty: already self-conscious about her changing body, she also had to contend with new, unwanted attention from school administrators who chastised her for wearing clothing that had drawn no attention just a few months earlier.

On paper, school dress codes can look both reasonable and even-handed: they apply to boys and girls alike and ban styles likely to be worn by each sex: for example, muscle shirts and offensive hats often worn by boys, along with short-shorts or low-cut tops typically favored by girls. Unfortunately, in practice, dress code enforcement almost always targets girls. For instance, roughly 90 percent of the two hundred students caught in the dress code dragnet at Tottenville High School were female. And this disparity isn't all that surprising given that many of the expressed rationales for high school dress codes assume female bodies are inherently distracting. For instance, Jim Bazen, principal of Plymouth Christian High School in Grand Rapids, Michigan, defended a dress code that focuses on girls as a way to keep them safe from boys: "[A] lot of bare skin . . . is a sexual distraction to the male . . . [and] leads him to treat women as sex objects. . . ." As if male libido were an uncontrollable force of nature, he blamed a litany of irresistible feminine temptations: "[E]xpecting the guys to keep their eyes off young ladies with shirts revealing their cleavage, shorts skirts, tight pants/leggings, shorty shorts or tight shirts is like walking out into the rain and expecting not to get wet. . . ." School administrators often insist that restrictive dress codes protect young women from predatory men, echoing the ancient belief that women are the source of all sin. Principal Bazen, for instance, implicitly blames women and girls for triggering the lust of men and boys: "[A] young man *may have no intention* [emphasis added] to lust, yet when an immodestly dressed girl passes him . . . he will think sexual thoughts." Accordingly, sexual harassment and objectification are not themselves misdeeds that should be kept in check by school rules but instead, following Augustinian dogma, the inevitable consequence of "man's total depravity . . . our once pure minds . . . corrupted by the fall." By this reasoning, women are to blame for original sin and morally responsible for ameliorating all of the sins that come thereafter: "[T]he only way you can help young men not to treat young ladies as sex objects is by telling the young ladies to cover up!"

High schools are far from the only places where women face scrutiny and censure for their clothing. In 2007, twenty-three-year-old Kyla Ebbert was told to "cover up" after boarding a Southwest flight from San Diego to Tucson. She was wearing a midriff sweater, scoop-necked T-shirt, and denim miniskirt. Just as the plane was about to taxi to the runway, a flight attendant insisted that she leave because her clothing was inappropriately revealing. Ebbert had no inkling that her attire was a problem until then: she had checked in for the flight, passed airport security, boarded in front of numerous Southwest employees, and passed flight attendants on the way to her seat. Humiliated and worried she would miss an important appointment, Ebbert covered up: after pulling the bottom of her skirt down and draping a blanket over her torso, she convinced the flight attendant that she was modest enough to stay on the plane. Later that same year a Southwest flight attendant chastised passenger Setera Qassim for her low-cut sundress (again, nothing too sexy for prime-time network TV), insisting that she cover up with an airline blanket or find another flight. In June 2012, Southwest employees stopped another young woman traveling from Las Vegas to New York, insisting that her dress was too low cut. Ironically, Southwest was shaming women for outfits less provocative than its *own uniforms* had been a few decades earlier. Southwest first made its name in aviation as the "love airline." In the 1970s the airline's advertising featured all-female flight attendants (Southwest eventually lost a discrimination lawsuit for excluding men from the position) wearing hot pants and go-go boots.

It's not as if these young women failed to meet the generally high standard of formality and elegance expected of airline passengers. Quite the opposite: slovenly dress, poor grooming, and lack of basic hygiene are all too common among airline travelers. For instance, in 2014, *Esquire*'s Max Berlinger noted with disapproval that some airline passengers remove their socks as soon as the plane pushes back from the gate, admonishing, "There was a time when men wore suits to fly. . . . While the glamour has worn off, the basic rules of civic behavior have not. Keep your socks on." Singing the same tune in fortissimo, *Slate*'s J. Bryan Lowder complained of "the cavalcade of pajama pants, tracksuits, nightgowns, painting rags and ill-fitting sweatshirts that one encounters in the world's terminals. . . . [P]ublic travel requires that we recognize that airplanes . . . are not extensions of our living rooms. . . ." Ultimately, though, *Esquire*, that bastion of sartorial refinement, threw in the hot towel: "There is no dignity left in air travel, so there is almost no compelling reason to try and look dignified."

Airlines tolerate this generally sorry state of sartorial affairs, but still single out women wearing miniskirts or bare midriffs. Why aren't the dress codes consistently enforced? Perhaps because the airlines don't actually have explicit rules about attire. For instance, Southwest vaguely prohibits "lewd, obscene or patently offensive" clothing. Similarly, before its merger with American Airlines, U.S. Airways banned "inappropriate attire." These vague dress codes effectively leave the regulation of attire to the discretion of individual employees, who in turn respond to complaints from other passengers, allowing the prejudice, jealousy, and petty resentments of individual employees and passengers to determine what is deemed "inappropriate" and who is singled out for shaming. These arbitrary, ad hoc airline decisions make high school dress codes look pretty good by contrast: at least the high schools provide students with some advance notice of what not to wear.

Strict dress codes that target women don't just encourage modesty: they define some types of clothing as immodest. When high schools ban yoga pants or bare clavicles, they aren't really reducing the amount of immodest attire; in a way they're *increasing* it, by sexualizing innocent clothing. Are yoga pants—the ubiquitous staple of soccer moms and their preadolescent daughters—really all that sexy? Do you think the typical airline passenger notices or cares that someone else is wearing a miniskirt while scrambling for overhead bin space? The real function of these dress codes is to insist that certain outfits are provocative, just as the moralists of the Renaissance insisted that "vanities" were the mark of the harlot. After all, there's no objective definition of provocative attire: it has changed dramatically over time. Consider the foot, the "heart of all male fixations" in the nineteenth century, which, as *Esquire*'s Max Berlinger ruefully notes, airline passengers now wantonly expose for all to see. *In olden days, a glimpse of stocking was looked on as something shocking,* as Cole Porter wrote. *Now, heaven knows* . . . it's collarbones and bare midriffs. That glimpse of stocking was shocking because it had always been kept under wraps: exposed to the light of day, it becomes mundane. The reverse is also often true—insist that those sexy collarbones must be covered for the sake of public morality and you just might encourage a clavicle fetish.

Modesty is, *by design,* always a moving target. Any group of women—no matter how they are dressed—can and will be divided into the virtuous and the sinful, the good girls and the bad girls (and because women carry the guilt of Eve's original sin, moralists will always find some bad ones). When high schools enforce overly strict, discriminatory dress codes, they're doing what schools know how to do best: they are *teaching* their students. They're teaching them that yoga pants aren't just casual attire—they're a sign of sin. They are teaching them by example to identify bad girls by what they wear and to treat those bad girls badly.

Crimes of Fashion

If clothing is a sign of vice and virtue, it's not surprising that judges and juries have blamed the victims of harassment, assault, and rape for wearing garments that supposedly enticed their assailants. Consider, for instance, the 1989 Florida trial of Steven Lamar Lord, accused of raping a young woman at knifepoint. The woman had been taken to a hospital shortly after the incident and treated for knife wounds. A physical examination proved that she and the defendant had had sexual intercourse. Another woman testified at trial that Lord had raped *her* at knifepoint in Georgia. But the victim's clothing—a miniskirt and high-heeled shoes—made this seemingly open-and-shut case into a case of "reasonable" doubt. After the jury acquitted Lord, the jury foreman explained: "We all felt she was asking for it, the way she was dressed." Lord later confessed to another rape, during which he told his victim while assaulting her: "It's your fault. You're wearing a skirt."

Sadly, this miscarriage of justice was not an aberration. Until the late 1970s and 1980s when states began to ban the tactic, defense attorneys in rape trials often introduced evidence of the victim's sex life or revealing clothing in order to suggest her loose morals, and jurors often assumed that immodestly dressed women enticed their attackers or simply ran an unnecessary risk—in other words, that they were "asking for it."

Indeed, sociological studies have revealed a widespread belief that women who are provocatively dressed or wearing heavy makeup are more likely to be raped or harassed. A 1991 study found that even professional psychiatrists believed that "revealing apparel does increase the risk of sex crimes against young females." In fact, provocative clothing does not increase the risk of sexual assault. As feminists have long insisted, rape is a crime of violence and aggression—not sexual desire. Rapists, like other criminals, look for vulnerable targets, not physically enticing ones. Indeed, to the limited extent clothing plays into it, *modest* attire seems more likely to draw the attention of sexual predators. A study of convicted rapists found that they were most likely to believe that women wearing "body-concealing clothing (i.e., high necklines, long pants and sleeves, multiple layers)" were passive and submissive and therefore easy targets for assault; by contrast, women in more revealing attire came across as assertive and more likely to fight back: "These results," the authors concluded, "conflict with the popular notion that females are at greatest risk when dressed in provocative, body revealing clothing." The idea that sexy clothing invites sexual assault is a myth. It is part of an unwritten dress code that blames women for the crimes of men. If sexy attire is risky, it's not because of the immutable nature of the male sex drive but because such stereotypes have made it into a justification for violence.

Thankfully, today's laws typically do not allow attorneys to point to a sexual assault victim's sexual conduct—or attire—to suggest consent. For instance, in response to the acquittal of Steven Lamar Lord, Florida banned evidence of a rape victim's "manner of dress . . . at the time of the offense" when used to show that the victim's attire "incited the sexual battery." A victim's attire is still admissible for other reasons; for instance, it may bolster or undermine a contested version of events: a garment that is difficult to remove easily may contradict a claim that the defendant undressed the victim quickly and without her assistance; a torn or soiled garment might support a claim that the assailant used force. This makes sense, but it also presents a risk that defense attorneys will look for excuses to introduce evidence of provocative attire under other pretexts, hoping to use social disapproval of immodesty to poison the opinion of juries.

Damned if You Wear It . . .

Ancient ideals of feminine decorativeness and feminine modesty still define respectable dress for women today. The woman who refuses decorativeness is belittled as unfeminine—a failed woman. The woman who rejects modesty is condemned as a tease, a temptress, or a slut—a fallen woman. These old norms collide with new demands as women seek social and political equality with men. To be seen as professional in a male-dominated enterprise, today's woman needs to renounce decorative attire—as men did centuries ago—but remain sufficiently decorative; she must adopt the form-fitting, tailored garments of industrious civic virtue while also retaining the traditionally feminine modesty characteristic of draped clothing. The dress codes controlling and defining women's attire express this ambivalence in language and in cloth, putting women in impossible double binds.

Sadly, this isn't just a matter of male chauvinism: some of the most withering criticisms of feminine attire come from other women, who, in opposing conventional notions of female beauty, can wind up enforcing a new, equally narrow, feminine ideal. Consider the dilemma of actress Emma Watson—Hermione Granger, to my twelve-year-old daughter—who has been such a successful advocate for the equality of the sexes that she is now a United Nations Goodwill Ambassador. Watson's considerable accomplishments as an actress and an activist didn't stop London radio host Julia Hartley-Brewer from belittling her on Twitter in 2017 because of a publicity photo in which Watson wore a revealing top: "Emma Watson: 'feminism, feminism . . . gender wage gap . . . why oh why am I not taken seriously . . . feminism . . . oh, and here are my tits!'"

Of course, male chauvinism is more commonplace. University of Exeter professor Francesca Stavrakopoulou, a historian with great expertise in ancient religion and the Hebrew Bible, faced similar criticism when she hosted a BBC television program titled *The Bible's Buried Secrets*. Television critic Tom Sutcliffe started his review of her show well, remarking that "it would be improper to mention . . . Stavrakopoulou's looks." But he then went on to mention them—indeed to obsess over them—describing Stavrakopoulou as "someone who looks as if she's shimmied out of one of the hottest passages of the Song of Solomon." In response, Stavrakopoulou noted such judgments about women's attire are all too common:

The implication is that . . . a woman who adopts a more feminine style is too preoccupied with pretty things to be a serious
academic, because a woman can't be both attractive and intelli-
gent. . . . [M]y heels are too high. My hair is too long. My smart
jeans are too modern. . . . I look too "glamorous," or too "feminine," to be an academic.

Stavrakopoulou recalled, "I've been criticized . . . by both men
and women . . . when it comes to my appearance. . . . [A] senior female professor suggested I should wear long skirts or looser trousers
and tie my hair back . . . because attendees would be able to concen-
trate . . . on what I was saying."

Were Stavrakopoulou's colleagues right? If she had worn less fashionable clothing, would potential critics have focused on her scholar-
ship instead of her physique? Two years before Stavrakopoulou was
deemed too sexy for prime-time TV, Mary Beard, a professor of classics at the University of Cambridge and an expert on ancient Rome,
appeared on the BBC in a program titled *Meet the Romans*. Unlike
Stavrakopoulou, Beard eschews any hint of feminine glamor:

I don't wear make-up . . . I don't dye my hair. . . . I'm every inch the
57-year old wife, mum and academic, half proud of her wrinkles,
her crow's feet, even her hunched shoulders from all those mis-
spent years poring over a library desk. . . . Like the great Greek
philosopher [Socrates] I look a mess. But if you took the trouble
to listen to him, he had something valuable to impart . . . [and] at a
lower level that analogy could apply to me.

Professor Beard had avoided the traps of sexy shoes and designer
jeans. Free of the distractions of feminine adornment, did people ignore her attire and focus on her ideas? To the contrary, television
critic A. A. Gill found Beard's unassuming, dressed-down appearance
a distraction: "[F]or someone who looks this closely at the past, it is
strange she hasn't had a closer look at herself. . . . The hair is a disas-
ter, the outfit an embarrassment. This isn't sexist," Gill insisted. "If

you're going to invite yourself into the front rooms of the living, then you need to make an effort."

Of course, it's possible that Beard *did* make an effort, that she internalized the kind of advice that Francesca Stavrakopoulou received and eliminated any hint of feminine vanity from her appearance. Or maybe, having experienced the can't-win scenario of women's professional dress, she long ago gave up trying to satisfy the contradictory demands of sexist men. Gill's statement—along with the diametrically opposed criticism that Stavrakopoulou faced in an almost-identical context—is proof that it's sexism that causes sexists to attack, harass, and belittle women and not sexy shoes, long shiny hair, bared clavicles, or low-cut blouses. When it comes to sexist dress codes, there is no "right" way for women to dress, only a lot of wrong ways, each of which provide an ever-ready supply of excuses to belittle and attack women.

Law Suits

One might think that lawyers, ever sensitive to the demands of justice and the threat of litigation, would avoid putting women in the double binds of gendered dress codes. Alas, the legal profession may be among the most intolerant when it comes to feminine attire. Female attorneys face all of the stringent and contradictory demands that confront any contemporary woman, in addition to the time-honored sartorial demands of a hidebound guild, all expounded with the unimpeachable authority of the law.

The Solicitor General—the lawyer who represents the interests of the federal government in the United States Supreme Court—must wear a distinctive and archaic ensemble when presenting oral arguments to the court. With one notable exception, to which I will turn shortly, every Solicitor General since the early 1800s has worn a morning coat—a cut-away coat with tails—with striped pants, vest, and ascot. According to the archives of the Supreme Court, the tradition began at a time when *all* attorneys arguing before the court wore formal attire as a matter of custom and respect. Woe betide the hapless advocate who failed to do so. When Senator George Wharton Pepper arrived to argue before the court in 1890 wearing "street clothes," Justice Horace Gray reportedly exclaimed, "Who is that beast who dares to come in here with a gray coat?" Pepper was refused entry until he returned in a morning coat.

Today, most attorneys who argue before the Supreme Court wear everyday business suits, but the Solicitor General and his or her staff carry on the older tradition and wear morning suits. The morning suit—as its name implies—is simply a variant of men's formal wear worn during the daylight hours (the more familiar black tie and tails being reserved for evenings). Today, of course, for the increasingly few people who have occasion to wear it, "formal" wear means a black or midnight-blue dinner suit with contrasting silk or grosgrain lapels and trouser side-seam stripe—what Americans call a "tuxedo." Strictly speaking, the tuxedo is semi-formal wear, a dressed-down version of tie and tails, once considered suitable only for more relaxed events at a private home (*Downton Abbey* fans might recall an episode when the Dowager Countess remarked disapprovingly on Lord Grantham's "pajamas" when he arrived for the evening meal in a semi-formal dinner suit, his formal wear having been misplaced by his valet). The morning coat is now a distinctive costume because fashions have changed and it has not—in this latter respect it is much like the nun's habits that began as copies of the modest attire of married women. All of this is to say that the Solicitor General's morning coat is a notable aristocratic anachronism, ensconced in a judicial system that imagines itself the guardian of the world's exemplary Constitutional democracy.

The sartorial traditions of the Anglo-American courts were established during an era when the legal profession was an exclusive boys' club. The morning coat, the bench wig, and even the judge's black robe were menswear. However affected and costume-like they look when worn by men today, they are an even more awkward fit for women. So, when a young lawyer named Elena Kagan became the first female Solicitor General in 2010, there was widespread concern and consternation surrounding her options for professional attire. Would she wear the morning coat? A lot was at stake because jurists in the Anglo-American tradition are often unforgiving when it comes to sartorial etiquette, as demonstrated by the English custom that barristers who fail to wear a bench wig are not "seen" by the judge and by Justice Horace Gray's outrage over the affrontery of a lawyer wearing a gray coat. Columbia Law School professor Patricia Williams recounted another example that was even more germane to Kagan's predicament. During the Clinton administration, a female deputy from the Solicitor General's office once eschewed the masculine morning suit and wore a "dove-brown" or "doe-beige" business suit when she appeared before the Supreme Court. Observers reported that Chief Justice William Rehnquist chastised her in open court for her attire and later sent an angry letter to the Solicitor General's office in which he demanded that such a breach of decorum not be repeated. In response, the office recommended that its female attorneys appear before the Rehnquist court in a "feminized" version of the traditional morning suit.

What exactly is a feminized version of the morning suit? Professor Williams speculated that it would be "more or less like the men's version, only with darts at the bust line . . . and instead of the classic striped charcoal trousers, a neo-classical striped charcoal skirt. Open question whether the same requires a Windsor-knotted tie with stretched winged collar." *Slate*'s legal commentator Dahlia Lithwick tackled the larger dilemma confronting Solicitor General Kagan, noting that, in historical terms, "the female equivalent to the morning coat is either an off-the-shoulder ball gown or a mother-of the-bride pastel confection." The problem for Kagan was that the morning suit became professional attire because it was the formal *masculine* attire of its era. It symbolized the virtues of sober judgment and industriousness that inspired the Great Masculine Renunciation. An indispensable part of the symbolism of masculine attire lies in the contrast with its opposite—feminine attire—which came to symbolize much of what the Masculine Renunciation renounced: ornamentation, display, fantasy, and vanity surrounding the physical body. The morning suit itself is unmistakably masculine and as a consequence, any woman who adopts it will unavoidably come off as if dressed in provocative drag, like Marlene Dietrich in the film *Morocco*. The symbolism of the morning suit is unmistakably masculine *by design*. There can be no feminine equivalent. As Lithwick points out, the feminine formal wear of the contemporaneous era is the symbolic opposite of the suit, as unsuitable to a courtroom appearance as the Chevalier d'Éon's full skirts were to a swordfight. Lithwick concluded that "Kagan should resist the impulse to don anything that suggests she is either a woman doing a man's job, or dashing off to a cotillion." For a woman, respecting tradition isn't an option when the tradition in question involves the exclusion of women. Kagan apparently agreed and wore a typical women's business suit as Solicitor General. Today, she has found a solution to the problem of traditional professional attire: as an Associate Justice of the Supreme Court, she wears a unisex black robe.

Or is that black robe really unisex? Associate Justice Ruth Bader Ginsburg told C-SPAN in 2009 that the standard judicial robe "is made for a man, because it has a place for the shirt to show, and the tie. So, Sandra Day O'Connor [the first woman to sit on the Supreme Court] and I thought it would be appropriate if we included, as part of our robe, something typical of a woman." Justice Ginsburg's lace collars, cravats, and jabots are now legendary among followers of the Supreme Court. She had an extensive collection, including a luxurious white beaded collar from South Africa, a colorful collar of blue and gold beads, and several white lace collars. She reserved a special austere black-and-gold collar for when she dissented from an opinion of the Court and another, more celebratory, gold-lace collar for when she read a majority opinion. Fans sent Justice Ginsburg handmade collars, her clerks gave her collars to commemorate their service together, and she purchased many as mementos and souvenirs herself. Like everything that concerns the nation's high court, Justice Ginsburg's fashion sense became the subject of ideological disputation: conservative attorney Ed Whelan accused the justice of "reinforcing sexist stereotypes" by drawing attention to her gender with

Supreme Court Justice Ruth Bader
Ginsburg in one of the collars she
wore to personalize and feminize
the traditional black robe.

her distinctive collars. For her own part, Justice Ginsburg wore her
"dissent" collar the day after Donald Trump, who infamously insisted
that women should "dress like women," was elected president of the
United States.

The morning suit was a safe uniform for male Solicitors General:
cumbersome and anachronistic but, because it was required, guaranteed to be appropriate. Elena Kagan had to blaze her own trail. Similarly, male lawyers always have available to them the tried-and-true
navy or charcoal suit, whereas women, by contrast, are faced with a
range of options, each and every one of which someone can object
to. Hence, dress codes, style guidelines, and wardrobe rules for female lawyers and aspiring lawyers, offering advice that could have
been taken from Edith Head's *How to Dress for Success* book. For

instance, in 2010 the Chicago Bar Association held a "What Not to Wear Fashion Show" in which, according to *Slate* reporter Amanda Hess, "a group of judges, law professors, and law students . . . nitpicked (mostly) female courtroom fashions." At another Bar Association event, "[A] panel of judges and lawyers convened to gripe about all of the sexy ladies in their midst. . . . Judge A. Benjamin Goldgar of the United States Bankruptcy Court for the Northern District of Illinois explained that female lawyers dressing too sexily is a 'huge problem . . . you don't dress for court as if it's Saturday night. . . .'" According to the legal news website *Above the Law*, in 2011, Duke Law School's Career and Professional Development Center cosponsored an event with the Women Law Students Association called "What Not to Wear: Interview Edition." The advice included the following:

Blouse:

A few rules: 1) never, ever, ever should it be low cut; 2) we meant that; 3) watch out for bows and ties, they usually look messy; 4) no wrinkles; 5) not low cut.

Makeup:

You really do need to wear makeup. Sorry. Keep your makeup understated and neutral. Eye shadow is okay, but don't wear too much. . . .

Hair/Other Grooming Misc.:

We like Deborah Lippmann nail polish and Sally Hanson's nail stickers. . . .

In 2012, *Above the Law* featured an interview with New York University professor Anna Akbari, who offered female law students helpful tips on how to score a coveted summer internship with a large law firm. Women, she insisted, need to dress to impress . . . men: "In male-dominated fields like law, skirts or dresses are particularly rewarded, as they are more appealing to men. In interview situations in particular, women should always wear a skirt or dress, as it is heavily favored by interviewers (many of whom are men.)" As for shoes, women should not wear heels "over 3.5 inches" but also must "avoid flats, except in emergencies. They do nothing for your stature or outfit, and they are some of the least powerful footwear you can wear." In 2014 the director of externships at Loyola Law School in Los Angeles admonished female students, "I really don't need to mention that cleavage and stiletto heels are not appropriate office wear. . . . Yet, I'm getting complaints from supervisors." Meanwhile, echoing Duke's "What Not to Wear" seminar, Professor Akbari insisted that women should "[w]ear at least a little bit of makeup. Studies have proven that women in makeup are rewarded in the workplace and perceived as more competent."

In response to the objection that such dress codes are out of date, a professional style consultant conceded, "[N]o one born after 1950 will have a problem with [pantsuits]. However . . . you're not always being interviewed by people who were born after 1950. . . . [W]e heard a story . . . of a blind judge who would make his clerks tell him when women lawyers were wearing pantsuits. And THAT is why we will always wear a skirt. . . . " Similarly, an article on the feminist website *Jezebel* complained that these dress codes were outdated and demeaning to women, but grudgingly conceded they were probably sound career advice: "[W]omen who don't dress the part might not land the job. . . ."

Meanwhile, some judges think women have it too *easy*. In 2013, Tennessee circuit judge Royce Taylor complained that "judges . . . weren't holding women to the same standard as the men. . . ." and issued a new dress code for his courtroom to eliminate such transgressions as miniskirts, revealing blouses, and sweatpants. It's true that women lawyers have greater freedom in their choice of attire than men, who are restricted by long-standing custom to the conventional suit and tie. But as a consequence, women are relentlessly judged on their choices—not only by judges but also by law firm partners, senior associates, mailroom clerks, and random men on the street. Women attorneys must wear skirts and heels, as long as the skirts are not too short and the heels not too high. They must wear makeup to please men, but also be sure not to look as if they are trying to please men. The good news is that anyone who can suss out and master all of these convoluted implicit rules should have no trouble at all with the intricacies of the law.

People will probably always judge each other based on their attire. In fact, because we dress to express ourselves, in a sense, we all invite judgment—we just prefer it to be positive in nature. Still, the judgment that often attaches to women's clothing is different: it is more unsparing, relentless, hypocritical, contradictory, and, worst of all, moralistic. But a growing number of women are unapologetically bringing the rich array of feminine styles to modern workplaces and the halls of power. For instance, in 2017, Democratic congresswomen organized a protest against a dress code that banned sleeveless outfits from parts of the Capitol building, and Arizona senator Kyrsten Sinema has become a fashion icon for wearing bright patterns, bold jewelry, stiletto heels, and form-fitting—and often sleeveless—dresses where most women feel the need to wear "solid neutral, structured sheath dresses and shapeless trousers" to be taken seriously (**Insert, Image #18**). As was true in the 1920s, fashion may provide a way forward to greater equality where ideological argument has failed.

While doing research for this book, I talked with *New York Times* chief fashion critic Vanessa Friedman at that newspaper's Manhattan offices. I couldn't help but notice that she was one of only a few women present. It was a cold, wet February morning and she was dressed casually but chicly in all black, with stylish motorcycle boots, a turtleneck, and a long skirt; a deft blend of fashion-insider chic and no-nonsense reporter's working garb. I asked her about the challenges facing working women, anticipating the insights of an expert on the rag trade and a woman in what is still a man's profession. Friedman offered a cautiously hopeful perspective:

Go through a history of what women were supposed to wear. [In
the 1940s and 1950s] they had to wear dresses and pumps and
pearls. . . . And then when they were in more traditionally male
roles . . . in the 1980s the power suit came in and there was the
idea that you needed the broad shoulders . . . [and] you needed
essentially to adopt a male uniform, but for a woman. . . . You
could wear a bright color, but you had to have a jacket; you could
wear a skirt, but not a sexy skirt. More recently . . . women . . .
are more willing to wear a classically feminine or softer style . . . a
less armored style and don't feel like that is ceding power in any
way. Marissa Mayer, when she was running Yahoo!, wore cardi-
gans and floral Oscar de la Renta skirts or Michelle Obama pretty
much always wore a dress when prior to her, first ladies always
wore a skirt suit. . . . I think that's helped open up a sense of what
women can wear as they start to feel more comfortable in their
own power positions and become more willing to define themselves according to what they want as opposed to what they think
will show men that they can be as good as them.

Dress codes in the late twentieth century perpetuated the age-old
strictures that have limited women's political, social, and sexual liberties by prescribing and proscribing their attire. Today, a dizzying and
conflicting array of rules governing that attire ultimately seek not so
much a single restrictive feminine ideal but rather a relentless state of
oversight—a set of commandments that change as soon as they are
satisfied. At the same time, fashion offers endless opportunities for
resistance and the subversive recycling of old symbols for new purposes, which in turn inspires a new generation of dress codes.

Chapter Fourteen

Recoding Gender

Clothing Not Belonging to Your Sex: Prom Night
Tuxedoes, Blue (or Pink) for Boys, Pink (or Blue)
for Girls, Miniskirts, Tutus, and Tailored Suits

THE ANCIENT PURPOSE OF DRESS AND DRESS CODES WAS TO make social status an extension of the body itself. Gender is the most fundamental and enduring of all social statuses, linking the biological function in sexual reproduction to a bundle of social roles. But in recent years, new technologies have made reproductive functions mutable and changes in social norms have challenged older gender roles. Women have been freed by medical advances and by changing mores from the demands of pregnancy and childcare to pursue careers outside the home. Men, displaced from the formerly exclusive roles of breadwinner and denied the exclusive privileges their fathers enjoyed, are also liberated to explore interests that might have been off-limits to their fathers. The new dress codes of the twenty-first century both reflect and resist these changes in gender roles.

Aniya Wolf of Harrisburg, Pennsylvania, found a conservative ensemble to wear to her prom at Bishop McDevitt High School in 2016: a black suit, bow tie, and gray vest. She added a teal pocket square that matched her date's dress. Wolf had worn pants and a shirt to school every day for the last three years and her outfit complied with the prom dress code, which outlined the various kinds of clothing that was acceptable—but didn't stipulate that girls couldn't wear suits. Indeed, Wolf's suit was a neat solution to the typical concerns about modesty that had plagued high school girls planning for proms nationwide: "You know a lot of girl's dresses . . . show a lot of skin," she mused. "I think I'm dressed pretty modestly." The school rewrote its dress code to require girls to wear dresses just days before the prom. When Wolf arrived to the prom in her suit, the school principal refused to admit her and threatened to call the police.

In that same year, in the small, conservative California Central Valley city of Clovis, a group of high school boys wore dresses to school to protest a school dress code prohibiting boys from wearing long hair, earrings, dresses, and skirts (sympathetic girls wore plaid flannel shirts and jeans in a show of solidarity with the boys and with transgender students generally). The protest was both a demand that the school accommodate transgender students and a call for more relaxed norms of gendered dress and grooming generally. Clovis Unified School District spokeswoman Kelly Avants spoke to the former concern, assuring the student body that transgender students could ask for exceptions to the dress code: "[W]e'll work with them to make sure they have an environment on campus that allows them to express themselves with the gender in which they identify." A school district trustee defended the dress code in less accommodating terms, insisting, "A woman's a woman and a man's a man, and there's a difference." But the California education code forbids discrimination based on gender expression and the American Civil Liberties Union duly threatened to sue the school district. Another district trustee, Ginny Hovsepian, advanced a novel legal theory in defense of the gendered dress code and against the non-discrimination mandate: "Just because it's a law doesn't mean we need to put up with it." But, of course, that's exactly what the term "law" does mean: the school district eventually gave in and adopted a more gender-neutral dress code. Boys can now have long hair and wear earrings; any other piercings—and any facial hair—are equally off-limits to both sexes.

Many other schools have struggled to enforce gender-specific dress codes in the face of growing opposition from students who accept transgender and nonbinary gender identifications and are frustrated with restrictive gender norms more generally. A new generation is using the tools of fashion to create new identities that complicate, subvert, or simply ignore the once-taken-for-granted gender distinctions. As they strive to rewrite the rules that define the apparel of sex and the meaning of gender, they are writing the dress codes of tomorrow.

How Dress Codes Fashion Gender

From ancient times until the present day, dress codes have required that clothing serve as a visible symbol of sex. Biblical proscriptions and legal strictures inspired uncompromising, sex-specific dress codes. Even as changing norms and ideals have weakened the symbolic links between clothing and most types of social status, law and custom have steadfastly ensured that the symbolic link between clothing and sex remains. But because fashions change, there is no specific type of clothing that inherently "belongs" to the male or female sex; moreover, these changes always threaten to erode any working distinction between masculine and feminine attire. The central purpose of gendered dress codes is not to ensure that people of each sex wear or refrain from wearing any specific type of clothing; instead it is to ensure that clothing clearly identifies the wearer as either male or female.

Occasionally, gender symbolism can be almost mimetic, as in the case of the phallic codpiece of the late Middle Ages and Renaissance era or, arguably, the long necktie, which one might interpret as a literal phallic symbol, both pointing to and mirroring the penis. But most sartorial sex symbols are more arbitrary, such as the idea that blue is a masculine color and pink a feminine one. This commonplace convention does not reflect any inherent masculinity or femininity in the respective colors; in fact, less than a century ago, this color symbolism was the reverse. A 1918 retail trade article insisted that "[t]he generally accepted rule is pink for the boys and blue for the girls," explaining that "pink, being a more decided and stronger color, is more suitable for the boy, while blue, which is more delicate and dainty, is prettier for the girl." What was important was —as it still is today— that boys wore *different* clothing from girls. Indeed, while the significance of a gender divide is ancient, the precise location of the dividing line has changed over time: in the late nineteenth and early twentieth centuries, infants and small children of both sexes wore white gowns, and young boys and girls alike wore long curls in their hair, pumps on their feet, lacy collars around their necks, and bonnets on their heads. Boys received their first haircut and graduated to men's clothing only when they achieved sufficient physical maturity—around age six or seven. Masculine attire wasn't linked to male sex per se but to male virility; children of either sex were considered delicate, innocent, and for those reasons were associated with domestic femininity.

The arbitrariness of such symbolism demonstrates that most gendered clothing doesn't refer to human biology; instead it reflects a social convention. "Women's clothing" isn't clothing that is especially suited to female bodies—it is simply any clothing that women typically wear. This means that every transgression of gender norms is also a potential revision of those norms: if enough women wear pants, then pants will become women's clothing.

Dress codes ensure that such changes don't erode the distinction in gendered clothing altogether. For instance, in the mid-twentieth century, hundreds of American cities had laws on the books specifically prohibiting cross-dressing, and many others used more general prohibitions against public indecency to ban it. Typically, these dress codes didn't enforce any *specific* type of gendered attire at all. Instead, they enforced a regime of *gendered symbolism*. Because the definition of gendered attire is both unclear and in flux, these cross-dressing bans were unavoidably vague. In practice, unlawful "cross-dressing" meant either intentional transgression of gender norms or a violation of certain well-established conventions. Both of these approaches to cross-dressing were problematic, and in the 1970s, people accused of cross-dressing began to challenge these laws as violations of civil rights.

Early challenges came from people who the medical profession recognized as "transsexual" (here I beg the reader's forgiveness—this term is understandably offensive to many, but it is the term that was widely used at the time and in the legal opinions in question). For instance, in *City of Columbus v. Zanders,* a court held that a male-to-female transsexual who wore women's clothing as psychological preparation for sex reassignment surgery lacked the mental culpability necessary to establish criminal intent under a local ordinance outlawing cross-dressing. The court opined, "For the true transsexual . . . dressing and posing as a female is more the result of an irresistible impulse or loss of will power than a deliberate violation of the provisions of the ordinance." This opinion was not a ringing defense of expressive liberty or the rights of transgender people. Indeed, in a sense it reinforced both the prohibition against "willful" cross-dressing and established conventions of gendered attire: Zanders was innocent of cross-dressing only because she desired and intended to wear feminine clothing in an essentially conventional way: *as a woman.*

Four years later, the same Columbus, Ohio, ordinance came under attack again: this time, the complaint was that it wasn't clear what type of clothing it prohibited or required. In *City of Columbus v. Rogers,* a court invalidated the law as unconstitutionally vague:

Modes of dress for both men and women are historically subject to changes in fashion. At the present time, clothing is sold for both sexes which is so similar in appearance that "a person of ordinary intelligence" might not be able to identify it as male or female dress. In addition, it is not uncommon today for individuals to purposely, but innocently, wear apparel which is intended for wear by those of the opposite sex.

As in *Zanders* four years earlier, this was no profound victory for freedom or tolerance. The court in *Rogers* didn't object to the goal underlying the cross-dressing ban; the only problem was that it was unclear precisely *what* the law banned. Because of changes in fashion, someone could violate the letter of the law without intending to do so, either by wearing a garment of ambiguous gender or by "purposely, but innocently" wearing a garment intended for the opposite sex as part of an ensemble that, as a whole, was appropriate to his or her own sex: for instance, in the 1970s, a man might wear a flowing blouse with ruffles to convey a fashionable romantic, "swashbuckling" effect; a woman might wear a necktie and blazer as part of the "Annie Hall look." It seems that for the *Rogers* court, an innocent violation of a gendered dress code would involve an ensemble in which the mix of elements—including the apparent physical characteristics of the human body—is clearly legible as masculine or feminine, even if certain individual elements "belonged" to the opposite sex.

Punishing Transgression

It's not always clear where the line between "innocent" transgression of gender norms and cross-dressing lies. During the "peacock revolution" of the 1960s and early 1970s, men experimented with flamboyant new fashions that recalled the masculine aesthetic before the Great Renunciation: bright floral prints, ruffled shirts, bold jewelry, and long, styled hair (though usually offset with facial hair and chest hair revealed through unbuttoned collars). By the 1980s, social anxiety about the masculine role in American society inspired a backlash and gender norms became more prescriptive. While artists, musicians, and fashion-conscious urbanities still experimented with unconventionally gendered grooming and attire, the typical American struggled to stay well within the established gender boundaries. Men worried that overly fashionable clothing would look effeminate or "gay" at a time when anti-gay prejudice was prevalent. Even inadvertent or playful transgressions of gender boundaries often met with ridicule and harassment. Today, although laws against cross-dressing have fallen into disuse, unambiguous cross-dressers still often suffer social contempt, ostracism, and even violence.

Ironically, perhaps the most reviled cross-dressers were those who the earlier laws might have exempted from prosecution because they wore their gendered attire conventionally and sincerely. Consider the tragic case of Gwen Araujo, who was born male by the conventional medical definition but identified as female. Araujo was seventeen years old when she went to a party at a friend's home in Newark, California. She typically wore a crop top and jeans, but that night she borrowed a peasant blouse and miniskirt from a friend. Araujo had begun a gender transition several years earlier. By outward appearances, she was an attractive young woman. But her mother worried about the miniskirt: Araujo had always worn jeans before and her bare legs might still look masculine. Moreover, Araujo had not had reconstructive genital surgery and a skirt offered less certain coverage than jeans.

Araujo's mother was right to worry. Things at the party took an ugly turn when José Merél—a boy Araujo had known and reportedly been intimate with earlier—began to grill Araujo. "Are you a man or a woman?" he demanded. The night went from bad to worse when another friend, Nicole Brown, offered to take Araujo to the bathroom to "check" whether she was male or female. Brown testified at trial that she reached up Araujo's skirt and "I thought I felt a penis." She then "freaked out" and ran into the hall screaming, "I can't believe this is a fucking man. I can't believe it. I can't cope with this."

Witnesses later reported that three men—José Merél, Michael Magidson, and Jason Cazares—beat and strangled Gwen Araujo, bound her hands and feet with rope and buried her body. At the subsequent murder trial, their defense attorneys asserted that the men acted in the "heat of passion" and were therefore not guilty of premeditated murder. "This is a case about deception and betrayal," one defense attorney told the jury. He insisted that his client was enraged "beyond reason" when he discovered Araujo was transgender: "His reaction was one of anger and rage, and shock and revulsion." The discovery of "Eddie's [Araujo's birth name] true sex" provoked a reaction "so deep it's almost primal. . . . Sexuality, our sexual choices, are very important to us . . . [and] the deception in this case . . . was such a substantial provocation—sexual fraud, a deception, a betrayal." José Merél's mother, Wanda Merél, told the press, "If you find out the beautiful woman you're with is really a man, it would make any man go crazy." One newspaper commentator took this line of argument to an even more contemptible extreme, insisting that because Araujo had been intimate with Merél and Magidson, she had assaulted *them*, provoking her own murder:

> The men did what they did because Araujo violated them. He used lies and deception to trick them into having sex. He was not honest with them and had he been, none of this would have happened. . . . These men were truly violated. They were raped.

Jason Cazares pled "no contest" to voluntary manslaughter. The jury deadlocked on the question of first-degree murder with respect to Merél and Magidson, resulting in a mistrial; in a subsequent trial the two men were convicted of second-degree murder. In 2006, California enacted the Gwen Araujo Justice for Victims Act, which scaled back the so-called "gay or trans panic defense" used in the trial. In 2014 the state eliminated the defense altogether.

Transgender activist and philosopher Talia Mae Bettcher points out that "the very gendered attire which is designed to conceal [the] body . . . [also] represents genital status. . . ." Bettcher argues that transgender people are punished for refusing to follow these conventional dress codes: "[G]ender presentation [through clothing] is a ubiquitous system of genital representation that transpeople opt out of." The history of gendered dress codes suggests that we might take Bettcher's idea that gendered clothing symbolizes genitalia a step further. Sex difference is not only a matter of genitalia: for instance, in mammals it is also defined by the ability to nurse infants after birth, and accordingly, much of feminine attire draws attention to female breasts. Moreover, because conventional stereotypes link certain psychological predispositions, such as aggressiveness or empathy, to sex, these ideas also inform gendered attire. Gendered attire can symbolize *all* of these characteristics and traits. What some find disturbing about transgender identity is that it often combines these attributes in unexpected ways. To a lesser but still considerable extent, this is also what some find disturbing about people who don't conform to gender stereotypes, such as Ann Hopkins or Darlene Jespersen.

José Merél's mother tried to explain her son's rage: *If you find out the beautiful woman you're with is really a man, it would make any man go crazy.* But here, a beautiful woman isn't an actual person whom Gwen Araujo deceptively impersonated: she's an erotic fantasy that no one could live up to—an ideal of femininity in which a host of attributes come together in one person. Gendered clothing doesn't just gesture toward the naked body it conceals—it fashions an idealized version of that body and indirectly, of the erotic and social relationships between bodies of different, complementary sexes. The so-called "deceptive" cross-dresser threatens this fantasy.

Indeed, unconventional expressions of gender of all kinds can often inspire violence, and many rationalize such aggression in terms remarkably similar to those used to defend Gwen Araujo's murderers. For example, on April 20, 2017, Wyoming senator Mike Enzi addressed a group of students at Greybull High School. He discussed a variety of topics, including what he saw as the excesses of the Affordable Care Act and his party's efforts to repeal it, and the overbearing regulations imposed on local schools by the Department of Education. The last question of the event came from sophomore Bailee Foster, who asked the senator what, if anything, he was doing for the LGBTQ community. Enzi replied that in Wyoming, "you can be just about anything you want to be . . . as long as you don't push it in somebody's face." To illustrate his point, Enzi mentioned "a guy who wears a tutu and goes to bars on Friday night and is always surprised that he gets in fights. Well, he kind of asks for it." Enzi didn't elaborate, but we can surmise that what the gentleman in a tutu *pushed in somebody's face* was the arbitrariness of the connection between human biology and gendered apparel. By combining the symbols of gender in unexpected ways, the "transvestite" (literally, one who transgresses vestimentary convention) draws attention to the artifice that underwrites our fantasies and ideals of sex and sexuality.

Dressing Naturally

Historically, a primary function of gendered clothing was to signal the reproductive role of the wearer. This explains not only attire designed to symbolize genital difference but also why prepubescent boys were dressed in gowns similar to those worn by girls, why unmarried women wore different clothing than married women, and why older women dressed differently than women of childbearing age. In monarchical and aristocratic societies where social status was transmitted through bloodlines, an important function of gendered attire was to symbolize the reproductive role on which the fate of dynasties, kingdoms, and empires depended. That doesn't mean that cross-dressing was ever "deceptive," but it did challenge social roles that had profound economic and in some cases geopolitical stakes.

But today, political power typically is not inherited and many people lead happy and fulfilled lives without producing offspring. Pleasure has eclipsed reproduction as the primary motivation for sex and at the same time, technology has made sexless reproduction possible. Our attire reflects these changes. Fashion historian Anne Hollander noticed this trend toward asexual dress:

> [T]rue parity of the sexes . . . has . . . been found in dressing everyone like children. A crowd of adults at a museum or park now looks just like a school trip. Everyone is in the same colorful zipper jackets, sweaters, pants and shirts worn by kids. . . . [These are] costumes connoting absolute bodily freedom and no responsibilities outside the self . . . an adult adaption of the former privileges of carefree children. . . . [Moreover they represent] freedom from the burdens of adult sexuality. . . . [M]en and women . . . dress exactly alike in versions of sand-box gear. . . . [They dress like] little boys and girls . . . at an age when their clothes need not differentiate the sexes because their activities are not supposed to, and neither are their thoughts. . . .

In contrast to desexualized, juvenile attire, deliberate transgression of gendered dress codes emphasizes the mature, sexual body. Cross-dressing and transgender identification (a distinct if related phenomenon) remixes conventional gender signifiers through a variety of novel, inventive uses. It's unsurprising that people will want to combine gendered symbolism in new—and, to some, disconcerting—ways. Indeed it is—dare I say?—natural that some people will psychologically identify with the symbolism of a gender that does not "belong" to their genital sex. The use of artifice in service of a gendered ideal does not in and of itself distinguish cross-dressers or transgender people: most of us deliberately exaggerate biological sex characteristics through clothing, and many do so through other interventions, such as cosmetic surgery or extreme bodybuilding. If this is "unnatural," then so is gendered clothing generally. As the famous drag queen RuPaul puts it: "[W]e're all born naked—the rest is drag, baby."

Today, a growing number of people—some who are transgender and many who are not—use the symbolism of gendered attire unconventionally. For instance, dancer Sara Geffrard favors stylish menswear and authors a blog called *A Dapper Chick* that features interviews with inspirational women and photos highlighting her own unique fashion sense. Geffrard finds the classic suit gives her self-confidence: "I'm a very, very shy person, but if I'm in a suit, I feel very confident. . . . Otherwise, I would walk in feeling sort of small." For Geffrard, the most important sartorial transition was from sportswear to tailored attire: "I used to wear more . . . urban streetwear, and I would get certain looks that I didn't really like . . . I would go into a store and someone would follow me. When I started dressing the way I do now, I didn't get that anymore." Geffrard isn't transgender and she doesn't think her suits are in tension with her gender. "These suits are actually women's wear," she says. Similarly, Danielle Cooper, author of the blog *She's a Gent*, who also favors men's suits, says, "I don't want to be a guy. I want to be a woman in menswear."

In 2015, Jaden Smith—son of Will Smith and Jada Pinkett Smith—

was the toast of the fashion scene when he wore a Louis Vuitton skirt for the designer's women's wear ad campaign. Smith was known for his unconventional style: *GQ* noted, admiringly, that "leopard print tights are his everyday jeans. Dresses are his T-shirts." The *New York Times* chief fashion critic Vanessa Friedman pointed out that Smith's style was notable precisely because "he's not a man in transition . . . or a man wearing clothing that looks as if it could be worn by either gender. . . . He is a man who happens to be wearing obviously female clothes. And while he doesn't look like a girl in them, he actually looks pretty good. It's not about the hairy legs in a skirt bro cliché." This is a harbinger, perhaps, of a future in which the dress codes of gender are more readily mixed and recombined. These new uses of gendered attire are among the many ways of imagining gender in today's world, suggesting novel social roles and new types of erotic fantasy.

Despite this unsettled equilibrium—or perhaps because of it—the efforts to control and regulate gendered attire are as numerous as ever. Gendered dress codes are changing to reflect new social norms, and new technologies, but they still shape our relationship to our bodies, our social encounters, our personalities, and ourselves.

Chapter Fifteen

Piercing the Veil

Outlawed as Indecent or Condemned as
Sacrilegious: Headscarves, Burkas, Burkinis, Bikinis,
Sexy Sheitels, Hip Hijabs, and CoverGirl Makeup

RELIGIOUS GARB MAY SEEM A STRAIGHTFORWARD APPLICA-
tion of an ancient, uncomplicated dress code, free of the kind of re-
mixing and borrowing that defines twenty-first-century fashion.
This conception informs most of the public conversation about religious dress, as well as our responses to conflicts surrounding it.
Many imagine that clothing prescribed by scripture or clerical edict
is a direct expression of belief—not a "mere" fashion statement but a
sacred mandate that no secular dress code should be allowed to in-
fringe upon. At the same time, for nonbelievers committed to secular civic ideals, religious attire can be seen as a threat, a wearable
dogma of moralistic intolerance and misogyny, justifying dress codes
that restrict or forbid such attire. But religious dress in the late twentieth and early twenty-first centuries is not a simple continuation of
a time-honored, sectarian dress code: instead it can combine traditional religious observance, anticolonial resistance, postmodern
identity politics, and a cosmopolitan fashion sense in a distinctively
contemporary amalgamation. Today, even the garments of ancient
religions have become part of the idiosyncratic self-expression of
modern fashion. The multiple and mixed messages conveyed through
religious garb are easily lost in translation, and every dress code that

either requires or proscribes sectarian symbolism has surprising side effects.

On March 3, 2004, the French Senate approved a law prohibiting conspicuous religious garb in public schools. Although the law applies to all religious symbols, no one doubts or denies that it was a reaction to the headscarves worn by some Muslim girls. The controversy surrounding the new law quickly became known as *l'affaire du foulard*— the scarf affair. The headscarf became a subject of conflict, not only because of the intensity of feeling it inspires but also because, over its long history, it has come to symbolize many different things to many different people. An ancient symbol of submission to faith, it is also a modern sign of resistance to secular authority. While some insist that the headscarf reflects the misogynistic conviction that a woman's hair and bare skin are obscene and unfit for public display, others believe it shields women against sexual objectification. Whether by design or by default, a garment created to be modest is now a form of exhibitionism, making its wearer conspicuousness in her effort to refuse attention. Can the dress codes that require it or those that prohibit it contain the profusion of meanings that threaten to escape any simple interpretation, like errant locks of hair from beneath an undersized mantilla? Can the women who wear a headscarf control its significance?

When I was in Paris as a visiting scholar at Sciences Po, in 2011, *l'affaire du foulard* seemed to be on everyone's mind. Many in France saw the headscarf as a reflection of an extreme, fundamentalist Islam that posed a distinct threat to republican values. In 2004, Justin Vaïsse, a professor at Sciences Po and consultant for the French Ministry of Foreign Affairs, warned of a "fringe of Islamist militants who . . . have obliged girls to wear a headscarf in school (often against their will) in order to create pressure for other girls to do the same . . . ." For some, the need to combat religious extremism justified laws banning the headscarf. For others, rhetoric linking peaceful religious observance with sectarian violence was evidence of anti-Muslim bias; for instance, the historian Joan Wallach Scott complained in a 2011 opinion piece that the headscarf ban was "part of a campaign to purify and protect . . . national identity, purging so-called foreign elements."

Some feminists saw the headscarf as a return to a compulsory modesty that European women themselves had only recently begun to escape. The French philosopher Sylviane Agacinski argued, "The [headscarf] law was made to protect the bodies of girls, of minors . . . the veil here isn't Islam, it's politics." Such concerns were not limited to Westerners unsympathetic to Islam and its traditions: for instance, Fadela Amara, a French Muslim and women's rights activist, insisted, "The veil is the visible symbol of the subjugation of women."

Many women who wore the headscarf—often referred to by the Arabic name *hijab*—insisted that it was not a symbol of women's subordination but just the opposite: an antidote to the objectification of women. For instance, one woman living in Ontario described her hijab as "a rejection of the society and their values and the sexual . . . it's the woman's power to take back her own dignity and her own sexuality." Another opined, "*Hijab* is a liberation from the tyranny of fashion. It is humanizing because it takes away the sex-appeal nonsense." In a sense, the popularity of the hijab mirrored a secular trend toward modesty that has caught on among women of a variety of faiths—and some of little or no faith. For instance, the creative director of a high-fashion house, describing her new line of "oversize, soft enveloping" clothing sounded a lot like a religious woman explaining her decision to wear a headscarf: "Images of women being intensely beautified, sexualized and shown like dolls over many years has had an impact on me." Similarly, podcast host Aminatou Sou echoed in secular tones the observations of many religiously modest women, remarking, "I really disagree with women who think walking around naked is liberation. . . . I'm sorry, but too many people get to enjoy this for it to be liberation."

Was the headscarf religious, cultural, or political? Or all three at once? Is it a symbol of Eastern misogyny or a feminist response to Western objectification of women? Is banning it coercive or liberating? The meaning of the hijab—and of the rules that required it and the laws that prohibited it—had yet to be decoded.

Veiled Meanings

As early as 1200 B.C., the laws of the Assyrian Empire made the veil a formal sign of social status, requiring married women and concubines to wear a veil when in public and prohibiting slaves and prostitutes from veiling themselves. Hair was of great spiritual significance in both pagan and early Christian rites, symbolizing vanity and sexuality: accordingly, cutting or covering hair was often a sign of chastity. The head coverings that modern Westerners associate with Islam were, until the fifteenth century, common in Christian Europe. European peasants wore simple scarves and aristocratic women wore more elaborate headdresses, such as the conical *henin* and the wing-shaped wimple (which later became an element of some nun's habits.) Today, the novices of the Catholic order of the Poor Clare Colettines shear off their hair on induction and place it in a basket with a crucifix. The Abrahamic religions—Judaism, Christianity, and Islam—share a commitment to modesty that some believe requires head coverings, particularly for women; hence, veiling is common to the most traditional or conservative sects of all three religions.

Islamic scholars disagree about whether the headscarf is an obligatory religious observance. Islamic Studies professor Sahar Amer notes that the Qur'an does not clearly require the hijab; the question "continues to perplex scholars. . . . [T]he lack of specificity in the actual Qur'anic text seems striking . . . [an] ambiguity, which is not a problem of translation . . . the Arabic text is perhaps even vaguer. . . ." Today the headscarf is also a reaction to a history of colonialism and cultural imperialism. European colonial powers saw the veil as a symbol of backward religious and cultural traditions from which Muslim women needed to be rescued. For example, Evelyn Baring, the British controller-general of Egypt from 1877 to 1879 and the consul general of Egypt from 1883 to 1907, insisted that veiling had "a baneful effect on Eastern society." He insisted that if Egypt was ever to be "persuaded or forced into imbibing the true spirit of western civilization," Europeans would have to first improve the status of Muslim women by overthrowing what he felt were retrograde Islamic customs—especially the veil. Ironically, though perhaps not surprisingly, Baring's feminism was conveniently limited to the colonies: back home in England, he was the founding member of the Men's League for Opposing Woman Suffrage.

Yet opposition to veiling was certainly not limited to colonists seeking to undermine local customs. Egypt became home to one of the earliest unveiling movements. The 1899 book *Tahrir al-Mar'a*, or *The Liberation of Woman*, insisted that the hijab was a "huge barrier between woman and her elevation, and consequently a barrier between the nation and its advance"—a play on the term *hijab*, which in Arabic means *barrier* or *partition*. In 1923, three prominent Egyptian women, returning home from the International Women's Alliance conference in Rome, dramatically stripped off their veils as they stepped onto the railway platform in Cairo—an event photographed and reported in the press as the *raf el-hijab*, or "shedding of the *hijab*." This inspired an Egyptian feminist movement that quickly spread to other majority-Muslim societies. The *raf el-hijab* was not, strictly speaking, a religious reform movement. Upper- and middle-class Egyptian women of all religions—Copts, Christians, and Jews—had worn veils for centuries, and during the *raf el-hijab*, women from all of these religious groups shed their veils in the name of liberation.

In some majority-Muslim countries, modernizing governments saw Western attire as the dress code for civilized nations. For instance, Mustafa Kemal Atatürk, founder of the Republic of Turkey, implemented a dress code for the civil service that required Western-style hats and suits, banning the traditional fez. He remarked in a 1925 speech, "[I]n some places I have seen women who put a piece of cloth or a towel or something like that over their heads to hide their faces. . . . [C]an the mothers and daughters of a civilized nation adopt this strange manner, this barbarous posture? It is a spectacle that makes the nation an object of ridicule. It must be remedied at once." Turkey banned the veil for civil servants and for university students in the 1980s. Similarly, Reza Shah Pahlavi, the shah of Iran from 1925 to 1941, outlawed the hijab in 1936; police physically removed veils from women and in some cases searched their homes for forbidden clothing. By the 1970s, prosperous and well-educated urban women in countries as diverse as Turkey, Iran, Morocco, and Egypt were typically unveiled. Ironically, lower-class rural women began to adopt the veil just as the elites were shedding it. According to Sahar Amer: "In the early twentieth century, a Middle Eastern woman who veiled . . . could afford to . . . stay at home and not work. . . . [Later] for rural women who were accustomed to hard work outside the home, the adoption of *hijab* represented urbanization and the hope for upward mobility." As a consequence, the veil, for centuries a signifier of high status, became identified with the lower classes.

When the veil made a resurgence in the late 1970s and 1980s, it was, in many cases, as much a political statement in reaction to European colonialism as it was a religious practice. In France, Algeria figures prominently in this colonial history. The French army took control of Algiers in 1830 and from then until Algeria became independent in 1962, French colonists sought to suppress the traditional customs and attire of the *indigenes*. One part of this assimilationist project was the ritualistic unveiling of Algerian women in staged events. The wives of French military officers would remove the veils of Algerian women—a symbolic demonstration of the civilizing influence of the West. In response, some Algerian women adopted the veil to demonstrate their opposition to French colonial rule. Similarly, veiling in Indonesia during the 1980s was, according to the anthropologist Carla Jones, "an expression of resistance and . . . a means of critiquing . . . [a] corrupt regime." Likewise, the Islamic Revolution in Iran began with demonstrations that included women defiantly wearing headscarves in violation of the legal proscription, making the headscarf a symbol of opposition to the corruption of the shah.

The defeat and exile of the shah and the rise of the Ayatollah Khomeini in 1979 brought a dramatic reversal. Today, Iran—along with Saudi Arabia, Sudan, and parts of Indonesia—requires that women veil. In 2014, Iranian law required all women to wear a black, blue, or brown *chador*—a robe that covers the body, head to toe—or its equivalent when in public, a dress code enforced by special morality police called the *Komiteh* or *Gashte Ershad*. According to the *New York Times*, the *Komiteh* has been known to arrest women for infractions as small as baring an ankle, wearing lipstick, or allowing a lock of hair to peek out from beneath a scarf. Iranian activist Masih Alinejad notes that in 2014, 3.6 million women were warned, fired, or arrested for their dress in Iran. Moreover, private enterprises are subject to legal sanction should they sell immodest clothing or serve women in violation of the dress code; as a consequence, businesses are the de facto deputies of the fashion police. For instance, the *Times* reported in 1990 that when a woman who was drinking tea in a hotel lobby let her headscarf slip to reveal her hairline, the waiter presented her with a printed card which read: "[F]ollowing Islamic laws helps keep the place of women in society so high—please respect the rules and let us have the pleasure of serving you"—a polite way of saying, *No hijab, no service.*

The hijab still divides Iranians. Traditionalists complain that the law requiring the chador is widely ignored. Some women have pushed the envelope, "combining tight coats with fluorescent scarves . . . from which locks cascade. . . . [H]ard liners . . . accuse some women of 'roaming the streets practically naked.'" In 2014 a Shiite seminary organized a protest of women clad in black chadors, to bring attention to the problem of lax morals: "Corruption and immorality have engulfed the nation," lamented one woman. In stark contrast, less than three years later in 2017, women frustrated by the restrictions on their dress protested by removing their scarves. "I took my scarf off because I'm tired of our government telling me what to do with my body," declared one protestor. The protests have inspired a social media campaign: *My Stealthy Freedom,* where women post images of themselves, heads uncovered, to demand an end to laws requiring the headscarf. Some protestors found new uses for their headscarves, tying them to the ends of sticks, the displaced scarves transformed into flags of defiance.

This history complicates the politics of the veil. Was the headscarf a patriarchal religious custom or a symbol of resistance to colonial rule? Did a decision to remove the veil reflect progressive feminist reform, the influence of European cultural imperialism, or an act of resistance to theocratic oppression?

The Indecent Burkini

Six years after *l'affaire du foulard*, in 2010, France passed a law that prohibits wearing the full-face veil, or *burka*, in public. France's ban was followed that same year by a similar law in Belgium. In 2015, the Dutch cabinet passed a ban on face-covering veils in public areas and on public transportation, and in December 2016, Germany's chancellor, Angela Merkel, publicly insisted that "the full facial veil is inappropriate and should be banned whenever it is legally possible." In January 2017 Austria moved to ban the full-face veil in courts and schools and planned to consider banning headscarves for all public employees.

European courts have upheld these dress codes in the face of challenges that they violate individual religious liberties. In 2014, France argued in the European Court of Human Rights that "the voluntary . . . concealment of the face is . . . incompatible with the fundamental requirements of living together in French society . . . contrary to the ideal of fraternity . . . [and] falls short of the minimum requirement of civility that is necessary for social interaction." The court agreed, holding that the burka ban served a legitimate purpose: "[T]he preservation of the conditions of 'living together' of all French citizens." In 2017, the European Court of Human Rights unanimously upheld Belgium's ban on "clothing that partly or totally covers the face," finding it plausible that the law was "necessary in a democratic society."

Some European cities, following the logic of the headscarf and burka bans, now also ban the full-body bathing suit favored by some Muslim women, dubbed the "burkini." The burkini—a two-piece ensemble that looks like a loose-fitting wetsuit, with long sleeves, leggings, and a cap—first appeared in 2004 when Aheda Zanetti, a Lebanese Muslim living in Australia, designed it for her daughter.

"When I thought back, I realized that we didn't really swim or play sports when I was growing up. Not because we didn't want to but because we just didn't have the clothing! So we never really enjoyed the summer life," said Zanetti. Her company, Ahiida Burqini Swimwear, was an instant success: "People went absolutely crazy. I wasn't prepared for it. Now we have sales all over the world. . . ." British merchant Marks & Spencer started selling a burkini in its stores in the United Kingdom and internationally on its website in 2016—it quickly sold out. Today, DKNY and Dolce & Gabbana offer high-fashion burkinis to the stylish observant woman and to a growing number of nonbelievers who just want a little extra coverage for a day at the beach.

Cities and towns in Austria, Germany, France, Italy, and Morocco have banned the burkini. In support of anti-burkini dress codes, the prime minister of France, Manuel Valls, said in 2016 that the burkini represented "the enslavement of women," while Laurence Rossignol, the women's rights minister of France, lamented that the burkini "promotes the shutting away of women's bodies." In answer to those who noted that the women in question choose to wear a burkini, she replied, "[O]f course, there are women who make the choice . . . [and] there were also . . . American negroes who were in favor of slavery." (She later apologized for the use of the term "negroes," but stood by the substance of her statement.) In the summer of 2016, police cited a woman sitting on a beach in Cannes wearing leggings and a headscarf for failing to dress in "an outfit respecting good morals and secularism." The same year, police in Nice ordered a burkini-clad woman to strip on the spot, citing a local law banning the garment.

Was a law that required women to strip in public really a victory for the equality of the sexes? Or was it just another dress code moralizing about what women wear? Ironically, some of the same towns that now effectively require modest women to strip not so long ago outlawed the bikini as scandalously immodest. In the not-so-distant past, Western norms of female modesty were as stringent as those of today's Iran. The respectable woman of the eighteenth and nineteenth centuries wore a cumbersome bathing costume with long sleeves, a long skirt, and bonnet. Some women even used a "bathing machine" designed for maximum modesty: a purpose-built cart that one could enter fully dressed and, once inside, change into her bathing costume. In 1805 the Irish author Walley Chamberlain Oulton described the bathing machines used on the beaches of Kent as

> four wheeled carriages, covered with canvas, and having at one end of them an umbrella of the same materials which is let down to the surface of the water, so that the bather descending from the machine by a few steps is concealed from the public view, whereby the most refined female is enabled to enjoy the advantages of the sea with the strictest delicacy.

In the twentieth century, women's bathing rituals and costumes gradually become less elaborate—but not without significant consternation. In 1907, the Australian swimmer and film star Annette Kellerman was charged with indecent exposure for wearing a form-fitting one-piece bathing suit on Boston's Revere Beach; the resulting legal fight encouraged American cities to relax their swimwear dress codes.

A woman about to enter a bathing machine.

By the 1920s the new flapper-era ideal of the trim, athletic woman inspired form-fitting, practical swimwear. Two-piece bathing suits appeared on the silver screen (and soon thereafter on beaches) in the early 1940s, but Hollywood's Hays Code, which governed morality in film, allowed two-piece outfits that exposed the midsection of the female torso only if the navel was covered. Fashionable American swimsuits copied those worn on screen and were, consequently, high-waisted.

The first "bikini" was unveiled in 1946, by French designer Louis Réard. In the argot of the 1940s, attractive women were "bombshells" and extreme sensations were "atomic." Réard deftly combined the two slang terms, with a nod to the testing of an American nuclear bomb in the Bikini Islands, naming his skimpy two-piece design *le bikini*. The bikini was an instant sensation but also an instant cause of moral panic. Americans considered the hip-hugging, navel-exposing bikini a symptom of European moral decadence when it appeared on Atlantic beaches in the early 1950s. In Europe, Pope Pius XII condemned the bikini after the first Miss World beauty pageant winner was crowned wearing one in 1951. Cities in France, Italy, Belgium, Spain, Portugal, and Australia, as well as in the United States, banned the bikini as a hazard to public morality and hygiene. Réard, betting that all publicity is good publicity, fanned the flames of outrage, advising that no swimsuit could be considered a real bikini "unless it can be pulled through a wedding ring." Cannes welcomed the scandalous swimsuits in 1953 when a young, bikini-clad Brigitte Bardot was photographed during that city's famous film festival, but in the prudish United States the bikini was still considered scandalous as late as 1957: *Modern Girl* magazine advised its American readership, "[I]t is hardly necessary to waste words over the so-called bikini since it is inconceivable that any girl with tact and decency would ever wear such a thing." By the early 1960s, the bikini had triumphed over moral outrage. Ursula Andress became an instant icon when she emerged from the Caribbean Sea carrying two conch shells and wearing a white bikini in 1962's *Dr. No*, the swimsuit having outlived the Hays Code. By 1965 *Time* magazine reported that it was "almost square" *not* to wear a bikini.

In the 1950s, skimpy swimsuits were considered a threat to public order; in 2016, it had become a breach of civility to wear *too much* clothing. Modesty, a religious virtue, had become a civic vice. The hijab, in all of its varied forms, was fraught because it meant so many different things to so many different people. It was a conspicuous symbol of ethnic and religious affiliation and as such set off debates about assimilation, national identity, and group pride. It was an exclusively feminine form of asceticism and self-abnegation, echoing long-standing practices of compulsory feminine modesty and implicating long-standing practices of exploitative sexual objectification. Its significance was a matter of context and perspective: it could be a defiant stance against Islamophobia or a symptom of a religious fundamentalism; an escape from sexual objectification or a moral fetish for religious misogynists; a matter of free individual choice or of overwhelming social pressure. Little surprise that every dress code that has attempted either to impose it or to restrict it has been marked by contradiction and the law of unintended consequences.

Hip Hijabs and Sexy Sheitels

When religious dress codes meet modern fashion, the novel combination of ancient symbols and contemporary sensibilities can transform signs of faith into elements of individual self-creation. The blend of the sacred and the profane worries religious hard-liners and the opponents of sectarian fundamentalism alike: both sides question the loyalties and legitimacy of these novel combinations. Nevertheless, new generations reject, respect, and repurpose religious dress codes, creating their own distinctive symbols of belief and transforming religious practice in the process.

The designer Anniesa Hasibuan argues that "fashion is one of the outlets in which we can start that cultural shift . . . to normalize the hijab in America and other parts of the West, so as to break down and demystify misconceptions." A growing number of religiously observant women have tried to retailor traditional religious dress to fit their modern, fashionable sensibilities. Nura Afia became the first Cover-Girl to wear a hijab in 2015 after making a series of popular YouTube makeup tutorials: "[T]here were still very few videos out there for the massive audience of observant Muslim girls who love beauty and are constantly on the hunt for cosmetics. . . ." Afia has helped create a new image for hijab-wearing Muslim women—and for herself: "[G]rowing up I felt like everyone would look down on me just because I wear a *hijab*. . . . [Makeup] has helped me feel confident in wearing a *hijab*. . . . It's my way of expressing myself. . . ." Or consider Halima Aden, who, in 2019, became the first *Sports Illustrated* swimsuit model to pose in a burkini. Like Afia, Aden made a modest dress code look glamorous and alluring by offsetting her covered hair, arms, and legs with jewel-toned silks, makeup, and dramatic jewelry. Young *hijabis* have even developed a distinctively urban pop culture: for instance, a group identified as #Mipsterz (Muslim hipsters) produced a music video that features women skateboarding, juggling, and doing headstands while wearing headscarves with Jackie O sunglasses, form-fitting capri pants, jean jackets, gold chains, rock concert T-shirts, high heels, and glittering, two-fingered "knuckle duster" rings.

The laws of religious modesty may be new to the fashion industry, but the laws of supply and demand are well understood: luxury brands such as Dolce & Gabbana, Oscar de la Renta, Burberry, and DKNY have rolled out modest high-fashion attire while H&M, Uniqlo, Zara, and Macy's make modest clothing for women with more modest resources. "Modest fashion" is a growth industry. According to the Global Islamic Economy Report, consumers spent $254 billion dollars on Muslim attire in 2017—Muslim women spent $44 billion on modest clothing items alone—and projections estimate the market will be worth $373 billion by 2022. Even laws prohibiting the garments have not cut into the market for them: according to burkini entrepreneur Aheda Zanetti, dress codes forbidding the burkini haven't reduced her sales: "[W]henever they ban it . . . people just buy more of them."

Of course, modest fashion is not without its detractors. For those who see the hijab as a symbol of sexism and repression, no effort to turn it into fashion can redeem it. Nura Afia's own—non-Muslim—grandparents disapproved of her hijab: "[W]earing the scarf was really, really hard, and still is, with my grandma... [S]he really thinks it holds me back." Mere hours after *Sports Illustrated* announced Halima Aden's inclusion in the annual swimsuit issue, critics complained that the magazine would "glamorize fundamentalist religious dress-codes" and was "celebrating a symbol of oppression." In 1998, the art and fashion historian Anne Hollander described a fashionable woman wearing a hijab in this way: "[A] silk scarf pinching her head and reducing her face ... above the shoulders, unattractiveness is the whole point. ..." For Hollander, when women combined a hijab with fashionable clothing, the scarf negated the expressiveness of the other parts of the ensemble: "[H]ow unnoticeable the attractions below the neck became without a personality to avow them. ... [T]he scarf completely depersonalized the shapely legs and curving torso displayed in contemporary clothes below it. The woman looks brainless, an antique statue of Venus with no head."

Other critics see modest fashion as a form of exploitative cultural appropriation. For instance, an opinion columnist in the *Guardian* complained that "eastern culture may only be celebrated when it is glamorised by western society. ... [This is] the same clothing that often leaves Muslim women perceived as 'extremist' and puts them at risk of being attacked or even criminalised. ..."

Meanwhile, religious traditionalists argue that fashion itself, with its emphasis on beauty and glamor, is inconsistent with the modesty that defines the hijab. Afia's parents and other Muslims disapproved of her use of cosmetics: "I hid it from my parents for a while ... I got yelled at for wearing makeup at my wedding by my Dad.... People told me I wasn't supposed to put myself out there. ..." As a consequence, Afia "understood why people within our faith decide to take off their scarves—because women who wear scarves in Muslim communities are always doubly judged.... [T]hey expect us to be perfect.... A lot of people say that I shouldn't wear makeup because beautifying yourself is kind of the opposite of covering. ..." Similarly, when Hamila Aden appeared in *Sports Illustrated* in a burkini, religious traditionalists insisted "the purpose of hijab is veiling (to cover up). What is this nonsense? She is completely and totally exposed. This is fashion, not Islam." Another complained that *Sports Illustrated* was "attempting the colonize and appropriate Islam. This is highly offensive." When Turkish fashion company Modanisa held its first "Istanbul Modest Fashion Week" in 2016, some conservative Muslims protested outside the venue: "[T]he reference point of the headscarf, which is seen as simple commodity or advertisement good for some people, is in fact chastity and identity," said Emine Nur Cakir, a leader of the demonstration. "The headscarf, which symbolizes a stand, an Islamic identity, is being sacrificed in the name of fashion." In reaction to the #Mipsterz YouTube video, one comment read, "WHAT? Hijabs and skin tight apparel? This is blasphemy!" Another remarked, "a lot of people think that wearing a hijab is enough . . . these kind of girls in the video is what you call part time moslims." Yet another detractor insisted, "This is not hijab. This is actually mocking the purpose of hijab. No where at all are these ladies modest or respect Islam." One comment was in keeping with the sense of fun the video exuded; it chided, "you never ride a skateboard with heels on. please respect the skateboard culture, sisters."

When ancient religious law collides with modern fashion, the faithful often find inventive, practical solutions that reconcile personal expression with piety. *Halakha*, or Orthodox Jewish Law, requires married women to cover their hair, a stricture similar to that which requires the hijab, and with common roots in Abrahamic doctrine. Many observant Orthodox Jewish women have adopted an expedient that satisfies the demands of the religious dress code and of their own fashion sense: a wig. The *sheitel* is virtually unknown to outsiders, but in Orthodox Jewish communities fashionable women discuss their wigs in the same way other women do their hair stylists: "[W]hen women get together at a wedding or a party they ask, 'Where did you get your shoes, dress and wig.'" One woman described hers as a "custom made, $1200 masterpiece of long silky layers dyed a deep, rich chocolate color . . . undeniably a sexy wig." Many even have their *sheitel* professionally styled: according to the *New York Times*, a Madison Avenue salon that specializes in *sheitel* grooming charges at least $600 for the service: "Orthodox women want something contemporary and realistic, and don't want a wig to look like what it is," said Mark Garrison, the owner. The famous hairstylist Frédéric Fekkai suggests that, in order to maintain verisimilitude, "an orthodox woman should have several wigs. A real haircut grows out at different lengths. You need more than one wig at different lengths." "I want my wig to look exactly like my hair," one young woman insisted.

Some see an emphasis on the form of observance over the substance (they wonder whether wigs that look exactly like one's own hair defeat the purpose of covering), but others see a sensible adaptation of traditional strictures to modern sensibilities. For instance, an advice column for Orthodox Jews asked: "Isn't Wearing a Wig Over Hair (Especially if the Wig is Nicer than the Hair) Pointless?" The columnist sided with the *sheitel* wearers, reasoning that wearing a wig was no more objectionable than wearing a shirt with flesh-colored sleeves. According to Rabbi Rafael Grossman, president of the Rabbinical Council of America, the practice is controversial but kosher: "[T]here are authorities who strongly object. A wig would seem to contradict the basic principal of avoiding incitement. But my personal view is that it is acceptable . . . though a woman should avoid wearing a wig that could appear to be sensual." According to the *Los Angeles Times*, a rabbi's wife who sported a "stylish, deep red bob with short bangs," insisted that "Judiasm doesn't equate modesty with unattractiveness . . . a *sheitel* allows a woman to look good without compromising her privacy. . . . [Even if no one else can tell] wearing a *sheitel* has a profound psychological effect on the woman wearing it. She is saying, 'I am not available to you.' By wearing the *sheitel*, a woman invests her true appearance and real self in the most important place in her life, her marriage."

The *sheitel* was a satisfactory form of quiet observance for many but some women have found even wigs too restrictive—not because of how they look but because of what they represent. Tova Ross, who purchased a luxurious, realistic *sheitel* she jokingly named "Esmeralda," wrote that she "grew to begrudge what I had been taught about the deeper reasoning behind the rule. . . . I sincerely doubted that my hair would drive any man wild to the point of intoxication . . . [and] why was it my job to advertise [my unavailability] to . . . men. . . . [C]ouldn't my married state be easily inferred from my wedding ring?" Ross also bristled at the hypocrisy of the religious dress code: "I had grown jaded watching the hordes of women in Flatbush in skin-tight skirts and $500 stilettos who told me they were capturing the essence of modesty as God prescribed it, because they also wore sheitels." And Ross found that wearing the *sheitel*, far from satisfying the demands of orthodoxy and freeing her from moralistic judgment, actually invited ever more demanding standards of modesty: "[P]eople stared at me when I wore the wig—so much for modesty. . . . If my skirt rested even slightly over my knees, they would adopt mock outrage as they tsk-tsked and waved a finger at me. . . . What I thought was my escape from preconceived expectations and whispering . . . turned out to be life under a different microscope. . . ." Eventually, Ross and "Esmeralda" parted company and gradually Ross abandoned covering altogether: "[T]hose *mitpachot* (Israeli headscarves) and bandanas became wide headbands and then thin headbands, and then no headbands. . . . I didn't want my sincere love of Judaism to be displaced by my bitterness over. . . rules."

With hip hijabs and the sexy *sheitels*, observant women satisfy ancient dress codes and still keep their personal style up to date. Some traditionalists object, arguing that these nods to fashion betray a lack of conviction: for instance, some would doubtless argue that Tova Ross's *sheitel*, a symbol of faith legible only to other observant Jews, made it all the easier for her to eventually leave her head uncovered. But perhaps an even greater, inarticulable worry is that such fashionable expressions of faith are symptoms of the seductive power of fashion and the individual-centered world it has helped bring into existence. Religious garments, like all significant ancient attire, are designed to

symbolize a social role and a commitment that transcends and su-
persedes self-assertion. Fashion tends to complicate and erode this
meaning, absorbing older status symbols and remaking them as signs
of individuality.

Consider the plight of Samantha Elauf, who, in 2008, interviewed
for a job at an Abercrombie & Fitch store in Tulsa, Oklahoma, wearing her headscarf. Abercrombie was a famously image-conscious
store that regulated which colors could be worn together, how employees roll up the cuffs on their jeans (no larger than 1.25 inches),
where on the arm they should push up the sleeves on their sweaters,
where on the hips the waistline of pants must fall (no sagging!), precisely how to "half tuck" in a shirt for a relaxed look, and how to "pop"
a shirt collar. A headscarf did not comply with the dress code. But
Elauf impressed the assistant store manager, who thought they should
make an exception for her. In fact, Title VII of the Civil Rights Act of
1964 *requires* employers to make exceptions to their dress codes to
accommodate religious garb. Nevertheless, according to court documents, supervisor Randall Johnson insisted, "You . . . can't hire her . . .
someone can come in, paint themselves green and say they were
doing it for religious reasons."

Elauf sued Abercrombie for religious discrimination and took her
case all the way to the Supreme Court of the United States. Abercrombie argued that it was entitled to enforce its dress code against
Elauf because she never said she wore her headscarf for religious, as
opposed to personal, reasons. The court found this excuse hard to
swallow. At one point during oral arguments, Justice Samuel Alito
posed this hypothetical question: "[F]our people [who] show up for
a job interview at Abercrombie . . . this is going to sound like a joke,
but, you know, it's not. So, the first is a Sikh man wearing a turban, the
second is a Hasidic man wearing a hat, the third is a Muslim woman
wearing a hijab, the fourth is a Catholic nun in a habit. . . . [D]o you
think . . . that those people have to say . . . we're dressed this way for a
religious reason? We're not just trying to make a fashion statement?"

Elauf prevailed in the Supreme Court and eventually settled
with Abercrombie for more than $25,000. As Justice Alito's rhetor-

ical question suggests, it was clear enough that Elauf wore a head-scarf as a religious observance. But the point was disputed all the way to the Supreme Court. Secular and religious dress codes were designed to eliminate just this type of vestimentary ambiguity. But rather than one straightforward meaning, even a garment as ancient and well-established as a hijab now has many.

Fashion doesn't undermine the religious significance of the hijab. But it does complicate that significance. In a sense, the fashionable Muslim woman, when she wears her hijab along with chic clothing or with makeup, contradicts the idea that the hijab is designed to obscure a female body that is a source of temptation: the fashionable hijab becomes a wearable argument in favor of theological liberalization. And, by complicating the stereotypical meaning of the hijab as an instrument of compulsory modesty, she insists on the primacy of its other meanings: the hijab becomes a symbol of cultural pride, a sign of post-colonial resistance or of opposition to Islamophobia.

In this respect, those who wish to defend the hijab as a pure signifier of religious modesty are right to be concerned about the fashionable hijab: fashion is anything but pure. The traditional hijab is a barrier. By contrast, the fashionable hijab is not a partition that conceals; like all fashion, it *reveals* a distinctive, individual personality. A hijab worn with full CoverGirl makeup, a hijab worn with chic clothing, a hijab worn with a hipster T-shirt and jean jacket while its wearer rides a skateboard—each of these sends a distinct and complex message in which the scarf evokes its traditional meaning as a symbol of religious devotion and modesty while other elements of the ensemble complicate, dilute, and even subvert that meaning. When inducted into the fashion system, religious attire becomes another cultural resource to be ripped from context and exploited for its power to evoke memory and emotion.

What's more (what's *worse*, from the perspective of religious orthodoxy), in giving voice to her hijab, the fashionable *hijabi* subtly but unmistakably suggests that all hijabs can have such an individual significance. Once the hijab becomes fashion, no hijab can ever again be an inscrutable partition; each now inevitably reveals something of its wearer, whether the wearer wants it to be revealed or not. Each becomes a fashion statement. In this sense, Emine Nur Cakir was right to complain that the hijab is "being sacrificed in the name of fashion." Fashion expropriates, dissects, and repurposes culture; it is voracious, profane, and irreverent. As traditional religious garb becomes an element of modern self-fashioning, as the hijab morphs from modest to modish, it is unavoidably transformed from a curtain that encloses to a banner that advertises—whether worn on the head or tied to the end of a stick.

In the late twentieth century, the ideal of expressive individualism came to dominate the development of fashion. In an inversion of past priorities, sartorial signs of status and even markers of sex differences became elements used to build and express personality. As attire became more closely associated with individual character, resistance to dress codes that reinforced older status distinctions grew. Women fought strictures based on feminine ideals of decorativeness and modesty. Older gender norms and even the idea of the male/female gender dichotomy itself were challenged. Religious garb took on an increasingly complex social and political significance. In reactions to these developments, businesses, schools, governments, and religious groups created dress codes designed to tame the disruptions of increasingly cosmopolitan fashions. And in the last years of the twentieth century, the growing centrality of individualism, combined with the renunciation of sumptuousness that began in the eighteenth century, gave rise to a new fashion trend: an ideal of ostentatious authenticity that would become one of the hallmarks of dress and dress codes in the twenty-first century.

Part Five

Retailored Expectations

You can have anything you want in life if you dress for it.

—EDITH HEAD

I don't design clothes. I design dreams.

—RALPH LAUREN

Chapter Sixteen

Merit Badges

Appropriate for the Workplace: Red-Soled
Louboutins, a 21 Club Tie, a Blue Blazer,
the Preppy Look, Red Sneakers, a Patagonia
Vest, a Gray or Black T-shirt. Inappropriate:
Designer dresses, High heels, Suits

THE DRESS CODES OF THE MIDDLE AGES AND RENAISSANCE ENSURED that aristocratic privilege was communicated through conspicuous opulence: the attire of the elite expressed an almost godlike magnificence. After the Enlightenment, unwritten dress codes communicated social status through elegance and refinement, reflecting humanistic civic virtues and a celebration of the human form. Today's dress codes include elements of both older traditions. Opulence lives on—especially in the attire of women—and, as always, the exclusivity of costly luxury goods makes them a sign of elite status. At the same time, the ethos of the Great Masculine Renunciation is reflected in unadorned tailored clothing (which nevertheless can contain a multitude of subtle status symbols: the minutia of internal construction, tailoring, button placement, and stitching) and, increasingly, in the predominance of casual sportswear in almost every setting (beachfront weddings in shorts and Hawaiian shirts, casual Friday every day of the workweek). The ideal of authenticity in fashion, a growing influence since the 1960s, encourages many people to adopt attire that seems practical and functional and to avoid any hint of sartorial artifice. Ironically, because this type of clothing is now a status symbol, many examples of it have become stylized and contrived, contravening the desired impression. The ethos of renunciation is carried to its logical extreme in a dressed-down aesthetic that pretends indifference to fashion while ascribing moral importance to it, reflected in the rumpled reverse snobbery of the university professoriat, the faux proletarianism of the so-called American heartland, and the pretentiously unassuming casual sportswear of California's Silicon Valley.

Marks of Distinction

According to the United States Court of Appeals for the Second Circuit, Christian Louboutin, S.A., "is best known for his emphasis on the otherwise-largely-ignored outsole of the shoe . . . Louboutin's shoes have been characterized by . . . a bright red outsole, which nearly always contrasts with the color of the rest of the shoe." The court emphasized that "in the high-stakes commercial markets and social circles in which these things matter a great deal . . . the 'flash of a red sole' is today 'instantly' recognizable to 'those in the know'. . . ." This bit of fashion esoterica was of interest to the court because "Louboutin, on March 27, 2007 filed an application . . . to protect . . . the 'Red Sole Mark'" as a registered trademark, thereby asserting exclusive rights to manufacture and market shoes with lacquered red soles. As a consequence, when Yves Saint-Laurent "prepared to market a line of 'monochrome' shoes in purple, green, yellow and red," in which the entire shoe—including the sole—was the same color, Louboutin sued to stop the sale of the red variation.

The dispute involved the obscure details of intellectual property law, in which arcane legal concepts such as "aesthetic functionality" and "acquired distinctiveness" play a large role. But the basic stakes of the dispute are easy to understand. Like many high-fashion brands, Christian Louboutin's business strategy was to make sure its products were both easily identified and exclusive. Thanks to Louboutin's tireless efforts, red soles had become a coveted status symbol. In order to ensure they stayed one, the company needed to control who could make—and, indirectly, who could wear—shoes with red soles. But Louboutin's success had inspired pretenders: the company had already fought to stop fast-fashion merchant Zara and several other companies from selling inexpensive red-soled shoes in Europe. Unlike Louis XIV, Louboutin could not simply decree that red-soled shoes were restricted according to social rank. Fortunately for Louboutin, today's laws offer a subtler but almost as effective dress code.

While medieval and Renaissance sumptuary laws fought against the unsettling changes of fashion, today's sumptuary codes ally themselves with fashion, harnessing its mercurial energy to sort and rank people. The widespread acceptance of Enlightenment values has made overt status hierarchy unacceptable: as a consequence, status has either been disguised or made to seem democratic. Accordingly, over the course of the eighteenth and nineteenth centuries, dress codes explicitly based on status gave way to a seemingly egalitarian meritocracy. Of course, fur, supple leathers, silks, cashmere, Egyptian cotton, to say nothing of precious metals and gems, still served to announce status, just as they always had. The difference was that the prerogative to wear sumptuous attire, once restricted directly according to social rank, was increasingly restricted only indirectly, by ability to pay. Here, the rapid changes of fashion *reinforced* rather than undermined the social hierarchy, facilitating what Thorstein Veblen dubbed conspicuous waste: by ensuring that clothing is out of style long before it shows signs of wear, the fashion cycle makes the ability to dress à la mode proof of wealth. These status symbols are, of course, still with us today, but by the nineteenth century, they had become unreliable: industrialization and mass production made the manufacture of clothing less expensive, allowing the average person to imitate the costly fashions of the elite. This trend accelerated in the twentieth century and today, synthetic materials mimic costly textiles at a fraction of their cost, bringing the look of luxury to a mass market, while fast fashion ensures that affordable copies of the most refined and avant garde designs are widely available days after fashion houses unveil them.

We now rely on other methods of marking status. Like many of the dress codes of the post-Enlightenment era, today's laws enforce social status under the guise of merit: in this case, the intrinsic quality of the luxury product. Ralph Lauren's horse and polo player insignia, Louis Vuitton's stylized initials, the overlapping "C"s of Chanel, the distinctive blue of Tiffany's packaging—these symbols are the purple silk and ermine trim of the twenty-first century. Likewise, the red sole of a high-heeled shoe—once exclusive to the French aristocracy—is now the exclusive trademark of designer Christian Louboutin and a status symbol for his well-heeled customers. These all signal exclusivity and high status, in large part because the law allows only a limited number of garments to exhibit them, much as the laws of Tudor England or the decrees of Louis XIV limited the circulation of sumptuous fabrics and precious gemstones. Elite fashion houses and luxury jewelers make sure their prices stay high by tightly controlling the distribution of the goods, from point of manufacture to point of sale. Supplies are limited. Contracts with retail sellers prohibit or strictly limit discounting and some companies reserve their most exclusive products for their own company-controlled boutiques. All of this is possible because the law gives each of these companies exclusive control over the use in trade of a distinctive status symbol: their trademark. The law does not directly dictate which individuals can display these high-status symbols. But, the effect of modern trademark law is to protect exclusivity and high status—just as the sumptuary laws of the past did. As trademark law expert professor Barton Beebe argues, "[S]umptuary law did not disappear with industrialization and democratization, as is generally believed. Rather, it has taken on a new . . . form" in modern trademark law.

Trademark law is supposed to link a company's name and logo to its products to promote accurate information for consumers and efficient, competitive markets. By giving a manufacturer an exclusive right to use a distinctive name or mark, the law prohibits unscrupulous sellers from "palming off" possibly inferior goods as those made by an esteemed competitor. In theory, both honest manufacturers and consumers benefit: a company with a reputation for quality goods enjoys the benefit of that reputation and the buyer knows that he is buying a product made by a trusted company—not an inferior imitation. This standard account of trademark law is in harmony with the ethos of meritocracy: we assign marks of distinction to communicate the quality of the product and the merit of its manufacturer.

However, a big part of trademark law is unrelated to the goal of ensuring consumers have accurate information. For instance, courts have held that cheap copies of pricier goods are unlawful because they "dilute" the exclusivity and high status of those goods, even if the actual consumers are well aware that the products in question are not what they may seem to be. Why are *obvious* knock-offs illegal? Consumers who buy "Pravda" handbags for $25 on Canal Street in Manhattan do not actually think they are getting a great deal on the wares of the prestigious Milanese fashion house Prada. The person who buys a $40 "Rolax" watch does not really believe it's a precision mechanical Swiss timepiece. These fakes are unlawful, not because the actual buyers might be misled, but because casual third-party observers might be: cheap copies make the real goods less exclusive. For example, in a case involving an inexpensive replica of a costly "Atmos" clock made by the esteemed Jaeger-LeCoultre watchmakers, a court noted disapprovingly that "customers would buy . . . [the] cheaper clock for the purpose of acquiring the prestige gained by displaying what many visitors would regard as a prestigious article. . . ." Similarly, in a decision prohibiting knock-off Hermès handbags, a court pointed out that "the purchaser of an original . . . is harmed by the widespread existence of knockoffs because the high value of the original, which derives in part from their scarcity, is lessened." Likewise, Christian Louboutin is entitled to stop its competitors from making shoes with red soles, even when those shoes are labeled and marketed under a different brand name, because a profusion of red-soled shoes would undermine the association of red soles with wealth and high status. The problem in these cases was not that purchasers of the cheaper products had been tricked; to the contrary, the worry is that they unjustly got a sort of counterfeit prestige while consumers of the genuine luxury product were robbed of the high status they had paid for. These buyers of cheap imitations are a bit like a Renaissance-era butcher's wife in a glittering crown—they confuse the meaning of an established status symbol.

Much of the value of a luxury good lies in its rarity. In fact, the economic market for such products is fundamentally different than the market for other, non-luxury products. Typical products—basic necessities, practical tools, run-of-the-mill clothes—are valuable because of their objective qualities. The classical economic laws of supply and demand apply. Demand for such products should typically reflect the quality of the product and the price: high-quality products that are inexpensive will be in greater demand than similar-quality products that are costlier, or than lower-quality products of the same price. Accordingly, manufacturers of similar goods will compete for customers on the basis of price, driving prices down, to the benefit of consumers. But many luxury goods are desirable as much for their rarity as for their intrinsic qualities. For these products, a higher price can actually *increase* the demand within the target market of luxury good consumers; accordingly, manufacturers may not compete on the basis of price but instead on the basis of exclusivity, resulting, in some instances, in a competition to charge the *highest*, rather than the lowest, price. Economists have a name for such exclusive, high-status products: *Veblen goods*. Named after the famous theorist of conspicuous consumption, Veblen goods derive their value from the rarity that accompanies a big price tag, and accordingly are desirable *because* they are expensive and therefore an exclusive status symbol. For instance, the buyer of a Hermès "Kelly" or "Birkin" handbag (who typically must wait for months or even years before being allowed the privilege of paying as much as $30,000 for one), the high price is an indispensable guarantee of exclusivity, serving the same social function that sumptuary laws once did.

Because Veblen goods derive their value from exclusivity, it is vital that the supply is strictly controlled. Trademark law allows manufacturers to control supply, creating a sort of artificial scarcity. Accordingly, the law prohibits not only inferior-quality copies but also copies that are *identical* to the authorized goods. For instance, even Gucci's own employees are unable to spot counterfeit handbags made by "super copiers;" nevertheless, such products are as unlawful as poorly made fakes. Similarly, when Tiffany sued eBay for facilitating the sale of counterfeit Tiffany-branded jewelry, the company had to concede that its own experts often could not distinguish the authentic products from the counterfeits. In fact, sometimes the factories licensed to make trademarked goods surreptitiously run off additional units to sell outside of authorized channels. These extra units are *exactly the same* as the licensed products: they are made in the same way, by the same people, using the same equipment and the same raw materials. But they are just as illegal as a cheap-quality knock-off because they threaten to dilute the carefully controlled exclusivity of the luxury product.

Luxury fashion houses enforce modern sumptuary law, guarding their privileges as zealously as a seventeenth-century tailors' guild. Their trademarks are the latest in a historical progression of sartorial status symbols, each more refined and abstract than the last. At the birth of fashion, status symbols required opulent display: elaborate construction, costly fabrics, and the use of precious metals and gems. After the Great Renunciation, status symbols became subtler, consisting of sumptuous but understated fabrics such as fine wools and cashmere, and refined construction that was apparent only to those who knew what to look for: the tailored suit was, in a sense, an expression of sumptuous attire refined to a pure form. The trademark takes the progression to its logical conclusion: all that remains of the spectacle of aristocratic display is an abstract symbol. Instead of cumbersome ermine and velvet, one carries a bag adorned with a single, telltale Hermès "H"; in the place of a flashy bejeweled crown, one can substitute an unadorned shoe with a flash of red sole.

Blazers of Glory

The subtler dress codes of the nineteenth century still survive, especially when it comes to tailored clothing. Although democratic values and mass production has created a sort of egalitarian professional uniform in the sport jacket, blue blazer, and business suit, social rank is still communicated through small sartorial variations. These finer points of style are stealth status symbols for a society that professes admiration of self-effacing modesty but rewards unapologetic self-promotion.

"It was a humid day, but every man seated in the Grill Room of the Four Seasons was wearing a jacket." In the dog days of the summer of 2013, according to the *New York Times,* the well-dressed diners at lunch included billionaire financiers, media moguls, and real estate robber barons—people who would command respect no matter what they wore. But the unwritten dress code was clear: "The few diners who arrived underdressed could request one of 30 navy blazers hanging in the upstairs coat room."

The "loaner" jacket was once a time-honored tradition in fine restaurants that enforced a formal dress code. It served two purposes: it preserved the genteel ambiance of the restaurant while also marking the wearer as something of a rube. The *Times* aptly described the typical loaners as "stained, ill-fitting polyester jackets of shame." The official dress code, which distinguishes the restaurant itself as an elegant establishment, works alongside a more intricate one, which makes distinctions among its patrons. Jackets and ties equal refinement, therefore the restaurant where jackets and ties are worn is refined—but some jackets and ties are more refined than others. A traditional cut sends a different message than a trendy one; subtle details of construction will be noticed by those in the know; the person who arrives wearing a well-tailored and stylish ensemble outranks someone in a poorly fitting, cheap-quality "loaner."

Even with respect to "loaners," there are additional nuances. For example, before it abandoned its mandatory jacket-and-tie dress code, the 21 Club in Manhattan would provide a shapeless blue blazer and a tie—often festooned with "21" emblems or images of the club's trademark lawn jockeys—to those who failed to arrive for dinner properly attired: a badge of shame. But the 21 Club loaner tie, worn anywhere *except* at the 21 Club, becomes a status symbol: it announces not only that one dined at the famous restaurant but also that one was so nonchalant about it as to turn up with an open collar (perhaps having just finished a game of squash at the racquet club?). Accordingly, for decades, students at the nation's elite prep schools, colleges, and universities have prided themselves on their 21 Club ties, "acquired" after meals with relatives, friends, or trust fund administrators.

The "loaner" jacket was almost always a navy-blue blazer. The blue blazer is a men's wardrobe staple; it suits everyone and matches almost everything. It is an ideal loaner because it homogenizes and differentiates; it is at once egalitarian and hierarchical. It can be an icon of both bourgeois respectability and aristocratic pedigree. A blue blazer may be worn as part of a chauffeur's livery or by the tycoon riding in the back seat, hence its universality and democratic symbolism. But God is in the details! There are slouchy polyester blue blazers and there are bespoke blue blazers from the London tailor that outfitted Captain Bligh himself; there are mass-produced stiff blue blazers, the default uniform of middle management the world over, and then there are ultra-lightweight silk and cashmere blue blazers handsewn by Neapolitan artisans, the choice of European aristocrats and venture capitalists. In its simplicity, subtlety, and ubiquity the blue blazer reveals how the details of clothing can signify social status, express political ideals, and convey individual personality.

The Four Seasons' lending library of blue blazers was a throwback: even in 2013, before the iconic restaurant was forced to vacate its home in the Seagram Building, it no longer required gentlemen to wear a jacket and tie. Indeed, the era of the formal dining room dress code was coming to an end: only two years later, the New York City Commission on Human Rights would declare that rules "requiring men to wear ties in order to dine at a restaurant" were a form of unlawful sex discrimination. Still, many patrons who arrived in their shirtsleeves chose to borrow a blazer. What was once an official dress code has become an unofficial, unwritten one—perhaps all the more potent as a marker of status for it.

Conventional sartorial terminology distinguishes the blazer and the sport coat. The latter traces its origins to jackets worn for sports such as hunting, rowing, and tennis—hence the name—and retains traces of its activewear ancestors: tweed fabrics, earthy plaids, and readily accessible hacking pockets derived from hunting; bold patterns and colors from crew and racquet sports. The navy-blue blazer is descended from the dress uniform of naval officers, which explains why it is traditionally worn with brass buttons and why it is the only "odd" jacket—a jacket without matching pants—that traditional sartorial mores allow to be double breasted. A long-lived account has it that the blazer got its name from a warship, the *HMS Blazer*, the captain of which outfitted his men in blue jackets adorned with brass buttons in order to impress the fashionable young Queen Victoria. Menswear authority G. Bruce Boyer playfully insists that "[t]he story has been told so many times, it almost deserves to be true." Alas, the name *blazer* more likely first referred to *red* jackets worn by rowing clubs at Cambridge, Oxford, and other English colleges and universities.

Nomenclature aside, the first *blue* blazers were the uniforms of eighteenth-century British naval officers. They were spare and functional: their wide lapels could be buttoned against cold sea air; their color was sober and unassuming. Law and custom restricted the blazer—an officer's uniform—to an elite, and as a consequence it became a status symbol. Then fashion took over. It became chic for officers to wear their jackets off-duty, and soon civilians embraced the garment too. Later, fashion houses produced myriad variations: some emphasized the blazer's nautical past with brass buttons, others its clubiness with emblazoned crests; still others simply reproduced its spare elegance in exquisite tailoring and sumptuous fabrics.

Traditionalists debate the appropriate type and placement of buttons. Brass buttons are traditional but can look clichéd. Horn is more subdued but undermines the blazer's nautical pedigree. Insignia buttons offer cachet, but only if the shield or crest in question belongs to one's own alma mater, private club, or family. Fake crests used by fashion designers are the mark of a parvenu, and as for "borrowed" crests, one need only consider *Esquire* creative director Nick Sullivan's cautionary story: "A friend was handed down a Savile Row-made wool serge reefer . . . with a set of Blackheath Golf Club buttons . . . [but] missing [a] single gold button. So he returned to the original tailor . . . 'Yes,' they said. They . . . would be happy to attach a replacement. All my friend needed to do was provide proof of membership in the Blackheath Golf Club."

Then there is the question of placement. For single-breasted blazers, two-button closures are standard but uninspired. Three-button closures are anathema—unless they are a three-roll-two closure, in which the top button is never used and the lapel is cut to roll open to the second button. Those are the height of relaxed elegance. In the case of double-breasted blazers, subtleties of button position separate the classic blazer from vulgar bastardizations. As menswear authority "Nicholas Antongiavanni" (the nom de plume, reportedly, of former Republican party speechwriter Michael Anton) explains, the six-two closure "forms . . . a double legged martini glass, which buttons in the middle row" and is rakish, having been worn by stylish men such as Fred Astaire, Humphrey Bogart, and *60 Minutes* news anchor Ed Bradley. It has the added advantage of versatility, as it can also be buttoned on the bottom row, "which effects a casual, relaxed look." Indeed, the unstudied chic of fastening only the bottom-row button on a six-two closure was celebrated in menswear journal *The Rake*, which devoted an entire article to the virtues of *doppiopetto trasformabile* blazer, pioneered by the Caraceni tailors of Rome: a "style of jacket . . . that . . . can be fastened at the middle button or closed using the bottom button." But take care! The *option* to button the bottom row on a convertible six-two blazer is quite different from the *necessity* of doing so on the déclassé six-one closure. The six-one "forms a keystone [rather than the double legged martini glass] that buttons *only* at the bottom row" and, according to Antongiavanni, is the ill-advised choice of the "Garment District huckster," along with such cautionary exemplars of poor taste as O. J. Simpson's defense lawyer Johnnie Cochran and game show host Alex Trebek. Even here, however, there is a notable exception: the renowned Parisian house of Cifonelli is famous for its six-one double-breasted jackets, which menswear authority Simon Crompton of the influential newsletter *Permanent Style* considers to be "absolutely exquisite."

I own four navy blazers at last count: an unlined tropical wool with white mother-of-pearl buttons, single-breasted with peak lapels (this combination is, admittedly, unorthodox, but rules are made to be broken); a heavier twill three-roll-two with patch pockets, smoked mother-of-pearl buttons and full canvasing; a medium-weight single-breasted two-button with relaxed construction and half-canvasing; and a double-breasted six-two in a slightly lighter-than-navy-blue flannel (again, anathema to purists, but what fun are they?). I won't deny an element of elitism: I'm partial to the Neapolitan shoulder—especially the fabled *spalla camicia*, in which the sleeve is gathered at the shoulder for a very subtle, almost pleated effect—and the surgeon's cuff with functional buttons. Both are markers of high-end tailoring: the former requires skilled handwork in manufacture; the latter requires, at a minimum, skilled custom alteration, as the sleeve must be shortened to fit the individual, and then the buttonholes added afterward—typically handsewn and cut. As always, there are mass-market copies of once-exclusive sartorial features: many inexpensive, mass-produced blazers now feature cuffs with working buttons, pret-a-porter. But in this case, the sleeve cannot be properly shortened at the cuff, leaving one with two unattractive choices: wear the sleeves too long—a dead giveaway that one lacks funds, cultivation, or both—or shorten the sleeve from the shoulder—a difficult and time-consuming operation even for a skilled tailor, who would charge more than the value of the jacket to do the job. The result of less-than-expert attempts at such alterations is inevitably a poor fit in the shoulder. Better to leave the sleeves long, turn them up, and call it sprezzatura.

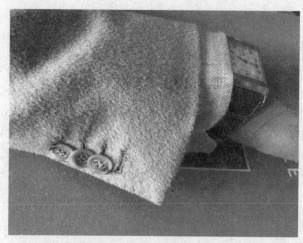

This jacket includes "surgeon's cuffs" with
working buttonholes.

My father took me shopping for my first "good" blue blazer just
before I left for college. We went to a few shops in San Francisco—the
kinds of places that also sold traditional men's accoutrements such
as shaving brushes, ivory-handled straight razors, horse-hair clothes
brushes, and over-the-calf dress socks. Even at these refined men's
haberdashers, some jackets didn't make the cut. A few were ventless.
Dad scowled at the salesman: "Left over from the days of the Conti-
nental style?" The man whisked the offending blazers away. One had
four buttons along the front. "The latest style!" the salesman said as
Dad looked at the fourth button quizzically. I liked it, having seen
four-button jackets worn by famous actors and musicians in magazines and on music videos.

"No," my father said firmly. "That will be out of style before you
are a sophomore."

Another had heavily padded shoulders and was made of a lightweight crepe fabric. I thought it was great and begged Dad to ap-
prove it.

"It's kind of like the one David Bowie wears. . . ."

This did not impress my father, who replied that actors and musicians may wear all sorts of outlandish costumes on stage, but we were not shopping for a theatrical audition. The salesman eventually admitted that he shared my father's dim view of the jacket, adding, apologetically, "But, this is what the young people these days want. . . ."

"Let them buy it, then." Before I could interject that *I* was such a young person, he added, "Those who want to pay for it with their *own* money." It was settled. We would get a blazer that would see me through four years of college (and perhaps graduate school!) and make me look presentable at collegiate dinners or cocktail parties. Having attended an especially raucous prospective students event that ended with Jell-O vodka shots in a dormitory hallway, I wasn't convinced that modern collegiate life required such a garment. But we finally settled on an acceptable jacket: three plain antiqued brass buttons—lapel rolling to the second, full canvas construction, in a tropical-weight navy-blue wool, double vents, patch pockets. We also bought several button-down collar oxford cloth shirts in white and sky-blue, a couple of striped ties, and a simple dark brown leather belt. We left the store and rounded the corner to buy cordovan loafers at a similarly old-fashioned shoe store. My ensemble was complete. It would take me from church to the theater in style. It was high quality but not overly luxurious—appropriate for a young man. It was much better than my father could afford when he went off to school. I was lucky to have it and I would be happy to have it when the time came.

The time came in my sophomore year at Stanford. I traveled thirty miles north for what would be the last-ever impromptu pre-game rally in San Francisco—a traditional start to the weekend of the Stanford–USC football game (the following year the city put a stop to it by insisting on a parade permit and a $1 million insurance guarantee against destruction of property). I played alto saxophone in the Leland Stanford Junior University Marching Band, an unconventional outfit whose repertoire included classic-rock songs. Before a game, we ate a breakfast of beer and doughnuts. The LSJUMB had been banned from several major hotel chains, two international airlines, and one foreign country on account of its antics—a point of pride celebrated by the posting of hate mail on a wall of shame in the "Band Shak" on the Stanford campus.

The weekend rally was an unplanned, pub-crawl-and-parade through the streets of San Francisco, which ended in a beach rally in Aquatic Park. My best friend and I had made a plan for the evening. I would "march" with the band until our wanderings took us somewhere near Union Square, where USC traditionally held *its* Friday night rally. There I would slip away from the group, change from the band uniform of bright-red jacket and Gilligan-style bucket hat into a something suitable for drinking and flirting with unescorted young women, and meet him at the upscale bar and Polynesian restaurant Trader Vic's. I was hopelessly shy and awkward and, accordingly, certain the plan would not work. My friend, on the other hand, was tall, good-looking, and exuded confidence—Holmes to my Watson—and insisted that we would both have the night of our lives if I simply followed his lead. It was decided: I packed the blue blazer, tie, shirt, gray flannels, and loafers in my saxophone gig bag and set off for the City that Knows How.

As planned, I peeled away from the parade at Union Square and, after changing clothes in a department store restroom, headed to Trader Vic's. A sizable crowd had gathered outside; inside the bar was packed. As we peered in, a group of unusually well-turned-out young women walked confidently into the bar. They had been with a group of young men in USC sweatshirts, jeans, and tennis shoes whom the host stopped as they tried to enter: "I'm sorry, but we're very busy— no one is allowed in the bar unless they have a dinner reservation." The men looked longingly after the young women who had just left them behind. They started to argue with the host. "You don't look old enough to drink, anyway—please stand aside."

My friend turned to me. "C'mon," he said, "let's get a drink." Without waiting for my response, he sauntered into the restaurant. Dressed in an impeccably cut blue blazer, oxford cloth button-down, knit tie, and gray flannels, he looked to the manner born (in fact, he was a real estate agent's kid from Vacaville) and acted the part. Just as he approached the host stand, he looked past the expectant host and cried, "Carol, is that you?" It wasn't, of course, but as the host turned around to look, my friend quickly scanned the reservation list, looking for late arrivals.

"Johanson, party of four—have our friends checked in?"

The host ran a finger down the reservation list. "No, sir, you are the first. I almost crossed you off as a no-show."

"Sorry, the traffic was unbelievable."

"Yes, these college students are everywhere this weekend. I'm afraid I don't have a table free just yet. As I said, we thought you weren't coming."

"I understand. We'll just wait at the bar."

We went to the bar and my friend continued the charade as we chatted with the young women—we were co-owners of an art gallery in Union Square—but after a drink and a few more minutes of playacting I couldn't keep it up. I admitted we were really college students. The women all burst out laughing. "Of *course* you are; so are we. I might have believed your story if you hadn't mixed up Monet and Manet. *Monet* did the waterlilies; Manet did the one with the picnic. But I'll give you this: you sure dressed the part."

Prepping for Success

I have a well-worn paperback copy of Lisa Birnbach's classic satirical reference, *The Official Preppy Handbook*. It was a style bible many years after my family moved from the northeast to California: as a teenager, the irony of an African American preppy from a Central California public school was too delicious to resist. More than that, preppies were a fascinating object of study. The apotheosis of the White Anglo-Saxon Protestant, the preppy was both exotic and strangely familiar to me. My father was certainly not white, much less Anglo-Saxon, but he was a mainline Protestant through and through. He was an ordained minister of the Presbyterian church. In the early 1970s he worked with a very traditional and well-established Presbyterian church in the northeast— so traditional and so well-established that the ushers in church wore morning suits. We were the only African American family in attendance at Sunday services and faced the predictable difficulties and awkwardness of being the first to integrate a venerable and somewhat hidebound institution, but my parents cherished the memories of the church and its dignified and refined approach to communal worship.

The *Preppy Handbook* chronicled a closed culture, barely legible to outsiders, yet one that could be understood and mimicked with sufficient attention to the rules—and exceptions. "Preppies dress alike because their wardrobes are formed according to fundamental principles that they absorb from their parents and peers. And although the Preppy Look can be imitated, non-Preps are sometimes exposed by their misunderstanding or ignorance of these unspoken rules," wrote Birnbach. Forty-five illustrated pages followed, detailing the importance of Madras cloth; mandatory and unacceptable types of tailoring, fabrics, and jewelry; the imperative to wear certain types of footwear without socks; and more. Reading the *Preppy Handbook* left one with something more than a list of dos and don'ts; one began to appreciate an inner logic, which would guide one through unforeseen challenges. The *Handbook* counsels an intricate combination of compulsive correctness (watchbands must match belts and shoes; hair must be neat; faces, clean-shaven) and very specific transgressions (clashing bright colors should be worn together, trousers must be one size too big). Garish color combinations and slouchy tailoring abound, each unflattering garment compensating for its aesthetic inadequacies with the enviable caché of association with a costly sport or exclusive school. There was a preppy aesthetic—or anti-aesthetic— of sorts, which underlaid the rules. At the heart of this aesthetic was something extremely familiar to someone raised in the Calvinist tradition: an abiding suspicion of pleasure and beauty, in tragic conflict with the universal human lust for the same.

This distinctively Protestant fusion of status and morality reached its apotheosis in the United States. By contrast, the English—from whom the preppy inherits his status but not his taste—have a celebrated sense of style. Masculine attire in particular owes many of its most enduring virtues to the denizens of the Sceptered Isle, from Beau Brummel to the Duke of Windsor. Indeed, the now world-renowned sartorial style of the Italians took shape when that nation's tailors sought to adapt classic English tailoring to the warmer climate of the Mediterranean. But the American colonists brought with them across the Atlantic not the lively eccentricity of Merrie Olde England but the repressed ethos and ostentatious drabness of English puritanism. As a result, in what is still the dominant culture of the United States, no sensual enjoyment can go unpunished. Around any activity or endeavor that involves pleasure—food, drink, and most of all sex and its stylish co-conspirator, fashion—an elaborate scaffolding of denial and misdirection must be built. Sex is tolerable as a way of continuing the family lineage and as an escape valve for healthy-if-inconvenient masculine drives, the less spoken of which, the better. Food is necessary and sometimes one must put on a show in order to keep up appearances, but once again, enjoyment is not the point and preparations should be accordingly lacking in unseemly finesse. Drinking is ubiquitous but one can't admit that it is simply a sybaritic indulgence, so in the hands of the preppy it becomes a competitive sport: it was the preppy-dominated American fraternity, with its hazing rituals, that invented drinking "games," beer bongs, and the like—scourges of every American university.

As for clothing, the imperative is to spend as much as possible while still looking somewhat haphazardly put together. Hence the proliferation of obscure cult labels that can only be purchased in places like Martha's Vineyard and that only those in the know will recognize as pricey; hence the reverse snob's practice of wearing threadbare suits and worn shoes so as to demonstrate that he has dressed like this for decades; and hence the adamant refusal of anything that might suggest one had actually made an effort.

The Preppy Handbook itself was a send-up but there are serious books and websites dedicated to convincing the reader that the old families of the Eastern Seaboard are great paragons of sartorial flair. To these exhortations it is typically added that preppy style is so refined, so subtle, so arcane in its aesthetics, that those not to the manner born might mistake it for the lazy, indifferent attire of a cloistered and complacent hereditary elite. It's in this way that the mystique

of preppy style has retained its staying power: anyone with the te-
merity to question it has, by his very skepticism, revealed himself as
untutored, too dim to appreciate the heightened sensibilities of the
blue-blooded. Preppies may feign offense at this description but they
will in fact take none because their aspiration is neither stylishness
nor beauty but exclusivity, which they brilliantly achieve. Tattered oxford cloth button-down collar shirts and "Nantucket red" chinos for
men; nondescript flat shoes and unimaginative pearl necklaces for
women—these are the choices of the preppy precisely because they
are both expensive *and* either bland or garish: a combination that
guarantees that no one outside the tribe will wear them.

Reverse Snobbery and the Red Sneakers Effect

The prestigious understatement of past eras informed Baldassare Castiglione's notion of sprezzatura: nonchalant excellence which conceals
the effort required to achieve it. This ideal only grew in importance
with the Masculine Renunciation. Today's sprezzatura typically involves
pricey bespoke tailoring and luxurious fabrics, treated with aristocratic
disdain. Unsurprisingly, stylish Italians epitomize it. Menswear blogs
and magazines pore over the seemingly accidental details of sprezzatura in a futile attempt to reduce effortless elegance to a formula that
anyone can follow. The Italian viscount's necktie is tied with a careless
asymmetry. The knot may be dimpled, but the dimple is never centered
in the knot. The narrow blade of the tie might be too long, peeking
out from behind the wider front blade, as if he couldn't be bothered to
retie it. Inevitably, despite these apparent flaws, the tie still manages
to look well-balanced and graceful. The collar of a button-down collar
shirt might be left unbuttoned; a wristwatch might be worn over a shirt
cuff, as the Fiat motors scion Gianni Agnelli wore his; the sleeves of a
sport coat might be unbuttoned and rolled or pushed up (demonstrating nonchalance and the presence of custom-tailored working cuff buttonholes at the same time). The common thread is the ability to convey
a casual familiarity with fine clothing.

This requires money, but also a certain confidence that must be earned, or perhaps inherited, but cannot be bought. Contrast this effortless panache to the labored and awkward attire of the 45th President of the United States, Donald Trump, who was photographed on several occasions with his necktie blades fastened together with *Scotch tape* (**Insert, Image #21**). The use of tape is required because Trump habitually ties his tie such that the front blade is far too long, dangling well below his waist. As a consequence, the too-short, narrower end cannot reach the loop on the over-long wider end and the two threaten to go off in separate directions, like Cabinet members with competing agendas.

This is a clear error, according to the canons of menswear decorum: one should fasten a necktie so that the front falls just at the waist, then thread the narrow end through the loop on the back of the wide end to keep it neatly in place and hidden. Of course, the stylish Italian with his tie askew and too-long narrow blade transgresses against this convention as well. The crucial difference is that unlike the Italian's devil-may-care attitude, Trump's tie betrays a devil who cares too much—and about the wrong things. Whereas the Italian's slightly askew tie demonstrates nonchalance—the mark of sprezzatura—Trump's mis-tied and taped tie suggests a desperate but failed bid to look impressive—a badge of insecurity. The former looks good despite an apparent lack of effort; the latter looks bad because of an evident lack of good taste. A taped necktie is worse than an honest, poorly tied one—it's not only a failure but also a fraud, a paper moon artlessly stuck over a cardboard sea.

Sprezzatura—the ancient art of seemingly effortless style—is both a status symbol and a way of turning a uniform into a mode of personal expression. It involves a fine balance of care and carelessness; respect and irreverence for older dress codes. There are rules, but rules are made to be broken—as long as they are broken in the right way, demonstrating mastery and casual disregard as opposed to either ignorance or belligerent defiance.

A less artful but equally effective mode of power dressing involves the total and conspicuous inversion of the conventional status symbol, turning a violation of the canons of elegance into a sort of merit badge. The English literature and law professor Stanley Fish noticed this type of reverse snobbery with respect to the cars favored by university faculty. Fish observes that at some point in the 1970s, "American academics stopped buying ugly Volkswagons and started buying ugly Volvos . . . [or] ugly Saabs. . . ." These cars "provided a solution to a new dilemma . . . how to enjoy the benefits of . . . affluence while at the same time maintaining the proper attitude of disdain towards the goods affluence brings." Fish saw the ugliness of Volvos as a coded form of virtue signaling that applied much more broadly: "In the collective eye of the academy, sloppiness . . . indifference and inefficiency are virtues, signs of an admirable disdain for the mere surfaces of things, a disdain that is itself a sign of a dedication to higher, if invisible, values." University professors enjoy a well-earned reputation for unfashionable attire, unkempt hair, and a disheveled appearance. Faculty offices are a riot of dog-eared books, teetering stacks of periodicals, piles of paperwork, and half-empty coffee cups. The absent-minded professor, tooling around on a ramshackle bicycle, wearing a threadbare corduroy sport coat is a fixture in cinema—and on most real-life college campuses.

There is something charming, perhaps even admirable, here: the life of the mind leaving no time for vanity; ideas crowding out image; substance triumphing over form. But the penchant for cars like Saabs and Volvos that are both ugly *and expensive* suggests that there's also a bit of snobbery involved. Tenured university faculty enjoy perhaps the greatest degree of personal freedom of any salaried professional in the capitalist world. We have no real boss—university administrators routinely, ruefully, and only half-jokingly say that *they* basically work for us—and no clients or customers to please (students don't count because, after all, *we* grade *them*). Professors who dress badly do so because they can get away with it: in this sense, sloppy, casual attire symbolizes their privilege. Indeed, as a rule, the more privileged the professor, the shabbier the clothing. Tenured professors typically dress more casually than junior faculty, who still feel the need to impress students and senior colleagues. At any national academic conference, the Ivy League professors are almost always the least well-dressed people in the room.

The power of reverse snobbery is so widespread that researchers have coined a name for it: *the red sneakers effect.* Professors Silvia Bellezza, Francesca Gino, and Anat Keinan found that university professors wearing garish red sneakers or a scruffy beard and a T-shirt were perceived by students as having higher status than those with a clean shave, polished shoes, and a tie. The red sneakers effect extends far beyond the ivied walls of academe: sales clerks at luxury boutiques thought a shopper wearing gym clothes was more likely to be a celebrity or VIP than a shopper in a dress and fur coat. "Wealthy people sometimes dress very badly to demonstrate superiority," one clerk noted. "If you dare enter these boutiques so underdressed, you are definitely going to buy something." An indifference to fashion is high status because it suggests the kind of seriousness of thought that is unconcerned with appearances generally and also because it suggests an indifference to the opinions of others. Like the VIP who shops at Hermès wearing gym clothes, the shabbily attired professor announces his high status by inverting conventional sartorial symbolism: he doesn't dress to impress because he doesn't *need* to impress.

Unsuitable

In March of 2019, David M. Solomon, John E. Waldron, and Stephen M. Scherr, senior executives of the venerable investment bank Goldman Sachs, sent an internal email with the subject line "Firmwide Dress Code." It reads, in part:

> Given . . . the changing nature of workplaces . . . in favor of a more
> casual environment, we believe this is the right time to move to a
> firmwide flexible dress code. . . . [P]lease dress in a manner that
> is consistent with your clients' expectations . . . we trust you will
> consistently exercise good judgment in this regard. All of us know
> what is and is not appropriate for the workplace.

For decades, a business suit has been required attire for professionals in banking and finance. Indeed, some say that the thin stripes on a pinstripe suit were originally meant to represent the lines on an accounting ledger. The suit reflected seriousness and practicality, following the symbolism of the Great Renunciation, and, through the sartorial details of cut, fit, and fabric, it conveyed a hierarchy of status. No other garment could accomplish this fusion of austerity and luxury; self-effacement and display. But in recent years suits have begun to fall out of favor. Goldman Sachs is far from the first firm to relegate the suit to ceremonial attire—indeed, it is one of the last. In March of 2019, the *Wall Street Journal* reported that sales of men's suits had plummeted by 8 percent in the preceding four years.

Perhaps the suit is no longer the default masculine professional attire because over time it has become a sort of costume, as obvious a status symbol as the opulent, aristocratic attire it displaced in the waning years of the eighteenth century. Moreover, its symbolic meaning is out of date. Today's high-finance world no longer values the prudence and sober judgment that the suit represents. Instead it prizes innovation and daring; not a fair and modest return on investment but the aggressive pursuit of a windfall. Accordingly, a new generation of money men (they remain overwhelmingly men) have abandoned the suit. What began in the 1960s as "Aloha Fridays" and spread nationwide in 1980s in the form of Casual Fridays has become a casual workweek dress code, punctuated only by rare "client-facing" occasions when a suit is still worn, like courtly dress at an affair of state. Business casual is the new norm.

One might imagine that financiers would use their newfound freedom to express themselves. Instead, with breathtaking speed, professional men from coast to coast have adopted a new uniform, more bland and austere than the plainest blue suit. The Instagram page @MidtownUniform features legions of professional men in various urban settings—crossing Manhattan streets, ordering coffee at generic business district cafes, standing in front of the glass doors of office buildings. They are all dressed almost identically. The Midtown Uniform consists of an oxford cloth shirt in white or blue (the daring

Two men wearing the Midtown Uniform.

may opt for pink or a subdued gingham), a pair of khaki or navy trousers, expensive loafers, and a Patagonia fleece vest, typically in gray, occasionally in black or navy.

For roughly two centuries professional men have worn a de facto uniform—a black, dark blue, or gray suit. The Midtown Uniform reflects an unwritten dress code that has rushed in to fill the void left by the demise of this older dress code. Khaki pants, oxford shirt, and loafers have a stylized informality. One can imagine that some people might actually dress like this when not at work but few people do. As a consequence, the Midtown Uniform seems unpretentious—just something one has tossed on—yet it is also immediately recognizable as professional attire. The all-important Patagonia fleece vest copies the function of a sport coat, blazer, or vest—it skims the body but also obscures it, flattering the physique. It suggests a rarified, out-doorsy athleticism: the fleece is designed for hiking, camping, and rock climbing—wilderness activities not easily accessible to urbanites and which, for that reason and for cultural reasons, are typically the activities of the affluent. The Midtown dress code would not allow a hoodie emblazoned with a sports team logo—the comparable garment of the working class—to substitute for the Patagonia fleece. Indeed, all evidence suggests that the fleece must be of the Patagonia brand, or one of equivalent price and practical unfashionableness (e.g., Vineyard Vines, Nautica—Moncler may be acceptable but is dangerously trendy, while anything made by a company that also sells women's handbags, cologne, or, it should go without saying, suits, is a mistake). A fleece emblazoned with the logo of a prestigious firm or professional conference is also an acceptable substitute, provided it is given out exclusively to employees or attendees and not sold to the general public. A *Patagonia* fleece emblazoned with an exclusive company or conference logo is especially prestigious.

Written dress codes are now almost unknown in the rarified circles of finance and management consulting, and when they do appear, they almost always omit any specific prescription or prohibition in favor of vague admonishments, such as the Goldman Sachs executives' freighted insistence: *All of us know what is and is not appropriate for the workplace.* Bloomberg.com finance reporter Matt Levine, a veteran of Goldman Sachs, decodes the dress code in this way:

> Goldman's dress code is that you should dress the way you're supposed to dress at Goldman. . . . The difference between a middling banker and a great one is this sort of tacit knowledge, a sense of appropriateness and nuance and savoir-faire. . . . [I]f you need explicit rules for how to dress then you'll never master the really hard parts. . . . *That* is the dress code.

The Midtown Uniform provides a solution for those uncertain of their savoir faire. Much better to be unimaginative than to be incorrect and show oneself to be outside the cozy fraternity of those who *know what is and is not appropriate for the workplace.*

The Midtown Uniform is, of course, in essence a reinterpreted business suit. Like the suit, the Midtown Uniform conveys practi-cality, masculine athleticism, and—by suggesting exclusive outdoor pursuits—social status, while also allowing for minor refinements that mark one's position in a hierarchy of equals. Hence, three hun-dred years after the Masculine Renunciation gave birth to the suit, we have arrived where we began, with a professional dress code based on subtle social hierarchy and masculine exclusivity.

By most accounts, the business-casual dress codes that inspired the Midtown Uniform were designed to cater to the laidback ethos of Silicon Valley, home to a growing share of investment bank clients. Today's techie dress code—or anti–dress code—was born in the 1960s, when the New York–based International Business Machines Corporation was the stereotypical tech company. IBM epitomized the mid-century corporate bureaucracy: its dress code required white shirts, black ties, and dark gray suits, suggesting employees were in-terchangeable parts of a well-calibrated machine. The small, scrappy software companies of Northern California brought a rebellious, hip-pie sensibility to tech, emphasizing flexible thinking and innovation over bureaucratic discipline. Intel, for instance, eliminated the layers of management typical of the twentieth-century corporation and en-couraged individual creativity and initiative: "[T]here would be no dress codes, no hierarchies, no protocols." Atari, Sun Microsystems, and, later, Microsoft all followed in this anti-bureaucratic mode. The elimination of professional dress codes went hand in glove with the individualistic ethos that these fledgling companies believed fostered innovation.

But a new, unwritten dress code quickly rose from the ashes of the old one. Conventional professional attire—epitomized by the suit—was thought to reflect old-fashioned thinking; consequently, the suit went directly from *de rigueur* to *verboten*. Tech entrepreneur Peter Thiel made this anti–dress code explicit in his 2014 book *Zero to One*, advising "never invest in a tech CEO that wears a suit." But new vesti-mentary strictures naturally followed. For instance, when tech executive Jorge Cortell (#brainsnotrequired) described high-heeled shoes as evidence of a lack of intelligence and inconsistent with a respect for "data, science, health . . ." he expressed not an indifference to fashion but an obsession with it—a determination to define his own, presumably sensible and honest attire, in opposition to the superficial artifice of high heels.

For all of their loudly announced opposition to corporate conformity, today's technology companies aren't exactly bastions of individuality. Indeed, there's a tech uniform, almost as unvarying as the Midtown Uniform. As he surveyed the crowd in downtown Palo Alto in 2014, software engineer Alexey Komissarouk told tech business reporter Queena Kim that he could tell whether someone worked in tech just by what they wore; in fact, he could even tell what kind of tech job each person had: "The engineers? T-shirt, jeans and hoodies." Another engineer agreed, "Hoodies signal young talent." A zippered sweater worn over a button-down (a refined version of the Midtown Uniform) was the tribal garb of the venture capitalist. Software designers—the creative types in tech—could risk designer sweatshirts and selvedge denim—"the engineer's outfit but with a bit more flair."

According to Silicon Valley insiders, "[I]n the fast-moving world of tech, the idea is to show you are not wasting precious time on something as vain as fashion." When Yahoo! CEO Marissa Mayer appeared in a 2013 *Vogue* magazine spread wearing a sapphire-blue Michael Kors dress and Yves Saint-Laurent stiletto heels, Silicon Valley's reaction was neither congratulatory nor indifferent; it was disapproving. One commentator summed up the indictment of Mayer's fashionable ensemble, saying she "comes off as if she's on vacation, she's relaxing while everyone else is doing work."

Similarly, Facebook founder Mark Zuckerberg, having become famous for a uniform of hoodie sweatshirt or gray T-shirt and flip-flops, was not content to simply enjoy his comfortable if uninspired wardrobe; he could not resist attributing moral significance to it:

I really want to clear my life to make it so that I have to make as few decisions as possible about anything except how to best serve this community [Facebook]. . . . [M]aking small decisions about what you wear, or what you eat for breakfast, or things like that . . . consume your energy. . . . I'm not doing my job if I spend any of my energy on things that are silly or frivolous. . . . [T]hat's my reason for wearing a grey T-shirt every day.

Zuckerberg in his uniform of gray T-shirts embodied the ideal ethos of Silicon Valley: an unselfconscious nerd too busy obsessively designing tomorrow's technology to worry about appearances. This has a naïve charm. But if the CEO of the company thinks he *isn't doing his job* if he spends *any* energy on the frivolous matter of attire, then what are we to think of the employee who arrives at work wearing a sharp tailored suit or a pair of high-heeled Louboutins? Here Zuckerberg's shift to the second person is revealing: he begins discussing his own ambitions but then insists that "making . . . decisions about what *you* wear . . . consumes *your* energy." Purported indifference to appearance becomes a reason to judge based on appearance; a new dress code displaces an older one.

Indifference to fashion has become the hottest trend. A host of clothing stores and services now cater to the tech sector promising to take the work out of workwear, "so you can spend your time doing awesome guy stuff." (One worries about what that might mean.) The BlackV Club, which specializes in . . . black V-neck T-shirts, markets its pricey cotton pullovers with the come-on "You're Too Busy to Worry about Clothes: the world's most successful people don't spend time choosing what to wear."

This grim asceticism extends beyond attire: the company Soylent promises to free busy tech professionals from the contemptible waste of time involved in eating solid food with a powdered substance that, when mixed with water and vegetable oil, purportedly contains "all the nutrients your body needs to be healthy." Soylent is the *reductio ad absurdum* of the reverse snob's conspicuous self-denial, disguised as tough-minded practicality. According to its boosters, Soylent (oddly, but perhaps appropriately, named after the science fiction film *Soylent Green,* in which a dystopian future society subsists on a mysterious food product that turns out to be made of human cadavers) offers choice and convenience. "Eat food when you want, drink Soylent when you want" proposes the company's advertisements. But when prominent executives can't waste time on choosing breakfast, how long will it be before Soylent or something like it becomes an obligatory sign of professional virtue?

When Mark Zuckerberg was summoned before the Congress of the United States in 2018 to defend his business practices, he wore a suit. It was a wise decision: lawmakers and public officials were inclined to take Zuckerberg's attire as a sign of respect—or lack thereof. For instance, on the day before Zuckerberg was about to appear, Donald Trump's chief economic advisor, Larry Kudlow, publicly wondered, "Is he going to wear a suit and tie and clean white shirt? That's my biggest question. Is he going to behave like an adult . . . or give me this phony-baloney—what is it?—hoodies and dungarees?"

The suit, it seemed, still had its uses, even for the unofficial prince of famously informal Silicon Valley.

That's because the suit offers advantages that no other ensemble can. Unlike a hoodie or the Midtown Uniform, a suit communicates seriousness of purpose. It conveys a familiarity with and respect for conventions. Because it requires at least a modicum of effort and because its tailoring gives the impression of improved stature and posture, it suggests a physical and mental discipline. Although a well-made suit can be as comfortable as jeans and a T-shirt, to say nothing of a Patagonia fleece, its true comfort comes from its ability to project competence. When Mark Zuckerberg was on his own turf he could afford to assert his status through the subtle signals of reverse snobbery. But when he was out of his element and under attack, he needed sartorial armor. He needed to come across as a responsible adult capable of running one of the world's largest companies and managing the unexpected challenge it posed for American democracy. When he had to care what other people thought—and needed them to know he cared—he put on a suit.

The suit was such a dramatic advance in sartorial form that all subsequent changes have been small refinements to the basic design established almost three hundred years ago. Because of the strength of that basic design, the suit has evolved while still retaining its essential form. Because it has been the ubiquitous uniform of the adult male, unchanged in its essential elements, for centuries, the suit can combine its conventional associations of practicality, industriousness, and civic virtue with many other meanings that it has acquired from the countless men—and more recently women—who have worn it over its long history.

For instance, the suit as an outdated bourgeois status symbol doesn't explain the roguish charisma of the unflappable Michael Caine's sharp tailoring in films such as *The Italian Job, The Ipcress File*, and *Get Carter*, or Alain Delon's steel-gray suits in the *nouvelle vague* classics *Le Samouraï* and *Le Cercle Rouge.* The constricting suit of the uptight, dutiful company man stands in stark contrast to the easy, irreverent besuited elegance of Frank Sinatra, Dean Martin, Sammy Davis Jr., and Peter Lawford—the infamous "Rat Pack"—that haunted bars, nightclubs, and casinos from Palm Springs to Las Vegas to Manhattan. And while the counterculture turned the term "suit" into an epithet, no hippie was ever hipper than Miles Davis, who personified cool disdain in his button-down oxford cloth shirts and sack suits with "jackets cut specifically for his . . . playing posture" from the legendary Andover Shop in Harvard Square. The elegant, fuller-cut suit can evoke a hidebound patriarch; the crisp, trim suit is the uniform of the federal G-man or, when paired with a turtleneck sweater or open collar, the garb of the dissolute playboy. This rich symbolism, acquired over the course of three centuries, is unique in the canon of Western fashion—no other garment is as iconic and evocative and at the same time as multifarious in affect.

The suit can even evoke armor, reflecting tailoring's ancient origins as sporting gear or formal court dress. This makes it the perfect attire for the gentleman spy, who must move unnoticed among aristocrats and captains of industry while still always ready to fight. James Bond—as well known for his style as for his secret missions—

provides one of the most well-known examples of the iconography of the suit. Sean Connery's Savile Row tailoring combined the best of long-standing sartorial tradition with contemporary styling to yield garments that were impeccably "correct" without being stuffy (among the best were the dinner suit with shawl collar and turnback cuffs from *Dr. No* and the glen plaid three-piece suit from *Goldfinger*). Most recently, Daniel Craig famously filled out Tom Ford's already snug tailoring with a bodybuilder's brawn, prompting the *New York Times* to dub the new look "006½." While Matt Spaiser, the editor of the website The Suits of James Bond, found Craig's suit "too fashionable in the cut . . . so tight, it pulls everywhere and it is unflattering. . . ." the costume designer for *Skyfall* felt the unconventional tailoring was a way of making the suit more versatile: "Suits are always associated with businessmen . . . [but] I wanted a cool suit. I wanted people to . . . say, 'I don't have any problem with Bond running or driving a motorcycle in a suit,' because a suit is a second skin in that case."

It's hard to imagine Bond trading in his suits for corporate casual or the Midtown Uniform. The suit remains a status symbol, because it can also be a subtler expression of individual personality. The strength of the design has allowed the suit to signify both worldliness and desk-bound insularity, sobriety and decadence, conventional decorum and countercultural defiance, formal ceremoniousness and virile rough-and-readiness—all with only slight modifications to the standard ensemble. The suit is a malleable icon, and a democratic one. Because of its long history as a symbol of professional competence and civic virtue, it has become an attractive option for people of all walks of life and both sexes. Accordingly, it has slowly lost its masculine exclusiveness as women have adopted the suit, not in the mode of provocative drag or transgressive cross-dressing, but as a natural adaptation of women's wear. Ironically, because of its history as the default uniform of authority, privilege, and success, the suit has been retailored to fit a diversity of personalities and lifestyles. Despite its origins as a sign of exclusively masculine virtue, today's suit is among the most egalitarian ensembles to emerge from over six centuries of Western fashion.

•   •   •

If even Mark Zuckerberg occasionally needs the sartorial stature of the suit, where does a norm of dressed-down informality leave people who struggle on a daily basis to be taken seriously? Reverse snobbery is the prerogative of those who don't need the good opinion of others. The red sneakers effect only works for those who can underwrite it with other, more obvious signs of status, such as their race and sex. It is rare that women can pull it off, as the experience of Mary Beard—the eminent historian of ancient Rome who was ridiculed by a TV critic for her unpolished appearance—proves. The idea that a polished appearance is evidence of frivolity leaves women, again, in a double bind. Like the suit once was, the Midtown Uniform is exclusively masculine. Its blend of sportswear and business casual expresses male athleticism, male understatement, and male privilege. A feminine equivalent would be as awkward as a feminine morning suit. A woman in the Midtown Uniform would be deemed sexless, frumpy, and butch or, perhaps, eroticized, because every feminine physical attribute would stand out in contrast to the implicitly masculine prototype. Maybe she could wear the sporty fleece and oxford cloth shirt with a skirt and pumps. Or, to retain the off-duty sportswear vibe, she might choose yoga pants—but the enduring controversy surrounding that simple, practical garment suggests that this would not achieve the desired result. Indeed, the Midtown Uniform is more immutably masculine than the suit, which women have adapted to their needs over the decades. As Susan Scafidi, director of Fordham University's Fashion Law Institute notes, "We've just achieved the parity of the pantsuit, and suddenly we're told the standard pantsuit is no longer workforce attire. Women will need to find another way to achieve parity in attire. . . ."

It is even rarer that people of color can achieve the red sneakers effect: a Black man in a hoodie and jeans is more likely to be treated like Trayvon Martin than like Mark Zuckerberg. Indeed, consider, the experience of one of the world richest women, Oprah Winfrey, when she dashed into a Hermès boutique in Paris after exiting a transcontinental flight. She was precisely the sort of person who would dare to enter a boutique underdressed and she was definitely going to buy something. She was used to being recognized and treated with the deference our society grants to the rich and famous. But here she was rebuffed—told the store was closed even as other shoppers completed their purchases inside—by a hapless salesperson who apparently did not recognize her and saw only a Black woman in casual attire. The snub was literally heard 'round the world: it was a public relations catastrophe for Hermès, prompting speculation about the salesclerk's motivations that ran the gamut from racism to exhaustion to Parisian *hauteur* (my own interpretation at the time). In any case, much of the public reaction to the incident suggested that Ms. Winfrey had suffered for violating a color-coded dress code. An anonymous source close to Ms. Winfrey insisted that the store would have accommodated Celine Dion or Barbra Streisand in similar circumstances. One blog post commenting on the incident read "Oprah Musta Forgot She Is Black," suggesting that people of color must dress to impress simply to be treated with respect. For some, refined attire is less an assertion of superiority than a bid for parity.

This, of course, is why the suit has begun to lose its preeminence. Because it was retailored to send mixed and multiple messages and to fit almost everyone, the suit became unsuitable as a status symbol. In its place, the casual Midtown Uniform and tech dress code, which suggest indifference to attire while also ascribing moral importance to it, have become the twenty-first century's expression of the ethos that inspired the Great Masculine Renunciation. But this mandatory asceticism does not reflect intellectual depth or practicality, far less free-spiritedness. Rather it is a form of reverse snobbery and a symbol of a severe work ethic, stripped of its spiritual pretensions and embraced as a new secular morality.

Despite a noisy pretense of egalitarianism and practical-minded indifference to the trappings of status, clothing today remains a sign of rank within a social hierarchy almost as elaborately stratified as that of Europe's anciens régimes. Brand names and trademarks distill conspicuous sartorial status symbols to their essence: pure signs of social rank, exclusive because they are costly and costly because they are exclusive. Tailoring, and its esoteric details, are subtle signs of distinction—now even more important within officially classless societies. Meanwhile, reverse snobbery takes the elitism of understatement to its logical extreme, making a highly stylized form of asceticism a sign of civic virtue. Today's dress codes have not renounced the hierarchical ordering that defined the sumptuary laws and social etiquette of the past; instead they have refined it, making it more insidious than ever before.

Chapter Seventeen

Artifice and Appropriation

Outfits for Cultural Tourism: Bleached Blonde Hair, Dreadlocks, Hoop Earrings, a Cheongsam, a Pink Polo, an Abacost, European Luxury Tailoring

SINCE THE LATE MIDDLE AGES, FASHION HAS RECYCLED THE symbolism of the past in service of new social movements, political projects, and modes of self-expression. New styles recombine fragments of older, once-unified ensembles, evoking their original meanings but also transforming them by putting them in a new context. Fashion absorbed and repurposed older markers of status, ethnicity, nationality, religion, and sex, incorporating their symbolic potency while also undermining aspects of their original meaning: for example, elite men and later, women, first adopted high-heeled shoes because they suggested military prowess, but in so doing, they transformed high heels, both in their meaning and in their physical form, from a martial riding shoe to a courtly status symbol and, later, to a sign of feminine sex appeal. This transformation of symbolic meaning in service of self-expression is the very essence of Western fashion.

As the pace of the fashion system—reflected in the clothing, industry, stylish individuals, and social groups—accelerated during the twentieth century, so did this creative reuse and destruction of older sartorial symbols. This profound and often deliberate challenge to the status quo was both opportunity and threat to people from all walks of life. Fashion disrupts ancient hereditary privileges only to create new forms of elitism; it undermines aging status hierarchies and the cherished affinities of downtrodden social groups with equal indifference. Dress codes at the dawn of the twenty-first century reflected and reacted to these incessant and kaleidoscopic changes.

Novel combinations of familiar sartorial elements combined with an aesthetic flair can be truly unique—at least until the look is picked up on Instagram and becomes a trend. The challenge is to find novel combinations of sartorial elements that are still familiar enough to evoke meaning. This often requires combining the fashions typical of one's own group with foreign elements, borrowing—one might say "appropriating"—garments, objects, and grooming that have long-standing associations with a social class, ethnic group, or religion to which one doesn't belong. This can yield striking and evocative results but at the cost of diluting the very associations on which they rely. Many of today's dress codes are a response to this struggle between the idiosyncratic use of sartorial symbols and the desire to safeguard their original meaning.

Blonde Ambition

On August 12, 2013, Farryn Johnson was fired from her job at Hooters Restaurant in Baltimore, Maryland, because her blonde hair violated the company's dress code. Anyone familiar with the Hooters brand can see the irony here. Hooters has created a global brand image around the "Hooters Girls": curvaceous waitresses who dress in tight, low-cut T-shirts and orange short-shorts, serving up PG-rated titillation with every order of curly fries. The prototypical Hooters girl, as depicted in the company's advertisements and represented in most of its restaurants, is a voluptuous *blonde*. For Hooters to ban blonde hair was as incongruous as for it to ban cleavage. Farryn Johnson, however, was not the stereotypical Hooters girl. She was African American. And her blonde hair violated a well-known, if unwritten, dress code.

The Hooters employee handbook sets out detailed standards for dress and grooming:

Part of being a Hooters Girl is maintaining the Hooters Girl image at all times. When you are in the Hooters Girl uniform, you are literally playing a role. . . . [Y]ou must comply with the Image and Grooming Standards that the role requires. . . .

Hair must be styled and worn down at all times with a glamorous appearance. No visible braiding, weaving, pony tails or similar styles will be allowed.

The Hooters dress code also prohibits "bizarre, outrageous or extreme . . . hair-cuts, styles or colors" and hair "more than two-shades in variance" from its natural color. Johnson's blonde hair probably violated this "two-shades" rule, but the arbitrator who heard Johnson's discrimination complaint found that the company didn't apply it evenhandedly: white women—including some in the company's own advertising campaigns—broke the rule with impunity. Johnson was fired for a different reason: "The manager told me black people don't have blonde hair," said Johnson.

In fact, plenty of Black people *do* have or have had blonde hair: Beyoncé, Nicki Minaj, and Dennis Rodman, to name just a few. They almost certainly bleach their naturally much darker hair—as do many Caucasian blondes. Peroxide blondes, bleach blondes, platinum blondes, bottle blondes, news-anchor blondes—all of these terms refer to the well-known fact that *most* blondes owe their fair hair to chemical processing, not to genetics. Indeed, blonde hair is, for most Black women, no more artificial than *straight* hair, which the restaurant effectively required: according to former Hooters waitress Rachel Wood, Black women felt obliged to straighten their natural hair or conceal it under a wig "to create an acceptable Hooters Girl image." If artificially straightened hair was practically a job requirement, why was Ms. Johnson's artificially colored hair a problem?

Hooters required a very specific type of artifice: a mix of conventional and unthreatening feminine attributes. Straightened hair reflects an ideal of feminine beauty that was already firmly established by the time Anne Moody sat in at the Jackson, Mississippi, Woolworth's: Black women who copy hairstyles designed for white women signal their acceptance of the norms and values of the mainstream society—especially the role of women as decorative. But blonde hair is a symbol of purity and desirability that remains the prerogative of the white race. Women of color who go blonde highlight the artifice underlying most blonde hair and transgress status boundaries to lay claim to a racially exclusive symbol. What Farryn Johnson's manager really meant when he said Black people *don't* have blonde hair is that Black people *shouldn't* have blonde hair.

The blonde has long held a distinctive place in the sexual imagination of Americans, whether the sexpot allure of Mae West, Lana Turner, and Marilyn Monroe or the innocent, girl-next-door charm of Sandra Dee and Doris Day. Alfred Hitchcock's famous "ice queens" are striking examples because the director was unusually self-aware and deliberate in his casting. Hitchcock deployed the symbolism of the classic blonde in all of its permutations: Eva Marie Saint's elusive and cunning minx in *North by Northwest*, Grace Kelly's society girl on a pedestal in *To Catch a Thief*, *Dial M for Murder*, and *Rear Window*, Janet Leigh's good girl gone bad in *Psycho*, and, most iconic of all, Kim Novak's unattainable mirage of the feminine ideal in *Vertigo*. Novak's dual roles in the film—the impossibly refined blonde Madeleine Elster and her worldly doppelganger, the brunette shop clerk Judy—provide a case study in the symbolism of blonde hair. When Jimmy Stewart's heartsick detective Scottie Ferguson begins his obsessive campaign to remake Judy into Madeleine, a trip to the hair salon is the final, crucial step in the transformation. As Scottie impatiently waits for Judy/Madeleine to emerge, the hairstylist tells him, reassuringly, "It's an easy color"—a wry allusion to the feminine artifice that plays such a pivotal role in the film.

As Hitchcock well understood, even as twentieth-century Americans worshipped the natural blonde, everyone knew that most blondes were made—not born. Over time, the blonde evolved: the immaculately artificial blondes of the early-twentieth-century Hollywood studio system, the platinum blonde of 1950s bombshells such as Jayne Mansfield and Mamie van Doren, and, later, of country-Western singer Dolly Parton, the self-consciously ironic bottle blonde of Debbie Harry, singer for the new-wave band Blondie (one album was titled *Once More into the Bleach*), and later, Madonna, whose conspicuous dark roots announced a knowing, postmodern relationship to blonde iconography (made literal in the name of her 1990 concert tour, Blonde Ambition). Blonde hair had become a floating signifier, unmoored from any consistent—much less natural—association with ethnic pedigree or biological predisposition. Blonde hair can only refer to other examples of blonde hair: Dolly Parton is an exaggerated iteration of Jayne Mansfield's already exaggerated blonde hair; Debbie Harry's blonde hair with dark roots deliberately subverts the glamorous and innocent blonde hair of the past; Madonna's blonde hair evokes and comments on sexiness by association with Marilyn Monroe and Lana Turner. Throughout the 1980s and 1990s unambiguously fake blondes proliferated and became less and less remarkable. Blonde hair was as commonplace as artificially straightened or curled hair.

It's no surprise that women of color wanted in' on the fun. Yet as late as 2013 one could be told that "black women don't have blond hair." It's hard not to see this prescription as a sort of racial sumptuary code, a twenty-first-century Negro Act prohibiting Blacks from dressing "above their condition." It's as if the social meaning of blonde hair would be confused, its status diluted, if a woman of color dared to crown herself in blonde tresses, like a butcher's wife wearing a jeweled tiara. Today's laws do not prohibit such status transgressions. They do, however, prohibit race discrimination: Farryn Johnson won a $250,000 civil rights judgment against Hooters.

Couturial Appropriation

If people of color can adopt blonde hair, should natural blondes be able to try out styles associated with people of color? During 2016's New York Fashion Week, the designer Marc Jacobs sent young women down the runway in seven-inch platform sandals, glittery hot pants, silver lamé trench coats, and cotton-candy-colored dreadlocks. The models looked like a steampunk-meets-glam-rock vision of the future: cosmic girls dressed for a laser battle, followed by a night out at the coolest disco in the galaxy. The *New York Times* described it as "a mosh pit of glam Rasta hippie froth" and "a singular, if somewhat out there, point of view." It was a fun, lighthearted, over-the-top collection that seemed destined to inspire at best, delight, at worst, bemusement.

But within hours of the show, Mr. Jacobs was pulled into the long-simmering controversy over race and hair: "Was super cool until I realized the pastel hair was in dreads . . . if that was the look you were going for, use models of color . . . " read one Instagram post. Others were even more pointed: "Why didn't you hire models with real dreads?! That are apart [sic] of their culture. . . . This is hideous and disappointing." Another asked "did Marc Jacobs really just build a whole fashion show around cultural appropriation?" Jacobs wasn't the first designer to face such an accusation. A year before, Valentino employed a predominantly white group of models in a show that featured an African-inspired collection and "corn row" hairstyles. In 1993 a Jean Paul Gaultier collection was inspired by the clothing of Hassidic Jews and in 1997 Hussein Chalayan offered a collection featuring the full-body chador worn by some Muslim women. All of these collections were condemned as cultural appropriation.

It's an ill-defined term, but "cultural appropriation" at its worst involves much more unambiguous transgressions. For instance, in 2014 an Arizona State University fraternity held a party on Martin Luther King Jr. Day at which "nonblack students mocked blacks by donning loose basketball jerseys, flashing gang signs and drinking from hollowed-out watermelons." A 2013 party at the Kappa Alpha fraternity in Randolph-Macon College in Ashland, Virginia, featured a "USA v. Mexico" theme where guests wore sombreros and large mustaches or border patrol costumes. That same year, Duke University's Kappa Sigma fraternity hosted an "Asia Prime" party where guests dressed in silk robes, fake sumo wrestler paunches, and chopstick hair accessories, and "mimicked stereotypically Asian accents." And then there was the Thanksgiving fraternity and sorority party dubbed "Colonial Bros and Nava-hos" held at Cal Poly, San Luis Obispo, where male students dressed as Pilgrims and women as Native Americans. Alas, this was not an original idea: Harvard students may have pioneered the concept with a "Conquista-bros and Nava-Hos" party held on Columbus Day in 2010. The University of Chicago's Alpha Delta Phi chapter also held an indigenous peoples–themed bash, where a Facebook page invited guests to "conquer, spread disease and enslave natives."

Understandably, Jacobs was stung by an accusation that put him into the same basket as these deplorables: "All who cry 'cultural appropriation' or whatever nonsense about any race or skin color wearing their hair in any particular style or manner—funny how you don't criticize women of color for straightening their hair. . . . I don't see colour, I see people. . . . I'm sorry to read that so many people are so narrow minded."

For Jacobs, the idea that white women who wear dreadlocks are guilty of cultural appropriation suggests that Black women who straighten their hair—or dye it blonde—are also wrong to wear hairstyles conventionally associated with other racial groups. The Black is Beautiful movement saw natural hair as an expression of ethnic pride and at the time many considered straightened hair a sign of self-hatred. But while Black is Beautiful pushed back against social expectations and standards of beauty that effectively *required* people to chemically alter their hair, the idea of cultural appropriation had become a new kind of dress code, one that would reserve certain styles for specific ethnic, racial, and cultural groups.

Figuring out which hairstyles belong to which races turns out to be harder than it may seem. Of course, some hairstyles are better suited to certain hair textures than to others and natural hair texture typically does differ according to race. But techniques designed to change hair texture are widely used by people of all races and have been for centuries: braiding, teasing, perms, curlers and curling irons, straighteners and straightening irons, dyes—to say nothing of artificial hair extensions and wigs—are commonplace and typically have little to do with racial identity. The use of artifice to change the appearance of one's hair is one of the most natural things in the world. And, of course, dreadlocks are a result of manipulation and technique—not natural hair texture. That's why it's easy for people of other races to "appropriate" them. Dreadlocks are associated with African Americans as a matter of custom, habit, and culture. But culture changes. In the 1960s and 1970s, during the height of the Black is Beautiful movement, a Black woman with blonde hair would have been seen by many as a self-hating sell-out. Today, blonde hair is simply a fashion choice for Black women, without such political overtones: for instance, no one thinks Beyoncé's blonde hair undermines her credibility as a proud Black woman.

A similar cultural shift could transform the meaning of dreadlocks. Marc Jacobs might relate to Chinese American basketball player Jeremy Lin, who drew the ire of former NBA player Kenyon Martin for his dreadlock hairstyle. "Somebody need to tell him, like, 'All right, bro, we get it. You wanna be black.' . . . but the last name is Lin," Martin said in an Instagram video, adding that he would not have tolerated a player "with that bullshit going on in his head" on one of his teams. Lin fired back with a subtle riposte: "It's all good. You definitely don't have to like my hair and definitely entitled to your opinion . . . At the end of the day, I appreciate that I have dreads and you have Chinese tattoos . . . I think it is a sign of respect. And I think as minorities, the more we appreciate each other's culture, the more we influence mainstream society."

The idea that certain hairstyles should be off-limits to certain racial groups is hard to defend. But Jacobs's critics had more sensible concerns as well. Some pointed out that Black women are pressured to straighten their hair because of racist standards of beauty—the same standards, they hinted, that led Jacobs to choose white women for his models: "If you don't see colour, then why are your models 95% white?" demanded one commentator. Others pointed out that while Jacobs used dreadlocks as a trendy fashion statement, people of color often suffer discrimination because of similar hairstyles: "I guess this means POC [people of color] can wear our locs freely now and not be blocked from a . . . job . . . ?" queried one Instagram user. These complaints reflected well-justified frustration over the underrepresentation of women of color in the modeling industry. The complaint was that even when using a style typically worn by Black women, Jacobs chose white models. Others referred to a racial double standard that Jacobs, perhaps unwittingly, exposed: styles that seem threatening or disreputable when worn by a Black or Latino person become cool or chic when adopted by whites. Just as a hoodie sweatshirt is threatening on Trayvon Martin but disarmingly unassuming on Mark Zuckerberg, dreadlocks are a sign of delinquency when worn by a Black person but become an edgy fashion statement when worn by a willowy Caucasian fashion model.

Similar concerns about a double standard inspired students at Pitzer College in 2017 to paint a strident demand on a public wall: "White girl, take off your hoops!!!" The missive was painted in large white letters on a campus wall set aside for graffiti and artistic expression. When baffled students asked for clarification, one student, Alegria Martinez, came forward to explain that white women wearing hoop earrings were guilty of "appropriating styles . . . that belong to the black and brown folk who created the culture. The culture actually comes from a background of oppression and exclusion." Martinez insisted that "the black and brown bodies who typically wear hooped earrings . . . are typically viewed as ghetto, and are not taken seriously by others in their daily lives . . . hooped earrings [have become] symbols . . . of resistance. . . ." and asked rhetorically, "[W]hy should white girls be able to take part in this culture (wearing hoop earrings . . .) and be seen as 'cute/Aesthetic/ethnic' . . . ?" As with the Marc Jacobs show, the complaint here was that a style that is seen as vulgar or menacing on dark-skinned women becomes fashionably edgy on a white woman. Another student added, "[I]f you didn't create the culture as a coping mechanism for marginalization, take off those hoops, if your feminism isn't intersectional, take off those hoops, if you try to wear *mi cultura* when the creators can no longer afford it, take off those hoops. . . ."

Some mocked the idea: for instance, Katherine Timpf, writer for the *National Review,* insisted, "[I]f you are going to try to tell me that I cannot wear a piece of metal . . . twisted into a circle, then I am going to tell you to shut up. . . . [N]obody owns circles." Maybe not circles, but the intersectional feminists of Pitzer College were far from the first to write a dress code dictating who could and could not wear earrings. Rules have accompanied earrings since their invention. Minoans used earrings as a status symbol in 2000 B.C.; earrings signified social rank in ancient Egypt and Greece and military allegiances in ancient Persia. Earrings have since been worn as signs of membership and identity by Hebrew slaves, Indian royalty, Russian Cossacks, and, of course, pirates of the high seas. Sometimes earrings carried a stigma for those unfortunate enough to be forced to wear them, such as for the Italian Jewish women in the late Middle Ages who were forced to wear earrings as a mark of their faith. In other cases, those with the right to wear earrings jealously guarded the privilege. The Pitzer College women were far from the first to claim an exclusive right to wear pieces of metal twisted into circles.

Alegria Martinez insisted that "white people have actually exploited the culture and made it into fashion." But could it be otherwise? New, incongruous combinations that suggest individuality—whether a modest hijab combined with dramatic CoverGirl makeup or vaguely "ethnic" jewelry worn by a blue-eyed sorority girl—are the essence of fashion. Like the religious purists who lamented that stylish young Muslim women had sacrificed the hijab to fashion, the women of Pitzer College demanded a dress code designed to define clothing as an expression of an orthodoxy. The contretemps over "cultural appropriation" was another example of the centuries-old anxiety about the corrupting influence of fashion on symbols of group identity and social status. Fashion is ready to sacrifice any convention in the tireless quest for novelty; it is indifferent to political struggles and claims of moral prerogative. No doubt: fashion exploits and appropriates, but it doesn't discriminate.

When high school student Keziah Daum posted photos of her Chinese style *qipao* dress on Twitter in the spring of 2018, she stood out from her peers in their conventional pastel taffeta and chiffon. Some

Asian American commenters did not appreciate her bid for individuality: "My culture is NOT your goddamn prom dress," read one post. A follow-up post intensified the criticism: "I'm proud of my culture. . . . For it simply to be subject to American consumerism and cater to a white audience, is parallel to colonial ideology." Another user insisted, "This is not ok. I wouldn't wear traditional Korean, Japanese or any other traditional dress and I'm Asian. I wouldn't wear traditional Irish, Swedish or Greek dress either. There's a lot of history behind these clothes. Sad."

The complaint of "cultural appropriation" seems to be unique to societies marked by conspicuous racial or ethnic hierarchy. Groups who are more secure in their social status tend to be more forgiving when outsiders borrow their fashions. For instance, in China, the birthplace of the *qipao*, Daum's choice of prom dress received a much warmer reception: "As a Chinese I really like your dress. And I think it's kind of a way to show respect to our culture," one post read. Another suggested Daum branch out and wear other traditional Chinese clothing as well: "I'm Chinese, most of us support you. We hope you can publicize the Chinese costumes a lot. Besides qipao, we have Hanfu." In an interview with the *New York Times*, Zhou Yijun, a Hong Kong cultural critic, said, "It's ridiculous to criticize this as cultural appropriation. From the perspective of a Chinese person, if a foreign woman wears a qipao and thinks she looks pretty, then why shouldn't she wear it?" For her own part, Daum said that she didn't mean to "cause any commotion or misunderstanding," and acknowledged "perhaps it [the issue of cultural appropriation] is an important discussion we need to have." Still, she insisted she didn't regret her choice and would wear the dress again.

Anna Chen, a London-based cultural commentator, pointed out that the *qipao* is itself a cultural hybrid: a traditional Manchu garment retailored with distinctly Western influences. "The current outcry could be compared to taking offence because someone in Asia wore a tuxedo," she opined. Indeed, the tuxedo itself was also a hybrid, combining elements of the traditional formal dinner suit with the sportier, more casual short jacket—and one unmistakably non-Western element. It was taken up as part of a relaxed, after-dinner ensemble by

The *cheongsam* or *qipao* combines
elements of Western and traditional
Chinese dress.

English aristocrats—possibly first and certainly foremost the Prince of Wales—and later adopted by a wealthy resident of Tuxedo Park, New York, the town which gave it its unofficial name. In an act of shameless cultural appropriation, fashionable men covered the waist of their new, modern dinner suits with a cummerbund—an accessory first worn in South Asia and adopted by the British military in colonial India (in Persian and Hindi, it is called a *kamarband*). Like a white person in dreadlocks or a *qipao*, these rakish men used an element of another cultural tradition to add individuality and panache to their wardrobe.

Fashion has always been a source of challenging cultural hybrids, in part because it grows and evolves from popular cultural and commercial practices, relatively unconstrained by the type of tradition-bound cultural institutions that control other art forms, such as theater, dance, literature, and the visual arts. This kind of borrowing and re-mixing has become more common in recent decades, as social identities, cultural traditions, and ethnic affinities have become more fluid and open to challenge and reinterpretation. In 2015, *New York Times* chief fashion critic Vanessa Friedman asked whether such cultural hybrids were "a frivolous response to serious problems: cultural appropriation of the worst kind? Or . . . an industry's legitimate attempt to deal with [the] real world [using] its own skill sets?" She concluded that fashion that crossed boundaries and raised uncomfortable questions that had social, political and artistic value: "Often the best fashion is about transgression. . . . At its most basic level, that's how we got women in pants and in miniskirts, all of which horrified plenty of viewers back in the day. . . . It takes risks. Otherwise . . . it risks irrelevance. Otherwise it's just clothes."

Preppy Appropriation

Cultural appropriation goes both ways: elites and dominant groups turn the styles of the marginalized into fashion trends, and marginalized groups return the compliment, remaking the customs of the upper classes and subverting their exclusivity and exploiting their symbolism for new, rebellious purposes. The results can be an improvement on the original in terms of both style and popular accessibility. For example, although the preppy look involves a fair amount of reverse snobbery, it can also be refined and elegant. But what many today admire in it is often mistakenly believed to be the exclusive creation of the moneyed elite of the northeastern United States. In fact, it reflects the relatively recent contributions of a group of talented photographers, discerning men and women of taste, and, of course, fashion designers who—while capitalizing on the mystique that comes along with old money—curated, edited, and retailored the attire of the New England blueblood into something genuinely rakish and chic. They include African Americans, such as Miles Davis, who made the sack suit and oxford cloth button-down collar shirt an icon of cool; Japanese, such as photographer Teruyoshi Hayashida and editors Shosuke Ishizu, Toshiyuki Kurosu, and Hajime Hasegawa, who applied their homeland's exquisite aesthetic sense to curate the selection of American sportswear shown in their book *Take Ivy*; and Jews, such as *Preppy Handbook* author Lisa Birnbach and, of course, Ralph Lauren, born Ralph Lifshitz to working-class parents in Brooklyn long before that New York City borough became fashionable.

In the 1980s, Lauren perfected the Ivy League look, distilling the Platonic ideal of preppy staples such as the khaki trouser, the deck shoe, the penny loafer, the duffle coat, the oxford cloth button-down collar shirt, and, of course, the polo shirt, after which he named one of his clothing lines. Like a Michelin-starred chef reimagining the cheeseburger, he remade and perfected these classics. In so doing he captured the imagined experience of the preppy lifestyle in his clothing, making it available to everyone as aspirational fantasy. Devotees purchased Polo shirts in every color of the rainbow, sometimes doubling down and wearing two at a time, collars flipped up; they paired them with Polo woven cloth belts, Polo madras-print pants, and Polo deck shoes. Aspiring preps took the sardonic *Preppy Handbook* as a serious guide to personal style and the most devoted even sought out Lauren's inspirations at old-school stalwarts such as J. Press, L.L.Bean, and Brooks Brothers, only to find that Lauren's copies were often more authentic than the long-since-degraded originals. Slowly but surely, the New England elites who had inspired Lauren began to take their inspiration *from* him. In 1980, *The Official Preppy Handbook* confidently declared that "the sport shirt of choice is Lacoste." By 2011 the blog *Ivy Style* described Ralph Lauren's polo shirts as "Lacoste, only better," and no less an authority than menswear legend Alan Flusser told a reporter that on weekends in the Hamptons, the shirt of choice is now "not Lacoste . . . but Polo."

Lauren's genius was not to copy preppy style but to take the all-American, democratic aspiration to aristocratic pedigree and attach it to his own aesthetic sense. Today's preppy look reflects the appropriation of a marker of an insular ethnicity by fashionable outsiders and the transformation of a status symbol into an aesthetic sensibility.

"But I'm doing pretty good, far as geniuses go, and I'm doing pretty hood in my pink Polo," quips Kanye West in "Barry Bonds." By 2007 the unlikely link between Ralph Lauren's pony-and-rider trademark and the culture of Black inner cities was so well established that every listener from Compton to Kennebunkport got the joke. Hip-hop artists, street gangs, and stylish kids had adopted a variation of the preppy look: polo and rugby shirts, ski sweaters, even blue blazers emblazoned with gilded crests and faux-aristocratic insignia.

In the early years of the second millennium, this was relatively new. Back in the mid-1980s, hip-hop style consisted of brightly colored sports jerseys and hats, tracksuits, basketball trainers, and showy gold and diamond jewelry, or somber, prison- and military-inspired looks such as black, navy, and gray pants, work jackets, and jumpsuits. Both styles involved straightforward references to Black urban life: professional athletes were heroes in Black communities, the quintessential local boys made good; prison grays were a sartorial comment on the all-too-common incarceration of young Black men, while workwear in SWAT-team black and navy expressed tough-guy proletarian solidarity with a nod to the martial chic of 1970s Black radicalism.

Hip-hop had always worn its pecuniary aspirations on its sleeve. The earliest rappers bragged about their wealth and sexual conquests: "checkbook, credit card, more money than a sucker could ever spend," boasted the Sugarhill Gang in 1979's classic "Rapper's Delight." From thick gold chains and diamonds in its early years to luxury cars, Cristal champagne, and charter jets in its more lucrative mature phase, hip-hop has always toggled between describing the challenges of ghetto life and an escapist fantasy of conspicuous consumption, where rappers take the ultimate revenge on a racist power structure by living larger than Wall Street financiers and *Fortune* 500 CEOs. Branding plays an important role in evoking the lush life: rappers name-drop their favorite fashion designers and luxury spirits to achieve verisimilitude much as F. Scott Fitzgerald did with posh hotels and Ivy League colleges, and as Ian Fleming did with 007's Bentleys, Aston Martins, Bollinger champagne, and dinners at London's exclusive men's club, Blades.

In the classic Veblenian mode, only the most showy status symbols would do—iconic trademarks, prominently displayed. The oversize Mercedes hood ornament became a medallion hung on a gold chain necklace; the gold-toned Cristal champagne bottle made appearances in numerous videos and on album covers. Gucci and Louis Vuitton—which had endlessly multiplied their trademarks to become a textile pattern—were cherished brands, both for high-end shopping by successful musicians and for creative appropriation by inventive entrepreneurs. Dapper Dan—Harlem haberdasher to hip-hop elites such as LL Cool J, Run DMC, Eric B. & Rakim, and Salt-N-Pepa—designed bomber jackets, tracksuits, boots, and even car upholstery from Louis Vuitton and Gucci fabrics, sometimes combining incongruous high-status trademarks (e.g., Louis Vuitton fabric overlaid with gold Mercedes-Benz symbols), prefiguring today's multi-brand collaborations (Mercedes x Vuitton?).

There was often a strong element of irony and critique in the way hip-hop culture adopted elite brands. As Dapper Dan recalls, "I was shut out . . . I wanted to make a statement that I could do the same thing that they're doing, but even better. . . . It was . . . an opportunity to thumb my nose at those big houses. . . ." Hip-hop's over-the-top consumerism put a klieg light on the already somewhat vulgar showiness of some high-end brands. Gaudy, trademark-covered handbags and gilded champagne bottles were low-hanging fruit for status seekers, critical commentators on capitalism, and those who were a bit of both. Eventually, Dan's success attracted the attention of the major fashion houses—and their lawyers. Facing multiple complaints and a lawsuit for trademark infringement, Dapper Dan closed his Harlem shop in the late 1990s and went underground; he wouldn't speak publicly again until a 2016 interview with a small, online fanzine. Then in 2017, the tables turned as Gucci introduced a collection inspired by

Dapper Dan's early designs. Some accused the high-fashion label of hypocrisy and appropriation, but Gucci's creative director Alessandro Michele openly acknowledged his debt and invited Dapper Dan to become an official collaborator with the label later that year. Dan opened an exclusive bespoke salon in his Harlem brownstone and launched a *Gucci x Dapper Dan* capsule collection for 2018.

The generation that came after Dapper Dan's heyday in the 1990s began to notice and emulate the somewhat subtler, blue-blood styling of Ralph Lauren. Thirstin Howl III was one of a group of young men from Brooklyn who, in the late 1980s, called themselves the "Lo Lifes" ("lo" short for *Polo*). According to Howl, the Lo Lifes were a fusion of two groups—Ralphie's Kids, from Crown Heights, and Polo USA, from the Brownsville projects—united by a shared love of Ralph Lauren's garments. Polo's image of upper-crust Americana was a big part of the appeal. The Lo Lifes weren't just wearing the colorful sportswear—they were adopting the image that countless magazine ads, billboards, and Polo boutiques had created for the brand. As Raekwon of the Wu-Tang Clan explains, "It expressed you had money. It's like when you think of that horse on your shirt, that horse symbolizes them cats out there playing polo. You know the majority of them is well-off—is comfortable. So it kinda made us feel like, if you got anything Polo on, you got money. You got a certain amount of status in the neighborhood. . . ." According to rapper Young Dro, who recorded the 2010 album *POLO Dro* (Players Only Live Once), Lauren's clothing offered a fantasy of upward mobility: "[O]nce we put that outfit on, we could go chill at the gables the white people. . . . I could go places. I'ma do this through my outfit, nah mean? I'ma go make a living and a life out of what I got through these clothes right here. . . ." Similarly, Thirstin Howl recalls, "[I]t started because there were a lot of people in Lo Lifes who were . . . the kid who got laughed at about his clothes when he was younger. The kid who didn't have nothin'. . . . That's what made the Lo Lifes. . . . [T]hat's what made them go get it and want to look the flyest. . . . [T]hey couldn't say nothin' back to you because your shit was extra sharp."

Some might look askance at the unapologetic embrace of branding that defines the aesthetic sensibility of the Lo Lifes and Dapper Dan. Isn't this just the sort of sycophantic status emulation Thorstein Veblen critiqued in *The Theory of the Leisure Class*, the escapist fantasy that E. Franklin Frazier exposed so unsparingly in *Black Bourgeoisie?* These critiques are both overstated and incomplete. Because so much of contemporary culture is mediated through branded commerce, such criticisms are a bit like condemning Renaissance artists for focusing on religious themes and aristocratic patrons. For better or for worse, brand names and logos have become an important part of our vestimentary vocabulary, a sort of shorthand for a multitude of sartorial symbols. A trademark can be a symbol of a design aesthetic, a sensibility, a personality, and a lifestyle. The bold "H" of Hermès conjures up old-world artisanship, equestrian exclusivity, and Parisian chic (as well as the brand's glamorous customers such as Grace Kelly and Jane Birkin, after whom the company has named two of its most exclusive handbags). Christian Louboutin's flash of red sole communicates sexy urbanity with an edge, the choice of trust fund socialites gone bad and platinum-selling rap divas. Ralph Lauren's Polo logo evokes a stylized preppy culture captured in scores of garments, retail stores, and advertisements.

These sartorial status symbols can be more than a means of one-upmanship: they are also evocative cultural signs. At its best, refined attire reflects a sophisticated aesthetic sensibility developed over the six-century-long history of fashion. Because this clothing was worn by important people on momentous occasions, it is part of our historical and cultural imagination: when we think of significant events or influential people, their wardrobe becomes a character in the drama. Attire communicates because we associate specific garments with their history—even if indirectly—and create new sartorial symbols from fragments of the old: for example, the button placement on a double-breasted blazer or the lapel notch on a sports coat are meaningful because of long-forgotten connections to military uniforms and patrician sports. Similarly, the trademark logo on a polo shirt, shoe, or handbag is a shorthand for these sartorial status symbols; it refers to a constellation of garments, design elements, and accompanying myths and fantasies. Accordingly, a trademark can be a sign of status, a social statement, and a reflection of individual personality. There is a popular interpretive process involved in making such attire meaningful, one that monarchs, religious authorities, politicians, merchants, and even today's multinational corporations can influence but never entirely control.

Fashion trademarks took on a new meaning in the hands of Dapper Dan and the Lo Lifes. Dapper Dan's creations were not really knock-offs of the designer brands: they were wry, even critical statements about those brands. Similarly, the Lo Lifes weren't exactly trying to pass themselves off as Andover students. Expensive designer clothing symbolizes elite privilege only if others assume one has actually paid for it; any suspicion that it has been begged or borrowed—to say nothing of stolen—undermines the prestige and suggests a life of hustling. The Polo-wearing gangs didn't always come by their Polo gear lawfully: Howl recounts, "Every day was a fashion show and a shoplifting spree throughout upstate malls and Manhattan stores." Moreover, they proudly announced the fact with names like "Polo USA (United Shoplifters Association)." For the Lo Lifes, expensive designer clothing conveyed a different kind of status: "[I]f you wanted to be fresh, you had to defend your shit. You had to know how to fight . . . cause [otherwise] you wouldn't be fresh that long."

Like the eighteenth-century commoners who adopted and adapted the aristocratic powdered wig, the Lo Lifes and Dapper Dan, with his unapologetic reuse of high-fashion trademarks, were appropriating a well-established luxury image for their own expressive purposes. The Lo Lifes aspired to the wealth and prestige that Polo represented, but on their own terms—they didn't want to climb the social ladder so much as to pull it down. In this they followed the example of the slaves of the eighteenth century, who wore European finery with a combination of pride and mocking contempt. As journalist Bonz Malone put it, "They challenged classism by wearing Polo—taking something that wasn't meant for them and making it their own."

Elegance as a Survival Skill

La Société des Ambianceurs et des Personnes Élégantes, or La SAPE, is
a league of extraordinary gentlemen dedicated to an exacting standard
of personal style. The *Sapeurs* follow a strict dress code—the "Code
of *Sapologie*," which dictates such details as the height of socks, the
style of a haircut, the telltale unfastening of a single button on a suit
jacket cuff. According to historian Ch. Didier Gondola, *Sapeurs* carry
ivory- or silver-handled walking sticks and wear finely tailored suits,
designer colognes, horn-rimmed glasses, silk pocket squares, "J.M.
Weston lizardskin loafers . . . Cartier watches. . . ." One *Sapeur* claims
to own over thirty suits from the best European tailors, to be sure
he never has to wear the same ensemble twice. Some *Sapeurs* dress
in the subdued tones of a middle-aged CEO while others prefer designer fashions in bold colors worthy of a fauvist painter. The *Sapeurs*,
dressed in their finest, congregate and promenade through the city
streets, living examples of vestimentary refinement and self-esteem,
dandies in the mode of Beau Brummel and the Comte D'Orsay.

The *Sapeurs* would be worthy of note—and a photo shoot—
in any of the world's great fashionable metropolises. But these
twenty-first-century boulevardiers hail from Brazzaville, capital
of the Republic of Congo, and neighboring Kinshasa, capital of the
Democratic Republic of the Congo (DRC), two of the poorest and
most troubled nations in the world: the DRC had a per capita Gross
Domestic Product of only $445 U.S. dollars in 2016, according to the
World Bank. Conspicuous elegance in the mode of nineteenth-century
Europe has a distinctive meaning in twenty-first-century Sub-Saharan
Africa. The *Sapeurs* have adopted—one might say appropriated—
European sartorial traditions, not in sycophantic emulation of former
colonists, but as an indigenous response to local conditions. In their
hands, fine tailoring is a ceremonial costume; high-fashion trademarks become signs of civic ideals and what appears to be a destructive struggle for status is in fact a choreographed dance, symbolizing
a peaceful competition for social esteem and expressing a critique of

a society plagued by endemic violence and poisoned by oppression and corruption.

According to Gondola, the *Sape* was born when the Congo was controlled by French and Belgian colonists. Much like white slave owners in the American South, some white colonists took pride in the sophistication of their servants and encouraged them to dress in European fashions. Fashionable attire became a status symbol for Black Africans, who adopted—and adapted—European fashions. As in the United States, Black people who dressed above their station faced censure and ridicule. In the early twentieth century, a European writer noted with chagrin: "[T]he locals in the region of Brazzaville dress up too much . . . to flaunt their wealth. Many pride themselves on following Parisian fashion . . . and now sport elegant panama hats." Similarly, a colonial governor wrote, with a condescending incredulity, that "the elite of Brazzaville dress sumptuously and even with a certain elegance." Today's *Sapeurs* are guardians of a long-standing Congolese tradition of sartorial elegance: "[T]he *sape* comes from our fathers and our grandfathers . . . my father was an elegant man," said one *Sapeur*. "He was the kind of person to put a breast pocket on his pyjamas."

The Congolese legacy of refined attire did not reflect lives of ease, wealth, or privilege. The Congo was subject to one of the more vicious and exploitative colonial regimes in history. First claimed by the Welsh adventurer Henry Morton Stanley, the Congo became the private property of the Belgian *Association Internationale Africaine*—ostensibly a philanthropic organization dedicated to scientific research and to improving conditions for the indigenous population, its main activity, in fact, was to extract ivory, rubber, and minerals for sale on the world market by exploiting the labor of the Africans. Between 1885 and 1908, millions of Congolese—some estimate as many as 50 percent of the population—died from inhumane working conditions, starvation, and diseases introduced by Europeans. Even by the standards of the colonial exploitation typical of its era, the atrocities of the Belgian Congo stood out and inspired international protest. Most famously, in 1899 Joseph Conrad wrote the classic *Heart of Darkness* describing the

horrors of life in the Congo. In 1905 Mark Twain published a satirical condemnation titled *King Leopold's Soliloquy*—a reference to the
ruler of Belgium at the time—and Arthur Conan Doyle, the creator of
Sherlock Holmes, published *The Crime of the Congo* in 1909. The two
greatest African American leaders of the day, Booker T. Washington
and W. E. B. Du Bois, put aside their infamously fierce disagreements
to join in condemning Belgian rule in the Congo. Reform was slow, un-
even, and incomplete. The Congo won independence in 1960 and in
1971 became the Republic of Zaire.

Kinshasa and Brazzaville are in different nations, but geographi-
cally they are essentially one city, separated only by the Congo River,
and the *Sapeurs* of both cities consider themselves part of a common
fraternity. Brazzaville *Sapeurs* tend to be more classical in their attire,
while the *Kinois* of Kinshasa favor bolder colors and more eccentric
styles, a difference historians attribute to a two-decades-long ban on
Western attire in Kinshasa during the 1970s and 1980s. During the
early 1970s, Zaire's president, Mobutu Sese Seko, imposed a series
of cultural reforms known as the *retour a l'authenticite* (return to authenticity) designed to rid the nation of European influences. Cities
named after Europeans and colonial officials were given new African
names: Leopoldville became Kinshasa; Stanleyville, named after the
Welsh explorer who established European rule, became Kisangani.
Mobutu's government encouraged citizens to change their Christian
names and threatened any parent giving a child a Western name with
five years' imprisonment.

Mobutu also banned European attire, imposing a sort of national
uniform, a Mao-style tunic called an abacost—short for *a bas le costume*,
or "down with the suit"—inspired by a visit to the People's Republic of
China in 1973. The *abacost*, along with thick horn-rimmed glasses, and
leopard-print fez, or *toque*, became a personal signature for Mobutu,
who controlled Zaire until 1997, when he was forced to flee following a
civil war—but only after siphoning billions of dollars from the national
economy as his people starved. Ironically the *abacost*, designed to unify
the nation and level social distinctions, became an international symbol
of the corrupt post-colonial autocrat (**Insert, Image #19**).

The country was renamed the Democratic Republic of Congo in 1997 and since has suffered two more brutal civil wars, ongoing ethnic and tribal conflict, and pervasive abject poverty. Against the backdrop of these horrors and deprivations, the *Sape* has reemerged. What might be a harmless indulgence in better circumstances can seem like reckless escapism amid the violence and poverty of the Congo: arguably, there is an element of desperation and even self-destructiveness in the *Sape*. For instance, one *Sapeur* "worked eight months at his part-time job . . . to earn enough for the single outfit, one of 30 he owns. . . . He lets an ex-girlfriend support their 5-year-old son and still lives with his parents, sleeping in . . . a closet with a mattress." Yet there is also a powerful dignity—even a moral conviction. Ultimately, the *Sape* is a *response* to the social and political conditions of the Congo rather than an escape from them. The Code of *Sapologie* is both a demanding dress code and a demanding ethical code: according to Spanish photographer Héctor Mediavilla, who has studied and photographed the *Sapeurs* since 2003, "a *sapeur* is, by definition a non-violent person, despite the three civil wars that have taken place since . . . independence. They stand for an exquisite morality . . . as they say, 'there can only be Sape when there is peace.' Their motto became 'Let's drop the weapons, let us work and dress elegantly.'" The *Sapeurs* deliberately refigure the physical violence that has scarred their nation for generations into a sartorial contestation: they stage "fights" in which "rival *sapeurs* will do battle with each other, flashing label after label, trying to best their opponents, stripping down, if necessary, to their underwear." According to Mediavilla, "It's combat, and the clothes are the weapons." Like the zoot-suited *pachuco*, the *Sapeur* uses the fantasy of fashion to imagine an alternative social order in which elegance and style replace corruption and violence. The *Sapeurs* find dignity, hope, and joy in grim circumstances. According to Mediavilla, the *Sapeurs* are minor celebrities in their communities: "Their presence is required at funerals, parties and other celebrations to bring a touch of stylishness to these events. . . . [E]verybody knows who they are, where they come from and where they live. . . . [T]hey perform an important social function for their fellow citizens."

The *Sape* reveals a very different Africa than the one of wars, famines, safaris, and caricatured primitive tribes typically portrayed in the Western media. The *Sapeurs* are the products of the colonial encounter in all of its exploitative brutality; they bear its scars and were shaped by its violence. The uncomfortable juxtaposition of the opulent display of the *Sapeur* and the abject poverty of his surroundings is a reflection of the contrast between first and third worlds, metropole and colony **(Insert, Image #20)**. The *Sape* is also a response to the betrayed promise of post-colonial liberation: if Mobutu's *abacost* symbolized a supposed return to a pre-colonial authenticity, the *Sapeurs'* European fashion signifies a rejection of reactionary cultural nationalism. There is something both heartbreaking and beautiful in the *Sape*: it demonstrates the resiliency of the human spirit and the penetration of modern marketing into every sphere of human life; it is an expression of remarkable creativity and of abject status seeking. The dress code of *sapologie* reflects both the best and worst of modern fashion.

Sartorial symbols do far more than signify social rank, position, and affiliation: they refer to stories, legends, personalities, lifestyles, and ideals. Because these symbols are familiar and evocative parts of the language of fashion, it is inevitable that individuals and groups will appropriate and recombine them to create new ensembles with new meanings. Today's dress codes continue a process that began in the late Middle Ages in which fashion absorbed, recycled, and recombined the traditional vestment and its relatively stable, easily legible symbolism to generate powerfully evocative yet ambiguous symbols. This process matured into something close to its present form in what philosopher Gilles Lipovetsky calls the "century of fashion" between the mid-nineteenth and mid-twentieth centuries; ever since, "what formerly appeared as signs of class and social hierarchy had . . . become . . . psychological signs, expressions of a soul or personality."

The Lo Lifes turned preppy Polo into an emblem of hip-hop street cred. The *Sapeurs* transformed the suit from a symbol of European

cultural hegemony into a flamboyant celebration of post-colonial re-
silience. Black and Latina women adopted the ancient hoop earring
as a fashion statement, and a symbol of ethnic pride, only to see it
taken up by white women as a domesticated form of edginess—a tat-
too without the pain or permanence. Similarly, "dreadlocks" became
popular as a vaguely Afrocentric statement, filtered through the international influence of Jamaican popular music; decades later, the
hairstyle had become a sign of soulful artistic idiosyncrasy, ripe for
reuse by the fashion industry. Blonde hair morphed from the crown-
ing glory of racially exclusive idealized womanhood to the sexualized
accoutrement of starlets, to a sign of assertive femininity, available
to all. Fashion's status symbols still mark the traditional allegiances
of class, kinship, faith, and nation. But they are also signs of individual personality and symbols of affinity for cliques, gangs, subcultures,
and countercultures.

The history of dress codes has been the story of this creative recycling of older sartorial signs: the earring of the exoticized and
stigmatized Jew becomes the adornment of the Christian elite; the
adventurous woman dons masculine tailored clothing to assert her
independence; the flamboyant wig of the French aristocrat becomes
the practical headwear of the petite bourgeoisie; African slaves adopt
elements of European formal dress in defiance of white supremacy;
the modest headscarf becomes an assertion of anti-colonial resistance; the red soles of Louis Quatorze become twenty-first-century
high fashion and, later, the "blood soles" of rap diva Cardi B. Exclusive
status symbols are the raw material for new statements of individual
dignity, personal reinvention, social critique, and political resistance.

Fashion is often described as the opposite of authentic: it's superficial, deceptive, and status conscious, whereas authenticity embodies depth, honesty, and down-to-earth meritocratic values. I hope
I've at least raised some doubts about this characterization. Typically,
when people impose or resist dress codes out of a concern for authenticity, their preferred clothing is no less contrived than the clothing they reject as inauthentic: we get Mobutu's *abacost* instead of
Western fashion; the Midtown Uniform instead of the business suit.

All clothing is artifice, contrived to convey meaning and produce an effect: the bland clothing of Thomas More's *Utopia* as much as the ermine and crimson silk of Henry VIII; the denim overalls of SNCC's young rebels as much as the Sunday-best attire of earlier civil rights activists; the sober suit as much as the slinky gown; the modest headscarf as much as the sexy miniskirt and stiletto heels; dreadlocks worn by people of African descent as much as dreadlocks worn by a blue-eyed fashion model. In a sense, each authentic individual is built from scavenged cultural materials and refined by the techniques of human civilization: psychology, philosophy, literature, theater, film, the visual arts, and fashion. The construction of countless unique individual personae from the chaotic storehouse of popular culture has been a miraculous accomplishment of modernity. Our deepest, most authentic selves are not born; they are fashioned.

Decoding Dress Codes

*Fashion is only the attempt to realize art in living
forms and social intercourse.*

—SIR FRANCIS BACON

Embodying Fashion

FASHION IS A WEARABLE LANGUAGE, AS ASTUTE OBSERVERS
from the French semiotician Roland Barthes to the Italian designer
Miuccia Prada have suggested. More than this, it is a tangible experience: the way our attire affects our movements and physical presence
is as important as what it communicates. Because clothing covers, ca-
resses, abrades, and constricts our bodies, it affects how we feel about
ourselves and our relationship to the world. A woman in a sexy dress
doesn't just evoke or suggest the idea of sexiness—she embodies it in
a way language cannot; moreover, if she not only looks sexy but also
feels sexy, she also experiences that embodiment for herself even as
she exhibits it for admiring or disapproving observers. By the same
token, a woman in a power suit or pair of mechanic's overalls may
embody freedom from conventional gendered expectations and expanded potential, her easy, unencumbered movements and grounded
posture physically acting out her liberation from the strictures of
patriarchy.

These fashioned experiences both reflect and inspire our views of
the world. The relationship between attire and ideas, clothing and so-

cial meaning, is a two-way street—or really, more of a chaotic mosh pit—with the aesthetics and tactile sensations of clothing inseparable from the more abstract concepts, ideals, values, and ways of being we associate with it. For instance, the Great Masculine Renunciation reflected Enlightenment-era ideals of practicality, civic equality, and industriousness, but just as importantly, reformed masculine attire also facilitated a new relationship between men and their bodies, changing the way they moved through the world: the light frock coat of the eighteenth-century English gentry offered a tangible bodily freedom that suggested and encouraged a liberation from political constraints. Similarly, when Black slaves in the early 1800s proudly wore the refined attire of European gentry, they turned their bodies—disparaged as brute and animalistic—into tangible, unimpeachable rebuttals to white supremacy. Reform of women's dress in the late nineteenth and early twentieth centuries not only reflected ideals of gender equality, it also embodied them by freeing women from physically cumbersome attire and from some of the symbolic burdens of vicarious display. In these cases and many others, fashion was more than a mode of expression—it was an act of self-creation. Fashion communicates, but more than this, it lets us physically feel and embody our ideals and social aspirations. New fashions transformed daily experience and in so doing, slowly and subtly, but surely, influenced new ways of thinking, which in turn inspired social change. This tangible and tactile aspect of dress is distinctive: it accounts for the allure of fashion, the enduring anxiety surrounding it, and the pervasiveness of rules about it.

The distinctive importance of attire is rarely acknowledged in scholarly accounts of social relations and political developments. To some degree, this may be the result of a narrow materialism, emphasizing wealth and resources over less measurable matters of culture, prestige, and psychological esteem. It also likely reflects the natural idealist bias of writers, scholars, and intellectuals: people who work with ideas and words tend to think of themselves in cerebral terms, as "brains-on-stilts" whose essential nature resides in a non-corporeal soul, a disembodied consciousness that knows itself by its own thoughts (*Cogito, ergo sum*) or, in today's imaginings, could soon be captured in a digitized artificial intelligence.

Today, it's fashionable to insist that technology, social media, and the growing importance of online and "virtual" interactions make clothing and the physical body in general less important: text messages replace face-to-face interactions and digital avatars stand in for flesh-and-blood, clothed individuals. But if anything, social media amplifies the importance of attire. The content of Instagram, for instance, consists primarily of personal images—still or moving—often crafted and curated with a great deal of effort to fashion a compelling self-image. Inevitably, a big part of that self-image comes from clothing, and it is clear that many users of social media choose what they wear in their online photos with at least as much care as the most dedicated style maven preparing for a night out during Fashion Week. Other social media platforms, once primarily text based, are now increasingly image dependent as well—indeed, this is what gives the impression that they could supplant face-to-face social interaction. We use implicit dress codes to make sense of what we find on social media: friends, prospective lovers, potential employers, and college admissions officers survey these digital records with a discerning eye, looking for clues to personality and disposition. Also, social media prolongs and renews the impact of attire—for better and for worse. It has always been true that one never gets a second chance to make a first impression, but now, that first impression is also a permanent impression; a poorly chosen outfit can never really be taken off— every triumph or crime of fashion lives on forever in a digital archive.

Digital communication attempts to mimic bodily presence but cannot replace it. Indeed, the socially desiccated interactions that occur online make the importance of physical proximity all the more obvious. The shelter-in-place orders imposed after the outbreak of COVID-19 in 2020 made the sad inadequacy of disembodied interactions inescapable. Work meetings were even more joyless than usual and online chats with friends and family members were a melancholy reminder of lost sociability. "Virtual cocktail parties" (log on and pour your own glass of wine!) with casual acquaintances or strangers were depressing and awkward despite the welcome effects of alcohol, proving that real social connection always includes the experience of another person's physical presence. Little wonder people grasped for any excuse to finesse the strictures of quarantine and seek the physical company of other people. Some suburbanites so relished their brief interactions with neighbors while taking the trash out to the curb that before long a tradition of trash day cocktail hour emerged, complete with dressy cocktail attire. Soon, dressing up for trash day became a global phenomenon, complete with Instagram pages and Facebook groups. Even standing six feet away from neighbors one had rarely spoken to before, a glass of rosé balanced on a can full of week-old trash, was better than a virtual interaction with a disembodied companion.

Our deepest selves are inseparable from our physical bodies—not only because of our bodily needs but also because our consciousness itself is formed by our bodily experience. The way we cover, embellish, and present our bodies influences how we come to understand our place in the world. Our clothing can transform us from subject into citizen; it can remake our interactions from a bestial struggle for survival into an Enlightened competition for excellence; it can elevate our sexuality from an animalistic urge into an expression of poetic connection; it can turn a social obligation into a glamorous adventure; it can make the solitary daily grind into a stylish personal biography. Our experiences, aspirations, and ideals are inseparable from our bodies and how we present them to the world.

Fashioning Individualism

Fashion tells the history of individualism in tailored cloth. The many and varied dress codes that have shaped the sensibilities of the modern world reveal that the cultural ideal of individualism was made tangible through the tailor's art and the dressmaker's skill. In the modern era, classical political liberalism put individual freedom at the center of a new political ideology, while both philosophy and psychology put individual cognition at the center of a new understanding of humanity. Fashion allowed people to express and experience this new ethos by clothing themselves in a way that both highlighted the unique contours of the individual body and exhibited the unique longings of the inimitable psyche. The free citizen of Enlightenment philosophy and the authentic self of modern psychology were not discovered or derived from human nature; they were *fashioned*.

This steady progression in fashion toward an ever-greater emphasis on individual expression has come largely at the expense of the use of attire to express social rank, biological sex, and group membership: to some extent, the importance of *status*, *sex*, and *power* have been overtaken by the imperative to express *personality*. But the former have not been eclipsed by the latter—instead they have been subsumed to become elements of individual expression. Novel combinations of clothing and grooming that convey individuality often do so through unfamiliar uses of styles traditionally associated with distinctive social statuses, social classes, races, and sexes. In fact, this sort of out-of-context "quotation" of older sartorial symbols is one of the most important ways the language of fashion expresses new sensibilities: the sartorial signs of status, sex, and power have become the building blocks from which we fashion personality. This can result in striking and evocative new individual fashion statements, but it also threatens the integrity of the older affinities, provoking unease, disgust, and accusations of appropriation. Indeed, fashionable individualism can come at the expense of social connection and social responsibility, at its worst curdling into selfishness and solipsism. Some of the familiar criticisms of fashion reflect this valid concern. Fashion, emblematic of the fast-paced, rootless, cosmopolitan modern world, is a conspicuous target for all of the well-worn objections to soulless modernity and alienated modern life. But fashionable individualism is not of a piece with the cold-blooded and calculating selfish individualism of laissez-faire economic theory. Fashionable individualism is exuberant, expressive, and affective; it may be self-centered, but it is not typically calculating—it seeks, above all, not rational self-interest but emotive self-assertion.

Of course, what looks like individual self-expression might just be a series of fashion trends, to which millions slavishly march in lock-step. Despite the unprecedented latitude we enjoy in our attire, people tend to gravitate toward a limited number of styles. Instead of individuality, one might see a procession of different cohorts, each one with its own distinctive—but internally homogeneous—costume. To the extent this is true, it may be because people seek safety in numbers. In more and more contexts, we are free to wear whatever we like, but we know we will be judged based on what we choose to wear. Dressing like other people is a good way of guaranteeing we won't be judged too harshly. Moreover, even for the intrepid, there are only a limited number of ways to dress that are socially intelligible. The history of fashion offers a vast but still limited vocabulary of clothing from which to select, and among these, many garments are clearly anachronistic—the sartorial equivalent of dead languages—while others are so inappropriate as to be illegible. As we choose from what's left, we express ambitions, ideals, and fantasies shaped by our present moment—as do our contemporaries. Inevitably, more than one person will hit on the same idea. This explains the zeitgeist of fashion trends, which often emerge before any designer or fashion magazine editor has time to identify or publicize them.

Perhaps true individuality in dress is almost never seen. But the *ideal* of individuality is everywhere, even if it is expressed in the same way by many different people. Contrast today's individualistic fashion to a true uniform, or even to a quasi-uniform such as the conventional business suit. A uniform is designed to suggest homogeneity: even if dozens of small details may differ from individual to individual, one wears it to signal one's *similarity* to other people. By contrast, modern fashion is designed to suggest individuality, even when the clothing is mass produced and worn in nearly identical combinations by hordes of other people. The Midtown Uniform is meant to suggest the absence of a dress code, even though it is in fact less individuated than the suit it displaced. When a software designer in the Silicon Valley chooses an ironic T-shirt (e.g., "Mr. Bubble"), the shirt suggests quirky individuality—not uniformity—even if it is produced in the hundreds of thousands and worn by a large number of people in similar jobs, all of whom also wear other similar clothing (flip-flops, cargo shorts, a plaid shirt worn unbuttoned, as a jacket).

Fashion highlights the importance of artifice in individuality, provoking the anxiety that what seems a natural and sincere reflection of personality may in fact be contrived and inauthentic. The ideal of human individualism posits that each of us have an essential and unique personality by design: like snowflakes, our defining traits are the product of intrinsic nature and no two of us are alike. Understandably, then, many yearn to look beyond fashion to see the true character of the individual. But much of the evidence of an individual character comes in the form of stylized self-presentation—in other words, fashion. Fashion is an unwelcome reminder that individual personality, which we cherish as a natural and inalienable birthright, may be a fragile creative project; a product of culture, not a law of nature.

This anxiety about the authenticity of our individuality leads many to resent the influence of fashion even though we can't do without it. In the early eighteenth century, just as men renounced conspicuous artifice in their attire, the English poet Alexander Pope made this analogy between deceptive rhetoric and inappropriate dress:

> Expression is the dress of thought and still,
> Appears more decent as more suitable
> A vile Conceit in pompous words express'd
> Is like a clown in regal Purple dress'd

Ironically, perhaps, dress codes have often been attempts to undermine fashion's influence, to make clothing itself less significant by ensuring it is simply a sign of deeper, less conspicuous individual virtues or faults: purple and red silk symbolized nobility; modest attire was a sign of sexual propriety; vanities, a sign of loose morals; respectable dress, evidence of social respectability; and gendered clothing, a symbol of biological sex and reproductive role. Throughout fashion's history, dress codes have been a way of making sure that attire offers an accurate sense of the authentic individual.

And there is a lot of fashionable artifice to root out. Even fashions that don't misrepresent may still deceive, by allowing people to enjoy an advantage while also disavowing it: the clown in purple masquerades but even the king seizes an unearned advantage because his prestige comes, in part, from his wardrobe rather than exclusively from his character. Likewise, a woman in an eye-catching dress or sexy shoes inspires resentment from the po-faced and the prudish, in part because of the suspicion that she quietly benefits from sex appeal when she deserves to be judged based on merit alone. Its ability to visually transform the body gives clothing a bit of the power of illusion: our attire is not a statement to be analyzed or assessed; it is a demonstration that persuades on a subconscious level before the observer can deliberate. This explains much of the association of fashion with decadence and even underhandedness, as well as the relentless calls to resist the seductions of fashion in favor of honest virtue. Meanwhile, many have tried to rebuff the ever-present suspicion that fashion is a ruse designed to get an undeserved edge by adopting subtle sartorial status symbols, stealth fashions disguised as practical or functional attire, like a Patagonia fleece on a Midtown Manhattan financial analyst, facilitating an insidious form of social hierarchy that need never justify itself.

Refashioning Dress Codes

The primacy of individualism leads us to feel that any restriction on self-expression is a gross injustice; meanwhile, the widespread notion that attire is trivial makes any attempt to control it seem petty and meddlesome. All of this cuts against dress codes, which censor individual expression and give superficial self-presentation seemingly undue weight. I've certainly found many examples of overbearing, mean-spirited, and discriminatory rules in my study of dress codes. But I've also discovered many defensible collective attempts to shape and exploit the expressive power of fashion—some relatively inconsequential; others quite profound. If clothing matters, there will sometimes be good reasons to control it. Indeed, many dress codes are simply a group's way of using attire to as a means of collective expression and group self-fashioning. Formal dress codes for special events create a refined atmosphere and ensure that everyone demonstrates appropriate respect for the occasion. Workplace dress codes allow businesses to shape a cooperative working culture, convey professional values, and create distinctive experiences for customers. School dress codes can reduce adolescent cliquishness and mute the competition for status. Activist movements for social justice and civil rights have used dress codes to send a unified message of self-respect and make a cohesive demand for dignified treatment. Even accusations of appropriation are, in essence, dress codes, designed to preserve the exclusivity of certain adornments for members of a select cadre. Dress codes can be an important way for groups to use the power of fashion.

Moreover, explicit dress codes can benefit individuals and promote equality by providing clear advance notice of social expectations. Although we usually think of dress codes as a constraint on personal freedom, they can liberate us from the tyranny of judgment surrounding our fashion choices. Ironically, today's culture of relaxed informality and individualized quirkiness can demand conformity as urgently as the most rigid corporate dress code. These informal standards of attire can be more demanding and more treacherous than any written dress code: failure to respect conventions of good taste marks one as an ignorant and tasteless boor, but too-slavish adherence to the rules can be a sign of insecurity, and hence poor breeding. While an explicit dress code demands only simple adherence, its absence leaves one adrift, forced to navigate ineffable standards of taste, elegance, and style—many vague and unwritten or overdetermined and contested. As the historian Anne Hollander observes, although "we are not required to respect the occasion itself in prescribed ways; we must make up our own version of what the occasion requires of us personally. . . . [W]e are forced to reveal ourselves. . . . [O]ur [clothing] choices now make a picture story, a personal illustration of our innermost sense of our relation to the world. . . ." The pressure to get that story straight—down to the most minute details of studied nonchalance—increases as the freedom to choose expands. *All of us know what is and is not appropriate. . . .* We are free to wear anything we choose, but slaves to the judgments of others. The United States Environmental Protection Agency reports that since 1960—precisely when large parts of American society began to abandon explicit common norms of dress—the volume of discarded clothing has increased by 750 percent, a reflection, perhaps, of millions of frantic and ultimately failed searches for an appropriate outfit in a world free of rules but full of judgment.

Casual attire promises indulgence of both expressive individualism and physical comfort, so it is no surprise that designer "athleisure" wear is now the ultimate luxury fashion. But there are signs that the pendulum may be swinging away from the misleading permissiveness of the casual and back toward sartorial refinement and decorum. I spoke with *Esquire* magazine's creative director Nick Sullivan in 2018 while researching this book, and he observed that "we're bombarded with images of people in fantastic cars and sweatshirts and sneakers . . . [but] young people are now saying *my Dad is wearing . . . sneakers. I can't be seen dead in sneakers. . . .* When everyone's wearing a T-shirt, it's rebellious to put a tie on." Sullivan sees an inversion of an older generational opposition. In the 1970s when a father and his college-age son met for a drink, the father would wear a jacket and tie and the son would wear jeans and a sweatshirt. Today parent and child are likely to have swapped wardrobes, the boomer dressing like the countercultural teenager he once was, the twentysomething dressing in anticipation of the mature adult he aspires to be. Young people are, for the first time in close to half a century, discovering the refined pleasures of tailored clothing: suits, blazers and sport coats, finer fabrics, leather shoes—in short, they are experiencing the privilege of dressing like adults. Many are happy to relinquish the superficial comfort of elastic waistbands and cotton jerseys with this rediscovery of the deeper social and psychological comfort that accompanies dressing well, and with care and creativity.

Our dress has political, professional, and social ramifications, making every new ensemble a strategy, designed to produce an effect.

But our attire is almost never entirely strategic because it also reflects our sincere self-image. Renaissance-era upstarts in red silk and dramatic trunk hose wanted to impress strangers but they also wanted to feel good about themselves and their own social position; colonial Americans wore modest homespun to liberate themselves from British imports but also because it reflected their individual sense of thrift and modesty; civil rights activists dressed in their Sunday best to set an example of respectability but also because elegant attire brought a sense of psychological comfort and self-esteem; some women wear high heels to look professional or to please men but many just feel that their shoes contribute to their sense of competence and stature. This makes every critical judgment about fashion both an assessment of a strategy and, potentially, a form of character assassination; every dress code, a form of social control and, perhaps, a personal insult.

Before I studied the history of dress codes, I—like many lawyers dedicated to weighty and profound issues of social justice and equality—underestimated how much some dress codes can undermine self-esteem. For instance, although I personally disapproved of dress codes that banned all-braided hairstyles, like the workplace rules Renee Rogers and Chastity Jones challenged in court, I didn't think they were burdensome enough to violate civil rights. After all, I thought, it's just a hairdo when all is said and done and a lot of people of all races have to change their hair and attire for work.

Studying the centrality of hair and grooming in political struggles throughout history—and especially in the Black Power movement—has made me rethink this. Given dominant standards of beauty and professionalism based on Caucasian phenotypes, braided hairstyles have become important symbols of racial pride for African Americans. Moreover, Black women have developed a wide array of flattering, glamorous, and evocative all-braided hairstyles. There are short and severe braids that stop at the collar; full manes of rope-like, cascading "locs"; dramatic, waist-length braids embellished with decorative beading; and a host of other styles: some sensible and others sexy; some hard-edged and others whimsical; some all business and others bohemian and romantic. As the styles have multiplied, a growing number of women—and more than a few men—have adopted them. What was once a somewhat unusual fashion statement even among Black women is now a common-sense approach to personal grooming. In fact, the styles are so popular among Black women that a dress code prohibiting them can only be seen as a racial insult. That's why a growing number of cities and states are passing new laws to prevent businesses and schools from banning them. These new laws, often passed under the name "The CROWN Act," are a welcome recognition of the centrality of hair and grooming to individual dignity and racial esteem.

Some might see the CROWN Act as vindication of the belief that hair and grooming are just too unimportant to merit consideration by employers—or anyone else. But wouldn't this suggest that they are also too trivial to merit legal protection? A better way of thinking about the CROWN Act is as a call for employers to reexamine prejudices and racially exclusive standards of beauty and professionalism, not to ignore personal appearance altogether; a demand for better dress codes, not for eliminating all dress codes. In this respect, our inspiration should be the Black is Beautiful movement, which demanded a new Afrocentric aesthetic, rather than the color-blind ideal that urges that we ignore certain aspects of appearance—a goal that has proven to be elusive, to say the least. As the Black is Beautiful movement insisted, if Black people were truly judged based on our whole selves—essence and appearance, character and skin color— we would be recognized as beautiful. Complexion and hair texture have never been the problem, nor is the fact that people will see, assess, and evaluate them. The problem is standards of evaluation that have been warped and corrupted to serve as a justification for racial hierarchy.

One could say something similar about standards of beauty more generally: the conventional criteria of human beauty—particularly with respect to women—are remarkably narrow and unsophisticated. I suspect much of the reason that most people have failed to cultivate more nuanced sensibilities is that we've been taught to deny that personal appearance is worth considering at all. To take the most obvious example, contrast the typical, cartoonishly simplistic ideal of feminine beauty, which feminists rightly attack, with the rich, complex, and varied ideals of beauty that inform the fine arts, architecture, design, and fashion (including the bold, challenging styles developed outside the fashion industry from which fashion designers take much of their inspiration—what some call "the fashion of the street"). These practices could inform more expansive notions of beauty and professionalism, and therefore better dress codes.

The law can't require such nuance. But it could encourage it through a general but limited right to personal autonomy in grooming and attire. For an example of how this could work, recall the case of Chastity Jones, who was rejected as an applicant for a job in a call center because she refused to cut her dreadlocks. The letter of the law offered her no refuge: the dress code was not discriminatory as written and she could not prove that it was applied in a discriminatory manner. But the real problem was that the dress code was simply unreasonable. Locs are not a part-time hairstyle that Jones could take out for work and redo in her free time: to comply with the dress code, she would have had to cut them off. Effectively, the dress code didn't just dictate how Jones needed to present herself for work; it required her to make a permanent change in her appearance to qualify for a position as a *call center operator* who no customer would ever see. And locs are an expression of racial pride for many, akin to religious raiment as a reflection of personal conviction. All of the practical equities cut against the dress code. But none of them were legally relevant.

They should be. Modest legal guidelines could address the many dress codes that don't obviously involve discrimination or speech-like expression, not by banning them indiscriminately but by weighing the costs and benefits. Demands for long-term changes in personal appearance are clearly more burdensome than requirements that easily can be reversed and forgotten after work. There's a stronger argument for a strict dress code in the case of a highly visible position in an image-conscious business than for a stockroom or call center employee. Similar considerations should govern school dress codes and dress codes for customers of restaurants or entertainment venues: "no shoes, no shirt, no service" requires less justification than a dress code requiring high-heel shoes and nylons or suits and neckties (and if such formality is justified, why not let everyone choose whether to wear the heels or the tie rather than assign one or the other based on birth sex?).

Of course, it won't always be easy to tell a sensible dress code from an unreasonable one. But it is a better goal than the abolition of all dress codes, not only because it is more realistic but also because it gives fashion its due. When people spend time and creative energy on their self-presentation, they want other people to notice it—not to ignore it. Fashion, in the broad sense I have used the term in this book, is a demotic and quotidian art, one of the few available to us all, which we are able to exhibit every day, rent-free, on our bodies. It has helped to shape the way we think of ourselves and our place in society in a profound, if often indirect and subtle, way.

This may seem objectionable to those who believe in some Platonic ideal of virtue, merit, or personality unsullied by its earthly and embodied manifestation. But if artifice and skill must inevitably play their part in the miracle of self-fashioning, then it instead describes a remarkable achievement of human civilization. The notion that personal appearance is trivial and should be irrelevant is an insult to the millions of people who labor to create practical garments of expressive beauty, not to mention everyone who takes care with their appearance. I suspect that the renunciation of fashion is mistaken for a virtue—and interest in it taken as a vice—not because fashion is "trivial" in the sense of unnecessary to survival (after all, so is literature, the fine arts, haute cuisine, and indeed the vaunted physical comfort to which fashion's impracticality is so often contrasted) but because fashion involves the human body, which from ancient times has been an object of irrational shame and moral anxiety. It's not a tough-minded practicality or a high-minded egalitarianism that inspires the renunciation of fashion but a prudish and ill-conceived attempt to quarantine the profane body from the sacred intellect.

How the Law of Fashion Made History

We all benefit from fashion's triumph every time we slip on a stylish jacket, a rugged pair of boots, an elegant sport coat, a sexy dress, a dashing scarf, or a chic pantsuit and feel a little bit more confident, more centered, more *ourselves* because of it. Whenever someone chooses her attire with care and purpose and wears it with confidence and conviction, it is a small victory for human flourishing. I'm a partisan of creative, daring, and provocative fashions, whether avant garde or elegant, refined or tacky, severe or sexy, haute couture or edgy streetwear. This doesn't mean I like every eye-catching ensemble or that I think you should. But even clothing choices that may seem vulgar, bizarre, or ill-advised can communicate important messages, create new modes of self-conception and ways of being, and contribute to a richer public culture. The history of dress codes tells the story of medieval cross-dressers, Elizabethan upstarts, Renaissance courtiers, and colonial American slaves dressing above their condition; of Victorian dandies, Industrial-era social climbers, seriously sexy flappers, and disaffected zoot suiters; of earnest activists in their Sunday best, chic radicals, and radical feminists; of blonde African American bombshells and natural blondes in dreadlocks; of hipster *hijabis*, preppy street gangs, and high-tech fashionistas. Each has given us something invaluable, even if many were misunderstood and maligned in their time.

When I first started on this unorthodox and idiosyncratic project, the puzzled looks and bemused expressions of many of my colleagues—lawyers and scholars dedicated to weighty disputes and serious topics—let me know I had some work cut out for me in making the case that dress codes were worthy of prolonged study and analysis. Indeed, at first, I had only a vague intuition as to why the topic was important. Over the years I have spent writing this book, I've come to realize that the story of dress codes is a parallel history of modernity and political liberalism. Today, what political philosophers call classical liberalism—at its essence, the belief that individual liberty and human flourishing must be at the center of any decent social and political order—seems under attack from all sides: from a reactionary ethno-nationalism that celebrates primitive tribalism based on blood and soil and from a corrosive skepticism that skillfully identifies every weakness and hypocrisy in liberal societies in order to suggest their fundamental degeneracy. Against these enemies, allied with the powerful emotions of disillusionment, alienation, and *ressentiment*, an analytical defense of liberal values and ideals rooted in ethical philosophy and jurisprudence has proven to be no defense.

Perhaps the profound cultural, artistic, and aesthetic legacy of liberalism is. The greatest accomplishments of modern humanism aren't to be found in the political polemics and philosophical treatises of learned figures or even in the courageous struggles of social movements for justice and equality. They are in the daily lives of ordinary people who fulfilled the promise of self-realization by insisting that their stories were worth telling and that their bodies were sources of pride and beauty rather than objects of shame or sin. Accordingly, the history of fashion isn't only in the grand garb of nobility, the artful creations of famous fashion designers, and the global marketing campaigns of multinational corporations, though they all played their part. It is also, and perhaps most of all, in the daring and subtle, heartfelt and contrived, skillful and stumbling self-fashioning of billions of people who let their imaginations inspire their wardrobes and wore their personal aspirations on their sleeves. The heroes and heroines— or at least the central protagonists—of the history of dress codes are not royalty, clergy, captains of industry, courtiers, or revolutionaries; they are people like Richard Walweyn, whose wardrobe so upset the power structure of Elizabethan England that the constable was dispatched to track him down; like the Chevalier d'Éon, who discovered feminist virtue through the sartorial discipline of a corset and petticoats; they are the flappers who made feminism fashionable; the Black men and women whose sense of style was a visual refutation of white supremacy; the Lo Lifes, who transformed the preppy look from a sign of elite insularity to a statement of disruptive class mobility; and the *Sapeurs*, who deftly sidestepped both the authoritarianism of post-colonial cultural authenticity and the violence of tribalism with well-shod feet. Fashion isn't a defense against oppression and exploitation. But it is an answer to them because fashion insists that human flourishing matters first and foremost—more than the ambitions of the powerful, the burdens of tradition, or the prescriptions of moral authority. Fashion may not help us fight the enemies of humanity. But it gives us a glimpse of what we're fighting for.

Dress Codes Stripped Bare

OUR FAMILY VISITED SAN FRANCISCO REGULARLY WHEN I was growing up, taking in the many attractions of the big city. One chilly San Francisco summer, as we were walking along Geary Street toward the theater district, we encountered a nudist. The man was making a great effort to behave as if he was doing nothing out of the ordinary, as if to say: *I am the sensible one in this crowd—it is the rest of you, in your ridiculous and cumbersome clothing, who look silly.* He stood next to my dad at an intersection as we waited for the light to change, and turned to look at us, defiantly. My mother turned her head and pulled me and my sister toward her, almost covering our eyes. But my dad turned to the man, glanced up and down, and said, without a trace of consternation in his tone, "Aren't you cold?"

"You get used to it," the man replied.

"Do you really?" my dad asked, the skepticism in his voice, referring, I think, to more than just the temperature.

The San Francisco Bay Area is home to one of the more active nudist movements in the United States. Every year, nudists defy public decency laws, walking the streets of San Francisco and Berkeley stark naked and marching unclothed into the meetings of local government to protest the tyranny of compulsory attire—the most enduring dress code. They insist that clothing is unnatural and uncomfortable and that our obsession with covering the body is an irrational moralism. So far, the nudist movement has not attracted a lot of followers. In one sense, this is surprising: the ethos of the nudist is precisely the same as that of the legions of people who insist that fashion is silly and irrelevant. If clothing is simply a distraction from substance, then why bother with it at all? The nudists outdo Mark Zuckerberg's wardrobe of gray T-shirts, dispensing with even the effort and thought required to choose and put on an ascetic uniform. In terms of comfort, in California's seasonable climate, nudity is, for much of the year, a perfectly viable option.

I suspect the reason their example has not inspired much imitation is that nudity can never achieve what the nudist aspires to: freedom from fashionable affectation, the innocence of nature stripped bare. This, the biblical story informs us, we lost forever when we acquired self-awareness. Because we are self-aware, we are inevitably self-conscious, anxious about our self-presentation, eager to fashion ourselves. Nudity, then, as scholars of painting and sculpture would assert, is not the same as the naïve nakedness of infants and small children: it is always self-conscious, cultured, deliberate, and laden with meaning. Whether the pose of Venus Unadorned or the stance of a middle-aged nudist protesting public decency laws, nudity is a fashion statement. Even by renouncing clothing, one can't escape the defining power of dress codes.

Notes

INTRODUCTION

1 *It was in evidence that Mr. Hetherington*: Original article on file with author.

2 *The riots engulfed the city from the Bronx to the Battery*: Neil Steinberg, *Hatless Jack* (New York: Plume 2004), 227–229.

2 *For instance, in 1999 to 2000*: "Percentage of Public Schools with Various Safety and Security Measures: Selection years, 1999-2000 through 2013-2014," National Center for Education Statistics, Digest of Education Statistics, https://nces.ed.gov/programs/digest/d15/tables/dt15_233.50.asp.

2 *the Starbucks barista must eschew*: "Making an Appearance: U.S. Retail Dress Code Guidelines," Starbucks Corporation, 2014.

2 *Consider the 2010 dress code*: "UBS Corporate Wear Dress Guide for Women and Men," UBS, 2010.

3 Your shirt should be of white marcella: Jason Chow, "The Rules for Tuxedos," the *Wall Street Journal*, November 24, 2010, http://blogs.wsj.com/scene/2010/11/24/tuxedo-rules/.

3 *"the implication that you would check"*: Antonio Centeno, "A Man's Guide to Black Tie: How to Wear a Tuxedo," *The Art of Manliness*, December 17, 2013, http://www.artofmanliness.com/2013/12/17/black-tie-how-to-wear-tuxedo/.

4 Ladies are kindly reminded that: "Style Guide 2015," Royal Ascot, 2015, https://www.ascot.co.uk/sites/default/files/documents/RA 2015_Style Guide_FINAL.pdf.

5 *In 2018, I asked Kate Lanphear*: Interview with Kate Lanphear, Hearst Tower, New York City, April 30, 2018 (on file with author).

5 *Even the Silicon Valley style of casual wear*: E.W., "Suitable Disruption," *The Economist*, August 4, 2014, https://www.economist.com/schumpeter/2014/08/04/suitable-disruption?fsrc=scn%2Ftw%2Fte%2Fbl%2Fed%2Fsuitable disruption.

12 *people who wore a white lab coat*: Hajo Adam and Adam D. Galinsky, "Enclothed Cognition," *Journal of Experimental Social Psychology* 48, no. 4 (2012): 918–25, https://doi.org/10.1016/j.jesp.2012.02.008.

12 *dressed up for a job interview*: Michael L. Slepian, Simon N. Ferber, Joshua M. Gold, and Abraham M. Rutchick, "The Cognitive Consequences of Formal Clothing," *Social Psychological and Personality Science* 6, no. 6 (2015): 661–68, https://doi.org/10.1177/1948550615579462.

12 *In 1967 the semiologist Roland Barthes*: Roland Barthes, Richard Howard, and Matthew Ward, *The Fashion System* (London: Vintage, 2010).

13 *From the earliest days of organized society*: *Miller v. School District No. 167*, Cook County, Illinois, 495 F2d. 658 (7th Cir. 1974).

14 *Indeed, many years ago when I first wrote*: Richard Ford, *Racial Culture: A Critique* (Princeton: Princeton University Press, 2005), 205–206.

15 *The dress codes this edict legally proscribes*: "Legal Enforcement Guidance on Discrimination on the Basis of Gender Identity or Expression: Local Law No. 3 (2002); N.Y.C. Admin. Code § 8-102(23)," Legal Enforcement Guidance on Discrimination on the Basis of Gender Identity or Expression: Local Law No. 3 (2002); N.Y.C. Admin. Code § 8-102(23). New York, 2015.

16 *She sued, claiming race discrimination*: *EEOC v. Catastrophe Management Solutions* (11th Cir. 2016).

Part One

CHAPTER ONE: ENCODING STATUS

25 *For his crime of fashion*: Wilfrid Hooper, "The Tudor Sumptuary Laws," *The English Historical Review* XXX, no. CXIX (1915): 433–49.

25 *Historian Victoria Buckley describes trunk hose as*: Victoria Buckley, "Mandillions and Netherstocks—Elizabethan Men and Their Dress," *Shakespeare's England*, January 13, 2010, http://www.shakespearesengland.co.uk/2010/01/13/mandillions-netherstocks-elizabethan-men-their-dress/.

25 *"could often be . . . ludicrous"*: Ibid.

25 *A royal proclamation in 1551*: Hooper, "The Tudor Sumptuary Laws," 439.

26 *The court that heard his case*: Ibid., 441.

27 *The Romans*: Catherine Kovesi Killerby, *Sumptuary Law in Italy, 1200-1500* (Oxford: Clarendon Press, 2005), 10–12.

27 *The earliest medieval European law*: Ibid., 34.

28 *[A] great number of young gentlemen*: Queen Elizabeth I, "Proclamation against Excess of Apparel by Queen Elizabeth I," *A Booke containing all such Proclamations, as were published during the Raigne of the late Queen Elizabeth*, British Library, London, June 15, 1574.

28 *The sumptuous and costly array*: Christopher Breward, *The Culture of Fashion* (Manchester, UK: Manchester University Press, 1995), 54.

29 *The English "Statute Concerning Diet and Apparel"*: Alan Hunt, *Governance of the Consuming Passions: A History of Sumptuary Law* (New York: St. Martin's Press, 1996), 154.

29 *Milan's sumptuary law of 1396*: Killerby, *Sumptuary Law in Italy*, 87.

29 *Genoa banned the use*: Ibid., 24.

29 *The papal legate of the Romagna*: Ibid., 63.

29 *In 1375 in Aquila*: Ibid., 73.

29 *In late-thirteenth-century France*: Ibid., 24–25.

29 *Outrage over the misuse of crowns*: Ibid., 81.

30 *"One can make a gentleman"*: Ibid., 61; Niccolò Machiavelli, *Opere Di Niccolò Machiavelli* (Milano: Mursia, 1983).

30 *In cities up and down*: Killerby, *Sumptuary Law in Italy*, 38; Hunt, *Governance of the Consuming Passions*, 29–33.

30 *Spain had only two sumptuary laws*: Hunt, *Governance of the Consuming Passions*, 30–32.

30 *a 1656 law empowered the police*: Jennifer M. Jones, *Sexing La Mode: Gender, Fashion and Commercial Culture in Old Regime France* (Oxford: Berg, 2004), 31.

31 *Meanwhile, a thriving market in used*: Daniel Roche, *The Culture of Clothing: Dress and Fashion in the Ancien Régime* (Cambridge: Cambridge University Press, 1996), 335–45.

31 *the global pandemic of the plague*: Samuel K. Cohn, "Black Death, Social and Economic Impact of the," in *The Oxford Dictionary of the Middle Ages*, ed. Robert E. Bjork (Oxford University Press, 2010).

31 *As the plague subsided*: See Walter Scheidel, *The Great Leveler: Violence and the History of Inequality from the Stone Age to the Twenty-First Century* (Princeton: Princeton University Press, 2017).

32 *The basis on which good repute*: Thorstein Veblen, *The Theory of the Leisure Class* (New York: Mentor Books, 1953), 70, 119.

32 *Most Europeans during the late Middle Ages*: David Mitch, "Education and Skill of the British Labour Force," in *The Cambridge Economic History of Modern Britain*, eds. Roderick Floud, Jane Humphries, and Paul Johnson (Cambridge: Cambridge University Press, 2004), 332–56.

33 *In 1510 the first Parliament*: Hooper, "The Tudor Sumptuary Laws."

33 *Even the common people*: Ibid.

33 *Historian Wilfrid Hooper*: Ibid., 436.

34 *to reinforce the point*: Ibid., 441.

34 *Elizabethan sumptuary laws*: Ibid., 435–36.

34 *A proclamation of May 6, 1562*: Ibid., 439.

34 *Ther conynually to remayn and watche*: City Corporation Records, Jo. 18, fo. 283 b (1566); Jo. 20 (2), fo. 348 b (1577); Jo. 21, fo. 19b (1579); Jo. 21, fo. 36 b (1580); cf. Malcolm, *Londinium Btdivivum*, ii. 60; Hooper, "The Tudor Sumptuary Laws," 443.

35 *For instance, a proclamation of 1580*: Hooper, "The Tudor Sumptuary Laws," 445.

35 *Those who aided and abetted vestimentary villains*: Ibid., 440.

35 *Under the provisions of the Act of Apparel*: Ibid., 436.

35 *Henry VIII's Lord Chancellor*: Thomas More, *The Complete Works of St. Thomas More: Vol. 4, Utopia* (New Haven: Yale University Press, 1965), 127, 133.

35 *In Utopia, gold and silver*: Ibid., 153.

35 *The Utopians gave gems to small children*: Ibid., 153.

35 *In More's imagining*: Ibid., 157.

38 *when ordered to remove*: Emanuele Lugli, "Fashion's Measure: Preaching, Chronicle-Writing, and the New Look of the 1340s," *Fashion Theory: The*

Journal of Dress, Body and Culture, 20 (2019), https://doi.org/10.1080/13627 04X.2019.1627758.

36 *In reaction to these contrast changes*: Hunt, *Governance of the Consuming Passions*, 37.

CHAPTER TWO: SELF-FASHIONING

39 *In the ancient world, trousers were rare*: Glenys Davies and Lloyd Llewellyn-Jones, "The Body," in *A Cultural History of Dress and Fashion: Vol. 1, Antiquity*, ed. Susan J. Vincent, (London: Bloomsbury, 2017), 59.

40 *Elite men adopted this*: Anne Hollander, *Sex and Suits: The Evolution of Modern Dress* (New York: Knopf, 1994), 43.

40 *The historian Stephen Greenblatt notes*: See Stephen Greenblatt, *Renaissance Self-Fashioning: From More to Shakespeare* (Chicago: University of Chicago Press, 1980), 2.

41 *According to philosopher Gilles Lipovetsky*: Gilles Lipovetsky, *The Empire of Fashion Dressing Modern Democracy* (Princeton: Princeton University Press, 2002), 46–47.

43 *What they lacked was our modern sense*: See Michel Foucault, *Madness and Civilization: A History of Insanity in the Age of Reason; Discipline and Punish: The Birth of the Prison; The History of Sexuality, Vol. 1*.

43 *But this idea, which the historian of sumptuary law Alan Hunt*: Hunt, *Governance of the Consuming Passions*, 68–69.

44 *Today, empirical study has discredited*: See, e.g., Diana Crane, "Diffusion Models and Fashion: A Reassessment," *Annals of the American Academy of Political and Social Science* 566, no. 1 (1999); George A. Field, "The Status Float Phenomenon: The Upward Diffusion of Innovation," *Business Horizons*, no. 13 (1970), 45.

44 *As historian Daniel Roche writes*: Daniel Roche, "*Apparences revolutionnaires ou revolution des apparences*," in *Modes & Revolutions, 1780–1804*, ed. Madeleine Delpierre (Paris: Editions Paris-Musées, 1989), 111.

CHAPTER THREE: SIGNS OF FAITH

47 *How do you know where to borrow money?*: Diane Owen Hughes, "Distinguishing Signs: Ear-Rings, Jews, and Franciscan Rhetoric in the Italian Renaissance City," *Past & Present*, no. 112 (1986), 51, 54.

48 *He railed against the use of hair dyes*: Elizabeth Kuhns, *The Habit: A History of the Clothing of Catholic Nuns* (New York: Doubleday, 2005), 58.

48 *"[J]ust as Nimrod"*: Collegio S. Bonaventura, ed., *San Bernardino of Sienna, Opera ommia*, 9 vols. (1950-65), 77.

48 *According to one medieval parable*: Breward, *The Culture of Fashion*, 37.

48 *Accordingly, many laws forbade prostitutes*: Ibid., 36.

49 *Similarly, in 1434 after a religious committee*: Hughes, "Distinguishing Signs,"

25, 26, note 74 (citing *Trattato degli ornamenti delle donne* (Treatise on the ornaments of women), ed. Aniceto Chiappini.)

49 *In the summer of 1416*: Ibid., 22.

50 *Allegra was a Jew*: Ibid.

50 *According to historian Diane Owen Hughes*: Ibid., 16.

50 *Not only had Jews become socially integrated*: Ibid.

50 *In 1322, Pisa required*: Ibid., 18.

51 *In a 1423 speech in Padua*: Ibid., 19; Bernardino de Siena, *S. Bernardini Senensis Ordinis fratrum minorum Opera omnia iussu et auctoritate R.mi P. Augustini Sépinski,* Quadragesimale de evangelio aeterno: Sermones LIV-LXV · Volume 5 (Quaracchi, Florence: Collegio San Bonaventura: 1950–65).

51 *According to historian Richard Sennett*: Richard Sennett, *Flesh and Stone* (New York: W. W. Norton, 1994), 225.

51 *For example, Friar Giacoma della Marca insisted*: Hughes, "Distinguishing Signs," 28.

51 *The anti-Jewish campaign of segregation*: Ibid., 19.

52 *According to Hughes, in northern Italy*: Ibid., 11.

52 *In 1397, Venetian law required Jews*: Sennett, *Flesh and Stone*, 240.

53 *In Viterbo, any Jewish woman*: Hughes, "Distinguishing Signs," 30.

53 *In 1418 they devised their own dress codes*: Ibid., 27.

53 *in 1520, the Venetian surgeon*: Sennet, *Flesh and Stone*, 225.

54 *For instance, in 1401 Bologna forbade all women*: Hughes, "Distinguishing Signs," 47.

54 *Similarly, a Venetian decree of 1543*: Sennett, *Flesh and Stone*, 240.

54 *Meanwhile, some of the most devout Christians*: Kuhns, *The Habit*, 3.

55 *According to historian Elizabeth Kuhns*: Ibid., 40.

55 *Indeed, in the early Christian church*: Ibid., 66.

55 *a letter from the Archbishop of Canterbury*: Ibid.

55 *According to Kuhns, as some religious devotees began to succumb*: Ibid., 93.

55 *For instance, King Alfonso X of Castile*: Ibid., 93–94.

56 *A fifteenth-century English mystic claimed*: Ibid.

56 *The color of the garments has significance*: Ibid., 16, 68; Veronica Bennett and Ryan Todd (illustrator), *Looking Good: A Visual Guide to the Nun's Habit* (London: GraphicDesign&, 2016), 24–25.

56 *According to Kuhns, some habits*: Kuhns, *The Habit*, 2.

57 *Indeed, some nun's habits*: Consuelo Maria Aherne, *Joyous Service: The History of the Sisters of Saint Joseph of Springfield* (Holyoke, MA: Sisters of Saint Joseph, 1983); Susan O. Michelman, "Fashion and Identity of Women Religious," in *Religion, Dress and the Body*, ed. Linda B. Arthur (Oxford: Berg Publishers, 1999), 137.

57 *A reception following her induction*: Kuhns, *The Habit*, 25.

57 *By the Middle Ages, the "life religious"*: Ibid., 93.

57 *Historian Helen Hills describes the practice of veiling*: Helen Hills, "The Veiled Body: Within the Folds of Early Modern Neapolitan Convent Architecture,"

Oxford Art Journal 27, no. 3 (January 2004): 269–90, https://doi.org/10.1093/oaj/27.3.269.

57 *Nuns were forbidden to leave their convents*: Ibid., 276.

57 *Intriguingly, the closed convents featured*: Ibid., 284.

58 *According to Hills, the stone enclosure of the convent*: Ibid., 283.

58 *As the day in which she must take the religious habit draws near*: Francesco Vargas Maciucca, *Degli Abuis introdotti ne monastery delle monache per le doti e per le spese che ogliono dale donzelle . . . e loro Riforma, Dissertazone scritta d'ordine degli Eccellentissi mi Signore Eletti di Napoli* (1745).

59 *But, according to Hills, "the richness of the decoration"*: Hills, "The Veiled Body," 278.

60 *Sensationalistic accounts of convent life*: Rene Kollar, *A Foreign and Wicked Institution?: The Campaign Against Convents in Victorian England* (Havertown: James Clarke & Co, 2014), 19–38.

61 *Similar literature circulated in other countries*: Cassandra Berman, "Wayward Nuns, Randy Priests, and Women's Autonomy: "Convent Abuse" and the Threat to Protestant Patriarchy in Victorian England," dissertation, Macalester College, May 1, 2006 (copy on file with author); Kuhns, *The Habit*, 120.

62 *Meanwhile, the nun's habit became a fetish object*: Kuhns, *The Habit*, 130.

62 *In some cases, the elaborate designs*: Ibid.

62 *Meanwhile, the pressure for distinctiveness*: Ibid., 134.

62 *Echoing this concern, in 1950 Pope Pius XII advised*: Ibid., 138.

62 *After Pius XII's admonishment*: "Modernizing Nun Habits," *Life* 33, no. 24 (December 15, 1952), 16–17.

63 *"shake off the dust"*: "Nuns to Wear New Garb by Dior," *New York Times*, August 31, 1964, https://www.nytimes.com/1964/08/31/archives/nuns-to-wear-new-garb-by-dior.html; Kuhns, *The Habit*, 142.

63 *Religious orders looked to fashion for help*: Kuhns, *The Habit*, 145.

63 *"the religious habit . . . must be simple"*: Kuhns, *The Habit*, 144.

63 *In 1968*, The Church and the Second Sex *theologian Mary Daly*: Mary Daly, *The Church and the Second Sex* (Boston: Beacon Press, 1985), 53.

63 *"for some sisters"*: Kuhns, *The Habit*, 142.

64 *In 1972, the Sacred Congregation for Religious*: Kuhns, *The Habit*, 156–7.

64 *By the late 1970s, the habit had become a political symbol*: Ibid., 159–60.

CHAPTER FOUR: SEX SYMBOLS

69 *citing Saint Thomas Aquinas who allows an exception*: Thomas Aquinas, *Prima Pars Secunde Partis Summe Theologie*. Uenetijs impssa: P Andream de torresanis de Asula, Bartolemu de blauijs de Alexandria, Mapheum de peterbonis de salodio socios, 1483.

69 *Similarly, Saint Hildegard von Bingen had written*: Hildegard av Bingen, *Scivias* (New York: Paulist Press, 1990), (Book II, vision 6), 77.

70 *According to historian Anne Hollander*: Hollander, *Sex and Suits*, 45.

70 *According to historian Valerie Hotchkiss*: Valerie R. Hotchkiss, *Clothes Make the Man: Female Cross Dressing in Medieval Europe* (New York: Routledge, 2012), 15.

71 *Some costumes truly concealed the wearer's identity*: Killerby, *Sumptuary Law in Italy*, 64; Hunt, *Governance of the Consuming Passions*, 137–38.

71 *For instance, the Renaissance-era Italian writer Baldassare Castiglione*: Baldassare Castiglione, *The Book of the Courtier: The Singleton Translation* (New York: W.W. Norton, 2002), (Book II, sections 11-12).

71 *Historians Judith Bennett and Shannon McSheffrey note*: J. M. Bennett, and S. McSheffrey, "Early, Erotic and Alien: Women Dressed as Men in Late Medieval London," *History Workshop Journal* 77, no. 1 (October 2014), 10–13.

71 *The attire of* upper-class *"matrons"*: Ibid., 13.

71 *According to one account of such* cross-class *dressing*: Edward Hall, *Hall's Chronicle: Containing the History of England, During the Reign of Henry the Fourth, and the Succeeding Monarchs, to the End of the Reign of Henry the Eighth, in Which Are Particularly Described the Manners and Customs of Those Periods* (London: Printed for J. Johnson, 1809), 513.

72 *A 1507 law in the city of Gubbio*: Killerby, *Sumptuary Law in Italy*, 64.

72 *For instance, in 1395 John Rykener*: Bennett and McSheffrey, "Early, Erotic and Alien," 2.

73 *Similarly, in fourteenth- and fifteenth-century London*: Ibid., 3.

Part Two

CHAPTER FIVE: THE GREAT MASCULINE RENUNCIATION

79 *According to historian Farid Chenoune*: Farid Chenoune, Richard Martin, and Deke Dusinberre, *A History of Men's Fashion* (Paris: Flammarion, 1995), 10.

79 *In 1930, the English psychologist and dress reformer*: J. C. Flügel, "'The Great Masculine Renunciation and Its Causes,' from *The Psychology of Clothes* (1930)," in *The Rise of Fashion: A Reader*, ed. Daniel L. Purdy (Minneapolis: University of Minnesota Press, 2004), 102.

80 *Max Weber's famous account*: Max Weber, *The Protestant Ethic and the Spirit of Capitalism: A Classic Study of the Fundamental Relationships between Religion and the Economic and Social Life in Modern Culture* (New York: Scribner, 1958), 169.

81 *In place of the ostentatious clothing of court*: Anne Hollander, *Sex and Suits*, 80–81.

81 *Chenoune notes that, in eighteenth-century England*: Chenoune, *A History of Men's Fashion*, 9.

81 *According to historian David Kuchta*: David Kuchta, *The Three-Piece Suit and Modern Masculinity: England, 1550-1850* (Berkeley: University of California Press, 2002), 79.

82 *According to an early-eighteenth-century observer*: César de Saussure and Ber-

thold van Muyden, *Lettres Et Voyages De Monsr César De Saussure En Alle-magne, En Hollande, Et En Angleterre, 1725-1729*, pp. xlvi, 390. (Lausanne: 1903), 57–58.

82 *For example, an English tourist*: Norah Waugh, *The Cut of Men's Clothes: 1600-1900* (London: Faber and Faber Limited, 1977), 105.

83 *When geopolitical conflict between France and England dampened*: Chenoune, *A History of Men's Fashion*, 19.

83 *Echoing the rationale that Queen Elizabeth advanced*: Silence Dogood, *New-England Courant*, June 11, 1772, 45th ed.

84 *As historian Michael Zakim notes*: Michael Zakim, *Ready-Made Democracy: A History of Men's Dress in the American Republic, 1760-1860* (Chicago: University of Chicago Press, 2003), 21.

84 *Nor was this the only echo of an older dress code*: Ibid., 32.

84 *The new French Republican government rejected*: Philippe Perrot, *Fashioning the Bourgeoisie: A History of Clothing in the Nineteenth Century* (Princeton: Princeton University Press, 1996), 20. (Le Moniteur universel, no 39, Ire decade de Brumaire, l'an II (30 October 1793)).

84 *As John Carl Flügel noted*: Flügel, "The Great Masculine Renunciation," 104.

85 *Political egalitarianism, combined with a new respect*: Ibid.

86 *By the early nineteenth century, the term*: Zakim, *Ready-Made Democracy*, 203.

86 *As historian Benedict Anderson argues*: Benedict Anderson, *Imagined Communities: Reflections on the Origin and Spread of Nationalism* (London: Verso, 1998), 5–7.

87 *That . . . no man or boy*: The Act of Abolition and Proscription of the Highland Dress, 19 George II, cap 39, sec. 17, 1746.

88 *New legislation disarmed the Highlanders*: Heritable Jurisdictions (Scotland) Act 1746.

88 *A mid-nineteenth-century commentary made these observations*: "Scottish Culture and History: The Story of Tartan Day," *The Royal Caledonian Society of South Australia*, http://www.rcs.org.au/content/history/cultureandhistory /The%20Story%20of%20Tartan%20Day.pdf.

89 *According to historian Hugh Trevor-Roper*: Hugh Trevor-Roper, "The Highland Tradition of Scotland," in *The Invention of Tradition*, eds. Eric John Hobsbawm and Terence Ranger (Cambridge: Cambridge University Press, 1983), 23.

89 Let others boast of philibeg: John Telfer Dunbar, *History of Highland Dress* (Edinburgh and London: Oliver & Boyd, 1962), 185–186.

90 *In 1727 an English officer posted in Scotland*: Trevor-Roper, "The Highland Tradition of Scotland," 23.

90 *A letter from one Ivan Baille*: Dunbar, *History of Highland Dress*, 12–13.

90 *There is some evidence of regionally distinctive tartans*: Allan Ramsay, *Tartana*, 1718, http://www.tartansauthority.com/tartan/the-growth-of-tartan/the -origin-of-clan-tartans/a-case-for-clan-tartans/.

90 *the Scottish author Martin Martin writes*: Martin Martin, *A Description of the*

Western Islands of Scotland (1703), http://www.tartansauthority.com/tartan/the-growth-of-tartan/the-origin-of-clan-tartans/thoughts-on-clan-tartans/.

90 *But the weight of opinion seems to be on the side*: Trevor-Roper, "The Highland Tradition of Scotland," 20. See also James Scarlett, MBE, "The Origin of Clan Tartans," Scottish Tartan Authority, http://www.tartansauthority.com/tartan/the-growth-of-tartan/the-origin-of-clan-tartans/: "Whatever inferences enthusiastic protagonists may draw from the totally inadequate evidence, there is no clear reference to the use of tartan in the 'clan' context before the '45."

91 *without fear of the Law*: Dunbar, *The History of Highland Dress*, 8.

91 *But by then the Highland costume had fallen into disuse*: Trevor-Roper, "The Highland Tradition of Scotland," 24.

92 *For instance, Trevor-Roper reports that*: Ibid., 30.

92 *By 1822, King George IV was painted wearing Highland tartans*: Robert Mudie, *Historical Account of His Majesty's Visit to Scotland* (Edinburgh, 1822).

92 *in 1853 Queen Victoria established a royal tartan*: "The Scottish Register of Tartans," https://www.tartanregister.gov.uk/tartanDetails?ref=182.

93 *According to historian Daniel Leonhard Purdy*: Purdy, *The Rise of Fashion*, 87.

93 *Similarly, Justus Möser, renowned jurist and advisor to the prince-bishop*: Ibid., 88.

93 *Möser's national uniform*: Ibid., 89.

94 *He observed that clothing was more than a sign of social status*: Ibid., 76.

94 *A law mandating a civilian uniform*: Ibid., 78; Samuel Simon Witte, "An Answer to the Question: Would it Be Harmful or Beneficial to Establish a National Uniform?", 1791.

96 *indeed, the great eighteenth-century authority on French culture*: Denis Diderot, *Encyclopedie Ou Dictionnaire Raisonne Des Sciences, Des Arts Et Des Metiers*, 1751–72.

96 *According to historian Michael Kwass, in 1771*: Michael Kwass, "Big Hair: A Wig History of Consumption in Eighteenth-Century France," *The American Historical Review* 111, no. 3 (January 2006): 631–59, 636, https://doi.org/10.1086/ahr.111.3.631.

96 *Even by the standards of the day*: Ibid., 635.

97 *According to historian Daniel Roche, Jean-Baptiste Thiers*: Daniel Roche, *The Culture of Clothing: Dress and Fashion in the Ancien Regime* (Cambridge, UK: Cambridge, 1996), 30.

97 *This left the bewigged cleric unable*: Ibid., 30–32.

97 *According to Kwass, the gentleman-economist*: Kwass, "Big Hair," 635.

97 *Another observer lamented the proliferation of wigs*: Ibid.

97 *Social critics, fashion experts, civility guides, and wigmakers themselves*: Ibid., 645.

98 *Far from an object of Veblen-style conspicuous consumption*: Ibid., 650.

98 *The wigmakers' art*: Ibid.

98 *No explicit dress code required barrister's the wig*: James G. McLaren, "A Brief History of Wigs in the Legal Profession," *International Journal of the*

Legal Profession 6, no. 2 (1999): 241–50, 241, 245, https://doi.org/10.1080/09
695958.1999.9960465.

CHAPTER SIX: STYLE AND STATUS

100 *In the early sixteenth century, Baldassare Castiglione*: Baldassare Castiglione,
The Book of the Courtier: The Singleton Translation (New York: W. W. Norton,
2002).

101 *Similarly, the seventeenth-century English poet Robert Herrick advised*: Robert
Herrick, "Delight in Disorder," in *Hesperides*, 1648.

102 *The French intellectual and diplomat Michel Chevalier wrote*: Michel Chevalier, *Society, Manners and Politics in the United States* (New York: A. M. Kelley,
1966), 341-42.

102 *In the mid-ninteenth century, the English poet Lady Emmeline Stuart-Wortley
remarked*: Emmeline Stuart-Wortley, *Travels in the United States During 1849
and 1850* (New York: Harper & Bros., 1851).

102 *for example, Thomas Ford, who would later become the governor*: Thomas Ford
and James Shields, *A History of Illinois from Its Commencement as a State in
1818 to 1847: Containing a Full Account of the Black Hawk War, the Rise, Progress and Fall of Mormonism, the Alton and Lovejoy Riots, and Other Events*
(Chicago: S. C. Griggs & Co., 1854).

103 *For instance, one American critic complained*: Gordon S. Wood, *The Creation
of the American Republic: 1776-1787* (Chapel Hill: University of North Carolina
Press), 1998.

103 *By the mid-nineteenth century, elite New Yorkers openly worried*: Nathaniel
Parker Willis, "Walk in Broadway," *New Mirror*, October 21, 1843.

104 *When asked the yearly cost to maintain the wardrobe*: *The Laws of Etiquette; or,
Short Rules and Reflections for Conduct in Society* (Philadelphia: Carey, Lea, &
Blanchard, 1836), 136.

104 *Brummell was, according to one of his contemporaries*: Chenoune, *A History of
Men's Fashion*, 21.

104 *Historian Phillippe Perrot observes*: Perrot, *Fashioning the Bourgeoisie*, 86.

105 *According to one French guide on the* comme il faut: Ibid., 89. (de Serieul, Eliane.
Le Diable rose 3, no.4 (July 20 1862).)

106 *An etiquette treatise from nineteenth-century France*: Ibid., 91-92. (Despaigne,
Le Code de la mode.)

106 *the "Comtesse de Bassanville" warned that*: Ibid., 99. (Comtesse de Bassanville,
La Sciences du Monde.)

107 *"Comtesse Drohojowska" admonished her readers*: Ibid., 100. (Comtesse Drohojowska, *De la politesse*.)

107 *According to Perrot, the aristocratic families of France's Second Empire*: Ibid., 129.

107 *As "Comtesse Dash" advised her readers*: Ibid., 135. (quoting Comtess Dash,
Comment on fait son chemin dans le monde.)

CHAPTER SEVEN: SEX AND SIMPLICITY

109 *As historian Anne Hollander points out*: Hollander, *Sex and Suits*, 41.

112 *Consequently, male tailors controlled*: Ibid., 66.

112 *Seamstresses could make only draped garments for women*: Jones, *Sexing La Mode*, 82–83.

113 *According to Jones, in one especially dramatic conflict*: Ibid., 77.

113 *Tellingly, the seamstresses countered*: Ibid., 84.

113 *The new craft of dressmaking*: Hollander, *Sex and Suits*, 66–68.

114 *For instance, in his influential treatise* Emile: Jean-Jacques Rousseau, *Emile, or, Education*, (New York: E.P. Dutton & Co., 1762).

114 *One author mockingly suggested*: Jones, *Sexing La Mode*, 98.

115 *men who hold the needle*: Ibid., 98. (quoting Mercier, Tableau de Paris, 177–78.)

115 *The argument succeeded*: Hollander, *Sex and Suits*, 68.

118 *As historian Anne Hollander puts it, "the male body received"*: Ibid., 54.

118 *"The difference between a man of sense and a fop"*: Philip Dormer Stanhope Chesterfield, *Letters to His Son; On the Art of Becoming a Man of the World and a Gentleman* (Tudor, 1917).

118 *Echoing this sentiment almost a century later*: Henry Lunettes, *The American Gentleman's Guide to Politeness and Fashion: Or, Familiar Letters to His Nephews, Containing Rules of Etiquette, Directions for the Formation of Character, Etc., Etc.* (New York: Derby & Jackson, 1859).

118 *the well-dressed gentleman left his appearance*: George P. Fox, *Fashion: The Power that Influences the World. The Philosophy of Ancient and Modern Dress and Fashion* (New York: Sheldon & Co., 1871).

120 *He received the Order of Saint Louis for his military service*: Simon Burrows, Jonathan Conlin, Russell Goulbourne, and Valerie Mainz, eds., *The Chevalier d'Eon and His Worlds: Gender, Espionage and Politics in the Eighteenth Century* (London: Continuum, 2010).

120 *But after running up large debts*: Linda Rodriguez McRobbie, "The Incredible Chevalier d'Eon, Who Left France as a Male Spy and Returned as a Christian Woman," *Atlas Obscura*, July 29, 2016.

120 *The French quietly abandoned the effort to arrest him*: Simon Burrows, *Blackmail, Scandal, and Revolution: London's French Libellistes, 1758–92* (Manchester: Manchester University Press, 2009).

122 *That narrative—which was widely accepted*: Rodriguez McRobbie, "The Incredible Chevalier d'Eon."

122 *This story would allow d'Éon to return to France*: Gary Kates, *Monsieur d'Eon Is a Woman: A Tale of Political Intrigue and Sexual Masquerade* (Baltimore: Johns Hopkins University Press, 2001).

122 *Although the new government decreed on October 29, 1793*: Perrot, *Fashioning the Bourgeoisie*, 20.

123 *Was d'Éon, as National Portrait Gallery curator Lucy Peltz put it*: Mark Brown,

"Portrait Mistaken for 18th-Century Lady Is Early Painting of Transvestite," *The Guardian*, June 6, 2012, https://www.theguardian.com/artanddesign/2012/jun/06/portrait-18th-century-early-transvestite.

123   *"to some extent tricked into"*: Rodriguez McRobbie, "The Incredible Chevalier d'Eon."

123   *According to Kates, d'Éon referred to his gender transition*: Ibid.

125   *Although French society hailed d'Éon as a heroine*: Ibid.

CHAPTER EIGHT: THE "RATIONAL DRESS" MOVEMENT

126   *Echoing the ethos of England's Beau Brummel*: Zakim, *Ready-Made Democracy*, 192.

126   *For men, freedom of movement*: *Mirror of Fashion* 12, no. 5 (May 1850).

127   *Numerous bulky underskirts made navigating narrow passages challenging*: Zakim, *Ready-Made Democracy*, 200–01.

127   *Susan B. Anthony insisted, "I can see no business avocation"*: Ibid., 201.

127   *Apparently some employers agreed that reformed attire*: *The Lily*, July 1851, 53, https://www.accessible.com/accessible/print.

127   *The* Lily *reported that the association*: *The Lily*, May 1856, https://www.accessible.com/accessible/print.

128   *The January 1889 issue*: *Rational Dress Society's Gazette*, no. 4 (January 1889), 1.

129   *Rational Dress Society founder Lady Harberton*: Ibid.

129   *"The corset is the framework of a woman's body"*: Perrot, *Fashioning the Bourgeoisie*, 153.

130   *Similarly, the 1870 treatise* Hygiene for Fashionable People: Ibid., 156.

130   *For instance, in 1857 Dr. Auguste Debay published statistics demonstrating*: Auguste Debay, *Hygiène Vestimentaire: Les Modes Et Les Parures Chez Les français Depuis létablissement De La Monarchie jusquà Nos Jours. Précédés Dun Curieux parallèle Des Modes Chez Les Anciennes Dames Grepues Et Romaines* (Paris: Dentu, 1857), 170–71.

131   *According to Flower, the corset not only threatened the health*: Benjamin Orange Flower, *Fashion's Slaves* (Boston: Arena, 1892), 15.

131   *"How many cases of gastritis"*: Perrot, *Fashioning the Bourgeoisie*, 154.

132   *For instance, one guide to "good form" advised women to wear a corset*: Perrot, *Fashioning the Bourgeoisie*, 157. (quoting Louis Verardi, *Manuel du bon ton et de la politesse francaise: nouveau guide pour se conduire dans le monde*.)

133   *An article in the* Rational Dress Society Gazette *lamented*: *Rational Dress Society Gazette*, no. 4 (January 1889), 2.

133   *He wrote a series on women's dress reform for the* Pall Mall Gazette: Oscar Wilde, "Slaves of Fashion," "Woman's Dress," "More Radical Ideas upon Dress Reform," and "Costume," in *Shorter Prose Pieces*, Project Guttenberg (2000) (originally in the *Pall Mall Gazette*, 1884); Oscar Wilde, "The Philosophy of Dress," *New York Tribune*, 1885.

133   *Starched collars were uncomfortable, suit coats were hot*: Joanna Bourke, "The

Great Male Renunciation: Men's Dress Reform in Inter-war Britain," *Journal of Design History* 9, no. 1 (1996): 23.

133 *As a consequence, men were*: Ibid.

133 *They advised that coats*: Ibid.

133 *According to historian Joanna Bourke*: Ibid., 24 [emphasis added].

133 *The implicit message, Bourke writes, was that*: Ibid., 26.

134 *A similar local ordinance passed in San Francisco*: Clare Sears, "Electric Brilliancy: Cross-Dressing Law and Freak Show Displays in Nineteenth-Century San Francisco," *Women's Studies Quarterly* 36, no. 3/4 (Fall-Winter, 2008): 170–87.

134 *Laws against disguise were also used to punish cross-dressing*: William Eskridge, *Gaylaw: Challenging the Apartheid of the Closet* (Cambridge, MA: Harvard University Press, 1999), 27.

134 *Many of these laws seemed designed to target deception*: Ibid.

134 *According to historian Clare Sears, cross-dressing bans were enforced*: Sears, "Electric Brilliancy," 171.

135 *Cartoons in an 1852 edition of* Harper's New Monthly: Zakim, *Ready-Made Democracy*, 201.

136 *Amelia Bloomer herself abandoned them*: Skye Makaris, "This Difficult-to-Wear Skirt Helped to Break Down Class Barriers" *Racked*, December 7, 2017, https://www.racked.com/2017/12/7/16717206/cage-crinoline-feminism-class.

136 *Although the United States had led the way in inexpensive ready-made men's suits*: See Zakim, *Ready-Made Democracy*.

137 *The predictable dynamic of status emulation and jealousy followed*: Malcolm Barnard, *Fashion as Communication* (Florence: Taylor and Francis, 2013).

137 *An essay in the* Dundee Courier *in 1862 called for legal regulation*: "Plunder Baskets," *Dundee Courier*, September 24, 1862.

137 *The crinoline quickly inspired the potent mixture*: *Petit Journal Pour Rire*, 1856, https://images-na.ssl-images-amazon.com/images/I/91oHNUtfM%2BL.jpg.

139 *society will fall to pieces*: Bourke, "The Great Male Renunciation," 29.

139 *In 1932, in a debate titled "Shall Man be Redressed?"*: Bourke, "The Great Male Renunciation," 30.

140 *This is why, as Anne Hollander pithily notes*: Hollander, *Sex and Suits*, 126.

140 *The stereotypical Pygmalion-like dictatorial fashion designer*: Ibid., 116.

140 *Ever since, to be sure, male designers have done a great deal*: Ibid., 121.

140 *It should not be assumed that all the women*: Ibid., 140.

CHAPTER NINE: FLAPPER FEMINISM

143 *In 1920, the* Saturday Evening Post *published a short story*: F. Scott Fitzgerald, "Bernice Bobs Her Hair," *Saturday Evening Post*, May 1, 1920.

145 *According to Dian Hanson, magazine editor and author of* History of Men's Magazines: Dian Hanson, *History of Men's Magazines* (London: Taschen, 2004).

146 *In 1926, with the flapper look a full-blown trend*: Emily Spivak, "The History of

the Flapper, Part 2: Makeup Makes a Bold Entrance," *Smithsonian Institution*, February 7, 2013, https://www.smithsonianmag.com/arts-culture/the-history-of-the-flapper-part-2-makeup-makes-a-bold-entrance-13098323/.

148 *The flapper look first appeared*: Lisa Hix, "'The Great Gatsby' Still Gets Flappers Wrong," *Collectors Weekly*, https://www.collectorsweekly.com/articles/the-great-gatsby-still-gets-flappers-wrong/.

148 *Indeed, critics lamented that flapper fashions*: Birgitte Soland, *Becoming Modern: Young Women and the Reconstruction of Womanhood in the 1920s* (Princeton: Princeton University Press, 2002), 25.

148 *More threatening still, flapper styles*: Ibid., 25–26.

148 *Another commentator made the implication explicit*: Ibid., 27.

148 *Newspapers and magazines blamed the unfeminine*: Gene Cohn, "Woman Always Pays, Says Girl of 14 In First Flapper Tragedy: Over-Sophistication of Modern Girl Blamed for California Tragedy," *Ogden Standard Examiner*, May 1, 1922.

149 *A characteristic opinion came from an unlikely source, the film actress Betty Blythe*: "Flapper Defends Daring Frocks," *Competitors Journal*, July 1926; republished in Glamourdaze.com, https://glamourdaze.com/2017/11/flapper-defends-daring-frocks.html.

149 *For instance, according to a 1922 article in the* Morning Tulsa Daily World: "Big Business Banishes the Flapper," *Tulsa Daily World*, July 16, 1922.

150 *The article also listed several other businesses and employers*: Ibid.

150 *Hairdressers multiplied from five thousand in 1920*: Spivak, "The History of the Flapper."

150 *A 1925 article in the* New Republic: Bruce Bliven, "Flapper Jane," *New Republic*, 1925.

151 *The* New Republic *saw flapper fashion as the uniform*: Ibid.

151 *The Symington Side Lacer, for instance, was a flapper-era brassiere*: Spivak, "The History of the Flapper."

Part Three

CHAPTER TEN: SLAVES TO FASHION?

157 *South Carolina's Negro Act of 1740*: David J. McCord, *The Statutes at Large of South Carolina, Vol. 7*, 1840 (containing the Act Relating to Charleston, Courts, Slaves and Rivers); see also Eulanda A. Sanders, "The Politics of Textiles Used in African-American Slave Clothing," Textile Society of America: Textiles and Politics (2012).

158 *According to historians Shane and Graham White*: Shane White and Graham White, "Slave Clothing and African-American Culture in the Eighteenth and Nineteenth Centuries," *Past & Present* 148, no. 1 (1995): 149–86, 153, https://doi.org/10.1093/past/148.1.149.

158 *In a similar vein*: Jonathan Prude, "To Look upon the 'Lower Sort': Runaway

Ads and the Appearance of Unfree Laborers in America, 1750-1800," *The Journal of American History* 78, no. 1 (1991): 124, 155, https://doi.org/10.2307/2078091.

158 *Black women in particular inspired calls for vigorous enforcement*: White, "Slave Clothing," 161.

159 *A 1772 letter to the editor of the* South Carolina Gazette: *South Carolina Gazette*, November 5, 1774.

159 *Well-dressed slaves—especially female slaves—suggested*: *South Carolina Gazette*, September 24, 1772.

159 *Indeed, according to Shane and Graham White*: White, "Slave Clothing," 160.

159 *A letter to the* South Carolina Gazette: *South Carolina Gazette*, August 27, 1772.

159 *For instance, "Bacchus," the personal servant of a Virginia plantation owner*: White, "Slave Clothing," 155.

160 *In eighteenth-century English slang, a "Macaroni" was*: Peter McNeil, *Pretty Gentlemen: Macaroni Men and the Eighteenth-Century Fashion World* (New Haven: Yale University Press, 2018), 13.

160 *His disgruntled former master described him*: White, "Slave Clothing," 155.

160 *The presiding judge, Lord Mansfield, having heard*: Somerset v. Stewart, 12 Geo. 3 1772, K.B. (May 14, 1772).

161 *A Black came in after dinner*: Gene Adams, "Dido Elizabeth Belle, a Black Girl at Kenwood: An Account of a Protegée of the 1st Lord Mansfield," *Camden History Review* 12 (1984).

161 *A Jamaica planter being asked*: Ibid.

161 *The slave owner, Stewart*: Somerset v. Stewart, 12 Geo. 3 1772, K.B. (May 14, 1772).

162 Somerset v. Stewart *repudiated the notion*: Pearne v. Lisle, Amb 75, 27 ER 47 (1749).

162 *in Massachusetts, several slaves sued for their freedom*: Robert M. Spector, "The Quock Walker Cases (1781-83)—Slavery, its Abolition, and Negro Citizenship in Early Massachusetts," *The Journal of Negro History* 53, no. 1 (January 1968), 12–32.

162 *In 1775, a North Carolina master described*: White, "Slave Clothing," 156.

162 *A Maryland man sought the return of two runaway slaves*: Ibid.

162 *Historian Jonathan Prude found, in a study of late eighteenth-century advertisements*: Prude, "To Look upon the 'Lower Sort,'" 143.

163 *Many runaways had expensive tastes*: Ibid., 155.

163 *in the 1780s one master, the Reverend Henry Laurens*: White, "Slave Clothing," 150.

163 *Shane and Graham White write of a "quasi-licit trade"*: Ibid., 160.

163 *Fashionable clothing could easily be sold or traded*: Ibid., 156.

163 *"pose as Methodist preachers"*: Ibid., 156–70.

163 *According to Prude, "Unfree laborers"*: Prude, "To Look upon the 'Lower Sort,'" 155.

164 *Jonathan Prude notes that "chattel laborers actively"*: Ibid.

164 *Shane and Graham White describe slaves using eclectic dress*: White, "Slave Clothing," 162.

164 *Descriptions of runaway slaves detailed*: Prude, "To Look upon the 'Lower Sort,'" 155.

164 *And Prude suggests that an "expression of anti-elite sensibilities"*: Ibid., 156.

164 *Free Blacks as well as many slaves avoided*: Ibid.

165 *In 1845 the prominent Philadelphian John Fanning Watson complained*: John F. Watson and Willis P. Hazard, *Annals of Philadelphia, and Pennsylvania, in the Olden Time: Being a Collection of Memoirs, Anecdotes, and Incidents of the City and Its Inhabitants, and of the Earliest Settlements of the Inland Part of Pennsylvania: Intended to Preserve the Recollections of Olden Time, and to Exhibit Society in Its Changes of Manners and Customs, and the City and Country in Their Local Changes and Improvements* (Philadelphia: J. M. Stoddart & Co., 1877).

166 *At the same time, popular depictions compared Black people in refined clothing*: Shane White and Graham J. White, *Stylin': African-American Expressive Culture, from Its Beginnings to the Zoot Suit* (Ithaca: Cornell University Press, 1999), 114–118.

166 *White schoolchildren taunted well-dressed blacks*: Ibid., 119.

166 *The police officer then warned Gordon against venturing into town*: Taylor Gordon, *Born to Be* (Lincoln: University of Nebraska Press, 1995), 116–17.

167 *When Black soldiers returned home from World War I*: White, *Stylin'*, 155.

167 *Alabama tenant farmer Ned Cobb, aka Nate Shaw*: Theodore Rosengarten, *All God's Dangers: The Life of Nate Shaw* (New York: Vintage Books, 2018), 161.

167 *One Black man living in South Carolina during the 1940s*: Hylan Lewis, *Blackways of Kent* (Chapel Hill: University of North Carolina Press, 1955), 54.

CHAPTER ELEVEN: FROM RAGS TO RESISTANCE

168 *"The zoot suit has become a badge of hoodlumism"*: "Ban on Freak Suits Studied by Councilmen," *Los Angeles Times*, June 9, 1943.

168 *One observer witnessed "a mob of several thousand soldiers"*: Carey McWilliams and Matt S. Meier, *North from Mexico: The Spanish-Speaking People of the United States* (New York: Greenwood Press, 1990).

169 *One account of the riots described a mob that stormed*: Stuart Cosgrove, "The Zoot-Suit and Style Warfare," *History Workshop Journal* 18, no. 1 (1984): 77–91, https://doi.org/10.1093/hwj/18.1.77.

169 *A typical article reported favorably that*: Ibid., 81.

170 *The* Times *speculated that the suit was inspired by Rhett Butler's clothing*: White, *Stylin'*, 249–51.

171 *The* Amsterdam News *quipped that*: Amsterdam News, May 29, 1943.

171 *Ralph Ellison's protagonist in* Invisible Man *begins his journey*: Ralph Ellison, *Invisible Man* (New York: Random House, 1952).

171 *That sartorial fraternity was not racially exclusive*: E. O. Pagan, "Los Angeles

Geopolitics and the Zoot Suit Riot, 1943," *Social Science History* 24, no. 1 (January 2000): 223–56, 244, https://doi.org/10.1215/01455532-24-1-223.

171 *It was also a sisterhood*: Clarissa M. Esguerra, "Putting on a Zoot Suit: A Case of Race and Class in the First Truly American Suit," *Vestoj*, December 13, 2016, http://vestoj.com/putting-on-a-zoot-suit/.

172 *As the poet Octavio Paz wrote of the* pachuco: Octavio Paz, *The Labyrinth of Solitude* (London: Penguin, 1990), 5–6.

172 *Baudelaire described dandies as*: Charles Baudelaire, "The Dandy" from *The Painter of Modern Life* (1863) in Purdy, *The Rise of Fashion*, 192.

172 *Barbey d'Aurevilly wrote that dandyism's*: Barbey d'Aurevilly, "The Anatomy of Dandyism with Some Observations on Beau Brummel" in Purdy, *The Rise of Fashion*, 174.

172 *Carlyle, in his idiosyncratic work* Sartor Resartus *(*The Tailor Retailored*)*: Thomas Carlyle, *Sartor Resartus* (1836).

173 *Dandies were, of necessity, rich*: Baudelaire, "The Dandy."

173 *California state senator Jack B. Tenney presided*: "Tenney Feels Riots Caused by Nazi Move for Disunity," *Los Angeles Times*, June 9, 1943.

173 *A witness testifying in the investigation*: "Watts Pastor Blames Riots on Fifth Column," *Los Angeles Times*, June 9, 1943.

173 *In an opinion piece in* The Crisis, *Chester Himes succinctly insisted*: Chester Himes, "Zoot Riots are Race Riots" in *Black on Black: Baby Sister and Selected Writings* (London: Joseph, 1975).

173 *while another editorial in* The Crisis *opined*: Ibid., 199.

174 *The novelist Ralph Ellison offered perhaps the most insightful comment*: Ralph Ellison, *A Collection of Critical Essays* (1974), 67.

175 *Indeed, for Frazier, almost every aspect of the culture*: E. Franklin Frazier, *Black Bourgeoisie: The Rise of a New Middle Class* (New York: Free Press, 1957), 176.

175 *The black bourgeoisie "are constantly buying things"*: Ibid., 189.

176 *Frazier lamented that these debutante balls were breathlessly reported on*: Ibid., 167–68.

177 *A group of high school boys pummeled the group*: Anthony David Moody, *Coming of Age in Mississippi* (New York: Dial Press, 1968), 238.

177 *"Before we were taken back to campus"*: Ibid., 239.

178 *Professor Anthony Pinn, an expert on the history of the Black church*: Aaron Howard, "There's a Deep Tradition behind Wearing Your Sunday Best," *Jewish Herald-Voice*, April 7, 2011, http://jhvonline.com/theres-a-deep-tradition-behind-wearing-your-sunday-best-p10854-147.htm; See also Anthony Pinn, *Black Religion and Aesthetics* (New York: Palgrave Macmillan, 2009).

180 *SNCC's new, more radical image included*: Tanisha Ford, "SNCC Women, Denim, and the Politics of Dress," *The Journal of Southern History* LXXIX, no. 3 (August 2013): 639–40.

180 *According to Tanisha Ford, a historian of the civil rights movement*: Ibid.

182 *When asked to define Black Power, Carmichael replied*: Stokely Carmichael and Charles V. Hamilton, *Black Power: the Politics of Liberation in America*, (1967).

182 *After the Greenwood rally*: Clayborne Carson, *In Struggle: SNCC and the Black Awakening in the 1960s* (Cambridge, MA: Harvard University Press, 1995).

183 *In 1962, Eldridge Cleaver, who later became a leader of the Black Panther Party*: Eldridge Cleaver, "As Crinkly As Yours," in *SOS—Calling All Black People: A Black Arts Movement Reader* (Boston: Boston University of Massachusetts Press, 2014), 135–144.

183 *"We must see ourselves as beautiful people"*: "Mainspring of Black Power: Stokely Carmichael," *London Observer*, July 23, 1967.

183 *He ruefully recalled his youthful attempts to meet*: Malcom X, *The Autobiography of Malcolm X* (London: Penguin Books, 1965), 55.

184 *As one contemporaneous article put it, natural hairstyles*: "Natural Hair: New Symbol of Race Pride," *Ebony*, December 1967, 137.

184 *In a 1965 speech, Malcolm X said*: Malcolm X, "Not Just an American Problem but a World Problem," address delivered in the Corn Hill Methodist Church, Rochester, NY, February 16, 1965.

186 *Many rural and small-town residents*: Ford, "SNCC Women," 643.

186 *Stokely Carmichael's then girlfriend and later wife*: Miriam Makeba, *Makeba: My Story* (Johannesburg: Skotaville Publishers, 1988), 155–56.

186 *In 1969, the Black radical sociologist Robert Allen complained*: Robert L. Allen, *Black Awakening in Capitalist America: An Analytic History* (Trenton: Africa World Press, 1992), 142.

187 *The journalist Tom Wolfe*: Tom Wolfe, *Radical Chic & Mau-Mauing the Flak Catchers* (London: Bantam, 1971), 7–8.

188 *By contrast, hippies slumming*: Roland Barthes, "A Case of Cultural Criticism," *Communications 14* (1969).

189 *In 1969, arguably the height of the Black is Beautiful movement*: "Report from Black America," *Newsweek*, June 30, 1969, 22.

189 *Black questioned radical politics generally*: Joe Black, "By the Way," advertisement in *Los Angeles Sentinel*, July 2, 1970.

189 *For instance, in 1969, one letter to* Ebony *magazine read*: "Back to the Hot Comb," Letters to the Editor, *Ebony*, November 1969, 15.

190 *Rogers argued that the cornrow hairstyle*: *Rogers v. American Airlines*, 527 F. Supp. 229 (S.D. N.Y. 1981).

190 *In addition, American Airlines didn't demand that Rogers cut her hair*: Ibid.

191 *In the 1972 book* Flying High: What It's Like to be An Airline Stewardess: Elizabeth Rich, *Flying High: What It's Like to Be an Airline Stewardess* (1970).

192 *The Disney Look flatly prohibits*: "The Disney Look," Walt Disney World Resort, http://wdw.disneycareers.com/en/working-here/the-disney-look/, archived June 20, 2015.

192 *Its "Service Values," to which every employee must commit*: "Looking Professional," Ritz Carlton, http://ritzcarltonleadershipcenter.com/2014/08/looking -professional-old-fashioned/, archived April 6, 2017. ·

192 *Although the hotel does not circulate its dress code to non-employees*: Kathryn

Bold, "Corporate Cleanup," *Los Angeles Times*, May 9, 1996, http://articles.la times.com/1996-05-09/news/ls-2388_1_corporate-america.

192 *According to a manager at the Ritz-Carlton*: Ibid.

193 *In 1986, Cheryl Tatum lost her job at a Hyatt hotel*: E. R. Shipp, "Braided Hair Style at Issue in Protests Over Dress Codes," *New York Times*, September 23, 1987.

193 *In response, almost fifty women picketed the hotel*: Ibid.

193 *the Eleventh Circuit Court of Appeals held that*: EEOC v. Catastrophe Management Solutions, 11th Cir. 2016.

193 *For instance, in 2013, seven-year-old Tiana Parker was sent home*: Rebecca Klein, "Tiana Parker, 7, Switches Schools After Being Forbidden From Wearing Dreads," *HuffPost*, September 5, 2013.

194 *The 2016 dress code for Butler Traditional High School in Kentucky*: Kiersten Willis, "Kentucky High School's Racist Hair Policy that Bans 'Dreadlocks, Cornrolls, and Twists' Sparks Controversy," *Atlanta Black Star*, July 29, 2016.

194 *In 2016 at Durham, North Carolina's School for Creative Studies*: Taryn Finley, "Parents Demand School Let Their Kids Wear African Head Wraps," *HuffPost*, February 9, 2016.

194 *And the Mystic Valley Regional Charter School*: Kayla Lattimore, "When Black Hair Violates the Dress Code," NPR.com, July 17, 2017, https://www.npr.org /sections/ed/2017/07/17/534448313/when-black-hair-violates-the-dress-code.

194 *Later that same year, California passed the CROWN Act*: Cal. SB-188 Chapter 58, July 3, 2019.

CHAPTER TWELVE: SAGGING AND SUBORDINATION

196 *Cosby harangued the crowd with a "get-off-my-lawn" style rant*: Bill Cosby, "Remarks at the NAACP's 50th Anniversary Commemoration of the *Brown vs. Topeka Board of Education* Supreme Court Decision," Washington, DC, May 17, 2004.

197 *He lamented that the rioters had "made shame on our race"*: Fredrick C. Harris, "The Rise of Respectability Politics," *Dissent*, 2014.

197 *Similarly, during a 2013 celebration of the 50th anniversary*: Ibid.

197 *In 2008, then-senator-and-presidential-hopeful Barack Obama*: Chris Harris, "Barack Obama Weighs in on Sagging-Pants Ordinances: 'Brothers Should Pull Up Their Pants,'" MTV.com, November 3, 2008, http://www.mtv.com/news /1598462/barack-obama-weighs-in-on-sagging-pants-ordinances-brothers -should-pull-up-their-pants/.

197 *In that same year, the police chief of Flint, Michigan*: Jessica Bennett, "Fashion Police: Flint Cracks Down on Sagging," *Newsweek*, July 17, 2008, http://www .newsweek.com/fashion-police-flint-cracks-down-sagging-93033.

197 *In 2007, Delcambre, Louisiana, prohibited*: Niko Koppel, "Are Your Jeans Sagging? Go Directly to Jail," *New York Times*, August 30, 2017; Haroon Siddique, "US Town Bans Saggy Pants," *The Guardian*, June 14, 2007.

197 *In 2008, Hahira, Georgia, banned wearing pants with the top*: Malynda Ful-
ton, "Hahira passes clothing ordinance," *Valdosta Daily Times*, March 6, 2008,
https://archive.is/20130205103015/http://www.valdostadailytimes.com/local
/local_story_066233535.html.

197 *In 2010, the city attorney of Albany, Georgia*: "Georgia City Gets Nearly $4000
from Sagging Pants Ban," Associated Press, September 27, 2011, https://
www.reviewjournal.com/news/georgia-city-gets-nearly-4000-from-sagging
-pants-ban/.

198 *Opa-locka, Florida, banned sagging in 2010*: Jim Forsyth, "Sagging Pants
Mean No Ride on One Texas Bus System," Reuters, June 2, 2011, https://www
.reuters.com/article/us-saggypants-texas/saggy-pants-mean-no-ride-on-one
-texas-bus-system-idUSTRE7517LK20110602.

198 *in 2012 Alabama judge John Bush sentenced*: Ruth Manuel-Logan, "Alabama
Judge Slaps Saggy Pants-Wearing Man with Jail Sentence," *NewsOne*, April 12,
2012.

198 *She noted that the ban "targets young African-American men"*: "Government
Should not Dictate Clothing Styles, Says ACLU," ACLU.org, September 7, 2010.

198 *In reaction to a Terrebonne Parish, Louisiana, sagging pants ban*: "Saggy Pants
Ban by Louisiana Town Opposed by ACLU," *Newsmax*, September 26, 2017,
http://www.newsmax.com/TheWire/saggy-pants-ban-Louisiana/2013/04/15
/id/499527/.

199 *Prosecutors have also argued*: See *People v. Romero*, 44 Cal. App. 4th, 386 (2008).

200 *Stephen Maciel—a father of four with no gang ties*: Malia Wollan, "Fresno State
Loves Its Bulldogs, But So Does a Gang," *New York Times*, November 7, 2013,
http://www.nytimes.com/2013/11/10/sports/ncaafootball/fresno-adopts-its
-college-team-but-so-does-a-gang.html?action=click&contentCollection
=Magazine&module=RelatedCoverage&region=Marginalia&pgtype=article.

200 *In 2015* New York Times Magazine *reporter Daniel Alarcón*: Daniel Alarcón,
"Guilt By Association," *New York Times Magazine*, May 31, 2015, 48.

201 *She remembered when the young son*: Ibid., 53.

201 *"I think the hoodie is as much responsible for Trayvon Martin's death"*: M. J. Lee,
"Geraldo: Martin Killed due to 'Hoodie,'" *Politico*, March 3, 2012.

202 *A neighborhood resident, George Zimmerman, thought*: "Exclusive: George
Zimmerman breaks silence on 'Hannity,'" Fox News Channel, July 18, 2012,
http://video.foxnews.com/v/1741879195001/.

202 *And according to Rivera, that sweatshirt was a symbol*: Lee, "Geraldo: Martin
Killed due to 'Hoodie.'"

203 It is our expectation that students who select Morehouse: Morehouse University, "MC Etiquette and General Behavioral Expectations," https://www.more
house.edu/media/studentconduct/MC-Etiquette-and-General-Behavioral
-Expectations.pdf.

204 *To its critics it was snobbish*: Elizabeth Gates, "Morehouse College's Gay Trav-
esty," *The Daily Beast*, October 20, 2009, http://www.thedailybeast.com/articles
/2009/10/20/morehouse-colleges-gay-travesty.html (as of March 25, 2015).

204 *It was discriminatory*: *"Morehouse is instituting a de facto"*: Reina Gattuso, Jess Fournier, and Sejal Singh, "Morehouse Bans Casual Clothes and Women's Clothing," *Feministing*, October 19, 2009, http://feministing.com/2009/10/19/morehouse-bans-casual-clothes-and-womens-clothing.

204 *It was repressive*: *"[O]nce you try to stop people's expression"*: Scott Jaschik, "What the Morehouse Man Wears," *Inside Higher Ed*, October 19, 2009, https://www.insidehighered.com/news/2009/10/19/morehouse.

204 *It was nothing less than a betrayal of the civil rights movement*: Frank Leon Roberts, "Morehouse's Crossroads Has Nothing to Do with 'Ghetto Gear' or Cross Dressing: New dress codes shrouds a lack of academic and financial vision that threatens the foundations of the college's pedigree," *The Root*, October 20, 2009, http://www.theroot.com/articles/culture/2009/10/morehouse_dress_code_sparks_controversy_over_ghetto_gear_and_crossdressing.2.html (as of March 25, 2015).

205 *Morehouse was an exception*: *one of a handful of colleges*: Among the others were Paul Quinn College in Dallas, which required business casual attire, and the University of West Alabama, which in 2007 imposed a dress code after university president Richard Holland noticed a pattern of inappropriate attire. Andy Guess, "No More Mr. Saggypants," *Inside Higher Ed*, October 9, 2007, https://www.insidehighered.com/news/2007/10/09/sagging.

205 *Indeed, Morehouse was a holdout in a more important way*: Peter Applebome, "The Final Four," *New York Times*, April 23, 2006, http://www.nytimes.com/2006/04/23/education/edlife/the-final-four.html.

205 *One of the others, Hampden-Sydney:* Trevor Starnes and Chris Ross, "Seersucker and Civility," *New York Times*, May 8, 2017, https://www.nytimes.com/2017/05/08/opinion/seersucker-and-civility.html.

206 Vibe *magazine picked up the allusion in an article*: "The Mean Girls of Morehouse," *Vibe*, October 11, 2010, http://www.vibe.com/article/mean-girls-morehouse (as of March 25, 2015).

206 *Morehouse's vice president for student services, William Bynum*: Jaschik, "What the Morehouse Man Wears."

206 *The co-president of Safe Space at the time*: Ibid.

206 *Instead, he argued, it targeted*: Roberts, "Morehouse's Crossroads Has Nothing to Do with 'Ghetto Gear' or Cross Dressing."

206 *A columnist for the news website* The Root: Deron Snyder, "Morehouse's Dress Code: Anything Goes, But Not Everywhere," *The Root*, October 15, 2010, http://www.theroot.com/articles/culture/2010/10/why_morehouse_has_the_right_to_enforce_a_dress_code.2.html.

210 *It insisted that "a black"*: Shosuke Ishizu, Toshiyuki Kurosu, Hajime Hasegawa, and Teruyoshi Hayshida, *Take Ivy* (Tokyo: Hachette Fujingaho, 1965), 130.

212 *In an interview, she corrected widespread misinterpretations*: Kimberly Foster and Evelyn Brooks Higgenbotham, "Wrestling with Respectability in the Age of #BlackLivesMatter: A Dialogue," *For Harriet*, October 2015, http://www.forharriet.com/2015/10/wrestling-with-respectability-in-age-of.html#axzz3pEQswiSR.

212 *The activist and philosopher Cornel West*: Cornel West, *Race Matters* (Boston: Beacon Press, 1993), 40.

213 *as the* Washington Post's *style critic Robin Givhan*: Robin Givhan, "The protesters are dressed as their unique selves—and that's part of their power," *Washington Post*, June 2, 2020.

213 *And in Columbia, South Carolina, a group organized a June 14 march*: Vanessa Friedman, "The Dress Codes of the Uprising," *New York Times*, June 17, 2020.

213 *Sociologist Zeynep Tufekci—who participated*: Issac Chotiner, "Has Protesting Become Too Easy?" *Slate*, May 8, 2017, http://www.slate.com/articles/news _and_politics/interrogation/2017/05/zeynep_tufekci_author_of_twitter_and _tear_gas_on_networked_protest.html.

214 *As Eddie Eades, one of the organizers of the march*: Friedman, "The Dress Codes of the Uprising."

Part Four

CHAPTER THIRTEEN: HOW TO DRESS LIKE A WOMAN

223 *In the 1967 book* How to Dress for Success: Edith Head and Joe Hyams, *How to Dress for Success* (New York: Random House, 1967), 1.

223 *It warned against fads and flamboyance*: Ibid., 10, 22.

224 *A subchapter titled "How to Hold on to that Husband"*: Ibid., 38.

224 *The overarching lesson of* How to Dress For Success *echoed*: Laura Regensdorf, "'There Are No Ugly Women, Only Lazy Ones': A New Beauty Exhibition Explores the Life and Legacy of Helena Rubinstein," *Vogue*, January 12, 2017, https://www.vogue.com/slideshow/helena-rubinstein-beauty-cosmetics -jewish-museum-exhibition.

224 *The chapter "How to Dress Your Family for Success" tells the reader*: Head, *How to Dress for Success*, 46.

224 *"[H]is apathy about his clothes"*: Ibid., 44.

225 *It required all bartenders to wear a uniform of black pants*: Jespersen v. Harrah's Operating Co., Inc., 444 F. 3d. 1104 (9th Cir. 2006).

225 *The dress code also contained a few other general guidelines*: Ibid.

226 *"sex object"*: Darlene Jespersen, "Case Is About Civil Rights and Sex Bias," *Reno Gazette*, February 4, 2004.

226 *"clown"*: Rhina Guidos, "Fashion Checklist: No Blush, No Lipstick . . . No Job," *Christian Science Monitor*, July 18, 2001. ("I was good enough to do my job for 18 years," says the bartender [Jespersen]. "Suddenly, I wasn't good enough to do my job because I refused to look like a clown." (alteration added))

227 *"I wear my hair long . . . it is below the ears"*: Fagan v. National Cash Register Co., 481 F.2d. 1115 (D.C. Cir. 1973).

227 *For instance, in 1971 an Ohio court held that*: Roberts v. General Mills, Inc., 337 F. Supp. 1055 (N.D. Ohio W.D. 1971).

227 *In 1972 a California court held that although an employer*: Aros v. McDonnell Douglas Corporation, 348 F. Supp. 661 (C.D. Cal. 1972).

227 *For instance, in 1972, a California court held that the employment discrimination law*: Baker v. California Land Title Company, 349 F. Supp. 235, 237-38 (C.D. Cal. 1972).

227 *Similarly, a court in Washington, D.C., opined in 1972*: Boyce v. Safeway Stores, Inc., 351 F. Supp. 402 (D.D.C. 1972).

228 *Likewise, in 1972 a federal court in Georgia insisted*: Willingham v. Macon Telegraph Publishing Company, 352 F. Supp. 1018 (Georgia M.D. 1972).

228 *And when focus groups suggested that makeover*: Craft v. Metromedia, Inc., 66 F.2d 1205 (1985).

229 *The federal court rejected Craft's claim*: Ibid.

229 *The partnership advised her to try again the next year*: Price Waterhouse v. Hopkins, 490 U.S. 228 (1989).

230 *According to the company, "[T]he essence of our business is the Hooters Girl"*: Jacob Shamsian, "The Strange Loophole That Lets Hooters Hire Only Female Servers," *Business Insider*, September 13, 2015, http://www.businessinsider.com /how-can-hooters-hire-only-women-2015-9.

230 *In 1963, a young Gloria Steinem wrote a damming exposé*: Gloria Steinem, "A Bunny's Tale," *Show Magazine*, May 1963.

231 *The Playboy clubs, needless to say*: St. Cross v. Playboy Club, Case No. CSF 22618 -70, Appeal No. 773 (N.Y. State Div. of Human Rights Dec. 17, 1971); *Weber v. Playboy Club*, Case No. CSF 22619-70, Appeal No. 774 (N.Y. State Div. of Human Rights Dec. 17, 1971).

231 *The Playboy clubs established the following guidelines*: Ibid.

232 *The board summarized the dispute and rendered its judgment*: Ibid.

232 *She had a comparatively blithe take on*: Shawn McCreesh, "Holy Cottontail! The Playboy Club Is Back Again," *New York Times*, September 6, 2018, https://www .nytimes.com/2018/09/06/style/playboy-club-gloria-steinem-lauren-hutton.html.

233 *"Why do women have to suffer physical pain"*: Sandra Chereb, "Casino Cocktail Waitresses Want to Give Show Rule the Boot," *Las Vegas Sun*, May 15, 2000.

234 *The cocktail servers considered high heels a health hazard*: "Casino Cocktail Waitresses Fight to Wear Comfortable Shoes after Hours in High Heels Causes 'Foot Damage,'" *MailOnline*, Associated Newspapers, June 10, 2013, http:// www.dailymail.co.uk/femail/article-2338906/Casino-cocktail-waitresses-fight -wear-comfortable-shoes-hours-high-heels-causes-foot-damage.html.

234 *according to an exposé in* Slate: Ann McGinley, "What Happened in Vegas?: Why Are Las Vegas Bartenders Now Mostly Women?" *Slate*, March 26, 2013, http://www.slate.com/articles/double_x/doublex/2013/03/las_vegas_bartender _went_from_a_male_to_a_female_job.html.

234 *one attendee complained that "even . . . older women"*: Andreas Wiseman, "Cannes: Women Denied Palais Entry for Wearing Flats," *ScreenDaily*, May 19, 2015, http://www.screendaily.com/festivals/cannes/cannes-women-denied-palais -entry-for-wearing-flats/5088395.article.

234 *Actress Kristen Stewart captured the mood of protest*: Andreas Wiseman, "Kristen Stewart, Julia Roberts Kick Off Their Heels in Cannes," *ScreenDaily*, May 13, 2016, http://www.screendaily.com/festivals/cannes/kristen-stewart-julia-roberts-kick-off-their-heels-in-cannes/5103878.article.

235 *More than 150,000 people signed the petition*: "London Receptionist 'Sent Home for Not Wearing Heels,'" *BBC*, May 11, 2016, http://www.bbc.com/news/uk-england-london-36264229.

235 *Like Nicola Thorpe, Japanese actress Yumi Ishikawa submitted a petition*: "Japanese Women Want a Law Against Mandatory Heels at Work," *ENM News*, June 4, 2019, https://www.enmnews.com/2019/06/04/japanese-women-want-a-law-against-mandatory-heels-at-work/.

235 *when the Manchus overthrew the Ming dynasty*: Kwame Anthony Appiah, *The Honor Code: How Moral Revolutions Happen* (New York: Norton & Company, 2011), 89–91.

235 *Some* chopines *were more than twenty inches high*: Fabritio Caroso, Julia Sutton, and F. Marian Walker, *Courtly Dance of the Renaissance* (London: Constable, 1995), 141.

235 *In 1430, Venice limited the height of* chopines *to three inches*: Margo DeMello, *Feet & Footwear: A Cultural Encyclopedia* (Santa Barbara, CA: Greenwood Press/ABC-CLIO, 2009), 311.

236 *According to Elizabeth Semmelhack, curator of the Bata Shoe Museum*: William Kremer, "Why Did Men Stop Wearing High Heels?" *BBC*, January 25, 2013, http://www.bbc.com/news/magazine-21151350.

236 *the Sun King declared that only members of his royal court*: Ibid.

237 *For instance, the English satirist and poet Alexander Pope*: Elizabeth Semmelhack, "Shoes that Put Women in Their Place," *New York Times*, May 23, 2015.

237 *For instance, a* New York Times *opinion piece from 1871*: "Make-Believe Shoes," *New York Times*, September 2, 1871.

238 *In the early twentieth century, dress codes proposed in Massachusetts*: "Will Seek State Law Against High Heels," *New York Times*, December 5, 1920.

238 *Utah, in 1921, considered a bill that provided*: "High Heels Prohibited by Proposed Utah Law: Limit of One and a Half Inches Set-Penalty is Fine and Jail Term," *New York Times*, January 21, 1921.

238 *Worst of all, the president of the society insisted*: "Stand By High Heels: Massachusetts Shoe Men Oppose Law Banning Them," *New York Times*, February 14, 1921.

238 *tweeted the photo along with the caption*: Megan Garber, "What Does it Mean to Wear Heels?" *The Atlantic*, October 23, 2013.

239 *their stiletto heels were a weapon in the battle*: Ibid.

239 *For instance, in 2000 my colleague Deborah Rhode wrote*: Deborah Rhode, "Step, Wince, Step, Wince," *New York Times*, October 18, 2000.

239 *For instance, in 2013 style consultant, Chassie Post*: Chassie Post, "Stilletos Are Power," *New York Times*, November 1, 2013.

240 *Louboutin was declared the most prestigious maker of women's shoes*: "Luxury Brand Status Index 2009: Footwear," *Reuters*, March 12, 2009, https://web.archive.org/web/20110602152627/http:/www.reuters.com/article/2009/03/12/idUS176686+12-Mar-2009+MW20090312.

240 *The novelist Danielle Steel reportedly owns more than six thousand pairs*: Lauren Milligan, "Louboutin Lover," *British Vogue*, August 14, 2019, https://www.vogue.co.uk/article/christian-louboutin-business-growth-and-celebrity-customers.

240 *Over the years, Louboutin has sued several rival shoemakers*: *Christian Louboutin S.A. v. Yves Saint Laurent America Holding*, 696 F.3d. 206 (2012).

241 *Hidden from view by dresses that skimmed the floor*: Perrot, *Fashioning the Bourgeoisie*, 105.

241 *The clever coquette danced along the boundary of propriety*: Ibid.

241 *By contrast, when too much was revealed*: Ibid.

241 *in 2015 Stephanie Dunn was sent to the principal's office*: Eun Kyung Kim, "Kentucky Student Violates High School Dress Code with Exposed Collarbone," *Today*, August 17, 2015, http://www.today.com/style/kentucky-student-violates-high-school-dress-code-exposed-collarbone-t39211; Caroline Bologna, "The Ridiculous Dress Code Rule that Made This Teen's Outfit 'Inappropriate,'" *HuffPost*, August 20, 2015.

241 *Earlier that year, Gabi Finlayson*: Eun Kyung Kim, "Teen Asked to Cover Up at School Dance: It Made me Feel Like I Wasn't Good Enough," Today.com, January 28, 2015.

241 *When sixteen-year-old Florida student Miranda Larkin*: Eliza Murphy, "Student Forced to Wear 'Shame Suit' for Dress Code Violation," ABCNews.com, September 4, 2014.

241 *In 2013, a Petaluma, California, junior high school held a special assembly*: Karina Ioffee, "Tight Jeans, Leggings OK, But Don't Show Your Underwear," *Petaluma Patch*, May 7, 2013, http://patch.com/california/petaluma/tight-jeans-leggings-ok-but-don-t-show-your-underwear.

241 *Such rigid dress codes may seem like a throwback*: "Digest of Education Statistics, 2015," National Center for Education Statistics (NCES), https://nces.ed.gov/programs/digest/d15/tables/dt15_233.50.asp.

242 *In the first two weeks*: Andrea Hay, "School's Strict Dress Code Nets 200 Detentions and a Rebellion," *New York Post*, September 14, 2014.

242 *Some studies have suggested that dress codes can promote*: "Research Brief, Student Dress Codes and Uniforms," *Educational Partnerships, Inc.*, 2009.

242 *Rules of thumb govern the length of skirts and shorts*: Bologna, "The Ridiculous Dress Code Rule that Made This Teen's Outfit 'Inappropriate.'"

242 *as Scott Hawkins of Woodford County High School put it*: Kim, "Kentucky Student Violates High School Dress Code with Exposed Collarbone."

243 *Brown observed that adults who arrived on campus*: Sarah Mervosh, "A Houston High School Has a New Dress Code. For Parents," *New York Times*, April 24, 2019.

243 *Outraged parents and bystanding commentators alike*: Antonia Noori Farzan,

"A High School's New Dress Code Bans Leggings, Pajamas and Silk Bonnets—for Parents," *Washington Post*, April 24, 2019.

243 *The president of the Houston Federation of Teachers said*: Ibid.

243 *She pointed out that many of the parents would not*: Staff, "High School Principal Stands by Creating Dress Code for Parents," *Inside Edition*, April 26, 2019, https://www.insideedition.com/high-school-principal-stands-creating-dress-code-parents-52502.

243 *Tennessee state representative Antonio Parkinson sponsored legislation*: Farzan, "A High School's New Dress Code Bans Leggings, Pajamas and Silk Bonnets—for Parents."

244 *The panel discussion centered on the publication of a report*: Dress Coded: *Black Girls, Bodies, and Bias in D.C. Schools*, National Women's Law Center, 2018, https://nwlc-ciw49tixgw5lbab.stackpathdns.com/wp-content/uploads/2018/04/5.1web_Final_nwlc_DressCodeReport.pdf.

244 *For instance, roughly 90 percent of the two hundred students*: Nick Canedo, "Staten Island High School Sends 200 Students to Detention for Violating 'Dress for Success' Policy," Syracuse.com, September 16, 2014, http://www.syracuse.com/news/index.ssf/2014/09/staten_island_high_school_dress_code_200_students_detention.html.

244 *As if male libido were an uncontrollable force of nature*: Jim Bazen, "Principal: Dress codes keep girls from becoming 'sex objects,'" *m.live*, October 29, 2015, http://www.mlive.com/opinion/grand-rapids/index.ssf/2015/10/principal_dress_codes_keep_gir.html#comments.

245 *"man's total depravity"*: Ibid.

245 *Humiliated and worried she would miss an important appointment*: Michael Ventre, "Southwest Reaction to Skimpy Outfit Out of Line," NBC News, September 7, 2007.

245 *Later that same year a Southwest flight attendant*: "Dress Code Debate: 2nd Passenger Censored," CBS News, September 13, 2007.

245 *In June 2012, Southwest employees stopped another young woman*: Katie J. M. Baker, "Cover Your Cleavage for Takeoff: Southwest Screws Up Again," *Jezebel*, June 14, 2012.

246 *Southwest eventually lost a discrimination lawsuit*: Wilson v. Southwest Airlines Co., 517 F. Supp. 292 (N.D. Tex. 1981).

246 *For instance, in 2014* Esquire's *Max Berlinger noted with disapproval*: Max Berlinger, "If You're On a Plane, Please Keep Your Socks On," *Esquire*, March 28, 2018, http://www.esquire.com/blogs/mens-fashion/socks-on-plane-1113?click=main_sr.

246 *Singing the same tune in fortissimo*: J. Bryan Lowder, "Stop Dressing Like a Slob When You're Traveling," *Slate*, September 9, 2014, http://www.slate.com/articles/life/a_fine_whine/2014/09/dressing_up_for_air_travel_in_defense_of_looking_nice_on_a_flight_or_train.html.

246 *Ultimately, though,* Esquire, *that bastion of sartorial refinement*: Editors, The

Fashion, "The Complaint: How People Dress on Planes Today," *Esquire*, October 11, 2017, http://www.esquire.com/style/mens-fashion/a29463/airplane-style -2014/.

246 *For instance, Southwest vaguely prohibits*: "Southwest Airlines Co. Contract of Carriage-Passenger, 19th revised, May 9, 2017," Southwest Airlines, https://www.southwest.com/assets/pdfs/corporate-commitments/contract-of -carriage.pdf, 16.

246 *"inappropriate attire"*: Justin Berton, "Grieving Passenger's Sagging Pants Lead to Arrest," SFGate.com, December 7, 2011.

248 *After the jury acquitted Lord*: "Rape Guilty Plea, After Acquittal: Man Gets Life in Georgia—Florida Jury Freed Him," *New York Times*, December 7, 1989.

248 *Lord later confessed to another rape*: Ibid.; Roger Simon, "Rape: Clothing is Not the Criminal," *Los Angeles Times*, February 18, 1990, E2.

248 *Indeed, sociological studies have revealed a widespread belief*: Ed M. Edmonds, Delwin D. Cahoon, and Elizabeth Hudson, "Male-Female Estimates of Feminine Assertiveness Related to Females' Clothing Styles," *Bulletin of the Psychonomic Society* 30, no. 2 (1992): 143–44, https://doi.org/10.3758/bf03330422; Roger L. Terry and Suzanne Doerge, "Dress, Posture, and Setting as Additive Factors in Subjective Probabilities of Rape," *Perceptual and Motor Skills* 48, no. 3 (1979): 903–6, https://doi.org/10.2466/pms.1979.48.3.903; Jane E. Workman and Kim K. P. Johnson, "The Role of Cosmetics in Attributions about Sexual Harassment," *Sex Roles* 24, no. 11–12 (1991): 759–69.

248 *A 1991 study found that even professional psychiatrists believed*: Donna Vali and Nicholas D. Rizzo, "Apparel as One Factor in Sex Crimes Against Young Females: Professional Opinions of U.S. Psychiatrists," *International Journal of Offender Therapy and Comparative Criminology* 35, no. 2 (1991): 167–81.

249 *by contrast, women in more revealing attire came across as assertive*: Lynne Richards, "A Theoretical Analysis of Non-Verbal Communication and Victim Selections for Sexual Assaults," *Clothing & Textiles Research Journal* 55 (1991).

249 *For instance, in response to the acquittal of Steven Lamar Lord*: See Fla. Stat. Ann. Ch. 794-022.

250 *didn't stop London radio host Julia Hartley-Brewer from belittling her*: @JuliaHB1, Twitter, March 1, 2017.

250 *But he then went on to mention them*: Tom Sutcliffe, "Last Night's TV: Katie: My Beautiful Friends, Channel 4; Bible's Buried Secrets, BBC2: Beauty that's not skin-deep," *The Independent*, March 23, 2011, http://www.independent.co .uk/arts-entertainment/tv/reviews/last-nights-tv-katie-my-beautiful-friends -channel-4-bibles-buried-secrets-bbc2-2249993.html.

250 *In response, Stavrakopoulou noted such judgments about women's attire*: "Female Academics: Don't Power Dress, Forget Heels—and No Flowing Hair Allowed," *The Guardian*, October 26, 2014, https://www.theguardian.com/higher -education-network/blog/2014/oct/26/-sp-female-academics-dont-power -dress-forget-heels-and-no-flowing-hair-allowed.

251 *Unlike Stavrakopoulou, Beard eschews any hint of feminine glamor*: Mary Beard, "Too Ugly for TV? No, I'm too Brainy for Men who Fear Clever Women," *Daily Mail*, April 23, 2012, http://www.dailymail.co.uk/femail/article-2134146/Too -ugly-TV-No-Im-brainy-men-fear-clever-women.html.

251 *To the contrary, television critic A. A. Gill*: Ibid.

253 *Pepper was refused entry until he returned in a morning coat*: "The Court and Its Traditions," Supreme Court of the United States, https://www.supremecourt .gov/about/traditions.aspx.

254 *Observers reported that Chief Justice William Rehnquist chastised her*: Patricia Williams, "Tripping on Obama's Coattails," *The Daily Beast*, January 9, 2009, http://www.thedailybeast.com/tripping-on-obamas-coattails.

254 *"more or less like the men's version"*: Williams, "Tripping on Obama's Coattails."

254 *"the female equivalent to the morning coat"*: Lithwick, "Law Suit."

255 *"Kagan should resist the impulse to don anything that suggests"*: Dahlia Lithwick, "Law Suit: Time to Do Away with Morning Wedding attire at the High Court," *Slate*, January 8, 2009, http://www.slate.com/articles/news_and_politics/juris prudence/2009/01/law_suit.html.

255 *Associate Justice Ruth Bader Ginsburg told C-Span in 2009*: "Supreme Court Justice Ginsburg: Supreme Court Week," *C-Span*, July 1, 2009.

255 *Like everything that concerns the nation's high court*: Ed Whelan, "Ginsburg's Lace Collars," *National Review*, July 31, 2014.

256 *For her own part, Justice Ginsburg wore her "dissent" collar*: Jamie Feldman, "No One Can Object that Ruth Bader Ginsburg's Collars are On Point," *HuffPost*, March 15, 2017.

257 *"[A] panel of judges and lawyers convened to gripe"*: Amanda Hess, "Female Lawyers Who Dress Too Sexy Are Apparently a 'Huge Problem' in the Court-room," *Slate*, March 21, 2014, http://www.slate.com/blogs/xx_factor/2014/03 /21/female_lawyers_still_must_dress_conservatively_to_impress_judges.html ?wpisrc=hpsponsoredd2.

257 *The advice included the following*: Staci Zaretsky, "A Message from Career Ser-vices: Ladies, Please Learn how to Dress Yourselves," *Above the Law*, November 21, 2011, http://abovethelaw.com/2011/11/a-message-from-career-services -ladies-please-learn-how-to-dress-yourselves/.

258 *In 2014 the director of externships at Loyola Law School*: Staci Zaretsky, "Law School Sends Memo About Inappropriate Student Cleavage, Hooker Heels," *Above the Law*, March 19, 2014, http://abovethelaw.com/2014/03/law-school -sends-memo-about-inappropriate-student-cleavage-hooker-heels/.

258 *"[w]ear at least a little bit of makeup"*: Staci Zaretsky, "Summer Associates: Please Don't Dress Like Fashion Victims," *Above the Law*, June 5, 2012, http:// abovethelaw.com/2012/06/summer-associates-please-dont-dress-like-fashion -victims/2/.

258 *In response to the objection that such dress codes are out of date*: Katie J. M. Baker, "Forget the Glass Ceiling, We Have Hemlines to Consider," *Jezebel*, June

8, 2012, http://jezebel.com/5916586/forget-the-glass-ceiling-we-have-hemlines-to-consider.

258 *Similarly, an article on the feminist website* Jezebel *complained*: Ibid.

258 *In 2013, Tennessee circuit judge Royce Taylor*: Cheryl K. Chumley, "Tenn. Judge Orders Dress Code for Female Attorneys," *Washington Times*, June 13, 2013.

259 *For instance, in 2017, Democratic Congresswomen organized a protest*: Stassa Edwards, "The House Has a 'No Sleeveless' Dress Code for Women," *Jezebel*, July 6, 2017.

259 *Arizona senator Kyrsten Sinema has become a fashion icon*: Christina Cauterucci, "Kyrsten Sinema Is Not Just a Funky Dresser. She's a Fashion Revolutionary," *Slate*, January 31, 2019.

259 *Friedman offered a cautiously hopeful perspective*: Interview with Vanessa Friedman, *New York Times* Building, New York City, February 7, 2018 (on file with author).

CHAPTER FOURTEEN: RECODING GENDER

262 *Indeed, Wolf's suit was a neat solution*: Alicia Richards and Sarah Newton, "Bishop McDevitt Girl Thrown Out of Prom for Wearing a Suit," *ABC 27*, May 21, 2016, http://abc27.com/2016/05/07/bishop-mcdevitt-girl-thrown-out-of-prom-for-wearing-a-suit/.

262 *When Wolf arrived to the prom in her suit*: Alenna Vagianos, "This Teen Was Kicked Out of Her Prom for Wearing a Tuxedo," *HuffPost*, May 9, 2016, http://www.huffingtonpost.com/entry/this-teen-was-kicked-out-of-her-prom-for-wearing-a-tuxedo_us_57309017e4b096e9f091ddfb.

262 *In that same year, in the small, conservative California Central Valley city*: Evie Blad, "Teen Boys Wear Dresses to Call for Changes to School Dress Code," *Education Week*, February 3, 2016, http://blogs.edweek.org/edweek/rulesforengagement/2016/02/teen_boys_wear_dresses_to_call_for_changes_to_school_dress_code.html.

262 *A school district trustee defended*: Mackenzie Mays, "Boys Wear Dresses at School to Protest Clovis Unified Dress Code," *Fresno Bee*, February 1, 2016, http://www.fresnobee.com/news/local/education/article57827983.html.

262 *Another district trustee, Ginny Hovsepian, advanced a novel legal theory*: Mackenzie Mays, "Clovis Unified Ready for a Legal Fight over Dress Code," *Fresno Bee*, January 27, 2016, http://www.fresnobee.com/news/local/education/article56972448.html.

262 *Boys can now have long hair and wear earrings*: Jessica Peres, "Clovis Unified Enacts New Dress Codes Changes," *ABC 30 Action News*, April 7, 2016, http://abc30.com/education/clovis-unified-enacts-new-dress-codes-changes/1281579/.

263 *A 1918 retail trade article insisted*: Jo B. Paoletti, *Pink and Blue: Telling the Boys from the Girls in America* (Bloomington: Indiana University Press, 2013).

264 *Boys received their first haircut*: Jeanne Magiaty, "When Did Girls Start Wearing Pink?" Smithsonian.com, April 7, 2011.

265 *For instance, in* City of Columbus v. Zanders, *a court held that*: City of Columbus v. Zanders, 25 Ohio Misc. 144; 266 N.E. 2d 602 (1970).

265 *In* City of Columbus v. Rogers, *a court invalidated the law*: City of Columbus v. Rogers, 41 Ohio St. 2d, 161; 324 N.E. 2d 563 (1975).

267 *But her mother worried about the miniskirt*: Kelly St. John and Henry K. Lee, "Slain Newark Teen Balanced Between Two Worlds: 3 Charged In Death of Youth Who Was Living His Dream as a Female," *San Francisco Chronicle*, October 19, 2002, http://www.sfgate.com/bayarea/article/Slain-Newark-teen-balanced-between -two-worlds-3-2782669.php.

267 *Things at the party took an ugly turn*: Kelly St. John, "Witness Tells How She Learned Transgender Teen Was Male," *San Francisco Chronicle*, April 21, 2004, http://www.sfgate.com/bayarea/article/HAYWARD-Witness-tells-how-she -learned-2765958.php.

267 *Brown testified at trial that she reached up*: Ibid.

267 *He insisted that his client was enraged*: Patrick Hoge, "Defense Calls Transgender Victim Guilty of 'Deception and Betrayal,'" *San Francisco Chronicle*, April 16, 2004.

267 *José Merél's mother, Wanda Merél*: Tim Reitman, Jessica Garrison, and Christine Hanley, "Trying to Understand Eddie's Life—and Death," *Los Angeles Times*, October 20, 2002.

268 *The men did what they did*: Zack Calef, "Double Standard in Reactions to Rape," *Iowa State Daily*, October 24, 2002.

268 *In 2006, California enacted the Gwen Araujo Justice for Victims Act*: Cal Assembly Bill No. 2501 (2014).

268 *Bettcher argues that transgender people are punished*: Talia Mae Bettcher, "Evil Deceivers and Make-Believers: On Transphobic Violence and the Politics of Illusion," *Hypatia* 22, no. 3 (Summer 2007): 43–65, 54–55.

269 *José Merél's mother tried to explain*: Reitman, Garrison, and Hanley, "Trying to Understand Eddie's Life—and Death."

269 *To illustrate his point, Enzi mentioned*: Mathew Burciaga, "Enzi Comments at Greybull High School Stir Controversy," *Greybull Standard*, April 25, 2017.

270 *Fashion historian Anne Hollander noticed this trend*: Hollander, *Sex and Suits*, 171–72.

271 *Similarly, Danielle Cooper, author of the blog* She's a Gent: Valeriya Safronova, "Women Who Prefer Men's Wear," *New York Times*, July 19, 2016.

271 *In 2015, Jaden Smith—son of Will Smith and Jada Pinkett Smith*: Vanessa Friedman, "Jaden Smith for Louis Vuitton: The New Man in a Skirt," *New York Times*, January 6, 2016.

272 *Smith was known for his unconventional style*: Jake Woolf, "Jaden Smith Tells Us Why He Wore a Batman Suit to KimYe's Wedding," *GQ*, June 23, 2015.

272 *"he's not a man in transition"*: Friedman, "Jaden Smith for Louis Vuitton: The New Man in a Skirt," *New York Times*, January 6, 2016.

CHAPTER FIFTEEN: PIERCING THE VEIL

275 *for instance, the historian Joan Wallach Scott complained*: Joan Wallach Scott, "France's Ban on the Islamic veil has little to do with female emancipation," *The Guardian*, August 26, 2010.

275 *The French philosopher Sylviane Agacinski argued*: Jane Kramer, "Taking the Veil: How France's Public Schools Became the Battleground in a Culture War," *New Yorker*, November 22, 2004, 69.

275 *Such concerns were not limited to Westerners*: Rose George, "Ghetto Warrior," *The Guardian*, July 16, 2006, http://www.theguardian.com/world/2006/jul/17/france.politicsphilosophyandsociety.

275 *For instance, one woman living in Ontario described her hijab*: Theodore Gabriel and Rabiha Hannan, eds., *Islam and the Veil* (London: Continuum, 2011), 167.

275 *"Hijab is a liberation from the tyranny of fashion"*: Ibid., 165.

275 *For instance, the creative director of a high-fashion house*: Naomi Fry, "Modest Dressing, as a Virtue: What's Really Behind Fashion's—and Women's—Love of Concealing Clothes?" *New York Times*, November 2, 2017.

275 *Similarly, podcast host Aminatou Sou echoed in secular tones*: Ibid.

276 *As early as 1200 B.C. the laws of the Assyrian Empire made the veil*: Sahar Amer, *What Is Veiling?* (Chapel Hill: University of North Carolina Press, 2017), 6.

276 *Today, the novices of the Catholic order*: Kuhns, *The Habit*.

276 *Islamic Studies professor Sahar Amer notes*: Amer, *What Is Veiling?*, 28.

277 *Ironically, though perhaps not surprisingly, Baring's feminism*: Leila Ahmed, *Women and Gender in Islam: Historical Roots of a Modern Debate* (Philadelphia: University of Pennsylvania Press, 1992), 152–153.

277 *The 1899 book* Tahrir al-Mar'a, *or* The Liberation of Woman, *insisted*: Ibid., 144, 160.

277 *In 1923, three prominent Egyptian women, returning home*: Amer, *What Is Veiling?*, 135.

277 *He remarked in a 1925 speech*: Ibid., 139.

278 *"In the early twentieth century, a Middle Eastern woman who veiled"*: Ibid., 135–36.

278 *One part of this assimilationist project was the ritualistic unveiling*: Katarzyna Falecka, "From Colonial Algeria to Modern Day Europe, the Muslim Veil Remains an Ideological Battleground," *The Independent*, January 27, 2017, https://www.independent.co.uk/news/world/politics/from-colonial-algeria-to-modern-day-europe-the-muslim-veil-remains-an-ideological-battleground-a7544786.html.

278 *Similarly, veiling in Indonesia during the 1980s*: Amer, *What Is Veiling?*, 144.

279 *In 2014, Iranian law required all women to wear a black, blue, or brown chador*: Ibid., 56.

279 *Iranian activist Masih Alinejad notes that in 2014*: Malhar Mali, "My Stealthy Freedom: The Hijab in Iran and in the West," *Areo Magazine*, July 12, 2017.

279 *For instance, the* Times *reported in 1990 that when a woman*: Philip Shenon, "In Iran, a Glimpse of Ankle Can Bring out the Komiteh," *New York Times*, July 16, 1990.

279 *Some women have pushed the envelope*: Thomas Erdbrink, "When Freedom Is the Right to Stay Under Wraps," *New York Times*, May 7, 2014.

279 *The protests have inspired a social media campaign*: Thomas Erdbrink, "Tired of Their Veils, Some Iranian Women Stage Rare Protests," *New York Times*, January 29, 2018.

280 *In January 2017 Austria moved to ban the full-face veil in courts*: Laurel Wamsley, "Austria Becomes Latest Country in Europe to Ban Full Face Veil," NPR, May 18, 2107, https://www.npr.org/sections/thetwo-way/2017/05/18/528948967/austria-becomes-latest-country-in-europe-to-ban-full-face-veil.

280 *The court agreed, holding that the burka ban*: S.A.S. v. France [2014] ECHR 695.

280 *In 2017, the European Court of Human Rights unanimously upheld*: Affaire Belcacemi and *Oussar v. Belgium*, [2017] ECHR 655.

281 *Today, DKNY and Dolce & Gabbana offer high-fashion burkinis*: Vanessa Friedman, "What Freedom Looks Like," *New York Times*, April 13, 2016.

281 *In support of anti-burkini dress codes*: Alissa J. Rubin, "Fighting for the 'Soul of France,' More Towns Ban a Bathing Suit: The Burkini," *New York Times*, August 17, 2016.

281 *Laurence Rossignol, the women's rights minister of France, lamented*: Kim Willsher, "French Women's Rights Minister Accused for Racism Over term 'Negro,'" *The Guardian*, March 30, 2016.

281 *In the summer of 2016, police cited a woman sitting on a beach in Cannes*: Chris Graham, "Women Forced to Remove Burkini on Nice Beach by Armed Officers," *The Telegraph*, August 24, 2016.

281 *The same year, police in Nice ordered*: Ibid.

282 *In 1805 the Irish author Walley Chamberlain Oulton described*: W. C. Oulton, *The Traveller's Guide; or, English Itinerary. Vol II* (Ivy-Lane, London: James Cundee, 1805), 245.

283 *Réard deftly combined the two slang terms*: Kelly Killoren Bensimon, *The Bikini Book* (New York: Assouline, 2006), 18.

283 *In Europe, Pope Pius XII condemned the bikini*: Brooke Magnanti, "Miss World Bikini Ban: Why It's No Victory for Feminists," *The Telegraph*, June 7, 2013.

283 *Cities in France, Italy, Belgium, Spain, Portugal, and Australia*: Leah McGrath Goodman, "Burkini Swimsuits Speak Anti-Muslim Outrage—and Fast Sales," *Newsweek*, August 6, 2016.

283 *Réard, betting that all publicity is good publicity*: "The History of the Bikini," *Elle*, April 23, 2012.

283 *By 1965* Time *magazine reported*: Julia Turner, "A Brief History of the Bikini," *Slate*, July 3, 2015.

284 *The designer Anniesa Hasibuan argues*: Christina Caron and Maya Salam, "Macy's Courts Muslims with New Hijab Brand," *New York Times*, February 8, 2018.

285 *Nura Afia became the first CoverGirl to wear a hijab*: Elizabeth Paton, "Cover-Girl Signs Its First Ambassador in a Hijab," *New York Times*, November 9, 2016.

285 *for instance, a group identified as #Mipsterz (Muslim hipsters)*: "Somewhere in America, #Mipsterz," YouTube, *Sheikh Bake*, November 20, 2013, https://www.youtube.com/watch?v=68sMkDKMias.

285 *luxury brands such as Dolce & Gabbana, Oscar de la Renta*: Caron, "Macy's Courts Muslims with New Hijab Brand"; Ruqaiya Haris, "D&G's Hijab Range Is Aimed at People Like Me—So Why Do I Feel Excluded?" *The Guardian*, January 16, 2016, https://www.theguardian.com/commentisfree/2016/jan/11/dolce-gabbana-hijab-collection-muslim-women-western-fashion.

285 *According to the Global Islamic Economy Report*: Ezzedine Ghlamallah, "State of the Global Islamic Economy 2017-2018," https://www.slideshare.net/EzzedineGHLAMALLAH/state-of-the-global-islamic-economy-20172018.

285 *according to burkini entrepreneur Aheda Zanetti*: McGrath Goodman, "Burkini Swimsuits Speak Anti-Muslim Outrage—and Fast Sales."

286 *Nura Afia's own—non-Muslim—grandparents disapproved*: Mi-Anne Chan, "This Muslim Blogger Makes an Important Statement About Beauty," *Refinery29*, November 9, 2015; Helin Jung, "Hijabi CoverGirl Nura Afia: 'More People are Smiling at Me' Since the Election," *Cosmopolitan*, December 9, 2016.

286 *"glamorize fundamentalist religious dress-codes"*: @LaloDagach, Twitter, April 29, 2019.

286 *"celebrating a symbol of oppression"*: @RitaPanahi, Twitter, April 29, 2019.

286 *For Hollander, when women combined a hijab with fashionable clothing*: Anne Hollander, "Veil of Tears: Why Islamic Women's Headscarves Are Less Anodyne than You Think," *Slate*, April 23, 1998.

286 *For instance, an opinion columnist in the* Guardian *complained*: Haris, "D&G's hijab range is aimed at people like me."

286 *As a consequence*: Chan, "This Muslim Blogger Makes an Important Statement About Beauty."

286 *Similarly, when Hamila Aden appeared in* Sports Illustrated *in a burkini*: @MalikObama, Twitter, April 29, 2019.

287 *Another complained that* Sports Illustrated *was*: @CrohnsBear, Twitter, April 30, 2019.

287 *"[T]he reference point of the headscarf"*: Irfan Ullah Khan, "Modanisa—Is Hijab Fashion Even Allowed in Islam? [A Critical Review]," *Happy Muslim Family*, https://happymuslimfamily.org/modanisa-hijab-fashion/.

287 *WHAT? Hijabs and skin tight apparel?*: "Somewhere in America" #Mipsterz posted Nov 20, 2013, https://www.youtube.com/watch?v=68sMkDKMias.

287 *One woman described hers as*: Tova Ross, "My Wig was Beautiful and Expensive, and Everybody Loved It—Except Me," *Tablet*, December 10, 2013, http://www.tabletmag.com/jewish-life-and-religion/151283/no-more-sheitel.

288 *according to the* New York Times, *a Madison Avenue salon*: Elizabeth Hayt, "For Stylish Orthodox Women, Wigs that Aren't Wiggy," *New York Times*, April 27, 1997.

288 *"I want my wig to look exactly like my hair"*: Ibid.

288 *For instance, an advice column for Orthodox Jews*: Allison Josephs "Isn't Wearing a Wig Over Hair (Especially if the Wig is Nicer than the Hair) Pointless?" *Jew in the City*, July 15, 2009.

288 *The columnist sided with the* sheitel *wearers*: Ibid.

288 *According to Rabbi Rafael Grossman, president of the Rabbinical Council of America*: Elizabeth Greenbaum Kasson, "For Devout Jews, a Zone of Privacy in the Sheitel," *Los Angeles Times*, October 31, 2010.

288 *According to the* Los Angeles Times, *a rabbi's wife who sported*: Ibid.

289 *And Ross found that wearing the* sheitel: Ross, "My Wig was Beautiful and Expensive, and Everybody Loved It—Except Me."

290 *Abercrombie was a famously image-conscious store*: Sapna Maheshwari, "Abercrombie's Preppy Police Enforce Rule for Staffers' Clothes, Internal Documents Show," *BuzzFeed*, May 2, 2013.

290 *Nevertheless, according to court documents*: Petitioner's Brief, *EEOC v. Abercrombie and Fitch Store, Inc.*

290 *Elauf sued Abercrombie for religious discrimination*: *EEOC v. Abercrombie and Fitch Stores, Inc.*, 575 U.S. 768, 135 S. Ct. 2028 (2015).

290 *At one point during oral arguments, Justice Alito posed this hypothetical question*: Shay Dvortezky, "Oral argument on behalf of the Respondent," *EEOC v. Abercrombie & Fitch Stores, Inc.*, February 25, 2015, 31.

290 *Elauf prevailed in the Supreme Court*: Michelle Gorman, "Abercrombie & Fitch Pays More than $25,000 to Settle Headscarf Lawsuit," *Newsweek*, July 21, 2015, https://www.newsweek.com/abercrombie-fitch-pays-25000-settle-headscarf-lawsuit-356004.

Part Five

CHAPTER SIXTEEN: MERIT BADGES

296 *According to the United States Court of Appeals for the Second Circuit*: *Christian Louboutin S.A. v. Yves Saint Laurent America Holding, Inc.*, 696 F.3d 206 (2d Cir. 2012).

298 *As trademark law expert professor Barton Beebe argues*: Barton Beebe, "Intellectual Property Law and the Sumptuary Code," *Harvard Law Review* 123, no. 809 (2010).

299 *For example, in a case involving an inexpensive replica*: *Mastercrafters Clock and Radio Co. v. Vacheron &* Constantin-Le *Coultre Watches, Inc.*, 221 F.2d. 464, 465 (2d. Cir. 1955).

299 *Similarly, in a decision prohibiting knock-off Hermès handbags*: *Hermès International v. Lederer de Paris Fifth Avenue, Inc.*, 219 F3d. 104 (2d Cir. 2000) (emphasis mine).

299 *Likewise, Christian Louboutin is entitled to stop its competitors*: Anne Hocking and Anne Desmousseaux, "Why Louboutin Matters," Donahue Fitzgerald

LLP, https://donahue.com/resources/publications/louboutin-matters-red-soles
-teach-us-strategy-trade-dress-protection-2/.

300 *Economists have a name for such exclusive, high-status products*: H. Leibenstein, "Bandwagon, Snob, and Veblen Effects in the Theory of Consumers Demand," *Quarterly Journal of Economics* 64, no. 2 (1950): 183, https://doi.org/10.2307 /1882692.

301 *For instance, even Gucci's own employees are unable to spot counterfeit hand-bags*: Gucci America, Inc. v. Daffy's, Inc., 354 F. 3d. 228 (3d Cir. 2003).

301 *Similarly, when Tiffany sued eBay for facilitating*: Tiffany Inc. v. eBay, Inc., 576 F. Supp. 2d. 463 (S.D.N.Y. 2008).

302 *But the unwritten dress code was clear*: Helene Stapinski, "Dress Up the Loaner Jacket," *New York Times*, August 19, 2013.

302 *The* Times *aptly described the typical loaners*: Ibid.

303 *For example, before it abandoned its mandatory jacket-and-tie dress code*: Glenn Collins, "A Last Bastion of the Necktie Throws in the Towel," *New York Times*, January 27, 2009.

303 *only two years later the New York City Commission on Human Rights*: "Legal Enforcement Guidance on Discrimination on the Basis of Gender Identity or Expression: Local Law No. 3 (2002); N.Y.C. Admin. Code § 8-102(23)," New York, NY, 2015.

304 *Conventional sartorial terminology distinguishes the blazer*: Nick Sullivan, *Mariner: The Call of the Sea* (Milan: Skira, 2012), 8–9.

304 *Menswear authority G. Bruce Boyer playfully insists*: Christian Baker, "The True Story of the Blazer," *The Rake*, September 2019, https://therake.com/stories /the-true-story-of-the-blazer/?utm_source=mailchimpBAU&utm_medium =newsletter&utm_campaign=rstory_19092019_the-true-story-of-the-blazer& goal=0_d02442ae5e-ce2d5a5869-141350241&mc_cid=ce2d5a5869&mc_eid =f6678e86f9.

304 *Alas, the name* blazer *more likely first referred to* red *jackets*: Jack Carlson, F. E. Castleberry, Adrian Krajewski, and Ursa Mali, *Rowing Blazers* (London: Thames & Hudson Ltd., 2014).

305 *as for "borrowed" crests*: Sullivan, Mariner: The Call of the Sea, 20.

305 *It has the added advantage of versatility*: Nicholas Antongiavanni, *The Suit: A Machiavellian Approach to Men's Style* (New York: Collins, 2006), 14–16.

305 *Indeed, the unstudied chic of fastening only the bottom-row button*: Wei Koh, "Going Both Ways," *The Rake*, November 2015, 68.

305 *The six-one "forms a keystone"*: Antongiavanni, *The Suit*, 14–15.

306 *"absolutely exquisite"*: Simon Crompton, "The Velvet Jacket and Modern Eve-ning Wear, in Cifonelli," *Permanent Style*, December 4, 2019, https://www .permanentstyle.com/2019/12/the-velvet-jacket-and-modern-evening-wear-in -cifonelli.html.

311 *"Preppies dress alike because"*: Lisa Birnbach, *The Official Preppy Handbook* (New York: Workman Press, 1981), 121.

315 *Fish saw the ugliness of Volvos*: Stanley Eugene Fish, *There's No Such Thing as Free Speech . . . and It's a Good Thing, Too* (New York: Oxford University Press, 1994), 273.

316 *Professors Silvia Bellezza, Francesca Gino, and Anat Keinan*: Silvia Bellezza, Francesca Gino, and Anat Keinan, "The Red Sneakers Effect: Inferring Status and Competence from Signals of Nonconformity," *Journal of Consumer Research* 41, no. 1 (January 2014): 35–54, 42–43, https://doi.org/10.1086/674870.

316 *"Wealthy people sometimes dress very badly"*: Ibid., 42.

316 *It reads, in part*: Max Abelson and Sridhar Natarajan, "Goldman Sachs Allows Bankers to Trade Bespoke Suits for Khakis," Bloomberg.com, March 5, 2019, https://www.bloomberg.com/news/articles/2019-03-05/goldman-sachs-allows -bankers-to-trade-bespoke-suits-for-khakis; "Firmwide Dress Code," Goldman Sachs, March 5, 2019.

317 *In March of 2019, the* Wall Street Journal *reported*: Suzanne Kapner, "Men Ditch Suits, and Retailers Struggle to Adapt," *Wall Street Journal*, March 25, 2019.

319 *Bloomberg.com finance reporter Matt Levine*: Matt Levine, "Be Careful Wearing Jeans at Goldman," Bloomberg.com, March 6, 2019.

320 *Intel, for instance, eliminated the layers of management*: Stephen Mihm, "Goldman's 'Flexible' Dress Codes Takes a Cue From Silicon Valley," *Bloomberg*, March 9, 2019, https://www.bloomberg.com/opinion/articles/2019-03-09 /goldman-takes-page-from-tech-sector-by-ditching-business-suit.

320 *Tech entrepreneur Peter Thiel made this anti–dress code explicit*: E.W., "Suitable Disruption," *The Economist*, August 4, 2014, https://www.economist.com /schumpeter/2014/08/04/suitable-disruption?fsrc=scn%2Ftw%2Fte%2Fbl%2Fe d%2Fsuitabledisruption.

321 *As he surveyed the crowd in downtown Palo Alto*: Queena Kim, "Silicon Valley has a dress code? You better believe it," *Marketplace*, January 28, 2014.

321 *Software designers—the creative types in tech*: Ibid.

321 *According to Silicon Valley insiders*: Ibid.

321 *One commentator summed up the indictment*: Anna Holmes, "Marissa Mayer and *Vogue* Couture in the C-Suite," *Time*, August 13, 2013.

321 *he could not resist attributing moral significance to it*: Vanessa Friedman, "Mark Zuckerberg Adopts Obama's Approach to Dressing," *New York Times*, November 12, 2014, https://runway.blogs.nytimes.com/2014/11/12/mark-zuckerberg -adopts-obamas-approach-to-dressing/?hp&action=click&pgtype=Homepage &module=second-column-region&region=top-news&WT.nav=top-news& _r=1 (as of March 17, 2017).

322 *The BlackV Club, which specializes in*: Nitasha Tiku, "Why Are Tech Workers So Bad at Dressing Themselves?" *ValleyWag*, August 1, 2014, http:// valleywag.gawker.com/why-are-tech-workers-so-bad-at-dressing-themselves -1613023344.

322 *This grim asceticism extends beyond attire*: Dylan Love, "Soylent Is Like a Productivity Cheat Code—and More Observations from Two Weeks on the Meal

Replacement Drink," *Business Insider*, July 14, 2014, http://www.businessinsider
.com/soylent-review-2014-7

323 *"Eat food when you want, drink Soylent when you want"*: Ibid.

323 *For instance, on the day before Zuckerberg was about to appear*: Vanessa Friedman, "Mark Zuckerberg's I'm Sorry Suit," *New York Times*, April 10, 2018.

324 *And while the counterculture turned the term "suit" into an epithet*: Christian
Chensvold, "Miles Ahead: Not Just a Jazz Genius, Miles Davis Was Also a Sartorial Chameleon, Easily Carrying Off the Ivy League Look and Slim-Cut European Suits with Ass-Kicking Charm," *The Rake*, October/November 2009, 54.

325 *Most recently, Daniel Craig famously filled out Tom Ford's already snug tailoring*: Cathy Horyn, "006 ½," *New York Times*, November 16, 2012, https://
runway.blogs.nytimes.com/2012/11/16/size-006-12/.

325 *While Matt Spaiser, the editor of the website The Suits of James Bond*: Ibid.

325 *the costume designer for* Skyfall *felt the unconventional tailoring*: Ibid.

326 *As Susan Scafidi, director of Fordham University's Fashion Law Institute*: Jena
McGregor, "New Goldman Sachs dress code points to a sartorial double standard in the workplace," *Washington Post*, March 21, 2019.

327 *But here she was rebuffed—told the store was closed*: Robin Givhan, "Oprah and
the View from Outside Hermès' Paris Door," *Washington Post*, June 24, 2005.

CHAPTER SEVENTEEN: ARTIFICE AND APPROPRIATION

330 *She was African American*: *Farryn Johnson v. Hooters of Harborplace, LLC.*,
Charge of Discrimination, Maryland Commission on Civil Rights, October, 21,
2013.

330 *The Hooters employee handbook sets out detailed standards*: Rachel Elizabeth Cook, "You're Wearing the Orange Shorts? African American Hooters
Girls and the All-American Girl Next Door," master's dissertation, Georgia
State University, 2011, 12, https://scholarworks.gsu.edu/cgi/viewcontent.cgi?
referer=https://duckduckgo.com/&httpsredir=1&article=1021&context=wsi
_theses; Rachel Elizabeth Cook, "Black Skin, Orange Shorts: A Hooters Girl
Narrative," *Ebony*, August 2, 2012.

331 *Johnson was fired for a different reason*: Joel Landau, "Hooters ordered to pay
$250,000 to black waitress who was told she couldn't have blond streaks in her
hair," *Daily News*, April 8, 2015.

331 *according to former Hooters waitress Rachel Wood*: Cook, "You're Wearing
the Orange Shorts?" 12; Cook, "Black Skin, Orange Shorts: A Hooters Girl
Narrative."

334 *The* New York Times *described it as*: Vanessa Friedman, "Marc Jacobs's Glitte-
rati," *New York Times*, September 15, 2016.

334 *"Why didn't you hire models with real dreads?!"*: Jenna Rosenstein, "How Will
the Internet React to Marc Jacobs' Rainbow Dreadlocks?" *Harper's Bazaar*,
September 18, 2016.

334 *"did Marc Jacobs really just build a whole fashion show"*: Nicole Bitette, "Marc

Jacobs blasted for cultural appropriation after sending models down the runway with fake dreadlocks," *DailyNews*, September 15, 2016, http://www .nydailynews.com/life-style/fashion/marc-jacobs-blasted-fake-dreadlocks -models-article-1.2794126.

334 *All of these collections*: Vanessa Friedman, "Should Fashion Be Politically Correct?" *New York Times*, October 14, 2015.

334 *For instance, in 2014 an Arizona State University fraternity held a party*: Fernanda Santos, "Arizona Fraternity Party Sires Concerns of Racism," *New York Times*, January 22, 2014.

334 *A 2013 party at the Kappa Alpha fraternity*: Raul A. Reyes, "Opinion: 'USA v. Mexico' frat party a big mistake," NBCLatino.com, November 26, 2013, http:// nbclatino.com/2013/11/26/opinion-usa-v-mexico-frat-party-a-big-mistake/.

334 *That same year, Duke University's Kappa Sigma fraternity*: Victoria Cavaliere, "Duke Fraternity suspended after hosting a party slammed as racist," *Daily News*, February 7, 2013, http://www.nydailynews.com/news/national/duke-frat -suspended-hosting-asian-themed-party-article-1.1257624.

334 *And then there was the Thanksgiving fraternity and sorority party*: "Frat's 'Colonial Bros and Nava-Hos' and 'Mexican and Americans' off-campus parties investigated for racism," *Daily Mail*, November 23, 2017.

335 *The University of Chicago's Alpha Delta Phi chapter*: Hannah Gold, "6 Disturbingly Racist and Sexist Frat Party Themes—from Just This Past Year!" *Salon*, March 4, 2014, https://www.salon.com/2014/03/04/6_disturbingly_racist_and _sexist_frat_party_themes_—_from_just_this_past_year_partner/.

335 *"All who cry 'cultural appropriation'"*: Afsun Qureshi, "Marc Jacobs: Cultural Appropriation Backlash 'Erodes Freedom of Speech,'" CNN.com, September 20, 2016.

336 *Lin fired back with a subtle riposte*: Scott Davis, "Jeremy Lin Posts Thoughtful Response with a Subtle Dig After Being Criticized by Former Player for Growing Dreadlocks," *Business Insider*, October 6, 2017.

336 *Some pointed out that Black women are pressured to straighten their hair*: Kevin Rawlinson, "Marc Jacobs Defends Himself in Dreadlocks-On-Catwalk Row," *The Guardian*, September 16, 2016, https://www.theguardian.com/fashion/2016 /sep/17/marc-jacobs-defends-himself-dreadlocks-furore.

336 *Others pointed out that while Jacobs used dreadlocks*: Valeriya Safronova, "Marc Jacobs's Use of Faux Locs on Models Draws Social Media Ire," *New York Times*, September 16, 2016.

337 *When baffled students asked for clarification*: Katherine Timpf, "Campus-Wide Email Tells White Girls to Stop Wearing Hoop Earrings Because It's Cultural Appropriation," *National Review*, March 8, 2017.

337 *"[I]f you didn't create the culture as a coping mechanism for marginalization"*: Elliot Dordick, "Pitzer College RA: White People Can't Wear Hoop Earrings," *Claremont Independent*, March 7, 2017, http://claremontindependent.com /pitzer-college-ra-white-people-cant-wear-hoop-earrings/.

337 *"[I]f you are going to try to tell me"*: Katherine Timpf, "Campus-Wide Email Tells

White Girls to Stop Wearing Hoop Earrings Because It's Cultural Appropriation," *National Review*, March 8, 2017.

338 *Earrings have since been worn as signs of membership and identity*: Margo De-Mello, *Encyclopedia of Body Adornment* (Westport, CT: Greenwood Press, 2007), 94.

339 *For instance, in China, the birthplace of the* qipao: @lin_chenhao, Twitter, May 11, 2018.

339 *Another suggested Daum branch out and wear*: @DengLeader, Twitter, May 4, 2018.

339 *In an interview with the* New York Times, *Zhou Yijun, a Hong Kong cultural critic*: Amy Qin, "Teenager's Prom Dress Stirs Furor in U.S.—But Not in China," *New York Times*, May 2, 2018.

339 *For her own part, Daum said*: Minyvonne Burke, "Utah Teen Who Wore Chinese-style Dress Hits Back at Critics," *Daily Mail*, May 2018.

339 *"The current outcry could be compared to"*: Anne Chen, "An American Woman Wearing a Chinese Dress Is Not Cultural Appropriation," *The Guardian*, May 4, 2018.

339 *It was taken up as part of a relaxed, after-dinner ensemble*: Ash Carter, "The Fascinating History of the Town Where the Tuxedo Was Born," *Town and Country*, January 1, 2012.

341 *She concluded that fashion that crossed boundaries*: Vanessa Friedman, "Should Fashion Be Politically Correct?" *New York Times*, October 14, 2015, https://www.nytimes.com/2015/10/15/fashion/should-fashion-be-politically-correct.html.

342 *By 2011 the blog* Ivy Style *described Ralph Lauren's polo shirts*: Matthew Benz, "Le Crocodile: How Lacoste Became the Preppy Polo of Choice," *Ivy Style*, June 8, 2011, http://www.ivy-style.com/le-crocodile-how-lacoste-became-the-preppy-polo-of-choice.html.

344 *As Dapper Dan recalls*: "Dapper Dan: The Hip Hop Tailor Of Harlem," *Sneaker Freaker*, November 8, 2017, http://www.sneakerfreaker.com/features/dapper-dan-the-hip-hop-tailor-of-harlem/#7.

345 *Dan opened an exclusive bespoke salon in his Harlem brownstone*: Matthew Schneier, "Did Gucci Copy 'Dapper Dan'? Or Was it 'Homage'?" *New York Times*, May 31 2017; Christine Flammia, "Gucci Is Officially Teaming Up with Street-Style Legend Dapper Dan," *Esquire.com*, December 14, 2017, http://www.esquire.com/style/mens-fashion/a14432993/dapper-dan-gucci-store/.

345 *According to Howl, the Lo Lifes were a fusion of two groups*: Dan Adler, "The History of Hip Hop's Obsession with Polo Ralph Lauren," *Esquire*, August 16, 2016, http://www.esquire.com/style/a47568/hip-hop-polo-ralph-lauren-history/.

345 *As Raekwon of the Wu-Tang Clan explains*: XXL staff, "Polo and Hip-Hop, an Oral History [Pt. 1]—XXL," *XXL Mag*, November 30, 2010, http://www.xxlmag.com/lifestyle/2010/11/polo-and-hip-hop-an-oral-history-pt-1/2/?trackback=tsmclip.

345 *Similarly, Thirstin Howl recalls*: Ibid.

347 *The Polo-wearing gangs didn't always come by their Polo gear lawfully*: Adler, "The History of Hip Hop's Obsession with Polo Ralph Lauren."

347 *For the Lo Lifes, expensive designer clothing conveyed*: Ibid.

347 *As journalist Bonz Malone put it*: Ibid.

348 *According to historian Ch. Didier Gondola,* Sapeurs *carry*: Ch. Didier Gondola, "Dream and Drama: The Search for Elegance among Congolese Youth," *African Studies Review* 42, no. 1 (1999): 23, 24, https://doi.org/10.2307/525527.

349 *According to Gondola, the* Sape *was born*: Ibid.

349 *In the early twentieth century, a European writer noted with chagrin*: Jehan de Witte, *Les Deux Congo. 35 Ans D'apostolat Au Congo français*. Pp. xii. 408. (Paris, 1913), 164.

349 *Similarly, a colonial governor wrote, with a condescending incredulity*: Gondola, "Dream and Drama," 27.

349 *Today's Sapeurs are guardians of a long-standing Congolese tradition*: Ibid.

351 *For instance, one* Sapeur: Edmund Sanders, "In Congo, Designer Cheek," *Los Angeles Times*, November 28, 2006.

351 *"a sapeur is, by definition, a non-violent person"*: Héctor Mediavilla, "The Congolese Sape," http://v1.zonezero.com/exposiciones/fotografos/mediavilla/index .html.

351 *The Sapeurs deliberately refigure the physical violence*: Anna Weinberg, "Paradise Is a Fabulous Suit: For the Congolese Sapeurs, Haute Couture Isn't Just an Abiding Passion, It's a Religion," *Colors*, no. 64, http://sites.colorsmagazine.com /64/01.php.

351 *According to Mediavilla, the* Sapeurs *are minor celebrities*: Mediavilla, "The Congolese Sape."

352 *This process matured into something close to its present form*: Gilles Lipovetsky, *The Empire of Fashion* (Princeton: Princeton University Press, 2002), 79.

CONCLUSION: DECODING DRESS CODES

358 *Soon, dressing up for trash day became a global phenomenon*: Leah Asmelash, "People Around the World Are Dressing Up to Take Their Trash Out as a Way to Enliven Their Self-Isolation," CNN.com, April 12, 2020.

361 *the English poet Alexander Pope made this analogy*: Alexander Pope, "An Essay on Criticism: Part 2," 1711.

363 *As the historian Anne Hollander observes*: Hollander, *Sex and Suits*, 192–93.

364 *The United States Environmental Protection Agency reports that*: Kendra Pierre-Louis, "How to Buy Clothes that Are Built to Last," *New York Times*, September 25, 2019.

364 *I spoke with* Esquire *magazine's creative director Nick Sullivan*: Interview with Nick Sullivan, *Esquire* Creative Director, Hearst Tower, New York City, April 30, 2018 (on file with author).

366 *These new laws, often passed under the name "The CROWN Act"*: The Official Campaign of the CROWN Act, https://www.thecrownact.com.

Selected Bibliography

Adam, Hajo, and Adam D. Galinsky. "Enclothed Cognition." *Journal of Experimental Social Psychology* 48, no. 4 (2012).

Adams, Gene, "Dido Elizabeth Belle, a Black Girl at Kenwood: An Account of a Protegée of the 1st Lord Mansfield," *Camden History Review* Vol. 12 (1984).

Aherne, Consuelo Maria. *Joyous Service: The History of the Sisters of Saint Joseph of Springfield*. Holyoke, MA: Sisters of Saint Joseph, 1983.

Ahmed, Leila. *Women and Gender in Islam Historical Roots of a Modern Debate*. Philadelphia: University of Pennsylvania Press, 1992.

Alarcon, Daniel. "Guilt By Association." *New York Times Magazine*, May 31, 2015.

Allen, Robert L. *Black Awakening in Capitalist America: an Analytic History*. Trenton, N.J: Africa World Press, 1992.

Amer, Sahar. *What Is Veiling?* Chapel Hill: University of North Carolina Press, 2017.

Anderson, Benedict. *Imagined Communities: Reflections on the Origin and Spread of Nationalism*. London: Verso, 1998.

Antongiavanni, Nicholas. *The Suit: A Machiavellian Approach to Men's Style*. New York: Collins, 2006.

Appiah, Kwame Anthony. *The Honor Code: How Moral Revolutions Happen*. New York: Norton & Company, 2011.

Barnard, Malcolm. *Fashion as Communication*. Florence: Taylor and Francis, 2013.

Barthes, Roland. *The Fashion System*. London: Vintage, 2010.

Barthes, Roland. "A Case of Cultural Criticism." *Communications 14*, 1969.

Beebee, Barton. "Intellectual Property Law and the Sumptuary Code." *Harvard Law Review* 123, no. 809 (2010).

Bellezza, Silvia, Francesca Gino, and Anat Keinan. "The Red Sneakers Effect: Inferring Status and Competence from Signals of Nonconformity." *Journal of Consumer Research* 41, no. 1 (January 2014).

Bennett, J. M., and S. Mcsheffrey. "Early, Erotic and Alien: Women Dressed as Men in Late Medieval London." *History Workshop Journal* 77, no. 1 (October 2014).

Bennett, Veronica, and Ryan (ill.) Todd. *Looking Good: a Visual Guide to the Nuns Habit*. London: GraphicDesign&, 2016.

Bensimon, Kelly Killoren. *The Bikini Book*. New York: Assouline, 2006.

Bettcher, Talia Mae. "Evil Deceivers and Make-Believers: On Transphobic Violence and the Politics of Illusion." *Hypatia* 22, no. 3 (Summer 2007).

Bingen, Hildegard av. *Scivias*. New York: Paulist Press, 1990. (Book II, vision 6, 77).

Birnbach, Lisa. *The Official Preppy Handbook*. Workman Publishing, 1980.

Burke, Joanna. "The Great Male Renunciation: Men's Dress Reform in Inter-war Britain." *Journal of Design History* 9, no. 1 (1996).

Burrows, Simon. *Blackmail, Scandal and Revolution: London's French Libellistes, 1758–92*. Manchester: Manchester Univ. Press, 2009.

Burrows, Simon, *The Chevalier D'Éon and His Worlds: Gender, Espionage and Politics in the Eighteenth Century*. Simon Burrows, Jonathan Conlin, Russell Goulbourne, and Valerie Mainz, eds. London: Continuum, 2010.

Carlson, Jack, F. E. Castleberry, Adrian Krajewski, and Ursa Mali. *Rowing Blazers*. London: Thames & Hudson Ltd, 2014.

Carlyle, Thomas. *Sartor Resartus*. 1836.

Carmichael, Stokely, and Charles V. Hamilton. *Black Power: The Politics of Liberation in America*. New York: Vintage, 1967.

Caroso, Fabritio, Julia Sutton, and F. Marian. Walker. *Courtly Dance of the Renaissance*. London: Constable, 1995.

Carson, Clayborne. *In Struggle: SNCC and the Black Awakening in the 1960s*. Cambridge: Harvard University Press, 1995.

Carter, Ash. "The Fascinating History of the Town Where the Tuxedo Was Born." *Town and Country*, January 1. 2012.

Castiglione, Baldassarre, *The Book of the Courtier: The Singleton Translation*. New York: W.W. Norton, 2002.

Chenoune, Farid, Richard Martin, and Deke Dusinberre. *A History of Men's Fashion*. Paris: Flammarion, 1995.

Chesterfield, Philip Dormer Stanhope. *Letters to His Son; On the Art of Becoming a Man of the World and a Gentleman*. Tudor, 1917.

Chevalier, Michel. *Society, Manners and Politics in the United States*. 1966.

Cleaver, Eldridge. "As Crinkly As Yours," in *S.O.S. Calling All Black People: a Black Arts Movement Reader*, Boston: University of Massachusetts Press, 2014.

Cohn, Samuel K. "Black Death, Social and Economic Impact of the." In Bjork, Robert E. (ed.). *The Oxford Dictionary of the Middle Ages*. Oxford: Oxford University Press, 2010

Crane, Diana. *Diffusion Models and Fashion: A Reassessment*, 566 ANNALS AM. ACAD. POL. & SOC. SCI. 13 (1999).

Daly, Mary. *The Church and the Second Sex*. Boston: Beacon Press, 1985.

Davies, Glenys and Lloyd Llewellyn-Jones. *A Cultural History of Dress and Fashion: Vol. 1, In Antiquity, "The Body."* London: Bloomsbury, 2017.

DeMello, Margo. *Encyclopedia of Body Adornment*. Westport, CT: Greenwood Press, 2007.

DeMello, Margo. *Feet and Footwear: a Cultural Encyclopedia*. Santa Barbara, CA: Greenwood Press/ABC-CLIO, 2009.

Diderot, Denis. *Encyclopedie Ou Dictionnaire Raisonne Des Sciences, Des Arts Et Des Metiers*, 1751–1772.

Dress Coded, Black Girl, Bodies and Bias in D.C. Public Schools, National Women's Law Center, 2018.

Dunbar, John Telfer, *History of Highland Dress,* Edinburgh and London: Oliver & Boyd, 1962.

Edmonds, Ed M., Delwin D. Cahoon, and Elizabeth Hudson. "Male-Female Estimates of Feminine Assertiveness Related to Females' Clothing Styles." *Bulletin of the Psychonomic Society* 30, no. 2 (1992).

Ellison, Ralph. *A Collection of Critical Essays,* Englewood Cliffs N.J: Prentice-Hall, 1974.

Ellison, Ralph. *Invisible Man,* New York: Random House, 1952.

Fish, Stanley Eugene. *There's No Such Thing as Free Speech: and It's a Good Thing, Too.* New York: Oxford University Press, 1994.

Flower, Benjamin Orange. *Fashion's Slaves.* Boston: Arena, 1892.

Flugel, J.C. "'The Great Masculine Renunciation and Its Causes,' from The Psychology of Clothes, (1930)" in Purdy, Daniel L. (ed.). *The Rise of Fashion: A Reader.* Minneapolis: University of Minnesota Press, 2004.

Ford, Richard, *Racial Cultures: a critique.* Princeton: Princeton University Press, 2005.

Ford, Tanisha. "SNCC Women, Denim, and the Politics of Dress." *The Journal of Southern History,* Vol. LXXIX, No. 3, August 2013.

Ford, Thomas, and James Shields. *A History of Illinois from Its Commencement as a State in 1818 to 1847. Containing a Full Account of the Black Hawk War, the Rise, Progress and Fall of Mormonism, the Alton and Lovejoy Riots, and Other Events.* Chicago: S.C. Griggs & Co., 1854.

Fox, George P. *Fashion, the Power That Influences the World: The Philosophy of Ancient and Modern Dress and Fashion.* New York: Sheldon & Co., 1871.

Frazier, E. Franklin. *Black Bourgeoisie: The Rise of a New Middle Class.* New York: Free Press, 1957.

Gondola, Ch. Didier. "Dream and Drama: The Search for Elegance among Congolese Youth." *African Studies Review* 42, no. 1 (1999).

Gordon, Taylor. *Born to Be.* Lincoln: University of Nebraska Press, 1995.

Greenblatt, Stephen. *Renaissance Self-Fashioning: From More to Shakespeare.* Chicago: University of Chicago Press, 1980.

Hall, Edward. *Halls Chronicle: Containing the History of England, during the Reign of Henry the Fourth, and the Succeeding Monarchs, to the End of the Reign of Henry the Eighth, in Which Are Particularly Described the Manners and Customs of Those Periods.* London: Printed for J. Johnson, 1809.

Hansen, Dian, *History of Men's Magazines.* Koln; London: Taschen, 2004.

Head, Edith, and Joe Hyams. *How to Dress for Success.* New York: Random House, 1967.

Hills, H. "The Veiled Body: Within the Folds of Early Modern Neapolitan Convent Architecture." *Oxford Art Journal* 27, no. 3 (January 2004).

Himes, Chester. "Zoot Riots are Race Riots" in Himes, Chester B. *Black on Black: Baby Sister and Selected Writings.* London: Joseph, 1975.

Hollander, Anne. *Sex and Suits the Evolution of Modern Dress.* New York: Knopf, 1994.

Holmes, Anna. "Marissa Mayer and *Vogue* Couture in the C-Suite." *Time*, August 13, 2013.

Hooper, Wilfrid. "The Tudor Sumptuary Laws." *The English Historical Review* XXX, no. CXIX (1915).

Hotchkiss, Valerie R. *Clothes Make the Man Female Cross Dressing in Medieval Europe*. New York: Routledge, 2012.

Hughes, Diane Owen. "Distinguishing Signs: Ear-Rings, Jews, and Franciscan Rhetoric in the Italian Renaissance City." *Past and Present Society* 112, 1986.

Hunt, Alan. *Governance of the Consuming Passions: A History of Sumptuary Law*. New York: St. Martins, 1996.

Ishizu, Shosuke, Toshiyuki Kurosu, Hajime Hasegawa and Teruyoshi Hayshida, *Take Ivy*. Hachette Fujingaho: Tokyo, 1965.

Jones, Jennifer M. *Sexing La Mode: Gender, Fashion and Commercial Culture in Old Regime France*. Oxford: Berg, 2004.

Kates, Gary. *Monsieur D'Eon Is a Woman: A Tale of Political Intrigue and Sexual Masquerade*. Baltimore: John Hopkins University Press, 2001.

Killerby, Catherine Kovesi. *Sumptuary Law in Italy, 1200–1500*. Oxford: Clarendon Press, 2005.

Kollar, Rene. *A Foreign and Wicked Institution?: The Campaign Against Convents in Victorian England*. Havertown: James Clarke & Co, 2014.

Kuchta, David, *The Three Piece Suit and Modern Masculinity: England 1550–1850,* Berkeley: University of California Press, 2002.

Kuhns, Elizabeth. *The Habit: A History of the Clothing of Catholic Nuns*. New York: Doubleday, 2005.

Kwass, Michael. "Big Hair: A Wig History of Consumption in Eighteenth-Century France." *The American Historical Review* 111, no. 3 (January 2006).

Leibenstein, H. "Bandwagon, Snob, and Veblen Effects in the Theory of Consumers Demand." *The Quarterly Journal of Economics* 64, no. 2 (1950)

Lewis, Hylan. *Blackways of Kent*. Chapel Hill: University of North Carolina Press, 1955.

Lipovetsky, Gilles, *The Empire of Fashion Dressing Modern Democracy*. Princeton: Princeton University Press, 2002.

Lunettes, Henry. *The American Gentleman's Guide to Politeness and Fashion, or, Familiar Letters to His Nephews: Containing Rules of Etiquette, Directions for the Formation of Character, Etc., Etc.* New York: Derby & Jackson, 1859.

MacWilliams, Carey, and Matt S. Meier. *North from Mexico the Spanish-Speaking People of the United States*. New York: Greenwood Press, 1990.

Makeba, Miriam. *Makeba My Story*. Johannesburg: Skotaville, 1988.

McCord, David J. *The Statutes at Large of South Carolina, Vol. 7.* 1840.

Mclaren, James G. "A Brief History of Wigs in the Legal Profession." *International Journal of the Legal Profession* 6, no. 2 (1999).

McNeil, Peter. *Pretty Gentlemen Macaroni Men and the Eighteenth-Century Fashion World*. New Haven: Yale University Press, 2018.

Mitch, David. "Education and Skill of the British Labour Force." *The Cambridge Economic History of Modern Britain*, 2004.

Moody, Anthony David. *Coming of Age in Mississippi*. New York: Dial Press, 1968.

More, Thomas. *The Complete Works of St. Thomas More 4, Utopia*. New Haven: Yale University Press, 1965.

Pagan, E. O. "Los Angeles Geopolitics and the Zoot Suit Riot, 1943." *Social Science History* 24, no. 1 (January 2000).

Paoletti, Jo B. *Pink and Blue: Telling the Boys from the Girls in America*. Indiana University Press, 2013.

Paz, Octavio. *The Labyrinth of Solitude*. London: Penguin, 1990.

Perrot, Philippe. *Fashioning the Bourgeoisie: A History of Clothing in the Nineteenth Century*. Princeton: Princeton University Press, 1996.

Prude, Jonathan. "To Look upon the 'Lower Sort': Runaway Ads and the Appearance of Unfree Laborers in America, 1750–1800." *The Journal of American History* 78, no. 1 (1991).

Richards, Lynne. "A Theoretical Analysis of Non-Verbal Communication and Victim Selections for Sexual Assaults," *Clothing and /Textiles Research Journal* (1991).

Roche, Daniel, *The Culture of Clothing: Dress and Fashion in the Ancien Regime*, Cambridge, U.K.: Cambridge University Press, 1996.

Rousseau, Jean-Jacques. *Emile, or, Education*, 1762.

Sanders, Eulanda A. "The Politics of Textiles Used in African-American Slave Clothing," Textile Society of America: Textiles and Politics. (2012).

Sears, Clare. "Electric Brilliancy: Cross-Dressing Law and Freak Show Displays in Nineteenth-Century San Francisco," *Women's Studies Quarterly* 36, no. 3/4, (Fall–Winter, 2008).

Sennett, Richard. *Flesh and Stone*. New York: W.W. Norton, 1994.

Slepian, Michael L., Simon N. Ferber, Joshua M. Gold, and Abraham M. Rutchick. "The Cognitive Consequences of Formal Clothing." *Social Psychological and Personality Science* 6, no. 6 (2015).

Soland, Birgitte. *Becoming Modern: Young Women and the Reconstruction of Womanhood in the 1920s*. Princeton: Princeton University Press, 2002.

Steinberg, Neil, *Hatless Jack*, New York: Plume 2004.

Stuart-Wortley, Emmeline. *Travels in the United States: during 1849 and 1850*. New York: Harper & Bros., 1851.

Sullivan, Nick. *Mariner: The Call of the Sea*. Milan: Skira, 2012.

Trevor-Roper, Hugh. "The Highland Tradition of Scotland," in Hobsbawm, Eric John, and Terence Osborn. Ranger eds. *The Invention of Tradition*. Cambridge: Cambridge University Press, 1983.

Vali, Donna, and Nicholas D. Rizzo. "Apparel as One Factor in Sex Crimes Against Young Females: Professional Opinions of U.S. Psychiatrists." *International Journal of Offender Therapy and Comparative Criminology* 35, no. 2 (1991).

Veblen, Thorstein. *The Theory of the Leisure Class*. Macmillan, 1899.

Waugh, Norah. *The Cut of Men's Clothes 1600–1900*. London: Faber And Faber, 1977.

Weber, Max. *The Protestant Ethic and the Spirit of Capitalism: A Classic Study of the Fundamental Relationships between Religion and the Economic and Social Life in Modern Culture*. New York: Scribner, 1958.

West, Cornel. *Race Matters*. Boston: Beacon Press, 1993.

White, Shane, and Graham J. White. *Stylin: African American Expressive Culture, from Its Beginnings to the Zoot Suit*. Ithaca: Cornell University Press, 1999.

White, Shane, and Graham White. "Slave Clothing and African-American Culture in the Eighteenth and Nineteenth Centuries." *Past and Present* 148, no. 1 (1995).

Wilde, Oscar. "Slaves of Fashion," "Woman's Dress," "More Radical Ideas upon Dress Reform" and "Costume." *Shorter Prose Pieces*, Project Guttenberg (2000) (originally in the *Pall Mall Gazette*, 1884).

Wolfe, Tom. *Radical Chic & Mau-Mauing the Flak Catchers*. New York: Farrar, Straus and Giroux, 1971.

Wood, Gordon S. *The Creation of the American Republic: 1776–1787*. Chapel Hill: University of North Carolina Press, n.d.

X, Malcolm and Alex Haley. *The Autobiography of Malcolm X*. London: Penguin Books, 1965.

Zakim, Michael. *Ready-Made Democracy: A History of Men's Dress in the American Republic, 1760–1860*. Chicago: University of Chicago Press, 2003.

Acknowledgments

Scholarly writing can be a solitary venture: lots of time spent alone in front of a computer, punctuated by time spent alone in the stacks of libraries. This book involved its fair share of such isolation, but thankfully it also attracted and held the attention of some of the most thoughtful, insightful, and generous people I've encountered in my career. I have joked about the attire of my colleagues in academia for comedic effect, but in fact as a group they dress quite well, and more important, they are rigorous but still kind, intellectually intrepid but still grounded, and generally fun to be around. I owe a great deal to their insights and willingness to discuss this project through its many years of development. Special thanks to Bernadette Meyler and Amalia Kessler for suggesting some first-rate historical sources, and to Deborah Rhode for consistently pointing out the indignities of women's fashions even as I celebrated their expressive potential. I had great fun with an energetic group of Stanford Law School 1Ls in my seminars on dress codes in 2019 and 2020. One of those students, Guillaume Julian, later became my research assistant and helped enormously with pounding the later drafts of the book into its final form, securing image permissions, assisting in French-to-English translations, and saving me from an embarrassing error by pointing out that George Washington, in all likelihood, did *not* wear a wig. I had the pleasure of working with three other terrific Stanford Law School students on this book: Sean Becker, who read drafts in the middle stages of development with keen insight and a sharp eye for structure, narrative coherence, and arresting verbal imagery; Heather Hughes, who tracked down lots of important sources, read early drafts with care, and gently corrected errors in terminology and etiquette from the perspective of the post-millennial generation; and Amy Tannenbaum, who helped me get the research off the ground and shaped the direction of the project. My administrative assistant Corissa Paris went above and beyond in helping to proofread and secure image permissions. The staff at Stanford Libraries was, as always, outstanding: thanks especially to law librarian Rich Porter for his energetic assistance, including suggesting sources I would not have thought to seek out.

I presented this project in various stages of development at Berkeley Law School, Georgetown Law Center, the University of Chicago Law School, the Roger Williams University School of Law, Stanford Law School, the Stanford Bungee Lunches and Stanford's Italic Program and benefited greatly from the conversations surrounding those lectures. I also enjoyed and profited from conversations and correspondence with chief fashion critic of the *New York Times* Vanessa Friedman; creative director of *Esquire* Nick Sullivan; creative director of *Marie Claire* Kate Lanphear; professional style consultant Jodi Turnadot; fashion and style consultant Mara Kolesas, PhD; and San Francisco's legendary *bons vivants* and proprietors of the cutting-edge retailer MAC (Modern Appealing Clothing) Ben and Chris Ospital. Special thanks to NYU School of Law professor Jeanne Fromer for alerting me to the existence of the *sheitel* and to Georgetown Law Center's professor Lama Abu-Odeh for her patience and advice on the politics of the hijab; I know Lama thinks what I wrote reflects the limitations of an ambivalent Western liberal postmodernist, and no doubt it does—despite my shortcomings, it is infinitely better than it would have been without her insights. Special thanks to the effortlessly chic and enviably witty Dawn Sheggeby, former integrated marketing director for *Esquire* and Hearst Men's Magazines and, most of all, very dear friend for decades, for her many insights into the world of fashion and the importance of personal style.

I was extremely privileged to have been able to work with the late, legendary Alice Mayhew at Simon & Schuster. Not only did she see the potential in this project in its earliest stages, when few others did, but she was also instrumental in making it into the book it is. Her insights into narrative structure were truly uncanny and I will greatly miss our lunches together at the Sea Grill in Manhattan. Nothing could really soften the blow of losing Alice as an editor, but working with Emily Graff has come close—Emily has been generous, gracious, and energetic in guiding me and the book through its critical final stages. Wendy Strothman, my literary agent for over a decade, was the first to see the potential in this idea; she has believed in me and my work through triumphs and failures and has gone well above and beyond the agent's generic job of finding a publisher and negotiating a deal, remaining a kind, comforting, and constant companion in all aspects of the long and often confusing publication process and post-publication publicity scramble. Her assistant, Lauren MacCleod, has been equal to Wendy's high standards: engaged, charismatic, and innovative in thinking about new audiences and the potential of social media (something I am too old to fully grasp on my own.)

My family has contributed in more than the typical sense of offering love and support. My mom, Nancy Ford, and my sister, Robin Ford, helped me clarify details and sharpen memories of Dad and reinforce his profound influence. My kids, Cole and Ella, besides being a source of joy and optimism, no doubt burnished my images as a "real" man in the *Esquire* contest by, respectively, sitting still and refusing to sit still for Marlene's photos. Finally, my wife, Marlene, who personifies the modern woman juggling family and career, is both the gravitational center around which our little brood orbits and an attorney practicing at the highest levels of the profession; she offered support, affection, and patient insight into the multiple and conflicting demands facing professional women as well as invaluable pointers with respect to trademark law. Incidentally, she looks stunning in a pair of Louboutins.

Index

Page numbers in *italics* refer to images.

abacost, 350, 352, 353
Abercrombie & Fitch, 290–91
Above the Law, 257
Aden, Halima, 285–87
affaire du foulard, 274, 280
Afia, Nura, 285, 286
African Americans, 20–21, 164–67, 173,
    208, 370
    Afrocentrism and, 185–87, 189
    Black is Beautiful movement and,
      183–85, 189, 335, 336, 366
    Black Power radicalism and, 21,
      182–84
    bourgeoisie, 174–77, 181–82, 196,
      209, 212, 214
    civil rights movement and, *see* civil
      rights movement
    flapper styles and, 148
    hair of, 179–80, 182–84, *185*, 186, 187,
      189–90, 330–31, 333–37, 353, 354,
      365–66
    hoodies and, 201–2, 326, 337
    Jim Crow system and, 166, 167, 204
    police violence and, 213–14
    and politics of respectability, 196–97,
      202, 211–12, 243
    racism and, 20, 164, 165, 167, 173,
      175, 178–79
    sagging pants and, 196–99
    slavery and, *see* slaves, slavery
    vagrancy laws and, 166
    in World War I, 166–67

Afros, 187, 189, 190, 194
Agacinski, Sylviane, 275
Agnelli, Gianni, 313
Ahiida Burqini Swimwear, 281
airlines, 190–91, 193, 245–47
Akbari, Anna, 257–58
Alarcón, Daniel, 200, 202
Alfonso X, King of Castile, 29, 55–56
Algeria, 278
Alinejad, Masih, 279
Alinsky, Saul, 209
Alito, Samuel, 290–91
Allen, Robert, 186–87
Amara, Fadela, 275
Amer, Sahar, 276, 278
American Airlines, 190–91, 193, 246
American Civil Liberties Union (ACLU),
    198, 262
American colonies, 83–84, 86, 162, 365
American Gentleman's Guide to
    Politeness and Fashion, The
    (Lunettes), 118
Amsterdam News, 171
ancient world, 27, 38
    draped garments in, 10, 39, *39*, 40, 67
    neoclassical influence, 116
Anderson, Benedict, 86–87
Andover Shop, 324
Andress, Ursula, 283
androgyny, 144, 152
    see also gendered clothing
Anthony, Susan B., 127–28

Anton, Michael (Nicholas Antongiavanni), 305, 306
appropriation, see artifice and appropriation
Araujo, Gwen, 267–68
architecture, 117
armor, 39–40, 68–70, 74, 110
artifice and appropriation, 329–54
　blonde hair, 330–33, 335, 336, 353
　cultural appropriation complaints, 333–41, 363
　dreadlocks, 333–37, 340, 353, 354
　hoop earrings, 337–38, 353
　preppy style, 341–47, 370
　Sapeurs, 348–53, 370–71
Art of Manliness, The, 3
Ascot, Royal Enclosure at, 4
Association Internationale Africaine, 349
Astaire, Fred, 305
Atatürk, Mustafa Kemal, 277
Athenians, 27
Atlantic, 239
authenticity, 353, 361
Avants, Kelly, 262

Bacchus, 159–60, 162
Bacon, Francis, 355
Baille, Ivan, 90
Balzac, Honoré de, 60, 77
Barbey d'Aurevilly, Jules-Amédée, 172
Bardot, Brigitte, 283
Baring, Evelyn, 276–77
Barnard, Malcolm, 137
Barthes, Roland, 12, 187–88, 355
Bata Shoe Museum, 236
bathing machines, 281–82, 282
bathing suits, see swimwear
Baudelaire, Charles, 172
Bazen, Jim, 244–45
Beard, Mary, 251–52, 326
beards, 29
　Vandyke, 13–14
beauty, 366–67
　Black is Beautiful movement, 183–85, 189, 353, 336, 366

Caucasian standards of, 183–84, 365
　see also makeup
Beauty Bias, The (Rhode), 233
Beebe, Barton, 298
Belle, Dido Elizabeth, 161
Bellezza, Silvia, 316
Bennett, Judith, 71–73
Berlinger, Max, 246, 247
Bernardino of Siena, Friar, 47–49, 51, 53, 237
"Bernice Bobs Her Hair" (Fitzgerald), 143, 148
Bettcher, Talia Mae, 268
Beyoncé, 331, 336
Bible, 68, 69, 263, 374
Bible's Buried Secrets, The, 250
bikini, 281, 283
Birkin, Jane, 300, 346
Birnbach, Lisa, 310–11, 342
Black, Joe, 189
Black Bourgeoisie (Frazier), 174–77, 346
Black Panther Party, 183, 184, 185, 187, 188
Blacks, see African Americans
black tie, 3–4
BlackV Club, 322
blazers, 302–10, 343, 364
　see also jackets
Blondie, 333
Bloods and Crips, 199
Bloomer, Amelia, 20, 126, 128, 136, 138, 142, 143, 222
bloomers, 126–28, 127, 134–36, 135, 136, 146
Blythe, Betty, 149
Bogart, Humphrey, 305
Bond, James, 324–25
Bond, Julian, 204
Book of the Courtier, The (Castiglione), 100–1
bourgeoisie, 177, 188
　Black, 174–77, 181–82, 196, 209, 212, 214
Bourke, Joanna, 133
bow ties, 7
Boyer, G. Bruce, 304

Bradley, D. Anthony, 139
Bradley, Ed, 305
Bradshaw, Thomas, 26, 27
brand names, trademarks, and logos,
    298–301, 328, 343–44, 346–47
brassieres, 151
Brazzaville, 348–50
Britain, see Great Britain
Brooks Brothers, 102, 136, 172, 342
Brown, Carlotta Outley, 242–43
Brown, Nicole, 267
Brown v. Board of Education, 196
Brummell, George Bryan "Beau," 103–4,
    126, 311, 348
Buckley, Victoria, 25
burka, 63
burkini, 280–81, 285–87
Burrows, Simon, 123
Bush, John, 198
business suit, 3, 10, 94–95, 117, 253,
    254, 302, 316–20, 322–27, 353, 354,
    360
Bynum, William, 206

Caine, Michael, 324
Cakir, Emine Nur, 287, 292
California State University, Fresno, 208
Calloway, Cab, 171
Cannes Film Festival, 234, 283
Cardi B, 240, 353
Carlyle, Thomas, 172
Carmichael, Stokely, 182, 183, 186
cars, 315
casinos, 233–34
Castiglione, Baldassare, 71, 100–1, 313
casual attire, 295, 317, 364
Catherine of Aragon, 71
Cazares, Jason, 267–68
CBS Sports Spectacular, 228
chador, 279, 334
Chalayan, Hussein, 334
Chanel, 298
Chanel, Coco, 219
Charles I, King of England, 80, 81
Charles II, King of England, 81, 236
Charles VII, King of France, 68

Chen, Anna, 339
Chenoune, Farid, 79, 81
cheongsam (qipao), 338–40, 340
Chevalier, Michel, 102
Chinese footbinding, 235, 236, 239
Chinese qipao, 338–40, 340
chopines, 235–36
Christians, Christian church, 32, 46–48,
    52, 55, 70, 72, 74, 80, 82, 86, 353
    Catholic, 54, 57, 59–60, 63–65, 80, 88
    clergy, 40, 42, 46, 47, 51, 55, 97
    head coverings and, 276
    Jews and, 50, 51, 53
    monks, 55, 56, 60
    nuns, 29, 54–66, 61, 64, 237, 276
    Protestant, 60–61, 80, 85, 88, 172, 311
    Protestant Reformation and Counter-
        Reformation, 57–60
    Puritans, 1, 79, 81, 83
Cifonelli, 306
City of Columbus v. Rogers, 265–66
City of Columbus v. Zanders, 265
Civil Rights Act, 230
    Title VII of, 226–27, 290
civil rights movement, 20–21, 177–81,
    204, 211, 212, 214, 215
    and class divisions among African
        Americans, 181–82
    lunch counter sit-ins, 177, 178, 189
    March on Washington, 179, 197, 214
    radical chic and, 182–89, 195, 215,
        343
    rebellious tactics in, 182–89, 194–95
    respectability strategy in, 177–82, 179,
        189, 194–95, 207, 215, 354, 363, 365
    working-class attire and, 181, 181,
        186, 354
clavicle (collarbone), 241, 242, 247
Cleaver, Eldridge, 183
Cochran, Johnnie, 306
cocktail waitresses, 233–34
codpiece, 263
collarbone, 241, 242, 247
collars
    Ginsburg's wearing of, 255–56, 256
    ruffled, 35

colleges and universities
    dress codes at, 5, 203–7, 209–11
    professors at, 5, 14, 296, 315–16
comfort, 139–41
comme il faut, 105, 108
Congo, 348–51
Congress of Racial Equality, 182
Connery, Sean, 325
Conrad, Joseph, 349–50
conspicuous understatement, 107, 108
conspicuous waste, 236, 297
Cook, Mya and Deanna, 194
Cooper, Danielle, 271
cornette, 62
cornrows and other all-braided hairstyles,
    190–91, 193, 194, 334, 365–66
Corset, Le (O'Followell), 131
corsets, 113, 114, 129–32, *131*, 139, 140,
    144, 151
Cortell, Jorge, 238–39, 321
Cosby, Bill, 196–97, 202, 209
cosmetics, *see* makeup
costumes and masquerades, 71, 72, 134
cotillions, 175–76
counterfeits, 299–301
COVID-19 pandemic, 357–58
Craft, Christine, 228–29
Craig, Daniel, 325
Crime of the Congo, The (Doyle), 350
crinolines, 136–40, *138*, 143
Crips and Bloods, 199
Crisis, 173
Crompton, Simon, 306
Cromwell, Oliver, 80, 81, 85
cross-dressing, 68–74, 133–34, 206,
    264–67, 269, 271
    d'Éon and, 120–25, *121*, 126, 370
    see also gendered clothing;
        transgender people
CROWN Act, 194, 366
crowns and tiaras, 29–30, 37, 44
cultural appropriation
    complaints about, 333–41, 363
    see also artifice and appropriation
cummerbund, 3, 340
Cunningham, Bill, 219

Daly, Mary, 63
dandyism, 172–74
Dapper Chick, A, 271
Dapper Dan, 344–47
Dark Ages, 30
Daughters of Charity of St. Vincent de
    Paul, 63, *64*
Daum, Keziah, 338–39
Davies, Glenys, 39
Davis, Miles, 324, 341–42
Davis, Sammy, Jr., 324
Debay, Auguste, 130
debutante balls, 175–76
*Declaration of Independence from the
    Despotism of Parisian Fashion*, 128
De La Cruz, Jesse, 201
Delmas, Casmir, 130
Delon, Alain, 324
d'Éon, Chevalier, 120–25, *121*, 126, 255,
    370
de Poorter, Nase, 72
Derek, Bo, 190
Descartes, René, 82
*Description of the Western Islands of
    Scotland, A* (Martin), 90
Diderot, Denis, 60, 96
Dietrich, Marlene, 255
Dior, Christian, 63, *64*, 152
discarded clothing, 364
disease, 53
    plague, 31, 53
Disney amusement parks, 191–92
DKNY, 281
Dolce & Gabbana, 281
D'Orsay, Comte, 103, 348
doublets, 26, 36, 37, 70, 110
Downton Abbey, 253
Doyle, Arthur Conan, 350
draped garments, 10, 39, *39*, 40, 67, 70,
    112, 116–17
dreadlocks, 16, 193–94, 333–37, 340,
    353, 354, 367
Dress Coded report, 244
dressmakers, seamstresses, 110–16, 140
dress reform movement (rational dress
    movement), 126–42, 143, 144, 356

Dr. No, 283, 325
Drohojowska, Countess, 131–32
Du Bois, W. E. B., 207, 212, 350
Duncan, Clyde, 170
Dundee Courier, 137
Dunn, Stephanie, 241

Eades, Eddie, 214
earrings, 52–54, 65, 338
    hoop, 337–38, 353
    Jews and, 49–50, 52, 65, 338, 353
eBay, 301
Ebbert, Kyla, 245
Ebony, 189
economy, 110–11, 119
Edward VIII, Prince (Duke of Windsor),
    170–71, 311
Edwardian era, 144, 146, 152
Egypt, 276–77, 338
Elauf, Samantha, 290–91
elegance, 106–8, 114
Elizabeth, Empress of Russia, 120
Elizabeth I, Queen, 27, 28, 33–34, 83,
    88, 141
Elizabethan England, 25–28, *26*, 33–34,
    71, 84, 370
Ellison, Ralph, 171, 174
Emile (Rousseau), 114
employee dress codes, *see* workplace
    dress codes
Encyclopédie (Diderot), 96
England, 80–86, 88, 102
    Elizabethan, 25–28, *26*, 33–34, 71, 84,
        370
    Glorious Revolution in, 81
    London, 34, 71–73, 81–82
    slaves in, 160–62
    see also Great Britain
Enlightenment, 19, 27, 43, 46, 80, 82, 85,
    100, 102, 108, 126, 153, 237, 295,
    297, 356
Environmental Protection Agency, 364
Enzi, Mike, 269
epics, 41–43
Equal Employment Opportunity
    Commission (EEOC), 193, 230

Esman, Marjorie, 198
Esquire, 246, 247, 305, 364
    Best Dressed Real Man contest, 7–9, *8*
ethnic and racial groups, 6, 86, 87, 92,
    155, 170, 215, 370
    cultural appropriation complaints
        and, 334–41, 363
    see also African Americans; Latinos
etiquette, 102, 105, 106, 158, 165, 166,
    328
European Court of Human Rights, 280
expectations, 21–22

Facebook, 214, 321–22, 335, 358
Fagan, Gerald, 227, 228
fashion
    birth of, 40, 41, 65, 74
    century of, 352
    cycle of, 297
    democratization of, 43–44, 103, 108
    indifference to, 322, 368
    limited number of styles in, 360
    men as followers of, 109–10, 118
    modest, as industry, 285–86
    pace of, 66, 329
    quotation of older symbols in, 359
    trends in, 360
    trickle-down view of, 44
    as trivial, 14, 15, 17, 362, 368, 374
    use of term, 40, 41
    women's association with, 114
fashion designers, male, 140
fashion magazines, 12
Fashion's Slaves (Flower), 130–31
Federal Reserve Bank, 150
feet
    as erotic objects, 241, 247
    footbinding, 235, 236, 239
Fekkai, Frédéric, 288
feminism, feminists, 20, 221–22, 239, 367
    Catholic, 63
    d'Éon and, 123, 126, 370
    flappers and, 20, 143–53, 370
    Muslim headscarves and, 275, 277
    rational dress movement and, 126–28,
        134

fez, 277
Finlayson, Gabi, 241
First Amendment, 15
first impressions, 5–6, 211
Fish, Stanley, 315
Fitzgerald, F. Scott, 143, 148, 344
flappers, 20, 143–53, *145*, 221–22, 227, 283, 370
Fleming, Ian, 344
Floyd, George, 213
Flower, Benjamin Orange, 130–31
Flügel, John Carl, 79–80, 84–85, 133
Flusser, Alan, 342
Ford, Tanisha, 180–81
Ford, Tom, 325
Foster, Bailee, 269
Four Seasons, 303
Fox, George P., 119
Fox & Friends, 201
Foxwoods, 233–34
France, 80–84, 104
    dressmakers in, 110–16
    Muslim clothing in, 274, 280, 281
    Paris, 30, 82, 96, 97
    Revolutionary, 84–86, 93, 102, 122–23
    Second Empire, 107
    wigs and wig production in, 95–99
Franklin, Benjamin, 83–85, 98–99
Frazier, E. Franklin, 174–77, 209, 212, 346
Frederick II, King of Sicily, 50
Friedman, Vanessa, 259–60, 272, 341

gangs, 2, 199–202, 242, 343
Garber, Megan, 239
Garrison, Mark, 288
Gaultier, Jean Paul, 334
gay community, *see* LGBTQ community
Geffrard, Sara, 271
gendered clothing, 6, 18, 20, 21, 67–75, 109–25, 140, 153, 261–72, 292, 359
    asexual dress and, 270–71
    and changes in gender roles, 261
    cross-dressing and, 68–74, 133–34, 206, 264–67, 269, 271
    d'Éon and, 120–25, *121*, 126, 370

divergence of masculine and feminine fashions, 115–16
    enforcement of, 134
    fashion changes and, 263
    flapper and, 144
    genital difference and, 268, 270
    Joan of Arc and, 68–70, 74, 122, 144
    mixing of, 272
    pink and blue, 263–64
    public decency laws and, 14
    reproductive roles and, 268, 270
    school dress codes and, 261–63
    simplicity and, 116–19
    symbolism in, 139–42, 263–64, 268, 270, 271
    transgender people and, 16, 69, 73, 206–7, 262–63, 265, 267–69, 271
    transgressions of, 266–69, 271
    workplace dress codes and, 15, 16
    see also men's clothing; women's clothing
General Mills Company, 227
George IV, King, 92
Giacoma della Marca, Friar, 51
Gill, A. A., 251–52
Gino, Francesca, 316
Ginsburg, Ruth Bader, 255–56, *256*
Givhan, Robin, 213
Global Islamic Economy Report, 285
Glorious Revolution, 81
Goldfinger, 325
Goldgar, A. Benjamin, 257
Goldman Sachs, 316–19
Gomez, Erick, 200–201
Gondola, Ch. Didier, 348, 349
Gone with the Wind, 170
Gordon, Taylor, 166
gowns, 39, 74, 115, 118, 139, 354
GQ, 272
graffiti tags, 199, 200
Gray, Horace, 253, 254
Great Britain, 88
    Tartan Act in, 87–92
    see also England
Great Feminine Renunciation, 150–52
Great Gatsby, The (Fitzgerald), 144

Great Masculine Renunciation, 79–99,
100, 101, 106, 109, 110, 117–19,
124, 133, 141, 144, 146, 151–53,
155, 222, 237, 254–55, 266, 295,
301, 313, 317, 320, 327, 356
Greece, ancient, 39, 116, 338
Spartans and Athenians, 27
Greenblatt, Stephen, 11, 40
Grossman, Rafael, 288
Guardian, 286
Gucci, 301, 344–45
guilds, 111–13
Gwen Araujo Justice for Victims Act, 268

hair, hairstyles, 16, 48, 95–96, 152
of African Americans, 179–80, 182–
84, *185*, 186, 187, 189–90, 330–31,
333–37, 353, 354, 365–66
Afros, 187, 189, 190, 194
blonde, 330–33, 335, 336, 353
bobbed, 143–45, *145, 148*, 149, 150
cornrows and other all-braided styles,
190–91, 193, 194, 334, 365–66
cultural appropriation criticisms of,
333–37
dreadlocks, 16, 193–94, 333–37, 340,
353, 354, 367
femininity and, 180
wigs, *see* wigs
workplace dress codes and, 190–94,
365–67
Hamer, Fannie Lou, 212
Hamlet (Shakespeare), 101
Hampden-Sydney College, 209, 210
handbags
counterfeit, 301
Hermès, 299–301, 346
Hanseatic League, 31
Hanson, Dian, 145–46
Harberton, Lady, 129, 142
Harper's New Monthly Magazine, 135
Harrah's Operating Co., 225–26
Harry, Debbie, 332–33
Hartley-Brewer, Julia, 250
Hasegawa, Hajime, 342
Hasibuan, Anniesa, 284

hats
fez, 277
straw, 2, 14
top hats, 1–2
Hawkins, Scott, 242
Hawthorne, Lyndsay, 200
Hayashida, Teruyoshi, 342
Hays Code, 283
Head, Edith, 223, 256, 293
head coverings, 276, 353, 354
hijabs, 274–80, 284–87, 289–92, 338
wimples, 62, 65, 276
Heart of Darkness (Conrad), 349–50
henin, 276
Henry VIII, King, 33, 35, 71, 354
Hermès, 346
handbags, 299–301, 346
Winfrey and, 326–27
Herrick, Robert, 101
Hess, Amanda, 257
Hetherington, John, 1
Hetzeldorfer, Katherina, 72
Higginbotham, Evelyn Brooks, 212
Highlanders, 87–92
hijabs, 274–80, 284–87, 289–92, 338
Hildegard von Bingen, Saint, 69
Hills, Helen, 57–59
Himes, Chester, 173
hip-hop, 44, 343–44
hippies, 174, 187–88
Hispanics, *see* Latinos
History of Men's Magazines (Hanson),
146
Hitchcock, Alfred, 332
Hollander, Anne, 39, 70, 109, 112–15,
118, 140–41, 270, 286, 363
Hollywood, Hays Code in, 283
Holy Roman Empire, 86
homespun, 83–84, 86, 102, 365
hoodies, 321, 323, 337
African Americans and, 201–2, 326,
337
Hooper, Wilfrid, 33–34
hoop skirts, 113
Hooters Restaurant, 230, 330–33
Hopkins, Ann, 229–30, 269

hospitality industry, 191–92, 225–26, 233–34
Hotchkiss, Valerie, 70
Hovsepian, Ginny, 262
Howl, Thirstin, III, 345, 347
How to Dress for Success (Head and Hyams), 223–25, 256
Hughes, Diane Owen, 50–52
humanism, 46, 85, 370
Hunt, Alan, 30, 43–44
Hutton, Lauren, 232
Hyatt, 193

IBM, 320
illiteracy, 32
immigrants, 173
individual, individuality, 40–44, 74, 75, 82, 124, 292, 358–64
    personality, 18, 43, 44, 75, 86, 124, 153, 359
    see also self-fashioning
Indonesia, 278
Industrial Revolution, 101
Instagram, 317, 330, 334, 336, 357, 358
Invisible Man (Ellison), 171
Iran, 278–79, 281
Ishikawa, Yumi, 235
Ishizu, Shosuke, 342
Islam, *see* Muslim attire
Ivy Style, 342

jackets, 7, 152
    in black-tie ensembles, 3
    blazers, 302–10, 343, 364
    buttons and buttonholes on, 304–8, *307*, 313, 346
    restaurant requirements for, 302–4, 368
    sport coats, 302, 304, 364
    surgeon's cuffs on, 306, *307*
Jackson, Samuel L., 204
Jacobites, 88, 89, 92
Jacobs, Marc, 333–37
Jaeger-LeCoultre, 299
James I, King of Great Britain (James VI of Scotland), 88

James Bond novels and films, 324–25, 344
    Dr. No, 283, 325
Jeanne of Navarre, 29
Jefferson, Thomas, 85–86, 95
Jespersen, Darlene, 226–27, 240, 269
jewelry, 48, 53, 54, 237, 298, 338
    earrings, *see* earrings
    flappers and, 151
    Jews and, 49–50
Jews, 50, 51, 276, 334
    Christians and, 50, 51, 53
    earrings and, 49–50, 52, 65, 338, 353
    laws on attire of, 49–54, 338
    Orthodox, wigs worn by, 287–89
    preppy style and, 342
Jezebel, 258
Jim Crow system, 166, 167, 204
Joan of Arc, 68–70, 74, 122, 144
job interviews, 12
John XXIII, Pope, 62–63
Johnson, Farryn, 330–33
Johnson, Randall, 290
Jones, Carla, 278
Jones, Chastity, 16–17, 193, 365, 367
Jones, Jennifer, 112, 113

Kagan, Elena, 253–56
Kant, Immanuel, 17
Kanteron Systems, 238
Kates, Gary, 122, 123
Kaunitz, Wenzel Anton von, 79
Keinan, Anat, 316
Kellerman, Annette, 282
Kelly, Grace, 223, 332, 346
Khomeini, Ayatollah, 278
kilts, 87–92
Kim, Queena, 321
King, Martin Luther, Jr., 182, 204, 207
King Leopold's Soliloquy (Twain), 350
Kinois, 350
Kinshasa, 348, 350
KMBC, 228–29
knock-offs, 299–301
Komissarouk, Alexey, 321
Kuchta, David, 81
Kudkow, Larry, 323

Kuhns, Elizabeth, 55, 56, 62, 63, 65
Kurosu, Toshiyuki, 342
Kwass, Michael, 96–98

lab coat, 12, 13
Ladies' Wreath, 134–35
Lanphear, Kate, 5
Larkin, Miranda, 241
Las Vegas, Nev., 233, 234
Latinos, 168–69, 243, 337
    hoodies and, 201, 202
Lauren, Ralph, 293, 298, 342–43, 345, 346
    Polo, 342, 343, 345–47, 352
Laurens, Henry, 163
Lawford, Peter, 324
laws, 2
    antidiscrimination, 16, 226–30, 333, 366
    on Jews' attire, 49–54
    public decency, 14
    sumptuary, *see* sumptuary laws
    vagrancy, 166
lawyers and judges, 14, 210
    dress codes for, 252–59
    English, 99
    judicial robes, 253, 255
    Supreme Court and, 252–53
    wigs worn by, 99, 253, 254
Lee, Spike, 204
leine, 89
leisure, 119, 148
Leland Stanford Junior University
    Marching Band (LSJUMB), 308–9
Levine, Matt, 319
LGBTQ community, 206, 269
    transgender people, 16, 69, 73, 206–7, 262–63, 265, 267–69, 271
Lily, 128
Lin, Jeremy, 336
Lindsay, John, 161
Lipovetsky, Gilles, 41, 352
literacy, 32
literature, 41–43
Lithwick, Dahlia, 254, 255
Llewellyn-Jones, Lloyd, 39

Locke, John, 17
logos, brand names, and trademarks, 298–301, 328, 343–44, 346–47
Lo Lifes, 345–47, 352, 370
London, 34, 71–73, 81–82
Lord, Steven Lamar, 248, 249
Los Angeles Times, 192, 288
Louboutin shoes with red soles, 240, 296–99, 322, 346, 353
Louis VIII, King, 29
Louis XIII, King, 95
Louis XIV, King, 95, 97–98, 236, 240, 297, 298, 353
Louis XV, King, 120–22
Louis Vuitton, 298, 344
Lowder, J. Bryan, 246
Luther, Martin, 59, 60
luxury, luxury goods, 48, 51, 53, 54, 74, 83, 101, 102, 295, 297, 298
    African Americans and, 176
    as effeminate, 114
    Great Masculine Renunciation of, *see* Great Masculine Renunciation
    imitations of, 299–301
    rarity of, 300
    renounced by elite, 81, 102, 108
    renounced by religious people, 55, 56, 59, 65
    replaced by elegance, 106, 108
    sumptuary laws and, *see* sumptuary laws
    wigs as, 97

"Macaroni," 160
Machiavelli, Niccolò, 30
Maciel, Stephen, 200
Madonna, 333
Magidson, Michael, 267–68
Makeba, Miriam, 186
makeup, 48, 53, 286
    flappers and, 146, 151, 152
    lipstick, 146, *147*
    men's use of, 79
Malcolm X, 171, 183, 190
Malone, Bonz, 347
Mansfield, Jayne, 332, 333

Mansfield, William Murray, Earl of, 160–62

March on Washington, *179*, 197, 214

Marie Claire, 5

Marks & Spencer, 281

Martin, Dean, 324

Martin, Kenyon, 336

Martin, Martin, 90

Martin, Trayvon, 201–2, 326, 337

Martinez, Alegria, 337, 338

Marx, Karl, 177

Mary, Queen of Scots, 88

Mashantucket Pequot Tribe, 233–34

masquerades and costumes, 71, 72, 134

mass production, 136, 297

Mayer, Marissa, 321

McLaren, James G., 99

McSheffrey, Shannon, 71–73

Mean Girls, 206

Mediavilla, Héctor, 351

Medici, Cosimo de', 23, 30

Meet the Romans, 251

Men's Apparel Reporter, 170

men's clothing, 126, 152
    dandyism and, 172–74
    Great Masculine Renunciation in, 79–99, 101, 106, 109, 110, 117–19, 124, 133, 141, 144, 146, 151–53, 155, 237, 254–55, 266, 295, 301, 313, 317, 320, 327, 356
    and men as followers of fashion, 109–10, 118
    modern, 81
    neoclassical, 116–19
    peacock revolution in, 266
    rational dress movement and, 132–33, 139, 141
    sexual appeal of, 140
    tailoring and, 32, 35, 37, 39–40, 67, 69, 74, 110–19, 126, 140, 301, 302, 312, 324, 325, 328
    women's donning of, 144, 236, 325, 353
    women's borrowing of tailoring from, 40, 110, 140
    see also gendered clothing; *specific items of clothing*

Men's Dress Reform Party, 133

mercantile economy, 110–11

Merél, José, 267–69

Merél, Wanda, 267–69

meritocracy, 297, 299

Merkel, Angela, 280

Mexican Americans, 168

Michele, Alessandro, 345

Middle Ages, 17–19, 27–32, 38–41, 46, 48–49, 55, 57, 62, 70, 72, 74, 75, 101, 144, 153, 263, 295, 297, 352

Midtown Uniform, 317–21, *318*, 323, 325–27, 353, 360, 362

Mies van der Rohe, Ludwig, 117

Miller, Elizabeth Smith, 127

#Mipsterz, 285, 287

Mirabeau, Marquis de, 97

Miss World, 283

Mobutu Sese Seko, 350, 352, 353

Modanisa, 287

Modern Girl, 283

modesty, 20, 21, 59, 62, 63, 70, 112, 113, 116, 240, 241, 247–50, 275, 276, 281, 284–86, 288, 289, 291, 292

monks, 55, 56, 60

Moody, Anne, 177–80, *178*, 189, 214, 331

More, Thomas, 35–36, 38, 49, 79, 354

Morehouse College, 203–7, 209–11

morning suit, 253–56

Morning Tulsa Daily World, 149

Möser, Justus, 93, 94

Murray, Elizabeth, 161

muscadin, 84

Muslim attire, 285
    burka, 280
    burkini, 280–81, 285–87
    chador, 279, 334
    hijab, 274–80, 284–87, 289–92, 338

My Stealthy Freedom, 279

National Cash Register Company, 150, 227

National Coalition of American Nuns, 64

National Dress Reform Association, 128

nationalism, 86–87

national uniforms, 86–95
  abacost, 350, 352, 353
  of Scottish Highlanders, 87–92
National Women's Law Center, 244
Nation of Islam, 183
neckties, 5, 7, 15, 263, 313, 314
  bow ties, 7
  restaurant requirements for, 303–4, 368
  Trump and, 314
Negro Acts, 157–59, 164, 333
Nelson, Norris, 168
neoclassical influence, 116–19
New Look, 152
New Republic, 150, 151
New York City Commission on Human
  Rights, 15, 194, 303–4
New York State Division of Human
  Rights, 231–32
New York Times, 170, 171, 202, 237–39,
  259, 272, 279, 288, 302, 325, 334,
  339, 341
New York Times Magazine, 200
New York Tribune, 133
Norteños and *Sureños*, 199–202
novels, 42–43
nudists, 373–74
nuns, 29, 54–66, *61, 64*, 237, 276
Nutter, Michael, 197

Obama, Barack, 197
O'Connor, Sandra Day, 229–30, 255
Official Preppy Handbook, The
  (Birnbach), 310–11, 342
O'Followell, Ludovic, 131
Oulton, Walley Chamberlain, 282

pachucas, 171
pachucos, 168–69, 172, 174, 215, 351
painter's coat, 13
Pall Mall Gazette, 133
pants, 39, 74, 84, 86
  black-tie, 3
  bloomers, 126–28, *127*, 134–36, *135,
    136*, 146
  Oxford Bags, 170–71
  sagging, 2, 174, 196–99

  women's wearing of, 145–46
pantsuits, 258, 326
Paracelsus, 53
Paris, 30, 82, 96, 97
  dressmakers in, 110–16
Parker, Tiana, 193–94
Parkinson, Antonio, 243
Parton, Dolly, 332
Patagonia fleece vests, 318–19, 323, 362
Paul VI, Pope, 64
Paz, Octavio, 172
Peltz, Lucy, 123
Pepper, George Wharton, 253
Permanent Style, 306
Perrot, Philippe, 104, 107, 241
Perry, Tyler, 197
personality, 18, 43, 44, 74, 86, 124, 153,
  359
Philippe le Bel IV, King, 29
Philippe le Hardi III, King, 29
piercing, 174, 192
Pinkett Smith, Jada, 271
Pinn, Anthony, 178–79
Pinnacle Peak Steakhouse, 5
Pitzer College, 337–38
Pius XII, Pope, 62, 283
plague, 31, 53
Plastics, the, 206
Playboy clubs, 230–33, *231,234*
police
  African Americans killed by, 213–14
  pretext stops by, 198–99
politics, 119, 356
  economics and, 110–11
  liberalism, 369–70
politics of respectability, 196–97, 202,
  211–12, 243
  in civil rights movement, 177–82, *179,
    189*, 194–95, 207, 215
Polo, 342, 343, 345–47, 352
Poor Clare Colettines, 276
Pope, Alexander, 237, 361
Porter, Cole, 247
Post, Chassie, 239
power, 18, 20, 74, 100, 153, 359
  see also status

practicality, 139, 295–96, 356
Prada, Miuccia, 355
preppy style, 310–13
    appropriation of, 341–47, 370
Price Waterhouse, 229–30
professors, 5, 14, 296, 315–16
prom, 261–62
prostitutes, 47, 49, 52, 71–73, 146, 237
Prude, Jonathan, 158, 162–64
psychology, 43
public decency laws, 14
Punch, 133
Purdy, Daniel Leonhard, 93
Puritans, puritanism, 1, 79, 81, 83, 312

Qassim, Setera, 245
qipao, 338–40, *340*
quelt, 90
Qur'an, 276

racial groups, *see* ethnic and racial
    groups
radical chic, 187, 195
    Black, 182–89, 195, 215, 343
Raekwon, 345
Rake, The, 305
Ramsay, Allan, 90
Ramsey, LaMarcus, 198
rape, 248–49
rational dress movement, 126–42, 143,
    144
Rational Dress Society, 128, 133
Rational Dress Society's Gazette, 128–29,
    132
Rat Pack, 324
Rawlinson, Thomas, 90, 91
ready-made garments, 102, 136
Réard, Louis, 283
red sneakers effect, 316, 326
Regina v. Whittaker, 99
Rehnquist, William, 254
religious clothing, 6, 16, 46–66, 72,
    273–92
    burkas, 280
    fashion and self-expression and, 273,
        284–85, 287, 289–92

modesty and, 275, 276, 284–86, 288,
    289, 291
    of nuns, 29, 54–66, *61, 64*, 237, 276
    school dress codes and, 274
    workplace dress codes and, 290–91
Renaissance, 13, 14, 17–19, 28–30, 32,
    33, 36, 37, 38, 41, 46, 49, 62, 71, 72,
    74, 101, 110, 129, 247, 263, 295, 297,
    365
restaurant dress codes for customers,
    302–4, 368
reverse snobbery, 102, 107, 217, 296,
    312, 314–16, 322, 323, 326–28
Reza Shah Pahlavi, 278
Rhode, Deborah, 233, 239
*Righteous Discontent: The Women's
    Movement in the Black Baptist
    Church* (Higginbotham), 212
Ringling, John, 166
Ritz-Carlton Hotel, 192, 194
Rivera, Geraldo, 201–2
robes and draped garments, 10, 39, *39,
    40*, 67, 70, 112, 116–17
Roche, Daniel, 44, 97
Rodman, Dennis, 331
Rogers, Renee, 190–91, 193, 365
Rome, ancient, 27, 39, 116
Root, The, 207
Ross, Tova, 288–89
Rossignol, Laurence, 281
Rousseau, Jean-Jacques, 17, 98, 114,
    125
Rubinstein, Helena, 146, 224
RuPaul, 271
Rykener, John, 72

Sacchetti, Franco, 36
sans-culottes, 84, 86
Sapeurs, 348–53, 370–71
Sartor Resartus (Carlyle), 172
Satcher, David, 204
Savile Row, 325
Savonarola, Girolamo, 53
Scafidi, Susan, 326
Scherr, Stephen M., 316
Schiaparelli, Elsa, 23

school dress codes, 2, 13–14, 193–94, 205, 241–45, 247, 363, 367–68
  college and university, 5, 203–7, 209–11
  gender and, 261–63
  girls targeted by, 244–45
  for parents of students, 243
  for prom, 261–62
  religious garb and, 274
Scotland, 88
  Tartan Act and, 87–92
Scott, Joan Wallach, 275
Scott, Walter, 92
Seagram Building, 117–18, 303
seamstresses, dressmakers, 110–16, 140
Sears, Clare, 134
Sebourn, Jesse, 200–1
self-fashioning, 11, 38–45, 55, 94, 356
  group, 363
  hairstyles and, 98
  politics and, 215
  religious dress codes and, 273, 284–85, 287
Semmelhack, Elizabeth, 236
Sennett, Richard, 51, 53
Seven Years War, 79
sexual harassment and assault, 245, 248–49
sexuality, 18
  cross-dressing and, 71–73
  and dress codes requiring modesty, 241, 247–48
  feet as erotic objects, 241, 247
  flapper styles and, 148–49
  menswear and, 140
  moral judgments about, 47–49, 65, 149
  nuns and, 60–62, *61*, 237
  promiscuity, 149
  prostitution, 47, 49, 52, 71–73, 146, 237
  school dress codes and, 244–45, 247–48
  sexual freedom, 144, 146, 222
  see also gendered clothing
Shakespeare, William, 77, 101, 210

Sharp, Granville, 160
sheitels, 287–89
She's a Gent, 271
shoes, 103, 139–40, 364
  brogues, 139
  chopines, 235–36
  high-heeled, 233–40, 321, 329, 365
  red-soled Louboutin, 240, 296–99, 322, 346, 353
"signature" items of clothing, 6
Silicon Valley, 5, 217, 296, 320–23, 327, 360
Silk Road, 31
"silk stocking," 86
simplicity, 103–8
  neoclassical, 116–19
Sinatra, Frank, 324
Sinclair, John, 89–90
Sinema, Kyrsten, 259
Sisters of Charity, 62, 63
Sisters of Loretto, 63
60 Minutes, 305
skirts, 127, 138–39, 152
  hoops and cage crinolines for, 113, 136–40, *138*, 143
  kilts, 87–92
  miniskirts, 152
Skyfall, 325
Slate, 234, 246, 254, 257
slaves, slavery, 14, 20, 157–66, 281, 347, 353, 356
  Emancipation and, 165, 166
  in England, 160–62
  Negro Acts and, 157–59, 164, 333
  runaway slaves, 159–60, 162–64, 166
Smith, Jaden, 271–72
Smith, Will, 271
social media, 357, 358
  Facebook, 214, 321–22, 335, 358
  Instagram, 317, 330, 334, 336, 357, 358
social status, *see* status
Sofaer, Abraham, 190
Solicitor General, 252–56
Solomon, David M., 316
Somerset, James, 160–62

Sou, Aminatou, 275

South Carolina Gazette, 159

Southern Christian Leadership Conference, 182

Southwest Airlines, 245–46

Soylent, 322–23

Spaiser, Matt, 325

Spartans, 27

sport coats, 302, 304, 364

sports, 146, 148

Sports Illustrated, 285–87

sports jerseys and hats, 199–200

sprezzatura, 101, 108, 306, 313, 314

Stanford University, 210, 211, 308–9

Stanhope, Philip Dormer, 118

Stanley, Henry Morton, 349, 350

Stanton, Elizabeth Cady, 127, 142, 222

Starbucks, 2

status, 18–20, 25–37, 38, 42, 44–45, 47, 74, 75, 93, 94, 100–8, 124, 153, 261, 263, 295–98, 359

    brand names and trademarks and, 298–301, 328, 343–44, 346–47

    democratization of fashion and, 43–44, 103, 108

    reverse snobbery and, 102, 107, 217, 296, 312, 314–16, 322, 323, 326–28

    sumptuary laws and, *see* sumptuary laws

    wigs and, 95–99

    see also luxury, luxury goods

Stavrakopoulou, Francesca, 250–52

Steel, Danielle, 240

Steinem, Gloria, 230–32

Stevens, John Paul, 13, 17

Stewart, Charles, 160–62

Stewart, Kristen, 234

Stormy Weather, 171

Stuart, Charles Edward, 88

Stuart-Wortley, Emmeline, 102

Student Nonviolent Coordinating Committee (SNCC), 180–82, 185, 186, 188, 354

Suenens, Léon Joseph Cardinal, 63

Sugarhill Gang, 343

suits, 10, 15, 94–95, 102, 117, 119, 136, 139, 144, 271, 301, 364

    business, 3, 10, 94–95, 117, 253, 254, 302, 316–20, 322–27, 353, 354, 360

    James Bond and, 324–25

    morning, 253–56

    pantsuits, 258, 326

    symbolism in, 324

    tuxedo, 253, 340

    women's wearing of, 325

    zoot, 168–74, *169*, 351

Sullivan, Nick, 305, 364

sumptuary laws, 25–30, 32–37, 44–45, 47, 49, 52, 54, 55, 65, 72, 84, 93, 106, 107, 155, 297, 328

    Negro Acts, 157–59, 164, 333

    trademarks as, 298, 301

Supreme Court, U.S., 229–30, 252–53, 290–91

    Miller v. School District No. 167, 13–14

    Solicitor General and, 252–56

Sureños and *Norteños*, 199–202

Sutcliffe, Tom, 250

swimwear, 282–84

    bathing machines and, 281–82, *282*

    bikinis, 281, 283

    burkinis, 280–81, 285–87

    two-piece, 283

syphilis, 53

Tahrir al-Mar'a (Amīn), 277

Tailor & Cutter, 139

tailoring, 32, 35, 37, 39–40, 67, 69, 74, 110–19, 126, 140, 301, 302, 312, 324, 325, 328

Tailor Retailored, The (Carlyle), 172

Take Ivy (Ishizu, Kurosu, and Hasegawa), 342

Tartana (Ramsay), 90

tartans, 87–92

tattoos, 174, 192

Tatum, Cheryl, 193

Taylor, Royce, 258

techies and Silicon Valley style, 5, 217, 296, 320–23, 327, 360

Tenney, Jack B., 173

Tertullian, 48

Theory of the Leisure Class, The (Veblen), 32, 174–75, 346

Thiel, Peter, 320

Thiers, Jean-Baptiste, 97

Thomas Aquinas, Saint, 69

Thorp, Nicola, 234–35

ties, *see* neckties

Tiffany & Co., 298, 301

Time, 283

Times (London), 1

Timpf, Katherine, 337–38

togas and other draped garments, 10, 39, *39*, 40, 67, 70, 112, 116–17

trademarks, brand names, and logos, 298–301, 328, 343–44, 346–47

trades, 110–11
  guilds and, 111–13

transgender people, 16, 69, 73, 206–7, 262–63, 265, 267–69, 271

Trebek, Alex, 306

Trevor-Roper, Hugh, 89–92

trews, 89–90

trophy wives, 237

trousers, *see* pants

Trump, Donald, 256, 323
  neckties of, 314

trunk hose, 25–27, *26*, 33, 36, 37, 38, 44, 168

Tudor era, 25–28, 33–36

Tufekci, Zeynep, 213–14

Turkey, 277–78

Turner, Lana, 332, 333

tuxedo, 253, 340

Twain, Mark, 350

21 Club, 15, 303

Twiggy, 152

undergarments
  brassieres, 151
  corsets, 113, 114, 129–32, *131*, 139, 140, 144, 151
  flappers and, 148
uniforms, 360, 374
  abacosts as, 350, 352, 353
  business suits as, 94–95, 360

Midtown Uniform, 317–21, *318*, 323, 325–27, 353, 360, 362
  national, 86–95
  of Scottish Highlanders, 87–92
  workplace, 15
Union Bank of Switzerland, 3
universities, *see* colleges and universities
U.S. Airways, 246
Utopia (More), 35–36, 49, 79, 354

Vaïsse, Justin, 274

Valentino, 334

Valls, Manuel, 281

Vandyke beard, 13–14

Veblen, Thorstein, 32, 43, 174–76, 195, 236, 297, 344, 346

Veblen goods, 300–1

veils, 29
  burkas, 280
  hijabs, 274–80, 284–87, 289–92

Vertigo, 332

Vibe, 206

Victoria, Queen, 92, 304

Victorian era, 60–62, 119, 142, 144, 151, 152

Vogue, 321

Vreeland, Diana, 155

Waldron, John E., 316

Wall Street Journal, 3, 317

Walweyn, Richard, 25–27, 38, 44, 470

Washington, Booker T., 350

Washington, George, 95

Washington Post, 150, 213

watch, 3

Watson, Emma, 250

Watson, John Fanning, 165

Watt, Ian, 43

Waverley (Scott), 92

Weber, Max, 80

West, Cornel, 212–13

West, Kanye, 343

whalebone, 113, 144

Whelan, Ed, 255

White, Shane and Graham, 158, 159, 163, 164, 166

white supremacy, 165, 183, 185, 353, 356, 370

wigs, 353
  in legal profession, 99, 253, 254
  powdered, 95–99, 347
  sheitels, 287–89

Wilde, Oscar, 132–33

Williams, Patricia, 254

wimple, 62, 65, 276

Windsor, Duke of, 170–71, 311

Winfrey, Oprah, 326–27

Witte, Samuel Simon, 94

Wolf, Aniya, 261–62

Wolfe, Tom, 187

women's clothing, 21, 152–53
  athletic silhouette and, 144, 151, 152, 283
  domesticity and, 119
  double-bind scenarios of, 249–52, 326
  and dressing for success, 223–25
  and dressing like women, 217, 221–60
  dress reform movement and, 126–42, 143, 144, 356
  in 1800s, 11–12
  fashion associated with, 114
  feminism and, see feminism, feminists
  flappers and, 20
  Great Feminine Renunciation in, 150–52
  hourglass silhouette and, 129, 132, 144, 151, 152
  legs and, 144–46
  masculine domination and, 140
  mass production of, 136
  menswear tailoring incorporated into, 40, 110, 140
  menswear worn as, 144, 236, 325, 353
  modesty and, 20, 21, 59, 62, 63, 70, 112, 113, 116, 240, 241, 247–50, 275, 276, 281, 284–86, 288, 289, 291, 292
  moral judgments and, 47–49, 65
  Negro Acts and, 158–59
  neoclassical, 116, 119
  prostitution and, 47, 49, 52, 71–73, 237
  pure womanhood ideal and, 119, 142, 152

religious faith and, see religious clothing
sexual harassment and assault and, 245, 248–49
see also gendered clothing; workplace dress codes; specific items of clothing

workplace dress codes, 2, 3, 190–94, 217, 222, 225, 259, 363, 367
  of airlines, 190–91, 193
  antidiscrimination laws and, 16, 226–30, 333, 366
  casual wear and, 317
  flapper fashions and, 149–50, 227
  hairstyles and, 190–94, 365–67
  high-heeled shoes and, 233–35
  at Hooters, 230, 330–33
  in hospitality industry, 191–92, 225–26, 233–34
  in legal profession, 14, 99, 210, 252–59
  at Playboy clubs, 230–33
  religious garb and, 290–91
  transgender employees and, 16

World War I
  African American soldiers in, 166–67
  women in the workforce during, 20, 139, 146

World War II, 170

Worth, Charles Frederick, 140

Wu-Tang Clan, 345

Yahoo!, 321

Yale University, 210

Young Dro, 345

Yves Saint-Laurent, 296

Zaire, 350

Zakim, Michael, 84–86, 136

Zanetti, Aheda, 280–81, 285

Zara, 297

Zero to One (Thiel), 320

Zhou Yijun, 339

Zimmerman, George, 201–2

zoot suits, 168–74, 169, 351

Zuckerberg, Mark, 321–23, 326, 337, 374

Image Credits

Text Page Credit

8   Williams Ford, Marlene. Rich Ford for *Esquire* Best-Dressed Real Men. 2009. Photograph. © Marlene Williams Ford.

26   *Trunk Hose | Bohemian*. The Metropolitan Museum of Art, Gift of Bashford Dean, 1923 licensed under Creative Commons 1.0.

39   Statues at the "House of Cleopatra" in Delos, Greece. *Man and woman wearing the himation*. By Heiko Gorski. Licensed under Creative Commons 3.0.

61   *Bluebeard*, Raquel Welch. 1972. © Everett Collection.

64   © Daughters of Charity Province of St. Louis, 1964.

121   Le Chevalier D'Éon, a man who passed as a woman: shown half in woman's, half in man's attire. Engraving. Welcome Library no. 275i. Licensed under Creative Commons 4.0.

127   Currier, The Library of Congress. *The Bloomer Costume*, 1851.

131   O'Followell, Ludovic. *Le Corset*. 1905.

131   O'Followell, Ludovic. *Le Corset*. 1905.

135   *Harper's Magazine*. 1852. January 1852 issue, 286.

136   *Harper's Magazine. A "Bloomer" (in Leap Year)*. 1852. January 1852 issue, 286.

138   *La crinolinomanie. Petit journal pour rire*, No. 037, 1856.

145   The University of Chicago Photographic Archive. *Students*. Circa 1940s. Photograph. © The University of Chicago.

147   Unknown.

169   1943. © Everett Collection.

178   Blackwell, Fred. *Salter, Trumpauer, and Moody at Lunch Counter Sit-in*. 1963. © Fred Blackwell.

179   Scherman, Rowland. Civil Rights March on Washington, DC. 1963. National Archives.

181   Library of Congress, Glenn Pearcy Collection. *Students March in Montgomery*. 1965. Photograph. © Glenn Pearcy.

184   UC Santa Cruz, Ruth-Marion Baruch and Prickle Jones Collection. © UC Board of Regents.

185   UC Santa Cruz, Ruth-Marion Baruch and Prickle Jones Collection. © UC Board of Regents.

231   *Playboy Bunnies*, 1975. © Associated Press.

256   Petteway, Steve, Collection of the Supreme Court. Ruth Bader Ginsburg, Official Supreme Court Portrait. Photograph.

282   Bain News Service. *Bather Posing for a Photo - Ostend*. 1913. Library of Con-

gress, Prints & Photographs Division, LC-B2- 2711-14 [P&P]. George Grantham Bain Collection.

307 © Richard Thompson Ford, 2020.

318 Sargent, Lee: @leecomptons. Photo for @midtownuniform on Instagram. 2019 © Lee Sargent.

340 Unknown (Woman wearing a cheongsam). 2009. Licensed under China Mainland Creative Commons 2.5.

Insert 1   Credit

1   Beach, Chandler B., ed. *The New Student's Reference Work.* Dress of Ancient Period. Illustration. Chicago: F. E. Compton and Company, 1805.

2   Unknown, Portrait of Queen Elizabeth, courtesy of Rijksmuseum, Amsterdam, 1550–1599.

3   Lynch, Albert. *Portrait of Jeanne d'Arc. Le Figaro Illustré.* 1903.

4   Bennett, Veronica, Ryan Todd, and GraphicDesign&. *Looking Good: A Visual Guide to the Nun's Habit.* GraphicDesign&: 2016. © Ryan Todd.

5   van Meytens, Martin. *Portrait of Wenzel Anton Graf von Kaunitz-Rietberg.* 1749–1750.

6   Batoni, Pompeo. Portrait of a Man in a Green Suit, 1760s. Oil on canvas, 39 ⅛ × 29 ⅛ in. (99.38 × 73.98 cm) courtesy Dallas Museum of Art, gift of Leon A. Harris, Jr., 1954.

7   Dighton, Richard. *George "Beau" Brummell*, watercolor. 1805.

8   *Women wearing crinolines which are set on fire by flames from a domestic fireplace.* Colored lithograph, ca. 1860. Wellcome Library no. 586198i. Licensed under Creative Commons 4.0.

9   Ellis & Walery. *Miss Camille Clifford.* 1906. Postcard. J. Beagles & Co. Ca.

10   Bain News Service. Louise Brooks. 1920-1925. Library of Congress, Prints & Photographs Division, LC-B2- 5474-15 [P&P]. George Grantham Bain Collection.

11   *Vanity Fair's* Bifurcated Girls, June 1903, from Public Domain review, https://publicdomainreview.org/collection/bifurcated-girls-vanity-fair-special-issue-1903.

Insert 2   Credit

12   Martin, David, Painting of Dido Elizabeth Belle and her cousin Lady Elizabeth Murray, courtesy The Right Honourable Earl of Mansfield, of Scone Palace, Perth.

13   © Sean Rayford, 2020.

14   Brooklyn Museum Costume Collection at The Metropolitan Museum of Art. *Chopines.* 1550–1650. Gift of the Brooklyn Museum, 2009; gift of Herman Delman, 1955.

15   *Persian*, 17th century. Collection of the Bata Shoe Museum. Image © 2020. Bata Shoe Museum, Toronto, Canada.

16   © Chris Luttrell.

17 Modern copy of Rigaud, Hyacinthe. *Portrait of Louis XIV*. 1701. © Everett Collection.

18 Senate Democrats. Sinema Reception. Licensed under Creative Commons 2.0.

19 Hall, Frank. U.S. Secretary of Defense Caspar W. Weinberger meets with President Mobutu of Zaire at the Pentagon, 1983.

20 Makangara, Justin and Héctor Mediavilla. Severin Mouyengo, aka the Salopard. © Justin Makangara.

21 Vucci, Evan. President-elect Donald Trump arrives at Indianapolis International Airport for a visit to the Carrier factory, Thursday, Dec. 1, 2016, in Indianapolis, Ind. 2016. Photograph. © Associated Press.

About the Author

Richard Thompson Ford is Professor of Law at Stanford Law School. He writes about law, social and cultural issues, and race relations and has written for the *New York Times*, the *Washington Post*, the *San Francisco Chronicle*, CNN, and *Slate*. He is the author of the *New York Times* Notable Books *The Race Card* and *Rights Gone Wrong: How Law Corrupts the Struggle for Equality*. He has appeared on *The Colbert Report*, *The Rachel Maddow Show*, and *The Dylan Ratigan Show*. He is a member of the American Law Institute and serves on the board of the Authors Guild Foundation. Quite to his surprise, he was one of twenty-five semi-finalists in *Esquire* magazine's Best Dressed Real Man contest in 2009. He lives in San Francisco with his wife, Marlene, and two children, Cole and Ella.